Rites of Realism

U8

ꝺq

RITES OF REALISM

Essays on Corporeal Cinema

Edited by I V O N E   M A R G U L I E S

DUKE UNIVERSITY PRESS   Durham and London 2003

The following are reprinted by permission: "La mort tous les après midi," by André Bazin, *Qu'est-ce que le Cinéma?* vol. 1, Paris, Editions du Cerf, 1958, © Cahiers du Cinéma, Editions de l'Étoile; "L'Ecran du fantasme (Bazin et les bêtes)," by Serge Daney, *La Rampe* © 1983, Editions Gallimard; "History of the Image, Image of History: Subject and Ontology in Bazin," by Philip Rosen, *Wide Angle* 9:4 (winter 1987–88): 7–34, © Ohio University, Athens, Center for Film and Video, reprinted by permission of Johns Hopkins University Press; "In Search of the Real City: Cinematic Representations of Beijing and the Politics of Vision," by Xiaobing Tang, in *Chinese Modern* © Duke University Press, 2000; "Pasolini on *Terra Sancta:* Towards a Theology of Film," by Noa Steimatsky, *Yale Journal of Criticism,* 2:1 (1998): 239–58, © 1998, Yale University Press and Johns Hopkins University Press; "Why Is This Absurd Picture Here? Ethnology/Equivocation/Buñuel," by James Lastra, *October* 89 (summer 1999): 51–68, © 1999 *October,* reprinted by permission; "Dreyer's Textual Realism," by James Schamus, © 1988, Museum of Modern Art, New York, reprinted by permission.

For Mark Cohen

Contents

Cultural Indices

Retracings

Acknowledgments

Along the way in this anthology many deserve thanks.

Mark Cohen, my closest reader, asked the right questions, pointed out the missing links, and made me sure of the project's worth. His love, warmth, and support are, as always, essential. Talks with Noa Steimatsky often got me closer to my own interests, even when the grand ambitions of a topic such as realism and cinema threatened to scatter the more pointed focus of this anthology. Catherine Russell's readings of the introduction and the essay on reenactment helped me enormously, with a last push to finish. Tim Corrigan was, as usual, a sharp reader, and his comments were especially helpful in shaping the book's introduction. My thanks also to Michael Gitlin, who was incredibly helpful in the preparation of illustrations for the book.

I would like to thank Elaine Charnov, David James, David Desser, Bill Nichols, Steve Fagin, Tom Gunning, Paul Arthur, and Richard Porton, who suggested contributors for this anthology's many shifting guises. I am also thankful for Ella Shohat's friendship and advice over so many years. She has made me feel at home in New York.

Richard Peña at the Film Society of Lincoln Center facilitated my contact with Abbas Kiarostami, and Godfrey Cheshire generously lent me his Kiarostami videos.

A grant from Hunter College (Shuster Award) paid for foreign copyright fees, translations, and stills. My thanks to Ana Lo Biondo at Hunter College for her help. Grants from the Research foundation of the City University of New York in 1999 and 2000 were invaluable in my research on reenactment films. In tracking films and related materials, I was aided at the UCLA Archive by Maria Rosa de Castro; at the Library of Congress by David Parker, Acting Head of the Curatorial Section; at the Pacific Film Archives by Kathy Geritz and Steve Seid; in Paris at the Centre National de Cinematographie Film Archives by M. Eric Leroy and Mme. Michelle Aubert; and at the Cinématèque Française by Mme. Danielle Kenzey.

My thanks also to Bernardo Carvalho, Joe McElhaney, Elaine Charnov, Bruni Burrest, and Jean-Paul Colleyn, who led me to wonderful examples of reenactment films. Candice Johnson, my assistant, helped with copyright and permission procedures. Thanks to Sudhir Mahadevan for his wonderful index.

Last, I want to acknowledge Ken Wissoker, my editor at Duke University Press, for his initial excitement about the project and support and friendship over the course of its various changes. The readers for the press gave expert advice on how to make my arguments more cogent, and I felt truly encouraged by their support. At the press, Leigh Ann Couch in the early stages and Fiona Morgan in the later stages of the book's production made me feel the work was worth it.

Rites of Realism

Bodies Too Much

Ivone Margulies

Under the general rubric of realism, *Rites of Realism: Essays on Corporeal Cinema* subscribes to the epistemological promise of referential images: that what we see refers to an existing reality and we can thus "know" a certain landscape, a suburb, a room, or a farming method. This anthology articulates, however, a more pointed intervention in the discourse on realism and film. The essays focus on issues that had become taboo in the 1970s theoretical equation of realism and essentialism. How can one recall an event's concrete peculiarity or reproduce its original urgency through a medium that so clearly defers? One way to invite such hard questions is to represent those events that most stubbornly resist the notion of duplication because of their close association with the carnality of the body and decay, to represent realities such as possession ritual, animal sacrifice, torture, or physical disability.[1] How is one to grant a corporeal weight to faces, places, and events through a medium that can imply but lacks depth? Where the body appears as theater, as third dimensional, it highlights cinema's constitutive hybridity.[2]

The title word *rites* is meant to invoke the ritual connotation of representations that have actual effects on reality and in particular the reality of profilmic bodies. When in *Sons* (1996) Zhang Yuan directs an actual Beijing family to reenact the last ten days before the sons commit their alcoholic father to a mental asylum, this restaging, two years after the fact, poses a number of questions having to do with the significance of retracing an original event in film. What is the status and purpose of this second time around? When Kazuo Hara follows his ex-wife, a feminist militant, in *Extreme Private Eros: Love Song, 1974* (1974), what exactly do we witness? How does the film performance of her private life differ from her public, politicized provocations in real life?

The essays in the book discuss makers who have, either in their subject choice or approach, engaged with the problem of originals. Literal representation may be, for instance, at the service of a faithful retracing of documents, places, and biographical events. And yet literal reenactment is shown to have little to do with accessing an original, pure past, working instead as an example offered to the audience with the aim of public betterment. The importance of these retracings lies in their present, performative efficacy.[3] They may be forms of psychodrama, provoked instances of acting out that produce a catharsis of a personal (*Sons*) or a historical nature (in Hara Kazuo's *The Emperor's Naked Army Marches On*, 1987); they may create a mutual contamination between a displaced text and its contemporary setting (in Pasolini's *The Gospel according to St. Matthew*, 1964); or they may mimic a host of discourses on a people ironically commenting on ethnography and its pseudo-objectivity (in Buñuel's *Land without Bread*, 1932). In each case, the film's reference to a preexisting event or text produces a form of provocative mimesis.

In an attempt to delineate a problematic of cinematic realism that bypasses questions of verisimilitude, this anthology is inspired by, and pays tribute to, André Bazin's thoughts on the dilemmas of performance (the once-only profilmic event) and filmic reproducibility.

Bazin was always wary of the ways in which conventions dull realism, and his choice of the terms *reality* and *the real* have a strategic rather than a descriptive function. He says: "the cinema has come a long way since the heroic days when crowds were satisfied with the rough rendition of a branch quivering in the wind!" Or, commenting on *Farrebique*'s impact, he asks why Rouquier has offended so many. "He has understood that verisimilitude has slowly taken the place of truth, that reality had slowly dissolved into realism. So he painfully undertook to rediscover reality."[4]

Bazin's own "rediscovery of reality" involves instead a heightened sense of the eclectic materiality of film. Images that bear the marks of two heterogeneous realities, the filmmaking process and the filmed event, perfectly illuminate his search for visceral signifiers for the real. And the registered clash of different material orders best defines for him, in turn, that which is specifically cinematic. In *The Bridge on the River Kwai* (1957), the bridge, which "really spans the River Kwai," could not survive the film: "the absurdity either had to be *in* the film or it had, finally, to be the film *itself*."[5] In *Kontiki* (1950), it is the missing and not the existing footage—"the negative imprints of the expedition" —that best represents the danger faced by the explorers.[6] It is the ellipsis in the last episode of *Paisa* (1946) that best tells us about the terror of being at war in one place instead of another. As Philip Rosen points out in his essay in this volume, such "markers of indexicality" attest to Bazin's continuous interest in contingency as the principal measure of the humanity (and reality) of cinema.

Bazin's images for the incidental and the contingent have usually served to exemplify the achievement of a surface realism through the putative inclusion of the marginal, nondramatic element. His description of the episode in *Bicycle Thieves* (1948) is exemplary: "in the middle of the chase the little boy suddenly needs to piss. So he does."[7] Siegfried Kracauer, another reputed defender of a realist ontology for cinema, finds similar examples for an inverted relation between those images that further the story and those that can do so precisely because they "retain a degree of independence of the intrigue and thus succeed in summoning a physical existence."[8] Within a different critical agenda, Roland Barthes has characterized literary references to objects that have no discernible narrative function except to give a material, worldly weight to the description as "reality effects."[9] While Bazin and Kracauer seem to note and celebrate these little escapes from narrative determinism, Barthes's functional analyses actually cast a shadow over those descriptive images that seem to be there merely to confirm an overall effect of naturalness. These formulations imply the potential co-optation of such irrelevant details for a realistic notation. But they may also define a critical impasse both in literature (with descriptions) and in cinema

1. The actual bridge explosion in *The Bridge on the River Kwai*, David Lean, 1957 (frame enlargement of video)

(with the contingent events): the category of verisimilitude is inadequate to define what modern realist films do beyond differing from classical realist representations.

Bazin's impatience with verisimilitude can suggest ways for theoretical speculation to account more adequately for modern realist films. His dismissal of verisimilitude is made clear in his frequent comments on the felicity of (mis)cast actors or the irrelevance of likeness for reenactment's moral projects.[10] He delves instead into the problematic of profilmic performances, taking special interest in production and reception contingencies. It is this interest that overlaps in an illuminating manner with materialist analyses of filmic images.

At the end of his reading of Jean Renoir's *La Marseilleise,* Bazin states: "An admirable touch, as he reviews the troops in the Tuilleries, Louis the XVI is hindered by the fact that his wig is askew."[11] Bazin adds a physical embarrassment to Louis's social predicament, and this material detail disturbs at once two forms of spectacle: Louis's and Pierre Renoir's royal attire and film costume. Bazin's admirable touch has to do with the seeming casualness with which he juxtaposes fictions, defining each through their shared physicality. In Jean-Louis Comolli's analysis of the same film, historical determinism uncovers the shakiness of appearances and lays bare the naked king: "The wig . . . is this part which first detaches itself from the disintegrating royal body. Never has this body stopped falling apart as it was constructed before our eyes . . . something undecidable floats around him [Pierre Renoir], a blur in the image, duplication: there is a ghost in this body. At any rate there is some historical knowledge, some referent constituting a screen for the image and preventing the actor and mise-en-scène from playing on self-evidence."[12]

Comolli's critical narrative is one of many materialist readings of film indebted to Bazin's insights into profilmic contingency.[13] His comments on the difficult referentiality of historical film indicate, however, where Bazin's thoughts about incidents of production and performance most productively lead—toward an understanding of the complex layering of referential modes.

What interests Bazin are precisely the rough edges of representation, the moment of encounter and productive maladjustment between representation and the actuality of filmmaking. The social and cultural resonances of this mis-fit are never lost in his criticism, and in the essays that follow one finds a similar attentiveness to the density of profilmic reality.

This anthology addresses referential genres and topics particularly prone to bodily discomfort. Historical film, but also portraiture, adaptation, and reenactment, create representations beset by competition with prior images (from portraits to filmic roles) and descriptive regimens (biographies, histories, and ethnographies) that vie to adequately represent a given reality. Because they refer to existing titles, events, and people, such films can eventually claim that they provide viable references for a critical understanding of one's culture and society. At the same time, since they are often perceived as parasitic of original sources, they also have an interesting aesthetic potential to betray a totalized or idealized version of reality.

Just as this anthology does away with verisimilitude as a working category appropriate to considering modern realist film, it also distances itself from the generalized indictment of realist aesthetics as a form of deception. The bodies brilliantly uncovered in Comolli's historical-materialist undressing are no longer "too much" or an excess worthy of ideological alarm. This excess is the question that moves several of the essays to rethink, not to condemn, realism.

The essays in this book look at films that make apparent use of straightforward recording, only to magnify how distant realism can be from a mere reproduction of appearances. The filming of possession rituals in Maya Deren's trance films and the infamous shot of the goat falling in *Las Hurdes* (*Land without Bread*) raise the prospect that what seems like a transparent record is not always a naive or deceptive form of representation. Even more forcefully than a reflexive comment on film language, a fully visible framing of reality may pose difficult questions about the relations between the clarity of vision and that of meaning.

This volume is divided into three parts: "Bazinian Contingencies," "Cultural Indices," and "Retracings." The essays resonate across sections, and their joint attention to the contingencies of reality and the film image will hopefully flesh out the changeable nature of realism and provide categories in which to consider new emerging representational aesthetics.

Bazinian Contingencies

For Bazin, nothing better illustrates the radical breach between the transience of existence and mechanical reproduction, which transcends it so obliviously, than a never to be repeated spectacle in flesh and blood.[14] *Rites of Realism* opens with one such image from Pierre Braubenger's documentary *The Bullfight* (*La Course de Taureaux,* 1949) and André Bazin's plaintive comment: "I cannot repeat a single moment of my life, but any one of those moments cinema may repeat indefinitely before me. . . . on the screen the toreador dies every afternoon."[15]

Mournful references to the unique moment are often cast as a theoretical throwback to an era before the structural-semiotic divide. Stephen Heath's text "Film Performance" is one example of the ways in which 1970s theoretical discourse talked about "performance." This discourse showed an obtuseness toward what was in front of the camera. Heath deploys Bazin's insight that cinema's fundamental obscenity is never as vivid as in its unique ability to reanimate dead bodies, that its remorse (in Bazin's pun *re-mords / re-morts*) lies in projecting on-screen the singular moment of a change to inert matter again and again.[16] But Heath only falsifies the thrust of Bazin's sensibility to the singularity of the recorded event. He opts for quite a different image of death to talk about the cinema, one that is from the start imbricated with capitalist commodification, an image that associates document, sensationalism, and profit. He rehearses Apollinaire's snuff film parable *Un beau film.* The narrator of "A Good Film," recounts how, after founding the International Cinematographic Company (CIC), the producers procured "films of great interest." The CIC had a "well-rounded program," but one subject was missing, the record of a crime. . . . giving up the possibility of licitly coming upon the spectacle of a crime, the producers decided to organize one."[17] "It is not by chance," notes Heath, "that Apollinaire's fascination with the new medium is immediately, in 1907 the story of a murder, the relation of cinema and crime." For the "crime of the good film is the film itself, its time and its performance . . . made of a series of stops in time, the timed stops of the discrete frames." Film depends, for its reconstitution of a moving reality, on "the *artifice* of its continuity and coherence."[18]

I paraphrase Heath's version of the inherent guilt of the "good film," frequently equated with classical Hollywood cinema (and in a further semantic/ideological slippage with realism *tout court*), in order to draw attention to a different crime scene. For in fact Heath has diverted us from the crime we are supposed to be seeing, from the murder actually perpetrated in front of the camera in this snuff film, to the presumed masked area of aesthetic production (editing) and reception. In this haste to indict a suspect ideology, we may have been inadvertently sidetracked.[19]

The repudiation of realist cinema as a worthy object of analysis represented, in 1970s theoretical writing, an unquestioned allegiance to a po-litical modernist agenda. As David Rodowick suggests in his analysis of the political modernist discourse, the dominant opposition at work here is that of realism versus modernism. This discourse polarized classical and countercinema practices, constantly pitching Hollywood cinema's decep-tiveness and illusionism against an avant-garde cinema whose task was the promotion of the critical awareness of the materiality of the medium.[20] This polarity has framed realist cinema as needing demystification rather than explanation.[21]

Ideological accounts of the camera have obscured important historical distinctions in ways of perceiving reality. Their explanatory power has been pervasive enough to create, in Jonathan Crary's words, "a confusing bifur-cated model of vision in the nineteenth century." "On the one level," he says "there is a relatively small number of advanced artists who generated a radically new kind of seeing and signification, while on a more quotidian level vision remains embedded within the same general 'realist' strictures that had organized it since the fifteenth century."[22]

At least in part, the impetus for the detailed historicization of media and reception has been a reaction to the technological determinism of appara-tus theories.[23] In *Sound Technology and the American Cinema: Perception, Rep-resentation, Modernity*, James Lastra carefully dismantles the ahistorical claim that the camera's production of spatially coherent images (from the Renais-sance's camera obscura to cinema) produces a transcendental subject and that the re-creation of the movement of objective reality could have the same effect "by each and every use of the cinema."[24]

Lastra, Tom Gunning, Miriam Hansen, Vanessa Schwartz, and Ben Singer, among others, have shown how broadly conceived historical ana-lyses can clear up well-worn cliches on cinematic practice and reception.[25] Most significant studies that align cinema with other popular media and forms of entertainment from the nineteenth and twentieth centuries have allowed a number of important questions to frame anew the issue of real-ism. What is cinema's response to the search for sensations apparent in turn of the century forms of spectacle such as the cabaret, the morgue visit, the wax museum, and the panorama? How is the spectator's body redefined by cinematic shock, and how does the reception of cinema compare with other physical and sensorial thrills of modern life? Such considerations have opened up the debate on realism to include other models not necessarily associated with film's lifelike qualities.

New film histories working on issues of performance and the body have also been instrumental in opening the field of inquiry beyond the operations of the camera lens, acknowledging that the camera does more than simply register a passive reality.[26] Distinctions between the notion of a captured moment in art, photography, cinema, and video have resulted in an enriched understanding of the relations of different media to the contingencies of reality, a reality that itself is subject to multiple levels of construction. Several considerations have qualified old critical paradigms based exclusively on the camera's agency: the acknowledgment that different perceptual regimens and interests inflect the reception of images, that profilmic and diegetic elements (staging, acting, and lighting as well as character development and narrative logic) are interlinked to, but not entirely accounted for by, editing or framing.

The selection of films and filmmakers for discussion in *Rites of Realism* is strategic regarding this renewed attention to profilmic operations. One of the most enduring effects of the simplistic proposal of apparatus theory lies in how effectively it associates depth perspective with "bourgeois" illusionism. The characterization of certain forms of representation as automatically suspect led the political modernist radar to miss important work operating in any other register than that subtended by the screen/surface analogy. As Ben Brewster and Lea Jacobs suggest in *Theatre to Cinema,* the emphasis on the shot and editing as the key defining features of cinema was linked to early cinema's need to define itself as art, not copy. The emphasis on editing at the expense of the content of individual shots (and at the expense of considerations of profilmic reality) was necessary in order to deflect the "suspicion that the moving-picture camera was no more than a sophisticated copying device, that any art there was in the cinema resided in the objects, people, events, and actions that had once been in front of the passive camera."[27] But it was only in the 1970s that formal strategies such as the foregrounding of surface flatness, the visible integrity of the shot, and breaks with cinematic verisimilitude such as direct address to the camera and graphic interruptions gained an overblown critical (and moral) valence. Conversely, any reading attentive to the reality in front of the camera, to the materiality shared by actor and individual, by a specific place and a dramatic setting, was somehow compromised by the illusory pull of verisimilitude.[28] Any work that did not seem to discursively parade formal quandaries was somehow suspect. Any film that embraced figuration and a discernible reference to external reality was dismissed along with a generically defined classical cinema. This led to a selective valorization of work, with more overt formal projects automatically disqualifying a number of films and issues from consideration.[29]

This book resists the segregation between avant-garde/modernist and realist films characteristic of the 1970s modernist agenda by looking at directors such as Luis Buñuel, Maya Deren, Carl Th. Dreyer, Peter Greenaway, Pier Paolo Pasolini, and Andy Warhol. Otherwise known for the experimental and formal qualities of their films, they are discussed here because of their confrontations with real existing bodies and their manipulations of profilmic realities.

The bullfight demarcates this book's alternative problematic, located this time in front of the camera in the profilmic area.[30] It is in this arena of "represented/actual bullfighting" that, like man and beast, different material registers productively clash.

It seems fitting, then, to open this anthology with a counterimage to Heath's anti-illusionist stance. In Bazin's "Death Every Afternoon" (*La mort tous les après-midi*) the difference between the dead and the living, central to the ontology of cinema and its uncanny animation, figures not simply as a perceptual trick set in motion by the projector but *also as* subject matter. The "permanent virtuality" of the bullfighter and the bull's death provides him with one more occasion to stress contingency as the central quality of the cinema. But Bazin has reminded us in another context that the subject matter should matter after all.[31]

The imminent death on-screen encapsulates the complexity of profilmic reality (its danger as well as its theatricality) at the same time that the long shot proffers its full visibility. Serge Daney's "The Screen of Fantasy (Bazin and Animals)" rethinks the consequences of such full visibility. He convincingly shows that Bazin's attention to subject matter is not simply a warning directed to the dangers of the *politique des auteurs*'s excessive formalism. Bazin's examples of the interdiction of montage — the encounter between man and beast framed together in a long shot — are, in their uncompromising figuration of heterogeneity, a favorite sign of violence and reality. Instead of an aesthetic safeguard for representing the integrity of the reality, the spatial and temporal expansions Bazin explores provide in fact the best conceivable stage for the emergence of the real, of its unpredictable heterogeneity.

Still focusing on how Bazin stages, in his descriptive examples, the unexpected event, Philip Rosen explains in "History of Image, Image of History:

Subject and Ontology in Bazin" how central time is to Bazin's cinematic ontology. It allows for a fantasy of convergence, the parallel unfolding of filming and event. But it also occasions a subjective investment, which is all the more active if there is a sustained ambivalence, a deferral of definition regarding where fact ends and fiction begins. Rosen draws out Bazin's interest in the viewer's gradual, subjective investment in the reading of an image, its temporality, but also on the critic's inspiring insights into the image's historicity. Bazin's articulation of the differential between a mythical and an existential dimension (Stalin and the actors that play him) and cinema's role in collapsing these categories becomes, through Rosen's reading, fundamental for thinking about two genres imbricated with time and actual existence—biographical and historical films.[32]

Sensitivity to the conjunction of cinema and history is central to much of the contemporary discussion around questions of realism and in particular to the evidentiary status of moving images. Renewed interest in notions of visible evidence and the rhetoric of authenticity of documentary modes epitomizes the way in which "fugitive images," defined by their indexical link with the real, have recently grown in importance.[33] The social gravity granted to representation in the Rodney King trial and the centrality of video in this case signaled the evidentiary relevance of record—to provide material proof of an event that might otherwise vanish from collective memory. Even though it became clear in that case that evidence was not self-sufficient and that framing verbal arguments defined the image's circumstantial significance, there was a firm desire to safeguard images as indisputably linked to truth.

The awareness that we have entered a postmodern era in which digitization has replaced the indexicality of photography has reawakened the debate around the authenticity of images. It has generated an ethically inflected preoccupation with the real revalorized as the residue of an accelerated technological and representational obsolescence.[34]

In "The Object of Theory," her essay in this anthology, Mary Ann Doane moves the discussion from a moral arena—whether indexically produced images are more trustworthy than digital ones—to a historical one. She historicizes the very concern with fugitive images that has animated some of the most interesting work in the last decade, linking the interest in contingency to a broader sensitivity to cinema's own suddenly foreshortened history. Cinephilia and the fastening on the indexically produced detail constitute a "safeguarding of the domain of the cinematic proper," the photographically based image menaced with extinction in the digital era.[35] The importance of the concept of indexicality in current film scholarship lies in its potential to make available "the particular, the singular, the unpredictable — in short, the antisystematic — within the cinematic domain."[36] It is this same unpredictability that charges the indexical sign with a value, crucial for cinephiles, for registering "something, that resists . . . existing networks of critical discourse and theoretical frameworks."[37]

Contingency — the barely grasped instant, which is nevertheless recorded — is the main measure of cinema's particular significance. Doane's insights concerning the renewed interest in cinematic specificity, the historicity of the medium, and the temporality proper to cinema significantly expand the theoretical implications of Bazin's sensitivity to the cinematic paradoxes of temporal freezing.

Cultural Indices

The book's second part extends the focus of Bazin's writings on neorealism, as well as his understanding of cinema's deep power to register and interpret particular nuances of history and place, into contemporary and classic realist films. These essays participate in the realist debate in two key ways. They raise issues conventionally thought to be residual to dramatic narrative and action plots — faces (portraiture and home movies), places (location and landscape, the representation of cities), or everyday banality. They also take into account the ways in which images develop their own genealogies and histories in dialogue with other national and international aesthetic traditions and forms of signification.

Fredric Jameson has proposed a neat periodization of film history corresponding to the development of global capitalism — realism, modernism, and postmodernism.[38] He suggests that the "moment of realism can be grasped . . . as the conquest of a kind of cultural, ideological and narrative literacy by a new class or group."[39] Given the implications of such a developmental model, it is to Jameson's credit that his categories keep breaking up to include alternate forms of what he terms "oppositional realism." *Oppositional realism* refers to films and film movements that present at the same time the self-referentiality of modernist art and the epistemological retrieval of a marginal reality. He exemplifies this tendency with a number of feminist and ethnic works from Akerman's *News from Home* to Stephen Frears and Hanif Kureishi's *My Beautiful Launderette*.[40]

What oppositional realism also suggests is that the equation of realism and a politics of identity is soon disqualified by a much richer and complex practice, one that often breaks the boundaries of the most readily utilized classificatory category—that of national cinemas.[41]

The essays grouped under "Cultural Indices" illuminate particular cinematic traits related to nationality, but their main purpose is not to make broad statements in line with a given national agenda or cultural sensibility. If anything, the emphasis on theoretical issues is meant to suggest the complexity of realist aesthetics, issues that are applicable to diverse realities.

The films analyzed here follow the thematic mandate of realism—to pay heed to underrepresented aspects of society. But they do so, at times, with a perverse excess (Warhol or Buñuel, Mike Leigh) or, and with similarly interesting results, with sincere earnestness (Stan Brakhage, direct cinema). Their representation of existing landscapes, physiognomies, and cityscapes yelds portraits that are as precise as they are defamiliarized.

Film can, because of its indexicality, guarantee the particularity of its object in time and space, its precise historicity. Time can operate, however, as a potent agent of "disfiguration."[42] It is extended time and an excess of contingency that after all destabilize Warhol's portraits. The camera shifts from merely recording and begins with time to "narrate [the subject's] anxious response to the process of being photographed."[43] As Paul Arthur describes, with a nuanced attention to detail, the facial expressions, the "orchestrated little comic fugues consisting of nods, lip movements, eye exercises,"[44] in avant-garde film, he posits the ways in which cinema, and certain referential modes in particular, are inordinately suited to unpredicted revelation.

Arthur's essay in this volume, "No Longer Absolute: Portraiture in American Documentary and Avant-Garde Films of the Sixties," follows Doane's incisive reflections on the nature of contingency in modernity. He recasts Bazin's central problematic—how to grant "presentness" to "embalmed time"—examining the particular affinity for a fluid identity evinced in both the 1960s countercultural ethos and the portrait film. Arthur explains how avant-garde cinema and direct cinema documentaries were particularly prone to the display of social diversity in an era that privileged spontaneity, unfettered self-expression, and personal idiosyncrasy.

The city is a recognized theme in discussions of realism.[45] As Kracauer continually suggested, "street and face open up a dimension much wider that that of the plots they sustain."[46] Kracauer refers here to contingency, the unpredictable flow of movement and expression likely to appear on the face and city. But even more significantly what qualifies it as an important setting for realist art is the fact that, like the face, the city is a socially inscribed landscape. Its constructed nature easily places it in a precise historical moment. Cities can thus be indicators of three main characteristics of realist drama and film according to Raymond Williams: the secular (the action played in exclusively human terms), the contemporary (the siting of actions in one's present), and a conscious movement toward social extension.[47]

The city's potential to serve as a barometer for shifts in the relation of individuals to the forces of modernization makes it an especially significant subject in contemporary China. The focus on contemporary urban life has often emerged as the trait that distinguishes the Fifth from the Sixth Generation filmmakers. Focusing instead on later films made by members of the Fourth Generation, filmmakers who made some of the most realistic films about rural China in the 1980s, Xiaobing Tang's close analyses suggest a more complex picture. His text evokes separate intellectual and aesthetic traditions: typicality in the case of *Good Morning Beijing* (Zhang Nuan, 1990) and modernist investigation of psychological depth in *Black Snow* (Xie Fei, 1989).

Also dealing with aspects of social geography, Richard Porton analyzes the intertexts for British realist Mike Leigh. He demonstrates how dramatic forms inherited from the theater intersect and reshape Leigh's modernist tale telling of everyday banality, thereby distinguishing his work most notably from the "kitchen sink" realism of the 1960s. Leigh's preference for claustrophobic interiors allows him a theatrically stylized but sociologically accurate depiction of the aspirations of petty bourgeois and working class characters. Using Henri Lefebvre's concept of "spatial politics," Porton suggests how Leigh's films reveal social alienation and class distinctions physically, through the "artifacts of social hierarchy." The kind of hors d'oeuvre served can suggest a person's anxiety about receiving a guest in *Abigail's Party*. But the accumulation of such cultural inscriptions, their excess, creates a distilled, critical version of that society.

There is no doubt a connection between the inventiveness of recent realist film and the anxiety felt by many around the world in the face of rapidly changing realities in their daily lives. Moreover, the attention to marginalized segments of urban societies, running the gamut from unemployment and urban anomie (Charles Burnett's *Killer of Sheep* and *My Brother's Wedding*, the Dardenne Brothers' *La Promesse* and *Rosetta*, Bruno Dumont's *Life of Jesus,* or Eric Zonca's *Dreamlife of Angels*) to the state of care for mentally handicapped children in China (Zhang Yuan's *Mama*), implicitly affirms the affinity of realism for social issues. It is, however, as important to note film's relative autonomy in interpreting and then forming fresh cultural images. As the filmmakers discussed here grapple with the complexities of this reality, they invent new forms of realism and additional aesthetic and social references.[48] Xiaobing Tang's essay on urban representation might seem, at first glance to describe a stable version of Chinese identity in the late 1980s. Nonetheless, his different emphases—on subjective representation in the case of *Black Snow* or on social mapping in the case of *Good Morning Beijing*—suggest in fact that realism is a plural aesthetics and not simply a way of recording signs of plurality.

These essays, then, have multiple tasks—they map both the referential horizons of a given moment, what is pressing as subject matter, and the aesthetic boundaries crossed on the way to representing particular issues. Hara Kazuo's provocative tracking of taboos and charged questions in *The Emperor's Naked Army Marches On* (cannibalism in World War II) or *Sayonara CP* (physical handicap) suggests the reach of Japanese documentary but also what constitutes a taboo in mid-1970s or early 1980s Japan. Abé Mark Nornes details the documentary tradition to which Hara responds as he creates an idiosyncratic, provocative dialogue with repressive elements in his culture.

The contributors to this anthology all examine realism as an aesthetic that effectively enacts cultural and social tensions. In "Why Is This Absurd Picture Here? Ethnology/Heterology/Buñuel," James F. Lastra traces Buñuel's 1932 film *Las Hurdes*'s aesthetic of equivocation to its dialogue with the film's avowed sources: Maurice Legendre's 1926 anthropological study and Miguel de Unamuno's 1922 travel essay. He suggests how Buñuel's depiction of the *hurdanos* is in fact a critical gesture aimed at the 1930s purist national discourses.

The anthology is organized so that each essay opening a section develops some of the questions broached in the next essay or section. For example, Arthur's "No Longer Absolute" discerns a cultural and historical particularity in 1960s portraiture—the genre's thirst for contingency and the consequent affinity for the thematic of wavering identities in that period. Arthur's insights on the parallel historical and aesthetic registers of the contingent in the production of 1960s identities significantly illustrates how Doane's work on indexicality and temporality matters for current readings of referential genres such as historical and portrait film. Lastra's essay closes the book's second part because of its focus on the cultural representation of the hurdanos in right-wing discourse. Buñuel's procedures of mimicry, yet another version of a provocative *retracing* initiates the next part's discussion. The extended discussion of the infamous goat shot in *Land without Bread,* a provoked, filmic, and filmed death, suggests once again the centrality of images of death in discussions of realism and cinema. This image of sacrifice is echoed in the essays' complex and layered forms of repetition and adaptation—in reenacted events, in transmuted locations, in possessed bodies, in "textual realism."

Retracings

In the last part of the anthology, the contributors discuss a number of realist genres that refer to actual, existing originals (documents, books, events, and people). The essays' questions have to do with the predicaments of performance (the once only of an event) in film (reproducible, circulating images). They consider the complexities of literal representation and embodiment.

Literal representation is associated with the faithful retracing of documents, places, and biographical events. It generates distinct projects and questions in the work of Dreyer, Pasolini, Antonioni, and Abbas Kiarostami.

In my essay, "Exemplary Bodies: Reenactment in *Love in the City, Sons, and Close Up,*" I discuss how reenactment functions as a form of atonement in public. Reenactment is not, for instance, enlisted in the retracing of past events but rather in the production of redemptive images and public examples for future action. The consciousness-raising appeal of these biographical re-creations lies in this on-screen repetition, which I define as a form of exemplary realism. I discuss two late neorealist films—Zavattini and Maselli's *Love of a Mother* and Antonioni's *Attempted Suicide*—and their use of reenactment to counter the perceived abuses of fiction cinema. I also analyze two contemporary films—Zhang Yuan's *Sons* and Abbas Kiarostami's *Close Up*—indicating these films' particular resistance to moralistic, redemptive functions.

Noa Steimatsky's "Pasolini on *Terra Sancta:* Towards a Theology of Film" focuses on Pasolini's *The Gospel according to Saint Matthew.* She integrates the film's production history in her interpretation of Pasolini's decision to film in Matera, Italy, after hunting for locations in Palestine and recording such images in his *Sopraluoghi di Palestina (Locations in Palestine,* 1963). The notion of a literal retracing of Christ's steps, here selectively transposed onto a different ground, is crucial to understanding the radicality of Pasolini's eclectic, impure realism. Steimatsky considers Pasolini's iconic stylistics, providing precise examples of the filmmaker's strategies of *analogy* and *contamination*.

Another significant move away from the problematic of faithful recording is apparent in Catherine Russell's "Ecstatic Ethnography: Maya Deren and the Filming of Possession Rituals." Russell looks at Deren's Haitian project, footage and texts, to identify the ways in which scenes of possession function as a catalyst in the development of cinema vérité, the formal affinity of melodramatic structures and spectacles of possession, and most importantly the challenge images of possession pose to cinematic epistemologies. She maps Deren's desire and failure to register the ritual spectacle of possessed subjectivity onto a more general difficulty—the invocation of subjective depth and the resistance to visibility present in possession scenes. She discusses how filmmakers engaging with possession rituals were interested in transformations of the self and how reflexivity and romantic self-expression were part of this intriguing combination of high visibility and utter opaqueness.

This anthology directly engages with films that assume cinema's problematic transparency and inherent hybridity. This is the explicit theme of Brigitte Peucker's "Filmic Tableau Vivant: Vermeer, Intermediality, and the Real," which looks at the *tableau vivant* as an apt trope for cinema's heterogeneity: "one of the tensions governing tableau vivant issues has its origin in an uncertainty about the boundaries that divide the representational from the real." Peucker closely analyzes the "embodiment" of Vermeer paintings in two films: Peter Greenaway's *A Zed and Two Noughts* (1985) and Wim Wenders's *Until the End of the World* (1991). The essay's particular focus on one of the oldest tropes of realism—the painting brought to life—allows her to examine these filmmakers' distinctively postmodernist problematics: an obsession with the "real" and their relation to intertextuality and intermedia. While intermediality forms a subset of this investigation, the tableau vivant introduces questions about the attempts to create fuller or embodied images of reality. That this search for presence only leads to greater artifice is discussed as part of these filmmakers' particular representational questions.

James Schamus identifies, in Dreyer's close adaptation of the original trial documents in *Passion of Joan of Arc,* a form of "textual realism," a second-degree referentiality, which, in dialogue with other forms of character-based realism, is itself informed by the filmmaker's search for authority. This search for authenticity translates into a particular form of realism: an attempt to replicate the "written traces" of a real person, a "reenactment of the documentary word." Focusing on the films' layered textuality (scripts based on notes, diaries, letters, and transcripts), the essay draws significant conclusions about the embattled relation of Dreyer's female characters (Joan of Arc, Gertrud) with this textual authority.

On the occasion of the 1997 International Week of Cinema, which was dedicated to contemporary European cinema, Jean-Louis Comolli revisited Bazin and some of the performative impasses raised in this book. Motivated by Rosselini and his predilection for representing traces of lost realities ("the ruins in *Germany Year Zero,* the paths in *Stromboli,* the bellies in *Voyage in Italy*"); Comolli considers realism to be a necessary "cruelty from cinematography: it needs to pass through the body."[49] He claims that since Rosselini modern cinema has treated motifs of ruin and restoration literally. Ruins, the expenditure of the material world, become at the same time the film's setting and its raison d'être. This form of compact reflexivity is at work in many recent films, whose most immediate characteristic is their descriptive, episodic narrative. The effects of the earthquake in *And Life Goes On* (1992) are an example. Kiarostami's pretext for filming was to look for actors from his previous film *Where Is My Friend's House?* who live in that region, to return to a place where the inhabitants were working to remake their homes and are therefore also moving stones for a film set—activities hard to tell apart. The ruins are an indexical trace of the actual catastrophe. But given the long-standing impact of broken mountains, rerouted roads, and destroyed villages, there is no way of knowing, except extratextually, how long ago the event took place or how urgent the quest is to find the children who once acted in a film by the director. Both reportage and fiction films are shown to have missed the earthquake. Kiarostami's film and the diegetic filmmaker are therefore always trailing after, telling a story in winding detours, traversing the many stops that will let us see as much as we can see, all we *can* see, traces of events.[50]

What is singularly brought home in such contemporary images of incidental events, staged in so many of Bazin's examples of cinematic specificity is the inherent heterogeneity of cinematic images—their awkward amalgams of literal materiality and reference.

"Modern cinema," notes Daney, can be characterized as "being always more or less documentary on the state of the materials to be filmed, always a dual operation, dialectical."[51] Contemporary realist cinema exercises pressure over this constitutive duality—the representational and literal aspects of cinema. Tsai Ming-liang's *The River* (1998) is an example. Caused perhaps by a brief stunt dip into a polluted river, or else by a dysfunctional family, the protagonist's sudden excruciating pain in the neck takes over every scene, contaminating more "dramatic" moments with an overwhelming physicality. This excessively charged sign, a symptom whose cause moves and evades the entire narrative, radically checks the film's fictive ground. The pain is a constant reminder of the actor's body, of its literalness.

Rites of Realism initiates an account of this layered materiality in its own promotion of an impure, corporeal cinema. Together the essays propose a methodological variant to work exclusively devoted to contextual research or detailed textual readings, a critical vocabulary attentive to the various contingencies of production and reception that form referential images and inform their readings.

Notes

1 See Elaine Scarry's argument on the difficulty of representing physical pain in *The Body in Pain: The Making and Unmaking of the World* (New York: Oxford University Press, 1985). For a discussion of the recent proliferation of theories about the body, see Carolyne Bynum, "Why All the Fuss about the Body? A Medievalist's Perspective," *Critical Inquiry* 22 (autumn, 1995): 1–34.

2 For an original consideration of cinema's hybridity, see Brigitte Peucker, *Incorporating Images: Film and the Rival Arts* (Princeton: Princeton University Press, 1995).

3 For Sandy Petrey, realist specificity is not "an impossible fidelity to a sociohistorical referent but a successful activation of the process by which sociohistorical collectivities make language appear referential." It is in part this active dimension of realism that I want to keep in my use of the term *performative realism*. See Petrey's *Realism and Revolution: Balzac, Stendhal, Zola, and the Performances of History* (Ithaca: Cornell University Press, 1988), 70.

4 André Bazin, "*Farrebique* or the Paradox of Realism," in *Bazin at Work: Major Essays and Reviews from the Forties and Fifties,* translated by Allain Piette and Bert Cardullo (New York: Routledge, 1997), 106, 108.

5 André Bazin, "High Infidelity (*The Bridge on the River Kwai*)," in Bazin, *Bazin at Work,* 227–28.

6 André Bazin, "Cinema and Exploration," in *What Is Cinema?* 2 vols., edited and translated by Hugh Gray (Los Angeles: University of California Press, 1967), 1:162. Both Philip Rosen and John Belton have used this example to suggest how "the greater reality" of a film equals, for Bazin, the spectator's investment in the construction of

meaning. See Philip Rosen, this volume, 70, especially 46, 48; and John Belton, "Bazin Is Dead! Long Live Bazin!" *Wide Angle* 9:4:78. Rosen's *Change Mummified: Cinema, Historicity, Theory* (Minneapolis: University of Minnesota Press, 2001) develops at length the relevance of Bazin's conception of indexicality and contingency. His discussion of Bazin, Barthes, and Comolli is an in-depth complement to my own take in this introduction. See also my analysis of realism in *Nothing Happens: Chantal Akerman's Hyperrealist Everyday* (Durham: Duke University Press, 1996).

7   André Bazin, "Bicycle Thief," in Bazin, *What Is Cinema?*, 2:52.

8   Siegfried Kracauer, *Theory of Film: The Redemption of Physical Reality* (Princeton: Princeton University Press, 1960), 231. See also Miriam Bratu Hansen, introduction to Kracauer, *Theory of Film*, xxxi. Hansen's work on Kracauer represents a historicized and highly sympathetic rethinking of cinema's affinity for the concrete. Rescuing Kracauer from his characterization as a naive realist, Hansen zooms in on the notion of materiality. She identifies Kracauer's concern as being "not with authenticity or verisimilitude but rather with film's ability to discover and articulate materiality, to enact 'the process of materialization' " ("Marseille Notebooks," 2.9, cited in Kracauer, *Theory of Film*, xvii. For another relevant reading of realism in the arts that departs from notions of lifelikeness, see Michael Fried, "Between Realisms: From Derrida to Manet," *Critical Inquiry* 21 (autumn 1994): 1–36.

9   Roland Barthes, "The Reality Effect," in *The Rustle of Language*, translated by Richard Howard (Los Angeles: University of California Press, 1989), 48–71.

10 See André Bazin, "Le Neorealisme se retourne," *Cahiers du Cinéma* 69 (March 1957): 45–47. See also Rosen's important reevaluation of Bazin's privileging temporality instead of "spatial similarity or dissimilarity between image and the world" as an indication of the irrelevance of life-looking qualities in Bazin's conception of realism in *Change Mummified*, 16.

11 André Bazin, *Jean Renoir*, edited with an introduction by François Truffaut, translated by W. W. Halsey II and William H. Simon (New York: Simon and Schuster, 1971–73), 67.

12 Jean-Louis Comolli, "Historical Fiction: A Body Too Much," translated by Ben Brewster, *Screen* 19 (summer 1978): 45, originally published as "Un corps en trop," *Cahiers du Cinéma* 278 (July 1977): 5–16.

13 See, for instance, "The Question Oshima" (as well as "Film Performance," which I discuss below), in Stephen Heath, *Questions of Cinema* (Bloomington: Indiana University Press, 1981), 145–64, 113–30. Many have pointed out the parallels between the teleological conceptions of cinema in apparatus theories and Bazin. See Rosen, this volume. Besides the essay on *La Marseilleise*, Jean-Louise Comolli bases his own take on contemporary realism on Bazin's emphasis on the encounter between the profilmic and the camera ("Du Realisme comme Utopie," in *Cine Europeo El Desafio de la Realidad*, 42 Semana Internacional de Cine [Valladolid: 1997], 107–17). Stephen Bann's "The Odd Man Out: Historical Narrative and the Cinematic Image" also returns to the wig in *La Marseilleise* for his analysis of the role of indexicality in historical representation (in *The Inventions of History: Essays on the Representation of the Past* [New York: Manchester University Press, 1990], 193). For an evaluation of Bazin's continuing relevance for a contemporary analysis of referential genres, see Rosen, *Change Mummified*, 3–41.

14 For an original interpretation of images of death in modernist narrative cinema, see Catherine Russell, *Narrative Mortality: Death, Closure, and the New Wave Cinemas* (Minneapolis: University of Minnesota Press, 1995).

15 André Bazin, "Death Every Afternoon," this volume, originally published as "La mort tous les après-midi," in *Qu'est ce que le cinema?* (Paris: Editions du Cerf, 1958), 1:65–70.

16 Bazin, "Death Every Afternoon," 31 n. 4.

17 Stephen Heath, "Film Performance," in Heath, *Questions of Cinema,* 113–14.

18 Ibid., 114–15.

19 As John Corner puts it succinctly: "At once and equally suspect are the projects of verisimilitude (being like the real) and of referentiality (being about the real)." "Presumption as Theory: 'Realism and T.V. Studies'," *Screen* 33:1 [spring 1992]: 98.

20 See the following relevant texts from *Screen:* Stephen Heath, "Lessons from Brecht," 15:2 (summer 1974): 103–28; Stephen Heath, "From Brecht to Film: Theses, Problems," 16:4 (winter 1975–76): 34–45; Stephen Heath, "Narrative Space," 17:3 (autumn 1976): 68–112; Colin MacCabe, "Realism and the Cinema: Notes on Some Brechtian Theses," 15:2 7–24; Colin MacCabe, "The Politics of Separation, 16:4 (winter 1975/61): 46–61; and Colin MacCabe, "Principles of Realism and Pleasure," 17:3 (autumn 1976): 7–28. For an excellent summary and critique of *Screen*'s positions on realism, see Dick Hebdige and Geoff Hurd, "Reading and Realism," *Screen Education* 28 (autumn 1978): 68–78.

21 Here I substitute Stephen Melville's formulation, applied to realism in literary and visual studies, to "realism in cinema," which seems even more blatantly to deserve "explanation." Melville's review of Michael Fried's *Courbet's Realism* also cites Fried's own statement on the need to inquire further into realist art. See Stephen Melville, "Compelling Acts, Haunting Convictions," *Art History* 14:1 (March 1991): 117.

22 Jonathan Crary, *Techniques of the Observer: On Vision and Modernity in the Nineteenth Century* (Cambridge: MIT Press, 1990), 4.

23 For basic arguments on the cinematic apparatus, see Jean-Louis Baudry, "Ideological Effects of the Basic Cinematographic Apparatus," 286–98; Jean-Louis Baudry, "The Apparatus," 299–318; Jean-Louis Comolli, "Technique and Ideology," pts. 3 and 4, 421–43; and Philip Rosen, "Introduction," 281–28, all in Philip Rosen, ed., *Narrative, Apparatus, Ideology: A Film Theory Reader* (New York: Columbia University Press, 1986). See also Stephen Heath, "The Cinematic Apparatus: Technology as Historical and Cultural Form," in *The Cinematic Apparatus,* edited by Stephen Heath and Teresa De Lauretis (New York: St. Martin's Press, 1980), 1–13. Two of the recent film histories that refer explicitly to the limitations of apparatus theories are: James Lastra, *Sound Technology and the American Cinema: Perception, Representation, Modernity* (New York: Columbia University Press, 2000); and Ben Brewster and Lea Jacobs, *Theatre to Cinema: Stage Pictorialism and the Early Feature Film* (New York: Oxford University Press, 1997). Annette Kuhn and Jackie Stacie note in their introduction to *Screen Histories: A Reader* that the journal's earliest forays into the "new" film history were all histories of technology and in particular of deep space cinematography, "which at that time formed part of the journal's overall theoretical agenda" (Oxford: Clarendon Press, 1998), 3–4. On the centrality of the concept of perspective to understanding the various theoretical stakes of realism, see Rosen, *Change Mummified,* 14–21.

24 Lastra, *Sound Technology and the American Cinema,* 11.

25 See, among others, Miriam Hansen, *Babel and Babylon: Spectatorship in American Silent Film* (Cambridge: Harvard University Press, 1991); Tom Gunning, "An Aesthetics of Astonishment: Early Film and the (In)credulous Spectator," *Art and Text* 34 (spring 1989): 31–45; Tom Gunning, "Tracing the Individual Body: Photography, Detectives, and Early Cinema," in *Cinema and the Invention of Modern Life,* edited by Leo Charney and Vanessa R. Schwartz (Berkeley: University of California Press, 1995), 15–45; Vanessa Schwartz, *Spectacular Realities: Early Mass Culture in Fin de Siècle Paris* (Los Angeles: University of California Press, 1998); and Ben Singer, *Melodrama and Modernity: Early Sensational Cinema and Its Contexts* (New York: Columbia University Press, 2001). For a comprehensive account of how significant early film scholarship was in changing the field of cinema studies, see "Early Cinema: From Linear History to Mass Media Archaeology," Thomas Elsaesser's introduction to *Early Cinema: Space, Frame, Narrative,* edited by Thomas Elsaesser and Adam Barker (London: British Film Institute, 1990), 1–10.

26 See, for instance, Rae Beth Gordon's *Why the French Love Jerry Lewis: From Cabaret to Early Cinema* (Stanford: Stanford University Press, 2001); Linda Williams *Hard Core: Power, Pleasure, and the Frenzy of the Visible* (Los Angeles: University of California Press, 1989); Linda Williams, "Corporealized Observers: Visual Pornographies and the 'Carnal Density of Vision,'" in *Fugitive Images: From Photography to Video,* edited by Patrice Petro (Bloomington: Indiana University Press, 1995); Judith L. Goldstein, "Realism without a Human Face," in *Spectacles of Realism: Gender, Body, Genre,* edited by Margaret Cohen and Christopher Prendergast (Minneapolis: University of Minnesota Press, 1995); Mark Sandberg, "Effigy and Narrative: Looking into the Nineteenth Century Folk Museum," in Charney and Schwartz, *Cinema and the Invention of Modern Life;* and Lisa Cartwright, *Screening the Body: Tracing Medicine's Visual Culture* (Minneapolis: University of Minnesota Press, 1995). See also Steven Shaviro's interesting take on corporeality in *The Cinematic Body* (Minneapolis: University of Minnesota Press, 1993). Linda Williams's work has been consistently important in the revaluation of the body in the cinema. See her "Film Bodies: Gender, Genre, Excess," *Film Quarterly* 44:4 (summer 1991): 2–12.

27 Brewster and Jacobs, *Theatre to Cinema,* 3, 4.

28 David Rodowick, *The Crisis of Political Modernism: Criticism and Ideology in Contemporary Film Theory* (Chicago: University of Illinois Press, 1988–94), xiv.

29 See ibid., xiv. In the preface to the second edition, Rodowick suggests how inseparable the "critique of realist form in Hollywood cinema as illusionistic, and the promotion of semiotic counter-strategies of modernism" are in the discourse of political modernism.

30 In his interesting chapter on research for fiction films, "Detail, Document, Diegesis," Philip Rosen points out that the profilmic is a significant area of scholarly attention elided in most antirealist theories since the 1960s (Rosen, *Change Mummified,* 147–99).

31 See, in particular, André Bazin, "On the *politique des auteurs,*" in *Cahiers du Cinéma, the 1950s: Neorealism, Hollywood, New Wave,*" edited by Jim Hillier (Cambridge: Harvard University Press, 1985), 248–59.

32 See André Bazin, "The Myth of Stalin in Soviet Cinema," in Bazin, *Bazin at Work,* 23–40. See also George Custen's definitive reading of the logic of biographical films, *BioPics: How Hollywood Constructed Public History* (N.J.: Rutgers University Press, 1992).

33 An essential contribution to this debate is present in Petro's *Fugitive Images: From Photography to Video.* See also Timothy Corrigan, "Immediate History: Videotape Interventions and Narrative Film," in *The Image in Dispute: Art and Cinema in the Age of Photography,* edited by Dudley Andrew (Austin: University of Texas Press, 1997), 309–27. The increase in the number of anthologies on documentary can be seen as a response of sorts to digitization. See Jane Gaines, "The Real Returns," her introduction to *Collecting Visible Evidence,* where she rethinks the reasons for the dismissal of realism and documentary issues during the 1970s, (edited by Jane Gaines and Michael Renov [Minneapolis: University of Minnesota Press, 1999], 1, 4, 10). See also Barry Keith Grant and Jeannette Sloniowski, eds., *Documenting the Documentary: Close Readings of Documentary Film and Video* (Detroit: Wayne State University Press, 1998); Kevin Macdonald and Mark Cousins, eds., *Imagining Reality: The Faber Book of Documentary* (London: Faber and Faber, 1996); Michael Renov, ed., *Theorizing Documentary* (New York: Routledge, 1993); and Brian Winston, *Claiming the Real: The Documentary Film Revisited* (London: British Film Institute, 1995). For a wonderful discussion of documentary and realism, see Dai Vaughan's *For Documentary* (Berkeley: University of California Press, 1999).

34 A few writers have importantly resisted and questioned the "technological argument," which sees in video or digital images the death of cinema. See Lynne Kirby's "Death and the Photographic Body," in Petro, *Fugitive Images,* 72–84; and Thomas Elsaesser's introductory essays in Thomas Elsaesser, ed., *Cinema Futures: Cain, Abel, or Cable* (Amsterdam: Amsterdam University Press, 1998). As other anthologies make clear, the emergence of digitization has led to a comparative impulse in rethinking cinematic specificity. See Dudley Andrew, ed., *The Image in Dispute: Art and Cinema in the Age of Photography* (Austin: University of Texas Press, 1997); and Dagmar Barnow, *Critical Realism: History, Photography, and the Work of Siegfried Kracauer* (Baltimore: Johns Hopkins University Press, 1994).

35 Interestingly, indexicality and André Bazin are frequently mentioned in 1990s work on the digital future of media technologies. In some historicist outlooks, the indexical gains a nondignified cast, where *instead* of being associated with the historical it becomes passé. See Philip Hayward and Tana Wollen, eds., *New Technologies of the Screen* (London: British Film Institute, 1993), especially the introduction.

36 Mary Ann Doane, this volume. She mentions in particular Paul Willemen, "Through the Glass Darkly: Cinephilia Reconsidered," in *Looks and Frictions: Essays in Cultural Studies and Film Theory* (Bloomington: Indiana University Press, 1998); and Miriam Hansen's introduction to Kracauer's *Theory of Film.* See also Hansen's " 'With Skin and Hair': Kracauer's Theory of Film, Marseille 1940," *Critical Inquiry* 19 (spring 1993): 437–69.

37 Willemen, *Looks and Frictions,* 231.

38 Fredric Jameson. "The Existence of Italy," in *Signatures of the Visible* (New York: Routledge, 1992), 155–229.

39 Ibid., 156.

40 Ibid., 167–74.

41 Discussions of British cinema exemplify the general tendency to subordinate issues of realism to considerations of national cinemas. See John Hill, *British Cinema in the 1980s:*

Issues and Themes (Oxford: Clarendon Press, 1999); and John Hill, *British Cinema: Sex, Class, and Realism, 1956–1963* (London: British Film Institute, 1986).

42 Miriam Hansen reads Kracauer's theories as a departure from an analogical realism: "Kracauer's investment in the photographic basis of film does not rest in the iconicity of the photographic sign, at least not in the narrow sense of a literal resemblance or analogy with a self identical object. Nor, for that matter, does he conceive of the indexical, the photochemical bond that links image and referent, in any positivist way as merely anchoring the analogical 'truth' of the representation. Rather, the same indexicality that allows photographic film to record and figure the world also inscribes the image with moments of temporality and contingency that *disfigure* the representation" (Kracauer, *Theory of Film,* xxv).

43 David James, *Allegories of Cinema: American Film in the Sixties* (Princeton: Princeton University Press, 1989), 69, cited in Arthur, this volume, 108.

44 See Arthur, this volume, 109.

45 See David James's analysis of urban representation, "Toward a Geo-Cinematic Hermeneutics: Representations of Los Angeles in Non-industrial Cinema—*Killer of Sheep* and *Water and Power,*" *Wide Angle* 20:3 (July 1998): 23–53.

46 Kracauer, *Theory of Film,* 303.

47 Raymond Williams, "A Lecture on Realism," *Screen* 18:1 (1977): 63.

48 Manthia Diawara acknowledges the broad range of aesthetic modes in representing black realities. Still his distinctions seem to forfeit the term *realism,* as it equates it with the conventions of classical Hollywood narrative or Italian neorealism. These cinemas, as well as realism, are conceived as unified, clear-cut blocs. See Manthia Diawara, ed., *Black American Cinema: Aesthetics and Spectatorship* (London: Routledge, 1993), 3–25.

49 Comolli, "Du Realisme comme Utopie," 115.

50 For a smart analysis of the correlation between the temporality of events and their media representation, see Mary Ann Doane, "Information, Crisis, Catastrophe," in *Logics of Television,* edited by Patricia Mellencamp (Bloomington: Indiana University Press, 1990), 222–39. See also Doane's "Screening Time," in *Language Machines: Technologies of Literary and Cultural Production,* edited by Jeffrey Masten, Peter Stallybrass, and Nancy Vickers (New York: Routledge, 1997).

51 Daney, *La Rampe,* 162.

BAZINIAN CONTINGENCIES

Death Every Afternoon

André Bazin

Translated by Mark A. Cohen

I understand that Pierre Braunberger nurtured the idea for this film for quite some time. The result shows that it was worth it. The chances are that a noted aficionado like Braunberger saw nothing more in this project than a way to honor and promote bullfighting as well as make a film his producer would not regret. From this point of view, it was probably a good invest-ment—deservedly so I must add—because bullfight lovers will rush to see it while the uninitiated will go out of curiosity. I do not think fans will be disappointed because the footage is exceptionally fine. They will find the most famous matadors in action, and the shots Braunberger and Myriam have compiled and edited are astonishingly effective. The bullfights must have been filmed copiously and repeatedly for the camera to convey the action of the bullring so completely. Many are the passes and coups de grâce filmed during top events featuring stars, which afford us long, practically uncut takes in which the framing of man and animal is never tighter than a medium shot or even an American shot. And when the head of the bull comes into the foreground it is not a stuffed head, the rest follows.

Perhaps I am a fool to be so astonished by Myriam's talent. She edited the footage with diabolical skill, and you have to pay careful attention to see that the bull that comes into view from the left is not always the one that left the screen from the right. So perfectly do the matches on action conceal the articulation of the shots that the film would have to be viewed with a moviola to distinguish with certainty between a single shot and a sequence created by patching together five or six different shots.[1] Without us noticing the switch, a "veronica" beginning with one matador and bull ends with a different man and a different animal. Since *The Story of a Cheat* (*Le Roman d'un Tricheur*) and especially *Paris 1900,* everyone knows that Myriam is a brilliant editor. *The Bullfight* has proved it yet again. When it is this good, the art of the editor goes well beyond its usual function—it is an essential element in the film's creation. Such a conception of montage film calls for further discussion. At issue here is something quite different than a return to the old primacy of montage over découpage (shooting script) as taught by early Soviet cinema. Neither *Paris 1900* nor *The Bullfight* are "Kino eye." They are "modern" works, aesthetically contemporary with the découpage of films such as *Citizen Kane, Rules of the Game, The Viper,* and *Bicycle Thieves.* The goal of the editing is not to suggest symbolic and abstract links between the images, as in Kulechov's famous experiment with the close-up of Moszhukin. If the phenomenon revealed in this experiment is to play a role in this neomontage, it is for a radically different purpose: to fulfill both the physical verisimilitude of the découpage and its logical malleability. The image of a naked woman followed by Moszhukin's ambiguous smile signifies salaciousness and desire. What is more, the moral significance in some sense preexists the physical one; the image of a naked woman plus image of a smile equals desire. No doubt the existence of desire logically implies that the man is looking at the woman, but this geometry is not there in the images. The deduction is almost superfluous; for Kulechov, moreover, it is secondary. What counts is the meaning given to the smile by the collision of images. In this case, the relationship is quite different. Myriam aims above all at physical realism. The deception of the editing supports the verisimilitude of the découpage. The linkage of two bulls in a single movement does not symbolize the bulls' strength; it surreptitiously replaces the photo of the nonexistent bull we believe we are seeing. The editor makes sense of her editing just as the director of his découpage, based solely on this kind of realism. It is no longer the camera eye, but the adaptation of editing technique to the aesthetics of the camera pen.[2]

That is why novices like me will find in this film the clearest and most thorough introduction imaginable. The footage was not edited randomly according to the shots' spectacular affinities but with precision and clarity. The history of bullfighting (and of the bulls bred for it) and the evolution of fighting styles up to and since Belmonte are presented with all the didactic resources of the cinema. When a figure is being described, the image is frozen at the critical moment and the commentator explains the relative positions of man and animal. Probably because they did not have access to slow-motion equipment, Pierre Braunberger relied on a truca, but the freeze frame is as effective.[3] Needless to say the didactic qualities of this film are also its limit, or so it would appear. The project is less grandiose and all embracing than Hemingway's in *Death in the Afternoon. The Bullfight* might seem nothing more than a feature-length documentary, a fascinating one to be sure, but still a "documentary." This view would be unjust and mistaken, unjust because the pedagogic humility with which it was carried out is less a sign of limitation than of a conscious refusal. Faced with such a grand subject, such rich material, Pierre Braunberger acted in all humility. The commentary restricts itself to explanation; it avoids a facile verbal lyricism that would be overwhelmed by the objective lyricism of the image. Mistaken, too, because the subject transcends itself, and this means that Pierre Braunberger's project is perhaps even greater cinematically than he could have imagined.

The experience of filmed theater—and its almost total failure until some recent successes redefined the problem—has made us aware of the role played by real presence. We know that the photographic image of a play only gives it back to us emptied of its psychological reality, a body without a soul. The reciprocal presence, the flesh and blood confrontation of viewer and actor, is not a simple physical accident but an ontological fact constitutive of the performance as such. Starting from this theoretical given as well as from experience, one might infer that the bullfight is even less cinematic than the theater. If theatrical reality cannot be captured on celluloid, what about the tragedy of tauromachy, of the liturgy and the almost religious feeling that accompanies it. A photograph of a bullfight might have some documentary or didactic value, but how could it give us back the essence of the spectacle, the mystical triad of animal, man, and crowd?

I have never been to a bullfight, and it would be ridiculous of me to claim that the film lets me feel the same emotions, but I do claim that it gives me its essential quality, its metaphysical kernel: death. The tragic ballet of the bullfight turns around the presence and permanent possibility of death (that of the animal and the man). That is what makes the ring into something more than a theater stage: death is played on it. The toreador plays for his life, like the trapeze artist without a net. Death is surely one of those rare events that justifies the term, so beloved of Claude Mauriac, *cinematic specificity.* Art of time, cinema has the exorbitant privilege of repeating it, a privilege common to all mechanical arts, but one that it can use with infinitely greater potential than records or radio. Let us be even more precise since there are other temporal arts, like music. But musical time is immediately and by definition aesthetic time, whereas the cinema only attains and constructs its aesthetic time based on lived time, Bergsonian "*durée,*" which is in essence irreversible and qualitative. The reality that cinema reproduces at will and organizes is the same worldly reality of which we are a part, the sensible continuum out of which the celluloid makes a mold both spatial and temporal. I cannot repeat a single moment of my life, but cinema can repeat any one of these moments indefinitely before my eyes. If it is true that for consciousness no moment is equal to any other, there is one on which this fundamental difference converges, and that is the moment of death. For every creature, death is the unique moment par excellence. The qualitative time of life is retroactively defined in relation to it. It marks the frontier between the duration of consciousness and the objective time of things. Death is nothing but one moment after another, but it is the last. Doubtless no moment is like any other, but they can nevertheless be as similar as leaves on a tree, which is why their cinematic repetition is more paradoxical in theory than in practice. Despite the ontological contradiction it represents, we quite readily accept it as a sort of objective counterpart to memory. However, two moments in life radically rebel against this concession made by consciousness: the sexual act and death. Each is in its own way the absolute negation of objective time, the qualitative instant in its purest form. Like death, love must be experienced and cannot be represented (it is not called the little death for nothing) without violating its nature. This violation is called obscenity. The representation of a real death is also an obscenity, no longer a moral one, as in love, but metaphysical. We do not die twice. In this respect, a photograph does not have the power of film; it can only represent someone dying or a corpse, not the elusive passage from one state to the other. In the spring of 1949, you may have seen a haunting documentary about the anti-Communist crackdown in Shanghai in which Red "spies" were executed with a revolver on the public square. At each screening, at the flick of a switch, these men came to life again and then the jerk of the same bullet jolted their necks. The film did not even leave out the gesture of the policeman who had to make two attempts with his jammed revolver, an intolerable sight not so much for its objective horror as for its ontological obscenity. Before cinema there was only the profanation of corpses and the desecration of tombs. Thanks to film, nowadays we can desecrate and show at will the only one of our possessions that is temporally inalienable: dead without a requiem, the eternal dead-again of the cinema![4]

I imagine the supreme cinematic perversion would be the projection of an execution backward like those comic newsreels in which the diver jumps up from the water back onto his diving board.

These observations have not taken me so far as it seems from *The Bull-fight*. One will understand me if I say that the film of a performance of Molière's *Malade Imaginaire* has no theatrical or cinematic value but that if the camera had been present at Molière's final performance it would be an amazing film.[5]

This is why the representation on screen of a bull being put to death (which presupposes that the man has risked death) is in principle as moving as the spectacle of the real instant that it reproduces. In a certain sense, it is even more moving because it magnifies the quality of the original moment through the contrast of its repetition. It confers on it an additional solemnity. The cinema has given the death of Manolette a material eternity.

On the screen, the toreador dies every afternoon.

Notes

1 A movieola is a playback machine.

2 Translator's note: Given that *The Bullfight* has a voice-over commentary written by Michel Leiris, it is probable that Bazin sees this as an essay film, as suggested by his use of Alexandre Astruc's term *caméra stylo.*

3 A truca is a special effects optical printer.

4 Translator's note: In the French this is *re-morts,* which is a pun on *re-mords,* meaning "remorse."

5 Translator's note: Molière died shortly after falling ill onstage during a performance of this play in 1672.

The Screen of Fantasy (Bazin and Animals)

Serge Daney

Translated by Mark A. Cohen

When André Bazin is asking questions about cinema, he often finds his answers in marginal films.[1] Documentaries, newsreels, "poetic" films, or "live-record" films allow him to formulate precisely what for him is a fundamental law: whenever it is possible to enclose two heterogeneous objects in the same frame, editing is prohibited. In that sense, we shall see that the essence of cinema becomes a story about animals. Judge for yourself: "It is true that other devices such as process shots make it possible to have two objects,[2] say the star and the tiger, *in the same shot,* a proximity which might cause some problems in real life."[3] Or again, "Here, to our surprise, we see the director abandon the series of close shots, which serve to isolate the protagonists from the dramatic action, and offer us simultaneously, *in the same long shot,* parents, child, and animal."[4] And last, "on the other hand in the same film [*Louisiana Story*] the sequence shot of the crocodile attacking the heron *filmed in a single pan* is simply wonderful."[5]

We can see that what justifies the prohibition of editing, of fragmentation, is not only, as has often been said, the exploitation of depth of field, the birth of cinemascope, or the ever-greater mobility of the camera in an increasingly homogeneous space but also, and above all, the *nature of*

what is being filmed, the status of the protagonists (in this case men and animals) who are
forced to share the screen, sometimes at the risk
of their lives. The ban on editing is a function
of this risk. There is no question for Bazin of
calling for the cinema to be completely free of
editing—such an extreme point of view is for-

eign to him—only that "there are cases where far from being the essence
of cinema, editing is its negation."[6] For the coexistence of crocodile and
heron, tiger and star, in front of the camera, is not without its problems
(particularly for the heron and the star), and to talk of "heterogeneous" elements is a euphemism when it is a question of a violent incompatibility, a
fight to the death.

It is therefore the possibility of filming death that "in certain cases" pro-
hibits editing, or at least the editing secretly hated by Bazin, a sort of generalized death, abstract, facile, automatically creating meaning, operating
in the blank spaces of the text. If it is forbidden, it is because it does not
let us read "what is said in between" because by moving in qualitative leaps
it deprives the obsessive-compulsive of his or her fantasy, to apprehend
(*saisir*) the passage of something not through a back and forth movement
from past to future but as an eternal present. Difference, rupture, discontinuity—they are not absent from Bazin's discourse nor from the cinema he
defends; they are in fact so present that they "burst the screen." A cinema
seeking continuity and transparency at all costs is identical to a cinema that
dreams of filming discontinuity and difference as such. And it can only do
it by reintroducing them as objects of *representation*.

We should not split up the screen but show the split occurring on it ("In
L'Afrique vous parle, a Negro gets eaten by a crocodile"),[7] not break continuity but make a rupture stand out on the conveyor belt of presence,
"deny by elevating, by idealizing, by sublimating in an amnesiac interiority, by *interning difference* in self-presence" (Derrida). Bring the forbidden fruit inside the frame and assign editing a demoted role: a practice
of making a "good connecting shot," meaning invisible editing, which,
in extremis, lets things speak of themselves. "To reveal the hidden meaning of beings and things without disturbing their temporal unity." In such
a sentence it is the second part that is imperative (unity), for the mean-

1. Predator and prey in *Louisiana Story,* Robert Flaherty, 1948 (frame enlargement of video)

ing itself can remain hidden or suspended with no harm done (things are chatterboxes but they talk drivel). This unity is never anything but that of the spatio-temporal continuum of representation. *To intern difference means saving representation.*

For Bazin, the horizon of cinema's history is cinema's disappearance. Until then, this history is indistinguishable from that of a small difference that is the object of a constant negation:[8] I know (that the image is not real) but all the same. . . . With each technical change, the transparency grows, the difference seems to get smaller, the celluloid becomes the skin of History and the screen a window open to the world. Sometimes he declares the limit has been reached: "No more actors, no more story, no more mise-en-scène, that is to say finally the perfect aesthetic illusion of reality: no more cinema."[9] Whoever passes through the screen and meets reality *on the other side* has gone beyond *jouissance.*[10] If he makes it back (but in what state? obsessional for sure) and if he is still speaking, it will be to talk at length about what he has missed the most: the prohibited.

Also this cinema of transparency only desires whatever limits it, impedes it. It only worships transparency because it knows that—all the same— there is no such thing. That is the price of fetishism. Certain proponents of this ideology of direct cinema, so widespread these days and to whose emergence Bazin contributed on the level of theory, are prisoners of this fetishism. Bazin, more savvy, always oscillated between "I know it" and "but all the same." At times, he clearly sees the realization of cinema's essence— aided by technique—in its move toward greater and greater realism: this is his famous "gain in reality." At other times, when he is readier to acknowledge his own fantasy, he points out that for every gain in reality there is a corresponding "loss of reality" in which abstraction insidiously returns. In volume 4 of *Qu'est-ce que le cinéma?* he admits that "it will always be necessary to sacrifice something of reality to reality."[11]

Sacrifice what? Precisely, the skin, the transparent. The transparent continuum that clings to the real takes its form, the bandages that preserve for us the mummy of reality, its still living corpse, its eternal presentness: that which allows us to see and protects us from what is seen: *the screen.* What overdetermines the Bazinian fantasy and, in its wake, a whole swath of idealist discourse on the cinema is a comical vision of the screen as the surface of a Teflon saucepan (in glass), capable of "sealing" [in the culinary sense] (*saisir*) the signifier. The screen, the skin, the celluloid, the surface of the pan, exposed to the fire of the real and on which is going to be inscribed—metaphorically and figuratively—everything that could burst them. If we have to save the screen so that representation can survive, what better to represent there if not the rescue itself?

That tiny difference, the screen: "Of course," says Bazin, "a woman who has been raped is still beautiful but she is no longer the same woman."[12] The obscenity perpetrated by the rape of reality cannot fail to send us back to the rape of the woman and the screen, the hymen. The fundamental ambiguity of the real is the uncertainty regarding virginity: the tiny almost nothing that changes everything. The attachment to representation, the taste for simulacra, a certain love for the cinema (cinephilia), all derive less from ontology than from obsessional neurosis. It is in the very essence of the latter to clothe itself in the former. "The predilection felt by obsessional neurotics for uncertainty and doubt leads them to turn to those subjects which are uncertain for all mankind and upon which our knowledge and judgments must necessarily remain open to doubt" (Freud, *The Rat Man*).[13] We think here of Buñuel, not because he is free of such a fetish (more or less the same as the immaculate conception) but because he managed to film the fetish as such. Take the scene in which, one night while his wife is asleep, the hero of *El* grabs ropes, the blade of a razor, thread, and a hooked needle.

The screen saved, representation brought home, montage humbled: it is from this homogeneous and continuous surface that—in the form of literary themes or contingencies/chance occurences during shooting—ruptures and differences will be stripped off.[14] They may refer to struggle (battles) or transformation (metamorphosis).

Struggle

MODEL: THE ONE/THE OTHER, MAN/BEAST

Who—for the sake of the cause and symmetry—is going to come and take this (always slightly questionable) place, to play the dummy part of the "wholly other"? Ethnocentrism—in fact any kind of centrism—would not be viable without collaborating/complicitous opposites. So: "I have no hesitation in stating that the cinema has rarely gone so far in making us aware of what it is to be a man. (And also, for that matter, of what it is to be a dog),"[15] says Bazin, writing about *Umberto D.* Bazin loved animals and lived with an iguana.[16]

Animal/Animal

"There is a sublime moment when, after having approached the sperm whales and tried rather brutally to make the contact that would cause two accidents in the herd, we gradually perceive the men starting to feel solidarity with the wounded mammals confronting the shark, which is, after all, nothing but a fish."[17] Let's look at that wonderful "after all." It tells us that out of two animals in a fight one is necessarily closer to us and that abstract knowledge—sperm whales (cetaceans) are mammals, like men—can fill in where perceptual evidence is no longer enough. The humans for whom this spectacle was intended will not be interested in it unless they

are represented in it: faced with two *others* there's still a choice to be made: *man/animal*.

"In *The Circus* Chaplin is truly in the lion's cage and both are enclosed within the frame of the screen."[18] As Bonitzer points out, the single frame "is very trenchant,"[19] and since it is clearly a question here of castration let us note that what one asks of the other is to confirm it in the certainty of its unity, therefore to castrate it.

Man/man

Or the bringing into play of what Freud has called the "narcissism of tiny differences." An (often very) minor contradiction becomes the axis around which the protagonists will be divided into two camps, with the frame as the shared space of their "life and death struggle," real or simulated. So-called classic cinema has rung infinite changes on these axes. In Ford, for example, the contradiction of majority/minorities can be applied (abstractly) to a large number of situations, with the minority represented, depending on the film, by explorers, Indians, the army, the Irish, or women. In Hawks, they are amateurs/professionals, in Renoir, masters/servants. The truth of this cinema and the moment when it begins to topple can be readily seen in the work of Jean Rouch, where it is almost as if the fiction/documentary pair were squared with the refinement of despair, cinematic practice as a game of black and white.

2. Man and animal in long shot, *The Circus,* Charles Chaplin, 1928 (frame enlargement of video)

Trip switch

"When a savage headhunter is shown in the foreground watching for the arrival of the whites, this necessarily implies that this person is not a savage because he has not cut the cameraman's head off."[20] With this witticism, Bazin indicates the exact spot where the cinema he would not dare dream of becomes a reality and then annuls itself, becomes itself the impossible. This is a limit that is not so distant, whose simple possibility valorizes the most banal image: the risk of death for the cameraman, of impossibility for the film: "occupational hazards."

When placing himself in danger, the filmmaker is not *so far* above the fray that he does not risk being swept away by the very real violence of what he films: "The cameraman runs as many risks as the soldiers, whose death he is supposed to film even at the cost of his own life (but who cares, as long as the reel is saved)."[21] Further on [in volume 1 *Qu'est ce le cinéma?*], he considers the first film about polar exploration to be all the more beautiful because its cameraman, H. C. Ponting, "had his hands frostbitten, while reloading without gloves in a temperature of −30°C."[22]

The trip switch is therefore the death of the filmmaker. In its more anodyne guise, this is also the fetishism of "filming as decisive moment," of filming as risk and of risk as what justifies the making of the film, which confers on it a certain surplus value. You have to go to the point of dying for your images. That's Bazin's eroticism. "It is no longer enough to hunt a lion unless it eats the bearers."[23]

Ways out

In their mise-en-scène of individual battles, of struggles and violent contradictions, the classic fictions have always hesitated between two solutions.

> —Both are reconciled. This is what occurs in humanist and recuperative discourse in which conflicts are absorbed into a superior unity, a larger community, a central state, and so on, all the fictions of the *Birth of a Nation* type.
> —One devours/is devoured by the other. This disappearing act becomes the object of a spectacle all the more beautiful because it is unbearable. It is no longer the complete reconciliation of everyone, but the aesthetic consolation of having looked death in the face without flinching, the death of the other, of course.

In both of these solutions "two merge into one."

In relation to its standard Hollywoodian foil, modern cinema, that is to say, postwar European cinema, has changed the terms of the problem somewhat. Its most characteristic feature, its lowest common denominator if you like, is its violent refusal of the dominant factor in American cinema: psychology as the explanation *nec plus ultra.* That is why modern cinema has sometimes been pulled toward mysticism (dissolution into the oneness of all things: Rossellini), sometimes toward pathology (the one is the other and the two are rift: Bergman). In both cases, what was released on the formal level was an entire logic of permutation and vicariousness, as can already be seen in the late work of Renoir (*The River, The Golden Coach*).

This is a logic whose fulfillment, almost to the point of parody, can be found in another great modern: Jean Rouch. When two groups (blacks and whites) are placed face to face, one mimicking the other, exchanging their positions to preserve rhyme and symmetry, this copresence reduces any struggle to an accelerated transfer of power, a humanist discourse, obviously antiracist, utopian, and contrived, where it is no longer a question of the class struggle but of the "struggle for position." In other words, the problems of neocolonial black Africa will not be resolved when the Dogons do ethnology in Brittany.

Politics. How to film the class struggle?

Transformation

MODEL: BEFORE/AFTER, LIFE/DEATH

"All that is necessary is that the spatial unity of an event be respected at the moment when fracturing it would transform the real into something purely imaginary."[24] The transformation, then, can be reduced to this: how are we to imagine a "change in plain view"? It is a question of magic, hypnotism, directing actors. It can be reduced to this, too: "Now death is one of those rare events that justifies the term, so beloved of Claude Mauriac, of cinematic specificity."[25]

EXAMPLES

Death as rupture, passage par excellence. But just as much everything that simulates death: the sexual act, metamorphosis. More generally, the main nodes of a story, the decisive moments when, under the impassive eye of the camera, something is unraveled, someone changes. Irreversibly. It is then that Bazin thinks we must not glide over the precise moment of transformation. It must be seen and "apprehended";[26] it must not be read or let itself be imagined in the back and forth movement of montage. Better still, the obstinate presence of the camera, far from being neutral, can provoke the transformation. At the end of his text on Allégret's film on Gide, Bazin writes: "time does not flow. It accumulates in the image until it is charged with an overwhelming potential whose discharge we await, almost with anguish. Allégret well understood this when he held back from cutting the last second of the shot in which Gide stares at the camera and lets out the desperate plea 'Cut!' Then the whole theater catches its breath, everyone fidgets in their seats, the storm has passed."[27] The prohibition of montage is wholly justified when the "Cut!" comes from the side of the filmed reality. Then we can orgasm.

Trip switch

Although the filmmaker sometimes risks death, it can also happen that he may film it without risk or even provoke it by means of his simple presence. Belief in the magic value of the camera, in the film as transformation of its protagonists, and, why not, in the cinema as transformation of society. The exorbitant power of the camera. You can die just to save face. This is what happened with Valentin, the birdman (in *Paris 1900*): "This is how it is in this prodigious birdman scene where the poor fool is obviously getting frightened and has finally realized that the bet was idiotic. But the camera is there to capture him for eternity, and he dare not disappoint its soulless eye. If there had only been human witnesses, a wise cowardice would certainly have won out."[28] The morality-masochism couple corresponds, then, to the aestheticism-sadism couple. Bazin even invents a sort of Freudian concept, the "Nero complex," the pleasure taken at the sight of urban destruction.[29]

Ways out

In "classic" cinema, transformation as the result of a quantitative accumulation *without* a qualitative leap, as a new state always given but never produced, is resolved or rather it does not get resolved.

— Either there is no transformation
— Or it occurs as a teleological coup

Here we should turn to Buñuel once more. Buñuel inscribes in the very first shot of his very first film (*An Andalusian Dog*) the castration that Bazin, via Chaplin, will seek in the lion's cage. As a filmmaker, he begins by finishing with sight, by announcing his respect for the hymen, his attachment to the Teflon pan, his fidelity to representation. But this is the fidelity of an impostor, the respect of a blind man. In Buñuel a general and ironic practice of "change in plain view" inscribes itself within the framework of a representation that will never be able to account for the change. Systematically in his last films (*Tristana, The Milky Way*) something is radically transformed within each scene and without any intervention from the outside. The reasons for these transformations are always multiple and undecidable. Representation is no longer the condition of a good exfoliation of the story but a sort of travesty that can say nothing about the nature of things, about their heterogeneity or the laws of their mutations. After all, if Nazarin seems so overwhelmed at the end of the film that bears his name it is perhaps because he loves pineapples.

Politics. How to film the "coming into consciousness"?

Notes

Translator's note: The notes cite English translations of Bazin taken from *What Is Cinema?* 2 vols., translated by Hugh Gray (Berkeley: University of California Press, 1967–72), and *Bazin at Work: Major Essays and Reviews from the Forties and Fifties,* translated by Alain Piette and Bert Cardullo (New York: Routledge, 1997), followed by French citations taken from *Qu'est-ce que le cinéma?* 4 vols. (Paris: Cerf, 1958–62). Where only the French reference is given, there is no English translation available. Gray's English translations have been modified.

1   He finds answers especially in *What Is Cinema?* in the following articles: "The Virtues and Limitations of Montage," (1:41–52; 1117–29); "Death Every Afternoon" (this volume and 1:65–70); "Le monde du silence" (1:9–64); "Le Paradis des hommes" (1:55–57); "On *Why We Fight:* History, Documentation, and the Newsreel" (*Bazin at Work* 1:31–36); and "A propos de Jean Painlevé" (1:37–39).

2   Translator's note: In French the technical name for a process shot is *la transparence,* which resonates with the concept of the cinema of "transparency" later referred to by Daney as one of Bazin's ideals.

3   Bazin, "Virtues," 1:45–46; 1:122.

4   Ibid., 49, n. 1; 1:126.

5   Ibid., 51; 1:128.

6   Ibid., 50, n. 1; 1127, n. 1.

7   Bazin, "Cinema and Exploration," in *What Is Cinema?* 1:155; 1:47.

8   Translator's note: *Dénégation* is a Freudian term meaning the formulation of a formerly

repressed thought that is then disavowed as a way of continuing to defend against it. J. Laplanche and J. B. Pontalis, *The Language of Psychoanalysis,* translated Donald Nicholson-Smith (New York: Norton, 1973).

9   Bazin, "Bicycle Thief," in *What Is Cinema?* 2:60; 4:59.

10 Translator's note: The phrase translated as "went beyond any conceivable pleasure" is "au-delà de la jouissance" in the original; *jouissance* of course means both pleasure and orgasm while the whole phrase itself alludes to the French translation of Freud's *Beyond the Pleasure Principle (Au-delà du principe de plaisir).*

11 Bazin, "An Aesthetic of Reality: Neorealism," in *What Is Cinema?* 2:30; 4:25.

12 Bazin, "Le Paradis des hommes," 1:57.

13 Sigmund Freud, *Notes upon a Case of Obsessional Neurosis (The Rat Man)* Case Histories 3. Translated by Alex Strachey and James Strachey (New York: Basic Books, 1959), 368.

14 Translator's note: the French translated as "stripped off" is *s'enlever,* which has the basic meaning of "to come off" and in relation to skin "to peel off" but whose nonreflexive form, *enlever,* can have (beyond its primary sense of "to remove") a sexual connotation of "to carry off, abduct, rape."

15 Bazin, "De Sica: Metteur en Scène," in *What Is Cinema?* 2:78; 4:91.

16 "De la difficulté d'être Coco," *Cahiers du Cinéma,* 91:303–5.

17 Bazin, "Le Monde du silence," 1:64.

18 Bazin, "Virtues," 1:52; 1:129.

19 See, in particular, Pascal Bonitzer, "Qu'est-ce que qu'un plan?" and "Les morceaux de la realité," in *Le Champ Aveugle: Essais sur le Cinéma* (Paris: Éditions Gallimard, 1982): 13–38 and 115–36. "Les morceaux" importantly complements Daney's essay, using many of the same examples from Bazin to articulate an understanding of the relation of the frame to reality.

20 Bazin, "Le Monde du silence," 1:62.

21 Bazin, "On *Why We Fight*," 188; 1:33.

22 Bazin, "Cinema and Exploration," 1:157; 1:49.

23 Ibid., 1:155; 1:47.

24 Bazin, "Virtues," 1:50; 1:127.

25 Bazin, "Death Every Afternoon," this volume and 1:68.

26 Translator's note: The term used here, *saisir,* is the same word used earlier in relation to the binding process of the Teflon pan.

27 Bazin, "André Gide," in *Qu'est-ce que le cinéma?* 1:74.

28 Bazin, "*Paris 1900,*" in *Qu'est-ce que le cinéma?* 1:41–42.

29 Bazin, "On *Why We Fight*," 188; 1:32.

History of Image, Image of History:

Subject and Ontology in Bazin

Philip Rosen

A Film Theorist from France

Since the 1960s, we have gone through a period in which Bazin bashing has become fashionable in film-theoretical discussion. Attacks have ranged in attitude from a virtual dismissal of André Bazin as theorist to measuring a respectful distance from his position.[1] Given the attack on realist arguments in recent critical thought, this widespread rejection is not surprising. But the insistent return to Bazin as the theoretical "other" to be attacked is also a kind of tribute. Somehow Bazin's history of style, his critical work, his explications of realism in film beginning from what he calls an ontology of the image have all remained required reading for anyone with a serious interest in cinema. Even given his rhetorical utility as an opponent, the repeated appearance of Bazin when referentiality has been under such suspicion in critical and theoretical discourse is striking.

If Bazin is still read, we must ask how one is to read Bazin. Despite local disagreements, the following reading is informed by commentaries on him already cited. But insofar as what follows is critique it does not start from an initiating condemnation or an unmediated outlining of contradiction but rather from the forms of coherence by which Bazin's writings claim our attention—appeal to us—as theoretically sophisticated. It is all too easy, having found something with which to disagree in a position, to stop thinking about it. But what is then missed is the relation between forms of coherence and contradictions that can provide for a symptomatic—a "historical"—placement of the argument. The final section of this essay proposes some moves in that direction.

The theoretical significance of Bazin's work is often said to begin from its stance as a phenomenological theory of film. Bazin established the mature foundations of his phenomenological view of cinema with the publication of "The Ontology of the Photographic Image" and "The Myth of Total Cinema" in 1945 and 1946. These essays formulated the ontological basis of Bazin's work, a basis sometimes too quickly read as a dialectic of the subjective (human) and the objective (materiality captured by the *objectif* of the photographic/cinematic apparatus for the human).

It is useful to recall that 1946 happens also to have been the year of publication of Jean-Paul Sartre's noted lecture, "Existentialism Is a Humanism." In this lecture, even while insisting on his radical differences with Descartes, Sartre said: "at the point of departure, there cannot be any truth other than this, *'I think, therefore, I am.'*" Dudley Andrew has emphasized that Bazin was conducting a debate with Malraux and Sartre.[2] However, what is important here is the common territory that was the ground of this debate: the centrality of the activity of the philosophical subject, the premise of all phenomenologies. If Bazin's theory is treated as yet another activation of the classical subject-object dialectic familiar from the history of continental philosophy, a *phenomenological* resolution of that split would take place on the ground of subjective intentionality. That is, any reading of Bazin on the image should begin from Bazin's view of the subject. Furthermore, this would have to be an *intending* subject, in the sense of philosophical phenomenology.

The "theory of the subject" is by now a catchphrase in Anglo-American film theory. But it comes to us as an intervention into our own intellectual history from such continental sources as German philosophy and, most intensively in recent years, French philosophy and textual theory. For example, Lacan's work (where the trace of Hegel is manifest) makes the Cartesian *cogito* its explicit target, seeking to divert not only psychoanalytic thought but also the course of French intellectual history by demystifying the allegedly fundamental nature of that category. On the other hand, in the institutional and pedagogical processes of the Anglo-American tradition, the role of the Cartesian cogito as an explicit, formal heritage is a less immediate issue than the practical dominance of empiricist and positivist standards in the human sciences generally, and this can affect readings of Bazin.

Thus, for example, in a critique that is enlightening for emphasizing the place of subjectivity, Colin MacCabe argues that Bazin's realism posits a subject of empiricism, reified out of the processes that form it. A counterexample is the critique of Bazin by the continental materialist Jean-Louis Comolli, who is able to read Bazin's "The Evolution of the Language of Cinema" in terms of the search by the subject for secure definition and positioning in the face of exteriority. Despite its source in Althusser, MacCabe's use of the term *empiricism* as under critique seems especially pertinent in the English-speaking theoretical tradition. But this polemical pertinence then prevents MacCabe from fully confronting existential phenomenology in one of its founding claims: the primacy of the *activity* of the subject; whereas in Comolli, Bazin's idealism is said to have at least the crucial virtue of exposing the struggle of the subject as the central issue.[3]

Now an opposition between continental and Anglo-American critiques of Bazin should not be overstated. The real point is to emphasize the relevance of the mode of thought in which Bazin worked. The subject's struggle for security, knowledge, and/or position is a problem not only for a psychoanalytic subject but also for the subject in a philosophical sense. It is a central issue posed in French philosophy from Descartes through at least existentialism and much of poststructuralism, and it is Bazin's context. It is true that in reading Bazin one must always be aware of his emphasis on the pregivenness of the concrete, objective real. However, another fundamental aspect of Bazin's theoretical work needs emphasis, and I would put it as strongly as possible: the processes by which human subjectivity approaches the objective constitute the basis of his position.

Of course, Bazin believes in the necessary coexistence and interaction of both "objective" and "subjective" aspects in the making and receiving/experiencing of films. However, what should not be ignored are the terms of this interaction. Bazin is quite consistent in his phenomenological solution to the subject-object split. For phenomenology, the subject's relations toward "exteriority" are definitive, and Bazin can almost always be read as analyzing the status of the objective *for* the subject. That is, "objective" here can be put in quotes with greater clarity, for the "objective" is always inflected by the "subjective," never available except through the processes of the latter. Bazin often expresses this with the terminology of abstract and concrete, which can remind us of his continental philosophical heritage: the world can never write itself apart from the abstracting drive of the subject to find meaning; the pure, brute, concrete real in its totality and apart from the intentionality of a subject is simply unavailable as such to humans. (This should not be confused with an automatic perceptual/mental processing of information, as in gestalt psychology, to which some important phenomenologists appealed.)[4]

Illustrations can be found in some of his most important critical work, such as "The French Renoir" and "An Aesthetic of Reality: Neo-realism."

> Given the fact that this movement toward the real [i.e., "realism"] can take a thousand different routes, the apologia for "realism" per se, strictly speaking, means nothing at all. The movement is valuable only insofar as it brings increased meaning (itself an abstraction) to what is created. . . . There is no point in rendering something realistically unless it is to make it more meaningful in an abstract sense. In this paradox lies the progress of the movies. In this paradox too lies the genius of Renoir, without doubt the greatest of all French directors.
>
> The same event, the same object, can be represented in various ways. Each representation discards or retains various of the qualities that permit us to recognize the object on the screen. Each introduces, for didactic or aesthetic reasons, abstractions that operate more or less corrosively and thus do not permit the original to subsist in its entirety. At the conclusion of this inevitable and necessary "chemical" action, for the initial reality there has been substituted an illusion of reality composed of a complex of abstraction (black and white, plane surface), of conventions (the rules of montage, for example), and of authentic reality. It is a necessary illusion. . . (wc2, 27, my emphasis)[5]

Such passages would seem to stand in direct contradiction to Bazin's notorious discovery of cinematic perfection in *Bicycle Thieves* (1948), "no more cinema." However, even that phrase, virtually always quoted out of the context of the sentence in which it appears, refers to "the perfect *aesthetic illusion* of reality" (wc2, 60, my emphasis). So there is something inevitably illusory in this apparently complete concreteness. Given the necessary abstraction, the physical-technical limitations of even cinema (e.g., black and white, plane surface), Bazin insists that realism is an aesthetic, or, rather, various realisms are various aesthetics. If readers are sometimes confused on this point despite Bazin's explicit insistence, it is perhaps because Bazin seems to propose that one can distinguish among various kinds of abstraction from reality and that some *illusions* of reality are to be valued over others. Is this not finally the point of his most influential essay, "The Evolution of the Language of Cinema," whose last paragraph proposes Hitchcock's (!) stylistic flexibility as an example of what the progressive realisms of the 1940s have made possible (wc1, 39)?

Bazin is a master of stylistic commentary, but formalistic distinctions can never be absolute for him, nor can the standards differentiating among kinds of illusions be held to an absolute criterion, a single view of reality. Even his often noted belief in reality's "ambiguity" works, among other things, to refuse the finality of constant criteria. If formal and stylistic procedures cannot provide an actual, unmediated access to the objective, then the basis for evaluating those procedures is located elsewhere than in the relation of text to its referent: in the processes of the subject, its modes of postulating and approaching "objectivity."

Thus, if we read Bazin in terms of the subject-object opposition, there is a fundamental move that must always be kept in mind: the "no more cinema" is *by and for the subject.* Bazin generally assumes a "subjective" assigning of significance to the concrete real, an activity that is inevitable and abstract with respect to the concrete. But the opposite term of this abstraction from the real is not an absolute concrete objectivity that cinema can somehow make immediately available; it is rather a subjective striving, the subject projecting itself, a subjective investment in the image precisely as "objectivity." This subjective projection is what serves Bazin's ontology in defining a cinematically specific phenomenological intentionality, and it is the stake of his analyses and his history of filmic style. It is a premise that can help maintain the complex interest of his theory even now.

"Mummy Dearest"

For example, consider what Bazin has to say about the import of Quattrocento perspective, which for at least two decades has been one of the central issues in accounts of "realism." Theorists such as Comolli and Stephen Heath cite its dominance in image technology ("normal" lenses) as stemming from the appeal of "centered" subject-position, understood through certain kinds of historical materialism and psychoanalysis. David Bordwell, on the other hand, has recently argued that even such sweeping sociohistoric claims must be grounded in an account of fundamental perceptual schemata.[6]

Notice what is common to both sides of this debate: though they may analyze "cues" for perception, both tend to assume a distinction between perception of actual depth and its perspectival representation, so both must account for spectators' finding enough in the basic iconic design of the image to invest in it as a sign or record of real space. Thus, the perspective discussions have tended to define the appeal of perspective in comparison with human *perception* of space, even if that comparison is to be bypassed. Bordwell explicitly calls on cognitive psychology, but at points even Heath draws on Arnheim's gestalt account for a description of the experience of the film image. Now, one would expect Bazin as realist theorist to be concerned with the comparison of image and the real, and of course passages can be found where he deals with the cinematic image by reference to perceptual-spatial accuracy. What needs highlighting, however, is how the centrality of this concern is ultimately diminished in the overall framework of his theory. In fact, Bazin invites us to displace consideration of the special appeal of cinematic "referentiality" from spatial similarity to temporal issues.

In "The Ontology of the Photographic Image," Bazin presents the development of Quattrocento perspectival representation as a key moment in the history of the representational arts, and the *camera obscura* as the direct ancestor of the photographic camera. In the history of culture, the power of this system does at first lie in its apparent spatial accuracy. In this sense, photography and cinema, as automated implementations of this mode, become "superior" developments of perspective and thereby divert painting away from achievements founded on spatial accuracy. Thus, Bazin describes perspectival representation of space as "the first scientific and already, in a sense, mechanical system of reproduction" (WC1, 11). And yet a basic thesis of his other crucial "ontological" essay, "The Myth of Total Cinema," is that scientificity has little to do with the development of cinematic technology. Is there a contradiction between these two essays?

Actually, even in "The Ontology of the Photographic Image" Bazin's early comments on perspective turn out to be ironic. We have already seen that Bazin was not afraid to remind his readers of the limits of cinematic representation, one of them being the distinction between a real space and the planar surface of the film image. In "The Ontology of the Photographic Image," the importance of perspective as a road to the real diminishes only a few paragraphs after its introduction. With the dominance of perspectival representation, "Painting was forced, as it turned out, to offer us illusion, and this illusion was reckoned sufficient unto art. Photography and cinema, on the other hand, are discoveries that satisfy once and for all and in its very essence, our obsession with realism" (WC1, 12).

In the distinction between likeness or mere illusion and the satisfaction of an obsession lies a key to Bazin's thought. The terms of "satisfying an obsession" can never be decided on the side of a concrete object; such satisfaction can by definition only be decided on the side of the *subject* whose obsession it is.[7] Quite consistently, Bazin associates the need for realism with "psychology" rather than "aesthetics"; hence "reality" itself is not the primary term of his ontology of the image, except insofar as it is an object of the obsession. The emphasis on the subject ("psychology") is what allows Bazin to indicate a surprising break between perceptual likeness to reality (usually associated with perspectival illusion) and the ontological status of the photographic image. That ontology is in operation, Bazin tells us, "no matter how fuzzy, distorted or discolored" the object may appear in the image (WC1, 14).

The impression of visual likeness through perspective, then, becomes merely a kind of prop, historically necessary for the development of the mechanically produced image. This historical function can almost be described by saying that perspective provides a sort of credible code—to put it in necessarily oxymoronic terms, a reliable illusion—whose credibility can then be lent to automatically produced images. But then, by a peculiar inversion, it ultimately becomes the *mechanical* process originally built on the illusion of likeness, which, once established, lends *its* credibility, a new kind of credibility, to the spatial configuration of the image. Thus, there is a distinction between perspective and the special credibility of the automatically produced image.

This new kind of credibility is productively described by Peter Wollen when he suggests that Bazin's view of the image answers to the description of an indexical sign in the semiotic typology of Charles Sanders Peirce. An indexical sign *indicates* or attests to the existence of something. In the case of a genuine index, the referent, or what Peirce calls the sign's object, is an existent whose presence is required in the formation of the sign. Among Peirce's examples of indexicality are a weather vane; a man's rolling gait, which indicates he is a sailor; a rap on the door; and a sundial signifying the time of day. As a film theorist, Wollen can point out that one of

Peirce's examples is a photograph, the definitional genesis of which is that light rays strike a chemical emulsion upon being reflected from the concrete objects in the actual spatial field to be pictured. But Wollen's Peircean description of Bazin is not followed through when he charges Bazin with stressing "the passivity of the natural world rather than the agency of the human mind."[8] It is precisely the activity and desire of the subject—"our *obsession* with realism"—that makes indexicality the crucial aspect of the image for Bazin.

Wishing to avoid the essentializing aspects of traditional accounts of cinematic signification, Wollen makes an attractive argument for a Peirce-influenced account of cinema as a complex of indexical, iconic (pictorial), and even symbolic (arbitrary, nonmotivated) aspects. But the Bazinian question would still be which aspects of the mix are basic *for the phenomenological cinematic subject,* and the answer is indexicality, that sign function that gives the photographic image its new level of credibility in relation to subjective obsession. Since an indexical sign is such by some existential connection between a specific referent and the signifier, the latter will always provide the subject with irrefutable testimony as to the real *existence* of the referent.

Most important for questions of space and perspective is that indexicality implies nothing necessary about the *form* of the signifier, even in relation to the referent, nothing, for example, about whether the signifier "looks like" the referent. (Does a weather vane "look like" the wind?) As Wollen notes, Peirce himself says that signs exist in various typological admixtures; indeed, according to Peirce, even that most "arbitrary" of signifying systems, verbal language, includes many indexical components, such as demonstrative and personal pronouns. Immediately pertinent here, Peirce allows for an indexical sign to include some degree of iconicity, that is, some aspect of similarity or analogy to its referent. But there are many forms of iconicity for Peirce. Thus, the particular kind of iconic system employed (e.g., the one-point perspective of dominant lenses as opposed to, say, some cubist configuration) is not mandated by the fact of indexicality.[9]

Quite complex relations between iconicity and indexicality are thus conceivable. In photography and film, this indicates, among other things, the continuing pertinence of investigating the impression of spatial likeness in relation to the dominance of perspective. But if the peculiarity of automatically produced images is that they are indexical images, what must be remembered is that perceptual markers of spatial likeness, whether thought to be conventional or natural, do not in themselves constitute that evidence for the existence of the referent that is definitive of indexical credibility. No matter how well it matches the spatial organization of a photograph, a painting does not have the former's degree of credibility since it cannot serve as evidence of the presence of the referent at some moment of production of the sign. This credibility therefore cannot be completely explicated by the relation of perspective as such to the ideal of centered subjectivity or to purely perceptual schemata. Spatial likeness and deviance are finally not quite the crux of Bazinian realism.[10]

In fact, on this account what is necessary to the special credibility of automatically produced images is not an apparently unmediated record of how reality appears, but rather markers of indexicality itself, which signify the presence of the referent at some point in sign production. To accept this account would mean, first of all, that the special credibility of automatically produced images depends on a certain prior knowledge on the part of the spectator — not so much of what the object actually looked like but of how the sign was generated. The process of diffusing that prior knowledge generally, of making known the presuppositions necessary to the workings of indexical signification, is not directly addressed by Bazin. It may well be possible to attribute it to cultural configurations. We will have to return to the question of the cultural underpinnings of indexicality.

For now, consider a related aspect that bears directly on photography and cinema. Some of Peirce's examples of an indexical sign, such as a weather vane or a sundial, attest to the action of a referent occurring at the moment one apprehends the sign. Others, such as the rolling gait of a sailor, require a reading based on a kind of history of the sign, for at least some of the referential presence occurred *before* the time of the reading. When Bazin compares cinema to such indexical significations as a fingerprint, a mold, a death mask, or the Holy Shroud of Turin, his examples consistently turn out to be the kind in which the referent was present in the past. If apprehending a sign as indexical is to recognize, to some degree, how it is produced, that apprehension in photographic and filmic images is of a production that has previously occurred, for the spatial field and objects depicted were in the camera's "presence" only at some point prior to the actual reading of the sign.[11]

That is, apprehending a photographic or filmic image as a photographic or filmic image involves a temporal dimension. The subject must necessarily read a past in the image — not a past as a signified (as in, say, a historical painting) but rather a past of the signifier, of the signifier-referent relation as one of a production. Here the referential credibility of indexicality assumes something absent from any immediate perception: a different *when* than that of the spectator. Since this different "when" cannot be immediately present, it must be "filled in," "inferred," "provided" by the subject. Thus, if indexicality is a crucial aspect of the image, we must assume some active capacity at work beyond perceptual activities, be it "memory," "mental activities," "subconscious investment," or whatever.

To summarize, Bazin must assume that the special credibility of photographic and cinematic images is based on a prior knowledge on the part of the subject of how any such images are produced. Furthermore, that production is apprehended as coming from some past moment, which makes temporality a crucial component of the process for the subject obsessively predisposed to invest belief in such a image. It is this tie between subjective obsession and temporality that is the fundamental importance of one of Bazin's most famous notions, the "mummy complex" with which he begins "The Ontology of the Photographic Image."

Bazin's Egyptian mummies reveal a universal unconscious human need that cultures must confront through ritual, religion, art, or in some other way. This is the need for some fantastic defense against time. For any human subject, the passage of time is the approach of death, the ultimate material limitation on subjectivity. On the one hand, the desire to defeat death is clearly an impossible one; hence, it can only continue to exist as an obsession, not a rational project. On the other hand, with greater or lesser degrees of conscious purpose, individuals in different cultures require imaginative indications of the possibility of defeating time to defend their existence, their subjectivities: "Civilization cannot . . . cast out the bogy of time" (WC1, 10). The mummies thus supply Bazin with a carefully chosen symptom. Of course, within a mode of argument that appeals to origins, Egyptian culture serves as a handy, quasi-figurative starting point for Western art history. But it thereby generalizes the subjective project described by Bazin all the way back to the foundation of the plastic arts and image culture.

To begin with, this putative origin of Western artistic representation is located in a religious context (not necessarily a Christian one, since the model is one of paganism). Its first vehicle is maintenance of the body against decay in the context of a belief in an afterlife, amounting to an obsession with the problem of "embalming time." Thus, we can call the founding obsession a *preservative* one. The history of the representational arts can then be seen as sublimations of this impossible impulse to defeat death: "It is no longer a question of survival after death, but of a larger concept, the creation of an ideal world in the likeness of the real, with its own temporal destiny. . . , man's . . . last word in the argument with death by means of the form that endures" (WC1, 101). When photography appears in Bazin's sketch of the development of visual media, its indexicality adds the appeal of endurance through time to the impression of likeness in perspective. "Likeness" is not being given cognitive value in itself but rather is being invoked as a support for fundamental needs of the subject vis-à-vis time. And cinema adds duration to the embalming of a temporal segment in still photography; this makes of cinema, as Bazin puts it in "The Myth of Total Cinema," the realization of a perennial compulsion, a virtually ageless dream of perfect realism, which would have to include duration, in the representation of real objects. But, as with any wish fulfillment, such preservation of the object is projectively converted into the preservation of the subject. Thus, again, we find that the cinema achieves its essence for Bazin through the relations of the subject.

But also, and more complexly, if indexicality gives the automatically produced image a special appeal this appeal is inseparable from those limitations of such images with respect to perfect reproduction of reality which Bazin so freely acknowledges. In fact, since it is grounded on subjective obsession, Bazin's ontology could not exist without a *gap* between referent and signifier; hence the famous asymptotic relation between film and reality. This gap serves central functions in Bazinian realism. It is precisely this gap that is filled in by subjective projection as variable manifestations of human imagination. This imagination is obsessively drawn to discover types of signs that can be invested with the credibility of the real and it is this objective gap that determines the inevitability of abstraction from reality even in the effort to make contact with it.

The mummy complex and the break between film and reality are the interlinked premises leading to Bazin's accounts of various components of the filmic process. At the level of spectatorship, it is from the desire to counter threats to its own existence, its own being, that the spectator is at least open to investing a nearly absolute credibility in the image despite its perceptible differences from the referent in real space; it is thus that the spectator affirms his or her own subjective being.[12] In a parallel way in Bazin's writings on the history of filmic textuality, the artist acknowledges and responds to this universal condition of the human subject by artistic means, especially through his or her style, including narrative form. These necessarily embody an attitude toward the world, since they respond to the inadequacies of the signifier (the gap between film and reality) in the face of the subjective demand for a fantastic control over materiality (locus of causation of death), a demand that is always the originating aim of mechanically produced images for the subject.

So what is usually regarded as Bazin's ontology describes a subjective intentionality for automatically produced images based on a preservative obsession. Of course, this means that the relation between such images and the physical world remains central for his theory: the special appeal to the subject rests on the preexistence of concrete objects, a preexistence offered by their preservation via indexicality. Nevertheless, once it is admitted that the referential force of such concreteness exists only for a subject, the indexical relation to the preexistent takes on a broader function. It can become a pervasive ideal or privileged model—that is, a manifestation of certain ambitions of subjectivity vis-à-vis signification beyond the basic level of the relation of a film image to its referent.

There are many illustrations of Bazin's recourse to this relation at key points in specific arguments. In his 1955 defense of Rossellini, for example, he defines neorealism not by the physical appearance of the image but by the subjectivity of the artist, which necessarily filters out aspects of literal reality, and he then explicates the *consciousness* of the neorealist by analogy to a black-and-white photograph: "a true imprint of reality, a kind of luminous mold in which color simply does not figure" (wc2, 98). Another striking example is his approach to literary adaptation in the dense, revealing essay "The Stylistics of Robert Bresson." For Bazin, Bresson treats *Diary of a Country Priest* (1950) as preexistent, "a pure reality" (wc1, 136). Since what is involved is not literally making images of Bernanos's writing, we have a gap between the filmic sign and a literal transmission of its object; hence, as always, abstraction from the preexistent reality is unavoidable. But the stylistics of Bresson fill in the gap by manifesting a subjective relation to the novel, which is not the assertion of his own capacity to construct a substitute for it found in Aurenche and Bost, not an imposition of his own categorical preconceptions; rather, his stylistics evince respect for the prior, independent existence of the novel.[13] Bresson thus shows how it is possible "for the existence of the novel to be affirmed by the film, and not dissolved into it. It is hardly enough to say of this work . . . that it is in essence faithful to the original because, to begin with, it *is* the novel" (wc1, 142–43).[14]

"It *is* the novel" corresponds to the more famous "no more cinema." Not physical reproduction, but the relation of the preexistent to the film as inseparable from preservation as an obsessive issue for the subject is central to the experience of reality through cinema and hence of an auteur's style. Thus, the Bazinian questions for adaptation may be phrased in a way consistent with Bazin's entire mode of thought: what are the various sorts of subjective projection toward the literary work, as they can be read within the history of filmic textuality?

Bazin's classic history of filmic style in "The Evolution of the Language of Cinema" begins with a discussion of *faith* in the image and *faith* in reality. Here this "faith" confronts cinematic "language," considered as historically shifting stylistic and formal systems, which must be employed given the unavoidable minimum of abstraction in any representational instance. The kind of faith in operation is thus readable in the progressive evolution of formal and stylistic systems, such as that of editing, through its historically significant strategies from montage to the long take. But one can here recall Bertrand Russell's remark to the effect that faith is belief in something for which there is no evidence. Since the ground for Bazin's position is an account of generalized subjective obsession, he must finally make imagination, fantasy, the illogical a root of any true realism. In "The Ontology of the Photographic Image," he even remarks on the affinity of photography with surrealism (WC1, 15–16).

Faith can move mountains — into the movie theater. This is why the fantastic and the religious can be legitimately invoked as kindred to those forces subtending the work of both the most distinctive realist artist as well as the spectator and why what Bazin sometimes calls "psychology" is the foundation of his ontology. This explains the extraordinary subjective investment in indexicality that is presupposed in his theory and critical work. But if the irrational leap of faith is the basis of Bazin's ontology of the cinema, then what must follow are accounts of the specific vicissitudes of this fundamental subjective investment. Bazin's construction of an evolutionary account of "film language" and his often brilliant analyses of the stylistics of individual filmmakers begin from here. He also treats this intentionality as having various manifestations as a collective, cultural, and/or social phenomenon that he often calls "myth," something we will consider shortly.

But at this point simply note the supple utility of Bazin's mode of proceeding from the phenomenologist's concern with an essential subjective project: the theorist of cinema's basic realism became our most influential producer of stylistic categories and the godfather of auteurism. The proclaimer of the special significance of photography and cinema for the *modern* world did so by means of sympathy for supposedly *timeless* needs met by fantasy, faith, religion, and myth.

"A Time to Live and a Time to Die"

Reading Bazin from the centrality of subjectivity leads one to emphasize the founding place of the preservative obsession and the mummy complex in his corpus; that is, time becomes central to his overall theory. This may seem odd, because some of Bazin's most important work can leave the impression of giving analytic priority precisely to *spatial* configurations and manipulations in film—for example, his metaphor of the frame as window, the significance of off-screen space, or his claim for the historical importance of deep focus cinematography. Given Bazin's sensitivity to manipulations of mise-en-scène and camera work, is it not necessary to acknowledge the fundamental significance of those instances when Bazin defines spectatorship spatially? We need only recall Bazin's controversial claim that the spatial continuity of deep focus long takes in a Welles or a Wyler film tends to bring the spectator's vision into a regime of choice, for it moves toward making every spectator into his or her own "editor" of the mise-en-scène. Given that reality is only ever available to the human in an ambiguous state, the need to choose would then put the subject in a more suitable or "realistic" relation with the profilmic.[15]

Yet, even where Bazin at last seems to illustrate his contentions about deep focus with reference to perception of real space, time is introduced to subtend the activities of the subject. Consider the following from his crucial 1948 analysis of William Wyler: "In reality, in fact, our eye adjusts spatially, like a lens, to the important point of the event which interests us; it proceeds by successive investigations, *it introduces a sort of temporalization* on a second level *by analysis of the space of a reality, itself evolving in time.*"[16]

To say such a passage demonstrates that for Bazin space and time are inseparable would be correct enough but finally bland and not very informative. However, the introduction of the notion of time here can also refer us back to the ontological essays, for it presents a metaphysical *partis pris,* related to that of the ambiguity of reality.[17] Any real existent in space is by definition in a temporalized state, a state of change. And given that partis pris, a happy coincidence of subjective processes and reality seems possible, for the perception/apprehension of the concrete on the part of the subject is also temporalized. Epistemologically, this proposition might enable a correspondence or reflection theory in the structures of subject and object on the common ground of time. This line would illustrate the beneficial aspects of the centrality of the subject in the ontology of automatically produced images insofar as this subjective given—the sense of time passing, of duration and the constancy of transformation—is also a sense of the actual "structure" or founding process of reality.

Yet, the context of Bazin's account of the subject in his ontology forces a more complex, and perhaps more telling, extrapolation. Time passing, duration, and change, are exactly what Bazin's ontological subject is driven to disavow, for they raise the problem of death. The lure of automatically produced images is attributable to subjective obsession precisely because time is a threat to the stable existence of the subject as well as the object. Hence, the paradox: automatically produced images are founded from a desire that the concrete be preserved, stopped in time, and this desire leads to the special appeal of cinema, when the subject is led to open itself to a revelatory experience of reality; *but* reality itself evolves in time and is even perceived in time.

This may be why respect for reality is such a cinematic value for Bazin. In the genuine realist attitude the impulse to control time is both exploited and checked. That is, the desire to master reality is achieved yet somehow sublimated so that the self-protective mechanisms motivating the projection toward the real are diverted from their defensive stance. Realism becomes an act of heroism. But this also throws into doubt the idea of realism as correspondence of subject and object on the grounds of temporality. For the subject's first interest in representations of time is in overcoming temporality itself. Thus, for example, Bazin's analyses of spatial constructions stem from the idea that spatial strategies can tend either to diminish or to highlight the temporality of perception, representation, and reality. The complication is that in the latter valued case cinema accords with its ontological purpose ("realism") by struggling against its ontology (defense against the victory of time). It is in order to deal with the continual onset of the *future,* which holds material death, that an investment in the possibilities of freezing the *past* is converted into the desires and imaginative projections involved in Bazin's cherished realism.[18]

A photographic or cinematic image always provides the spectator with absolute, irrefutable brute knowledge that the objects represented in the frame *were at one time* in the spatial "presence" of the camera. As Roland Barthes explicates photographic indexicality, every such image is a "certificate of presence," and the *noeme* of this kind of image is "that-*has*-been" (my emphasis). The essential attestation of the photograph is that the camera at one time had to be in the presence of *then* existing objects *now* represented—preserved for the subject—in the image.[19]

Thus, what is crucial is the presentation of something as preserved, as appearing from an irrefutable past existence. Since Bazin insists on the *pregivenness* of the universe to the human, the indexicality of mechanically produced images insures that such pregivenness can (at least potentially) be experienced as the temporal relation of the profilmic to the camera.[20] Thus, not only the temporality *of* the image but also the representation of temporality *in* the image (and sound)—the particular contribution of cinema to the evolution of image production—must receive its own consideration. Photography preserves a fragment of time for a subject, and cinema preserves a fragment that can be experienced as actual duration, wherein time itself is apprehended as captured: for Bazin, cinema is "objectivity in time . . . change mummified, as it were" (WC1, 14–15). But note the deliberately oxymoronic aspects of the phrase "change mummified."

Exploring the stylistics of temporality in Bazin's writings might lead one directly to familiar terrain, involving, for example, the significance of the long take; however, this should also encompass something emphasized by Brian Henderson, Bazin's less-noted interest in ellipsis.[21] While finding significant virtues in such instances as Bazin's analysis of narrative ellipsis in Rossellini (e.g., WC2, 34–38), Henderson objects that Bazin illegitimately applies the classical concept of narrative ellipsis to "reality" and sees this as part of an overall contradictoriness in Bazin's corpus. Contradictoriness there may ultimately be, but, as with all Bazin's accounts of stylistic and formal usages, temporal manipulations must be read through the special credibility of cinema for the subject, which is not definable in strictly formal, objective terms but is simply a prior condition of the cinematic experience.

As we have seen from his account of Wyler, while Bazin takes continuous temporal flow as a given of reality, he also believes that it is under constant subjective analysis even in perceptual activity. It could only be more so in the various illogical processes subjectivity brings to bear in representation. In a film, not only temporal continuity but also its *interruption* are unavoidably central. Henderson is puzzled when he finds in Bazin a suggestion to the effect that all cinema is based on ellipsis, but cinema always interrupts any literal impression of "real" temporal continuity. Even a hypothetical one-shot film must begin and end. So Bazin's often-quoted praise of Stroheim is double edged: when he writes "One could easily imagine . . . a film by Stroheim composed of a single shot as long-lasting and as close-up as you like" (WC1, 27), he points to what is imaginary, an ideal. All realisms are aesthetics because the myth of total cinema is impossible of objective realization.

Consequently, various cinema aesthetics involve various modalities of playing temporal continuity against its inevitable interruptions, no matter whether what is involved is diegetic, narrational, and/or (at another level) the purportedly referential time of a shot. A good cross-reference for Bazin's interest in narrative ellipsis in Rossellini is his commentary on *Kon Tiki* (1951) in "Cinema and Exploration." Here Bazin claims that realism is manifested by the film precisely because, at a moment when the filmmakers are depicted as being in danger, a chunk of time encompassing the events of most interest must be omitted. This frustration acts to draw a greater quotient of belief from the spectator, for the interruption serves as evidence that the danger was real. This reading hinges on indexical pastness (the camera and filmmakers were actually present at the moment of danger) and the special credibility of cinema for the subject. It is thus no accident that when Bazin concludes this essay with a comparison to another film *Annapurna* (1953), we find a constellation of familiar figures: mummy, religion, indexicality, and objective endurance of the preexistent—a virtual invocation of the mummy complex:

> then begins the long Calvary of the descent, with Herzog and Lachemal strapped like mummies to the backs of their Sherpas. This time the cinema is there like the veil of Veronica pressed to the face of human suffering. Undoubtedly the written account by Herzog is more detailed and more complete. Memory is the most faithful of films—the only one that can register at any height, and right up to the very moment of death. But who can fail to see the difference between memory and that objective image that gives it eternal substance? (WC1, 163)

Here we can clearly see that Bazin's aesthetics of style, so often summarized by reference to a temporally defined filmic device (the long take), is in fact not limited to a formalistic promotion of temporal continuity. His analytic flexibility and openness to a variety of filmic strategies do not derive from the willful theoretical slackness of a cinematic enthusiast but from the prior centrality of temporality as inseparable from the status of subjective projection, which underpins cinema per se. The specific indexicality of cinematic representation includes duration, so that the essential "realism" of this mechanically reproduced image lies in the relation of the subject to the future by something like a hallucinatory control over the past. The priority of temporality is necessarily manifested at another level, however, where the theoretical coherence of Bazin's work becomes problematic.

"Le Dieu au Corps" (or "From Here to Eternity")

In Bazin's work generally, the explicit concern with the flow of time and the various ways a subject obsessively apprehends the past is pertinent not only for the filmic subject but also for the theoretical/critical subject—such as Bazin himself. His own teleological accounts of the history of filmic style are consistently asymptotic pseudoteleologies since their end points always remain unattainable. Thus, his historical accounts of filmic textuality retain their own subject-object, sign-referent gaps. In his film theory, such gaps are what attract the special kind of subjective investment that founds the invention of cinema and the implications of cinematic style. In that case, the ontological centrality Bazin attributes to the relation between the subject and "pastness" in the cinema—the preservative obsession—may well be refracted into his own work, which takes the existence of cinematic signification in time, "film history," as *its* object. Bazin's mode of theoretical and critical work leads directly to problems of history—the "shapes of time."[22]

In this light, we may ask not only whether Bazin offers us an acceptable account of the subjective compulsions of film, and not only if his account of those compulsions is a fundamental factor for understanding film history, but also whether his work does not include a subtext on the compulsions and fascinations of history, the sublimations and attractions of the past, even outside cinema. Since this rarely receives any overt treatment by Bazin, it will illuminate his position in unanticipated ways, enabling us to shift from comprehending the general coherence of his work to a more symptomatic reading of that coherence.

It is possible to section Bazin's interest in historicity, considered as manifestations of the human concern with "pastness" carried to the prestigious knowledge claims of historiography. The most obvious and influential sector of this interest is surely his dialectical-evolutionary history of filmic styles. Outlined most directly in "The Evolution of the Language of Cinema," this history manifests itself in some of his most important critical work, for example, "An Aesthetic of Reality" and the essay on Wyler; as we have already seen, vicissitudes of filmic textuality are here accounted for by appeal to a fundamental subjective project. But another sector of Bazin's historical concerns is not often enough interrogated. This is what some Marxists might call the construction of "second nature" and what Bazin often calls "myth." Myths function in his writings as particular kinds of social or cultural usages of cinema that embody what we can tentatively label a *collective* subjectivity. It is clear that the word *myth* does not in itself carry necessarily negative or positive connotations for Bazin. In addition to the more universal "myth of total cinema," he is sympathetic to localized "myths" such as those embodied in the American Western and the best periods of Soviet cinema. Yet he is hostile to others, such as "The Stalin Myth in Soviet Cinema."[23]

Like an auteur's style, which embodies individual subjectivity within the overarching myth of total cinema, these collective subjectivities may or may not respect the pregivenness of the concrete in its ambiguity. That is, these myths can employ the abstracting side of subjectivity either to the detriment or benefit of the side that projects toward concrete objectivity and to which indexical image production makes its special appeal. For an analysis of a myth that goes too far toward the abstractive side, and one that reveals how a special relation between cinema and history might be embedded in Bazin's thought, consider his essay "The Stalin Myth in Soviet Cinema."[24]

The key symptom from which Bazin unpacks the Stalin myth is the fact that even while Stalin is living he is represented in Soviet cinema as a perfect subject, identified with the objective course of history. Stalin is alive, a historical being with the limitations that implies, yet he is represented as omniscient; hence, he embodies the end of contingency within history. This makes Stalin as subject the ultimate *telos* of human history, because he is given as being in a perfect relation of knowledge to objectivity. This is a way of describing the direction of any myth of total cinema, for example, that slogan implies a subject no longer alienated and threatened by objectivity ("death") but rather in perfect communion with it.

Bazin's analyses of myth thus highlight the conjunction of a transcendent, ontological function with an actual existent—here the person of Stalin; in this case, however, contradiction is not converted into one of

Bazin's beloved paradoxes, and it is therefore refused entry into his dialectic. Why? Because in this myth *there is no asymptote — with the subject-object split suppressed, the gap between sign and referent is closed off.* For if subject and object were united as the objective course of history in the person of Stalin then telos has been already objectively attained, and the desires of the subject perfectly realized. Such a victory of subjectivity would leave no place for further processes of subjectivity and hence no basis for realism.[25] So Bazin argues that this cinema is actually imposing telos by political fiat; it marks a fatal imbalance, whereby the side of subjectivity that projects toward the objective concrete is overwhelmed by the abstractive side of subjectivity.

The implications of the Stalinist cultural strategy are especially highlighted by its embodiment in cinema. In the present context, we can note Bazin's comment that the realistic appeal of cinema is used "to fix his [Stalin's] essence forever." This is explicitly compared to mummification, as Bazin dates the beginnings of this process from the embalming of Lenin's body.[26] But *this* mummy complex, culturally and politically imposed on cinema, hypocritically validates itself by laying claim to the achievement of an absolute, closed subjective (epistemological) security, that is, by pretending to abolish the original mummy complex, it suppresses the always unfinished aspiration which defines the appeal of pastness. The peculiar project of these films — historical films that abolish history — can thus be explained as a "bad" paradox: the claim to objective realization by a myth means that the myth suppresses the gap that stimulates the necessary imaginative projection toward actual, concrete objectivity.

This conjunction of myth and mummification in the relation to a past returns us to Bazin's ontological essays: Stalinist cinema clearly diverts the

1. Stalin's image addressed in *The Fall of Berlin* (frame enlargement of video)

2. Stalin embodied in *The Fall of Berlin* (frame enlargement of video)

3. Stalin represented as an image of fascism in *WR: Mysteries of the Organism,* Dusan Makavejev, 1971 (frame enlargement of video)

founding myth of total cinema, showing that the appeals of cinematic realism could be put to what an existentialist would call bad faith uses. As Comolli indicates, Bazin's theory is a theory of the *struggle* of the subject to maintain itself in the face of materiality. In Stalinist cinema, an undesirable hypertrophy is manifested in the representation of history, but it is a hypertrophy of a condition that pervades all cinema: the subject defends itself against time, seeking (among other things) to tame temporality. The extremism of Stalinism is that it purports to be a victorious conquest of the problem.

This is the special danger of a medium that, as we have seen above, claims an ontological purpose that is to be realized in paradoxical struggle with its ontology. If time must be captured because it is a threat, then the ultimate victory for subjectivity might seem to be to do away with time, to make it irrelevant. But for the phenomenologist Bazin this must be a perversion, a perversion that can occur in relation to historical representation as well as properly cinematic instances. As the case of Stalinist cinema makes clear, filmic and narrative strategies are readable for Bazin not only at the level of the individual subject (artist) but also at the interconnected level of culture and societies; subjectivity is both individual and collective.[27] On both levels, the gaps between subject and object, sign and referent, and the inevitability of realizing myths only asymptotically must be maintained; then contingency, subjectivity, cinema—and phenomenology—may all continue to exist and can register temporality in ways that keep the subject open to its fundamental action in reality.

Stalinist cinema, as one kind of limit case of the struggle of the subject, shows that human subjectivity cannot be posited as outside of time and outside of history. In "The Ontology of the Photographic Image" and "The Myth of Total Cinema," Bazin establishes a historically shifting hierarchy among image-producing media based on their relative capacities to appeal to the human desire for security against death. Further, in the medium of cinema the shifting relations among styles, definitively outlined in "The Evolution of the Language of Cinema,"[28] are similarly hierarchized on the basis of the types of credulity the aesthetic strategies elicit given the mummy complex. Thus, it is precisely a *history* of subjectivity that is to be read off of shifts in this hierarchy among media and/or styles. In fact, this historiographic project is the connection between Bazin's ontology and his critical work.

Now, this means that there are not two but three coexisting levels at which the history of subjective investment in images manifests itself. We have commented on the individual subject (artist, spectator) and the collective subject (society and/or culture, with the Western and Stalinist cinema as relatively pure examples). Throughout Bazin's writings, these are subsumed by a third, which in effect mandates the other two and functions as a universal, dating back to the origins of representation: the fundamental preservative impulsion of the subject to overcome time, with the consequent desire for "objective" representation. But if Bazin is driven by his project and his logic to posit a universal the question arises whether his history of subjectivity has truly evaded the dilemma of Stalinist cinema with its abstractive hypertrophy of the atemporal. Has not the desire to control time taken over his own formulations, perhaps from the other side of subjectivity, which projects toward the concrete?

Even if there are individual and cultural variations in the ways in which this projective desire of subjectivity is met, the desire is itself an *ahistorical* constant. Whether in ancient Egypt, Rennaissance Florence, or post–World War II Italy, the force of that desire remains consistent, not just the premise of an obsession but an obsessional premise explaining the pull of the image as realistic representation. Histories, cultures, and technologies may develop in various ways, and individual artists may propose distinctive, revelatory utilizations of representational possibilities, but that subjective obsession is always the ground. It serves Bazin's theory as a universal phenomenological intentionality, a constant existential projection of the subject into the material world, where it cannot find satisfaction—so therefore into representations that are materially distinct from that world and yet can be diverted toward a special credibility.

What kind of historian, then, is Bazin? Certainly he is not one who allows an emphasis on the vicissitudes of a fundamental phenomenological intentionality to blind him to economic, social, and technological determinants of film history and textuality; on the contrary, he often insists on their pertinence. However, the terms of that pertinence are ultimately secondary. For example, in "In Defense of Mixed Cinema," his noted metaphor of an equilibrium profile of form and style is embedded in something close to a technological determinism. He argues that a period of novelty in technique and form that lasted from the invention of cinema through the innovation of sound has been succeeded by an "age of the scenario," whose technical and formal equilibrium will only be shattered by some further technological innovation such as an advance in color or stereoscopy (wc1, 73–74). But how could Bazin explain the technological development that would have such a result? Even in "The Evolution of the Language of Cinema," when he announces that the equilibrium profile has undergone a vast disturbance associated with the profusion of deep focus cinematography and the new kind of realism it manifests, Bazin himself declares that the reasons for the shift cannot be found in technical determinants (wc1, 30). But then how does one explain why the shift to a categorically new realism occurs when it does—in Hollywood, Renoir, the Italians?

This illustrates a fundamental difficulty in Bazin. The insistence on a historicized outlook in his notions of a succession of media (and of styles within media) inevitably raises the question of the determinations of transformations within those successions; yet there is ultimately little theoretical space that would allow for explanations of even his own skeletal outlines of *change*. For example, "The Myth of Total Cinema" defines the delay in the efflorescence of optical machines synthesizing movement until the nineteenth century as a historical problem, since the necessary principles had been known for centuries. At first, this question is met by reference to the innovations of image chemistry (photography), which manifests a dominant impulse in "the imagination of the [nineteenth] century." But this move toward historical, localized explanation is then blocked, for the final claim organizing the essay is that the *idea* of cinema—of perfect, lifelike reproduction—long preceded its materialization. He compares it to the idea of flight, which "had dwelt in the soul of everyman since he first thought about birds" (wc1, 22).

The universality of the ambition for perfect reproduction is of course the universality of the preservative obsession, Bazin's founding theoretical axiom; thus, the axiom finds reconfirmation in history. But the consequence is a waffling on any historical explanation of transformations among media and styles. Nineteenth-century technological, industrial, and economic developments were important conditions for the emergence of cinema; yet that appearance is finally accounted for only by vague reference to a conjunctural convergence of obsessions (scientific, industrial, economic) into the general preservative obsession embodied in the mechanically produced image. It appears that every new realization of the fundamental preservative obsession described by the mummy complex can only be explained on the basis of a circular reference to that obsession.

There may well be no way that Bazin can satisfactorily answer questions proper to historical studies—about change, about shifts in the hierarchy of media and/or styles. For example, he cannot with theoretical consistency resort to the idea of an independent technical development of various media, with which he sometimes flirts. This would separate the history of technology from subjectivity, and hence his ontology as well as the coherence of his critical work with the ontology would collapse. At the crucial point, Bazin must suppress the temporal.

Yet, the omnipresence of time and change is inextricable from the virtues of the irrational projection toward the concrete basic to Bazin's account of subjectivity. This shows up in his often insightful strivings to integrate a more historicizing consciousness, especially when he embeds subjects in specific societies and cultures. This is the case not only with respect to the social mythifications associated with collective subjectivities; sometimes it appears even in the analyses of individual subjects, such as those cinema artists working in postwar Italy. Nevertheless, in the last instance Bazin's historical accounts remain variations on an ontological theme. Distinctions among periods and cultures there may be but not radical, qualitative differences of the premises of human subjective activity.

"Change mummified," indeed. Bazin's oxymoron aptly crystallizes his view of the paradoxical relations of cinema for the subject; it registers for his film theory the illogical processes and desire for *permanence* (of subjective existence, of identity) that can open the subject to the concrete, hence the flow of time and the fact of *change*. But applied to Bazin himself as historiographic subject it reveals a fundamental inconsistency. We have seen how his very account of the irrationality at the heart of the cinematic experience takes on a static quality, the character of an unchanging law. Thus, as the figure of the mummy complex assumes the logical position of a valid description Bazin's historiographic discourse presumes to the function of a rational metalanguage. That is, like much twentieth-century thought, by analyzing the illogicality or irrationality of a phenomenon it establishes its own logical and epistemological security, its superiority. In this case, the cognitive efficacy of the concept of the preservative obsession is rooted in its imputed universality.

Historiographically, there is something enabling about this. It follows from the claim for the universality of the mummy complex that the historian would share with all humans in all periods basic aspects of film viewing—those described by the mummy complex. (There may be limitations to such empathy insofar as some components of a film are historically localizable, but their extent is open to discussion.) So there is a theoretical basis

for identification between subjects of the past who are objects of historical investigation, and subjects of the present who may be conducting the
investigation. Some have argued that such identification is the basic assumption of historical writing.[29] Yet, it seems less of a delicious Bazinian
"paradox" than a critical contradiction that, in the aspiration to a kind of
knowledge crucial to his mode of thought, namely, historical knowledge,
Bazin desires a kind of security that would disjoin his historiography from
his cinematic presumptions about the limitations of subjectivity vis-à-vis
pastness.

Now a Bazinian might respond that the mummy complex has to do with
the experience of iconic or figurative representation and the writing of
history is a paradigmatically linguistic act whose cognitive rather than irrational claims define it. For some, this might be true enough, but for Bazin
this would split off the centrality of temporal experience in cinema from
the centrality of temporal understanding in his writings about cinema. He
would have to give up the theoretical rationale for the compulsive insistence, even in his critical work on individual filmmakers, on an overall
evolutionary, teleological, and/or dialectical account of film history.

So it is difficult to see how the appeal of the past to Bazin as historiographic subject could be completely divorced from the preservative obsession and the characteristics he attributes to the cinematic experience. But
in that case we find in Bazin himself a hypertrophy of abstract rationalization, the blockage of the static. In his own terms, it is as if temporality were
as fascinating a threat to Bazin the historian as it is to the cinematic subject, so that temporality must both be figured and mastered. Ultimately, if
Bazin's analysis has shown how the Stalin myth becomes a kind of "second
nature" for Soviet filmmakers, then so does the myth of total cinema for
Bazin as historian; and are the ultimate ideological consequences of these
myths, the abstract abolition of historical time, so dissimilar? Bazin's attempt to negotiate temporality through a timeless subjective intentionality
has as its consequence a theoretical blank spot around history.

From one point of view, much of this is only to say that Bazin is an
idealist. Yet, the extraordinary critical power, intelligence, and influence of
his idealism bring us back to the difficulties of simply dismissing all of his
work on the basis of a theoretical a priori. Further, a theoretical blank spot
around history is also a problem in more recent, influential film theory.
Bazin's difficulty is not so far from us. Thus, several years ago such a self-
proclaimed anti-idealist as Comolli could suggest we consider the possi-

bility that Bazin's obsessional premise, with its pull toward the ahistorical, may well reveal something crucial about the *historical* regime of the filmic.[30]

To historicize what Bazin requires as an ahistorical constant would mean beginning not from the image but from what precedes the image in Bazin —the preservative desire, the obsession with pastness, that Bazin universalizes. Is this simply an essentialist premise to be dismissed by those who oppose his phenomenology or can it be located more specifically? If the latter is the case, we can propose an interrogation of the media of automatically produced images that starts by asking when and how time becomes central and fatal, in many senses, for conceptions and experiences of human subjectivity.

"Once upon a Time in the West"

A "historical contextualization" in the sense of the "history of ideas" might seem appropriate at this point, for the question of the appeal of pastness compels a historical contextualization that deals precisely with ideas of history. Now this has been a crucial problem over the last two centuries in the West generally. For that reason, the imbrication of preservative ideals and notions of history requires a broader understanding than could be supplied by study of the biographical Bazin's specific intellectual, cultural, social, and institutional context. The exposition of such an understanding would carry us well beyond the limits of this reading of Bazin; however, a sketch of some of its elements can for now serve as a provisional conclusion.[31]

Bazin might well agree that the concept of a preservational obsession could not be explained as a product of French intellectual history. For him, nineteenth-century innovations throughout the West in indexical image-making must in the end refer us back to an obsession that is evidenced in the arts at least since the mummies and serves his theory as an apparently eternal human disposition. But suppose we took the opposite tack and placed our bet on the specificity of the period during which the photograph and cinema were invented? Leaving aside a number of necessary nuances and qualifications, this move would entail the position that if the mechanically produced indexical image establishes a representational relation to temporality and registers a preservative obsession, then the nineteenth century would have to be a period saturated with a concern with time that had a pervasive impact on representational forms and media.

In fact, there is a convincing staging of this thesis in a recent book,

Stephen Bann's brilliantly suggestive *The Clothing of Clio.* Bann argues that an ideal of representation as the transparent re-creation of a referent that had previously existed was a long-term aspect of post-eighteenth-century cultural formations in Britain and France. This goal was so widespread that its diachronic development is readable in various representational practices; as early as the 1840s, for example, it was already possible to treat it ironically or parodically. Bann compares rhetorical forms of determinant nineteenth-century developments in media and institutions such as literature, painting, architecture, the museum, and even taxidermy (think of Bazin in relation to the last). Of special interest here is the inevitable importance in his discussion of a number of image technologies, among them lithographs, dioramas, various photographic inventions, and, by the end of the century, cinema. Bann is thus in a position to make an important claim:

> The evidence goes to show, therefore, that photographic reproduction aroused no absolutely new types of response. On the epistemological level, photographs appeared to present no distinctive and unprecedented vision of the external world. Or rather, whatever was novel about them could be contained within the existing framework of responses to [purportedly] non-mediated forms of representation, which were already becoming established by the later 18th and early 19th centuries.

Thus, "the unique 'testimony' of the photograph remained as the extreme boundary of a continuum of forms of historical representation."[32]

Historical representation: Foucault identifies historical investigation as a master discipline in the vast rearrangement of Western disciplines and knowledges—the epistemic break—he finds in process by the beginning of the 19th century. He summarizes the specificity of this shift by describing a period when philosophy "will necessarily lead thought back to the question of knowing what it means for thought to have a history."[33] (Is this not one of our questions here?) This view is not unique to Foucault. It has long been a commonplace that an "Age of History" occurred in the West during the nineteenth century. This was not only the century in which photography and cinema appeared but also the century of Hegel, Marx, and Ranke.

The nineteenth century is thus the period of the diffusion of major concerns of Bazin: the indexical image and questions of historicity. Both are implicated in a fascination with representing the past and hence in the status of temporality. What consequences for "historicizing" our understanding of Bazin might stem from this? Here are a series of proposals that cannot be developed here but point toward a conclusion.

1. The effectivity of time surely was not a new question in the nineteenth century, for instance, in philosophy. But its diffusion throughout the West seems to have been pervasive in this period.[34] With Bazin in mind, it is revealing to consider the extent to which concerns around time are manifested in representational forms and intellectual formations throughout the century.

2. On one side, it would be possible to construct an account of a powerful drive to rationalize time from the beginnings of the industrial revolution in the eighteenth century through the Taylorism of the early twentieth century and later. The model of industrial rationalization of time effected the most significant changes in daily life, in the household as well as the workplace. Its impact can be read in a wide range of manifestations, from the new market for inexpensive watches to the geographical standardization of time within individual nations and establishment of worldwide time zones. That time is a resource to be controlled, managed, and made useful is probably one of the great cultural themes developed by the nineteenth-century West.[35]

3. The contemporaneous reconsiderations of time in science, philosophy, the human sciences, and the arts undoubtedly bear relation to the far-reaching processes of industrialization, new technologies, and so on. But by the late 1800s there was evidently another side to the rigorous organization of time and the positivistic, rationalizing confidence with which that was allied. For it had become well established that the ramifications of a radically conceived omnipresence of temporality could be radically unsettling. A standard reference is Darwin, whose fame led to generalized, breakthrough realizations throughout the culture of the sheer "quantity" of time and pastness. But additionally this was the period of a number of disciplines that were founded on, or refurbished by, the insistence on temporality: not just evolutionary biology, but archaeology, geology, and others, including, of course, history. And one cannot omit psychoanalysis, which decenters human subjectivity by submitting the conscious to the subject's past.[36]

4. Hence, in the nineteenth century temporality can be pictured as a crucial battle terrain, implicated both in ideals of rationalized human progress and in the corrosive decentering critiques of humanistic ideals associated

with modernism in philosophy, the arts, and social theory. This is a "context" for the profusion of representational forms and media concerned with transmission or recovery of the past.

5. In culture and philosophy, then, this period appears to probe and sharpen a seemingly unavoidable antinomy: *time-filled versus time-less.* Within historiography itself, this is a classic problem: does everything change in the flux of time, which means anything is specific to a given moment or period, so that history as the rule of time becomes the rule of the particular? Or are there general truths, laws, patterns, more or less "eternal" verities that can serve to center our knowledge and block the collapse of existence into particularities and disjunctions? By the beginning of the twentieth century, the former tendency would make the radical relativism of a modernist stance an unavoidable problem in the philosophy of history, as in the famous "crisis of historicism" in Germany.[37] The stakes of the struggle for control of time were high.

6. The opposition time-filled versus time-less is at the heart of the contradiction probed above in Bazin, but once again this only points to the consistency of Bazin's phenomenology. Phenomenology is in fact often read as a response to the epistemological crises of Western theory well established by the beginning of the twentieth century. As just one example, Foucault brings Husserl onto the scene at the conclusion of a chapter that describes the nineteenth century as the age of history, with a standard summary of the phenomenological solution as being to "give empirical contents transcendental value, or displace them in the direction of a constituent subjectivity." Consequently, the disjunction between transcendental timelessness and the stream of time of actual existence is a central problem in the constitution of the phenomenological subject. Thus, critics of phenomenology such as Adorno have long argued that the contradiction between the universal effectivity of temporality in existence and a timeless consciousness (hence essence) is only overcome by a logical sleight of hand impelled by sociohistoric circumstances. According to Adorno, such slippages, even in master thinkers such as Husserl are defensive: "Dread stamps the ideal of Husserlian philosophy as one of absolute security." This also accords with Bann, who cites Foucault on the nineteenth-century sense of deficiency and loss against which defenses had to be erected. It also could refer us to Benjamin's account of nineteenth-century shifts in subjective positionality entailed by the new media, for the loss of aura is a loss of the unique pastness of the object as it is apprehended for subjective life. These

divergent thinkers all depict the period that led to phenomenology and cinema as one in which the force of time is embraced but often in order to be displaced.[38]

Let us move toward a conclusion from this last emphasis on insecurity and defensiveness. The original rationale for the philosophical innovations of phenomenology was to find security against fundamental epistemological deficiencies. Bazin may indeed be positioned within this "context," both in his own theoretical obsessions and in the aspects of his privileged object, cinema, to which he shows special sensitivity. But then, as phenomenology is connected to the intensified time awareness in the nineteenth-century West, so is Bazin. To read Bazin is to constantly encounter privileged nineteenth-century discoveries and disciplines, from the evolutionary and dialectical approaches in his historical formulations to the archaeological and geological comparisons that mark both his literary and cognitive style.[39]

Bazin's sophistication is indicated by the fact that he thematizes the threats to secure human subjectivity posed by a radical time awareness that had become so evident by the end of the nineteenth century. The mummy complex is a center by means of which film theory incorporates and turns away the deficiencies motivating the drive toward an absolutely secure, preservative representation. Bazin's theory counters the dread described by Adorno, first by internalizing and essentializing it; second, by making the indexical image the basis of a valid response to the insecurities of subjectivity without eliminating them; and, third, by suppressing them on another level. For the mummy complex provides him with a stable truth, an epistemological security for the theorist's assimilation of the past, of a sort that he would identify as illogical and even perverse if it were claimed by the cinematic subject.

This view of Bazin could accord with a claim found in French film theory, from Merleau-Ponty through Metz, that there is a special correspondence or affinity between phenomenology and cinema, which circulates around definitions of *subjectivity*.[40] Bazin as historiographic subject is where the cinematic subject as described by him would like to be. Instead of a perfect correspondence between metalanguage and object, however, this parallel between phenomenology and cinema is here a floating, "historical" one in that it is based on historical overlaps and junctures. In many ways, Bazin's arguments constitute ideas whose time had come. Certainly, as Bann traces out, the ideal of lifelike, re-creative representation embodied in formal and technological developments of an imposingly large number of nineteenth-century arts, media, and institutions, it becomes difficult to resist the impression of a generalized cultural obsession close to that which grounds Bazin's ontology. Recalling our earlier point that investment in the special credibility of indexical images presumes a predisposing desire to believe and a prior knowledge of how such images are produced, we can begin to make out the shape of an account of how both of these were diffused as parts of large-scale sociocultural developments during the nineteenth century.

Hence, it is necessary to read Bazin with a sort of respectful complexity, for his work simultaneously explores a configuration historically crucial for cinema and registers it symptomatically. This is not to agree that we should ask how phenomenology and/or cinema achieves or embodies essence but rather to foreground the problem of how they attempt to produce essences, securities. We can thus share with Bazin the project of reading subjective relations off of the history of representations, which involves the presumption that such relations are inseparable from the latter. But we would not share with him the unification of the time-filled with a victory over time, so that "the" fundamental subjective relation to cinema as such is the same now as it was in, say, 1895, and can therefore give us a secure ground from which to commence inquiry. Instead the contradiction between the time-filled and the time-less requires its own understanding, in a peculiar balancing act whereby the very terms that drive us to conceive of cultural formations in a radically "historical" way are themselves under that kind of interrogation. As a response to their cultural and ideological power, then, we can begin by treating Bazinian conceptions as following from widespread nineteenth-century forces and representational conceptions that bear on cinema.

Is cinema a medium of the nineteenth century? Is Bazin a thinker of the nineteenth century? Perhaps—at least insofar as we admit that elements of this "nineteenth century" persist well into the twentieth and continue to require response. For example, the film titles to which I have alluded for section headings in this essay all have what might be regarded as "historical" subject matter; they dredge up, preserve, or restore events, settings, and/or situations that "really" existed. The long-lasting fascination of mainstream (but not only mainstream) cinema with the historical, the special construction of historical temporality in cinema as a central aspect of film culture—and therefore historical representation itself as a historical and cultural construction in relation to the appearance of cinema—are thrown into prominence by this consideration of Bazin. Once more, Bazin may point us toward something we wish to explore in ways different from him but which cannot be ignored. For in Bazin's ontology there is not only a history of the image but an image of history. And constructing this latter image is our problem today.

Notes

1   For examples of kinds of commentaries on Bazin, see James Roy MacBean, *Film and Revolution* (Bloomington: Indiana University Press, 1975), 101–3 and passim, on Bazin's ideological/metaphysical complicity; on his contradictory logic, see Brian Henderson, "The Structure of Bazin's Thought," reprinted in Brian Henderson, *A Critique of Film Theory* (New York: Dutton, 1980); on the blockages of his realism from the perspective of semiotics and psychoanalysis, see Colin MacCabe, "Theory and Film: Principles of Realism and Pleasure," *Screen* 17:3 (autumn 1976): esp. 9–17, reprinted in Philip Rosen ed., *Narrative, Apparatus, Ideology: A Film Theory Reader* (New York: Columbia University Press, 1986). On the partiality of Bazin's insights, see Peter Wollen, *Signs and Meanings in the Cinema* (Bloomington: Indiana University Press, [1969] rev. 1972), 125–36, 140–41; Christian Metz, *The Imaginary Signifier: Psychoanalysis and the Cinema,* translated by Celia Britton et al. (Bloomington: Indiana University Press, 1982); Jean-Louis Comolli, "Technique et idéologie: Camera, perspective, profoundeur de champ," intermittent series in *Cahiers du Cinéma* 229–41, especially the explication and comparisons of Bazin and Mitry in numbers 230 (July 1971) and 231 (August–September 1971); Brian Henderson, "Bazin Defended against His Devotees," *Film Quarterly* 32:4 (summer 1979): esp. 30–37. For a slightly different kind of critique from the perspective of narrational theory, see Edward R. Branigan, *Point of View in Cinema: A Theory of Narration and Subjectivity in Classical Film* (New York: Mouton, 1984), 198–212. On the other hand, for an admiring account, see our only book-length treatment of Bazin, Dudley Andrew, *André Bazin* (New York: Oxford University Press, 1978).

   Except for the last two and MacCabe's 1976 article, original publications of these (and there are more) all had occurred by 1975. Whatever the merits of the critiques (in my view there were many), it is as if the familiar constellation of breakthrough tendencies in post-1968 film theory (those associated with structuralism, semiotics, neo-Marxism, poststructuralism, and psychoanalysis) required an "other" in film theory to help define their own radical novelty and often found Bazin more than suitable. The translation of major work by Bazin in the two volumes entitled *What Is Cinema?,* in 1967 and 1971, was undoubtedly a factor both confirming Bazin's importance and making him more generally available as a target in the Anglo-American world.

2   Jean-Paul Sartre, "Existentialism is a Humanism" in *Existentialism from Dostoevsky to Sartre,* edited by Walter Kaufman (New York: Meridian, 1956), 302, emphasis in original; Andrew, *André Bazin,* 68–81. For an earlier American view of Bazin also sensitive to the connection with Sartre, see Annette Michelson's knowledgeable and presciently criti-

cal review of the first volume of English-language translations from *What Is Cinema?* in *Artforum* 6 (summer 1968): 67–70.

3 MacCabe, "Theory and Film." See the installments from Comolli's series cited above. Cf. Rick Altman, "Toward a Theory of the History of Representational Technologies," *Iris* 2:2 (1984): 111–26. While I question certain implications he draws, I think Altman is correct in reading Comolli in light of Bazin.

4 See, for example, Maurice Merleau-Ponty, "The Film and the New Psychology," in *Sense and Non-Sense,* translated by Hubert L. Dreyfus and Patricia A. Dreyfus (Evanston: Northwestern University Press, 1964), originally published in 1947, for example, the same period as "The Ontology of the Photographic Image."

5 Throughout this article citations from *What Is Cinema?* and *What Is Cinema?* volume 2 (Berkeley: University of California Press, 1967 and 1971) will be listed in the text as WC1 and WC2 respectively. The first passage is from André Bazin, *Jean Renoir,* edited by Francois Truffaut, translated by W. W. Halsey II and William H. Simon (New York: Delta, 1974), 85.

6 See the first part of Comolli's series "Technique and Ideology," translated by Diana Matias, in Bill Nichols, ed., *Movies and Methods,* vol. 2 (Berkeley: University of California Press, 1985), 40–57; "Narrative Space" in Stephen Heath, *Questions of Cinema* (Bloomington: Indiana University Press, 1981), esp. 24–54; and David Bordwell, *Narration in the Fiction Film* (Madison: University of Wisconsin Press, 1985), 100ff.

7 From *The World Walk,* a 1984 British Broadcasting Corporation (BBC) production about the war criminals imprisoned at Spandau, written by Jonathan Smith:

> HESS: Speer, I just realized my food can't be poisoned. After all, I could take any of the bowls offered.
>
> Yours, Schirach's. . . .
>
> SPEER: Or the Admiral's.
>
> HESS: Quite.
>
> SPEER: Good. So you're over that obsession at last.
>
> HESS: Of course not. If I were, it wouldn't be an obsession.

8 Peter Wollen, *Signs and Meaning in the Cinema.* The claim that Bazin deemphasizes "the agency of the human mind" is on page 131. On the pages immediately following, however, Wollen goes on to make points not opposed to those made here. Another important reading of Bazin, which hits on some motifs of my argument, is Wollen's " 'Ontology' and 'Materialism' in Film," reprinted in Peter Wollen, *Readings and Writings: Semiotic Counter-strategies* (London: New Left Books, 1982), esp. 205–6, 189–93. But there Wollen concludes that cinematic "language" is opposed to ontology for Bazin, who is said to have desired meaning to emerge completely and naturally from the profilmic. This again misses the possibility that the ontology proceeds from the subject's desire rather than a supposedly direct relation between apparatus and filmed object.

9 In fact, "likeness" or "resemblance" is itself a complicated notion for Peirce: "Peirce's theory of iconicity is not a sentimental appeal to 'natural resemblances' and, in fact, allows for changing mimetic conventions." Elizabeth W. Bruss, "Peirce and Jakobson on the Nature of the Sign," in *The Sign: Semiotics Around the World* edited by R. W. Bailey, L. Matejka, and P. Steiner (Ann Arbor: Michigan Slavic Publications, 1980), 88. For

Peirce's definitions of *indexicality* and its relation to iconicity, see pertinent passages in *Philosophical Writings of Peirce*, edited by Justus Buchler (New York: Dover, 1955), e.g., 102; also 108: "a genuine Index may contain Firstness, and so an Icon as a constituent part of it." (*Genuine* here is a technical term; Peirce distinguishes between "genuine" and "degenerate" indices.) On pronouns and indexicality, see 110–11. Part of the appropriateness of considering Bazin through Peirce is that Bazin's premise of the inevitability of a subjective project even in the apprehension of the most realistic media is paralleled by Peirce's insistence, emphasized by Teresa de Lauretis, that signification always includes the interpretant. See de Lauretis, *Alice Doesn't: Feminism, Semiotics, Cinema* (Bloomington: Indiana University Press, 1984), 179–80.

10   Since this argument regarding a special credibility of cinematic images is fairly abstract and restricted, two points might be glossed in passing. First, the question of synthesized movement, of which Heath and Bordwell are well aware, is not dealt with here. Briefly, depicted movement as a matter of spatial displacement is inconceivable outside temporality, and it is the centrality of temporality toward which I am moving.

   Second, the decentering of spatial likeness in an account of cinematic realism might seem inappropriate in a discussion of Bazin given, for example, the way in which he treats something like *The Cabinet of Dr. Caligari* (1919) as a film-historical "heresy" [wc1, 26]. On the other hand, the most striking and famous visual "distortions" of such a film take place at the profilmic level (expressionistic sets, stylized acting, etc.); these "distortions" are then conveyed to us, with an impression of faithful transmission, as a preexisting configuration of the profilmic. For example, it is appropriate for a viewer of *Caligari* to appreciate the work of the expressionist artists who served as set designers. Such trust even in images that do not always correspond to perspectival norms can occur only on the assumption of an indexical relation to a preexistent; it is how we take film images to be produced that might encourage this understanding of the image. The same kind of comment might be made about Bordwell's example (*Narration in the Fiction Film*, 107) of a photograph depicting depth according to a non-Western system, achieved strictly by arrangement of the profilmic and with little if any deviation from "normal" lenses.

11   The temporality of the image bears on a vacillation in this article between the theoretically familiar phrase "mechanically produced images" and "automatically produced images." While the former is applicable to photography and film, the main concerns of Bazin, it is not, strictly speaking, quite appropriate for video. Television certainly provides opportunities to extend Bazinian concerns, in that it is indexical and in its dominant forms partakes of graphic procedures such as Quattrocento perspective. But it also refuses to fit into some of the Bazinian account of the progress of the media. The potential for "liveness" means that television is not restricted to bringing us something from the past but introduces the possibility of simultaneity of sign and referent; hence, the mummy complex is not quite applicable to television. But in actuality the problem is more complex, since much mainstream television, as well as other kinds of video, is "prerecorded," whether on film or videotape, with "live" programming restricted to certain genres such as sporting events. The entire relation between prerecorded and "live" programming needs attention. See Jane Feuer, "The Concept of Live Television:

Ontology as Ideology," *Regarding Television,* edited by E. Ann Kaplan (Frederick, Md.: University Press of America and the American Film Institute, 1983). And see Pamela Falkenberg, " 'The Text! The Text!': André Bazin's Mummy Complex, Psychoanalysis, and the Cinema," *Wide Angle* 9:4 (1987): 35–55.

12 Since it is the spectator's being as subject that is at stake, one might well argue for a certain kinship between recent psychoanalytic formulations and Bazin. Bazin does intermittently show interest in psychoanalytic understandings of culture and spectatorship, but also this kinship is a product of a set of theoretical and discursive concerns (e.g., around the identity and self-knowledge of the subject) so important in much of the international post-1968 theoretical milieu, but which do have, precisely, a history that predates 1968 even in film theory. See, for example, "Theater and Cinema, part 2," in WC1, esp. 96–102. Bazin's motifs in these pages include the opposition presence-absence, identification, and the use of striptease as a counterexample of spectatorship in relation to these. Comparisons could be drawn with Metz in "The Imaginary Signifier.

13 A third category of the "free adaptation," exemplified by Renoir, need not detain us here.

14 Subjective projection is necessary but not sufficient. Bazin also argues that Bresson's fidelity would not be possible in a film about paintings. Since paintings do not include a temporal dimension, a film about a painting "cannot pretend to be [either] a substitute for the original or to share its identity." But novel and film "are both narrative arts, that is to say temporal arts" (WC1, 142–43). This reminds us of the medium-specific considerations in "The Ontology of the Photographic Image" for the subjective ambitions of indexicality (note the phrase "share its identity"). In the present context, it is also striking that Bazin places cinema closer to a verbal art than a pictorial art on the basis of temporality.

15 See WC1, 35–36, for the passage in "The Evolution of the Language of Cinema" that most concisely states this claim. However, a more extensive development of the argument is in the 1948 essay "William Wyler ou le janséniste de la mise-en-scène," in André Bazin, *Qu'est-ce que le cinéma?* vol. 1 (Paris: Ed. du Cerf, 1959), translation without Bazin's expository footnotes in Christopher Williams, ed., *Realism and the Cinema: A Reader* (London: Routledge and Kegan Paul, 1980), 36–52.

16 Bazin, "William Wyler ou le janséniste de la mise en scène," 157; translation in Williams, *Realism,* 42, my emphasis.

17 Early in *André Bazin* (18–25) Dudley Andrew notes the impact of the Bergsonian intellectual heritage on the formation of Bazin's thought and on Catholic thinkers read by the young Bazin such as Béguin and Maritain. In passing, Andrew briefly makes a point congruent with my argument here: the Bergson whom Bazin knew mainly through such critics "gave Bazin a deep feeling for the integral unity of a universe in flux," which led among other things to his critique of montage as part of the "analytical, *spatializing* tendency in man" (21, my emphasis).

18 It would be nonsense, of course, to say that space is not a basic Bazinian category. However, even a sentence such as "Our experience of space is the structural basis for our concept of the universe," (WC1, 108) is most understandable in terms of the spe-

cial—temporal—levels of representation and engagement that automatically produced images bring to spatial representation. The point is that photographic realism of *space* always has roots in a *temporal* relation inherent for the subject in such images. (In fact, immediately after this sentence Bazin notes that spatial correspondence between image and world is not the point.)

19 Roland Barthes, *Camera Lucida: Reflections on Photography,* translated by Richard Howard (New York: Hill and Wang, 1981), 77, 87. Barthes draws a sharper distinction between film and photography than Bazin, whom he cites; however, he strongly argues that a phenomenology of photographic credibility emphasizes the *temporal* chemistry of the image over its *spatial* physics (perspective and likeness).

20 On this pregivenness, see, for example, the discussion of *Paisa* (1946) in "An Aesthetic of Reality: Neorealism," WC2, 35–38.

21 Henderson, "Bazin Defended against His Devotees," 32ff. This is perhaps the only commentary that directly emphasizes the importance of ellipsis for Bazin.

22 The phrase "shapes of time" is appropriated from Peter Munz, *The Shapes of Time: A New Look at the Philosophy of History* (Middletown, Conn.: Wesleyan University Press, 1977).

23 In WC2, 148, he equates the mythical function of the best periods of Soviet cinema with that of the Western; therefore, his critiques of Stalinist cinema, discussed immediately below, should not be read as a reflexive anticommunism.

24 Included in Nichols, *Movies and Methods,* vol. 2. See also the discussion of this article in Janet Staiger, "*Theorist,* Yes, but What *of?* Bazin and History," *Iris* 2:2 (1984): 107–8.

25 An unexpected cross-reference: When Lukács in 1967 evaluated his classic 1923 text of humanist Marxism, *History and Class Consciousness,* he considered an overvaluation of the Hegelian notion of a perfect unity of subject and object as his fundamental error within Marxist theory. Given the subsequent complex events in Lukács's own relation to Stalinism, we can with some sense of irony point out that Bazin shows how Stalinist cinema manifests this "deviation" within Marxist conceptions. But, further, Lukács's 1923 account of alienation of the subject, which he would soon repudiate, had great impact (both against and for) in the intellectual milieu of existentialism, from Sartre to Heidegger, and in France particularly, where, for example, Bazin's mentor Mounier sought to overcome the subject-object split with his personalism. What is interesting here is not just the chain of thinkers that might underlie structural parallels in the thought of Bazin and Lukács but the general diffusion of certain problematics throughout the West, discussed in the last part of this article. See "Preface to the New Edition (1967)," in Georg Lukács, *History and Class Consciousness: Studies in Marxist Dialectics,* translated by Rodney Livingstone (Cambridge: MIT Press, 1971), esp. xxi–xxv, xxxv–xxxvi.

26 Bazin, "The Stalin Myth in Soviet Cinema," 38–39.

27 See Staiger, whose chronological discussion of Bazin's writings with respect to history places them in the political and social issues of his day. Janet Staiger, "Theorist, yes, but what of? Bazin and History", *Iris* 2:2 (1984): 107–8.

28 See also, for example, Bazin's "William Wyler, or the Jansenist of Mise-en-Scène" and "An Aesthetic of Reality."

29 For a classic example of the argument that empathy with human agents from the past is

the definitive component of historical investigation, see "Human Nature and Human History" in R. G. Collingwood, *The Idea of History* (New York: Oxford University Press, 1946), e.g., 215ff.

30 See notes 1 and 4 of this essay.

31 A fuller development appears in Philip Rosen, *Change Mummified: Cinema, Historicity, Theory* (Minneapolis: University of Minnesota Press, 2001): 3–43.

32 Stephen Bann, *The Clothing of Clio: A Study of the Representation of History in Nineteenth Century Britain and France* (New York: Cambridge University Press, 1984), 133, 136. This book may generate some quibbling in the particular ways it uses psychoanalysis; however, it is an important book for film studies, both as a new development in the study of reality effects—one that proposes a *historical* subtlety in differentiating their manifestations—and for Bann's ability to draw parallels and connections among a number of verbal and visual media. I am indebted to Christina Crosby of Wesleyan University, who alerted me to the pertinence of Bann's work for my concerns.

33 Michel Foucault, *The Order of Things: An Archaeology of the Human Sciences* (New York: Vintage, 1973), 219–20.

34 It is generally accepted that time became a fundamentally important concern in the natural and human sciences during this period; for example, "By about 1800, historical attitudes and ideas were ready to crystallize out in many fields from the matrix of 18th-century thought, as men [*sic*] began for the first time to recognize the full extent of time and the crucial importance of development." Stephen Toulmin and June Goodfield, *The Discovery of Time* (Chicago: University of Chicago Press, [1965] 1983), 125. This book is a useful, synthetic account of the chief conceptions of time in the context of scientific speculation and cosmology in the West since the ancient Greeks.

35 Thus, E. P. Thompson writes that in worker-manufacturer disputes over the temporal organization of the workday during industrialization, "the conflict is over two cultural modes or ways of life." *The Making of the English Working Class* (New York: Vintage, [1963] 1966), 305–6. On this shift and time technology, see David Landes, *Revolution in Time: Clocks and the Making of the Modern World* (Cambridge: Harvard University Press, 1983), 227–30. Regarding the geographical standardization of time, see Wolfgang Schivelbusch, *The Railway Journey: Trains and Travel in the 19th Century,* translated by Anselm Hollo (New York: Urizen, 1979), 48–50.

36 Toulmin and Goodfield, in *The Discovery of Time,* chap. 10, survey interrelations of conceptions of time in the physical and human sciences during this period.

37 On the crisis of historicism, see Georg G. Iggers, *The German Conception of History: The National Tradition of Historical Thought from Herder to the Present* (Middletown, Conn.: Wesleyan University Press, 1968), chaps. 6 and 7. See also John Berger, "Painting and Time," reprinted in his *The Sense of Sight* (New York: Pantheon, 1985), 205–11, for an indication of how this antinomy could penetrate the arts.

38 Foucault, *The Order of Things,* 248; Cf. Theodor W. Adorno, *Against Epistemology, a Metacritique: Studies in Husserl and the Phenomenological Antinomies,* translated by Willis Domingo (Cambridge: MIT Press, 1983), 217–228 (quoted phrase on 219); Bann, *Clothing,* 14. Walter Benjamin introduces his famous concept of aura in "The Work of Art in the Age of Mechnical Reproduction" through notions of subjective relations to

temporality—tradition, history, and so forth; see his *Illuminations,* edited by Hannah Arendt, translated by Harry Zohn (New York: Schocken, 1969), 220–22. Benjamin is an indispensable counterpoint for reading Bazin, and certain of his brilliant essays on the nineteenth-century West bear directly on the approach I am developing here. See Benjamin's comments on Bergson's appropriation of duration as a sociocultural configuration—a reaction against the new experiences of the nineteenth century, and one that excludes a genuinely historical approach, in "Some Motifs in Baudelaire," in Walter Benjamin, *Charles Baudelaire: A Lyric Poet in the Era of High Capitalism,* translated by Harry Zohn (London: New Left Books, 1973), 111, 144–45, 146–48 (in connection with the decay of the aura). See also his "Paris: the Capital of the 19th Century," included in the same volume. I am grateful to Miriam Hansen for reminding me of the pertinence of Benjamin's commentary on Bergson for my concerns.

39   In fact, Leopold von Ranke's famous 1824 statement, so often treated as marking the birth of modern historiography, that the historian is concerned only with "what actually happened" is underpinned by the problem of attributing sense to preexistent referents; hence, in von Ranke we find the opposition between description and explanation, object and subject—and the necessity of a leap of imagination or faith to bridge the gap—which we find in Bazin. The centrality of a historiographic project in Bazin might be illustrated by the set of broad parallels that could be adduced between certain Bazinian texts and von Ranke's landmark introduction to *History of the Latin and Teutonic Nations, 1494–1535,* in von Ranke, *The Secret of World History: Selected Writings on the Art and Science of History,* edited and translated by Roger Wines (New York: Fordham University Press, [1824] 1981), esp. 58–59.

On geology and evolution, see Andrew, *André Bazin,* 65–67, for the impact of Teilhard de Chardin on Bazin's thought with respect to geology and evolution. But within the present argument, Teilhard, a geologist and paleontologist who wished "to wed science and religion," can only appear as one more thinker trying to clean up the mess—in this case, in theology—after the shocks of the nineteenth century.

40   Maurice Merleau-Ponty, "Film and the New Psychology," in Metz, "The Imaginary Signifier," 52–53, esp. 59. Note again that the former (cited by Metz) was almost contemporary with Bazin's ontological essays.

The Object of Theory

Mary Ann Doane

My title is designed to evoke the multileveled modalities, the ambiguity as well as the seemingly contradictory obviousness and transparency of the term *object*.[1] While *object* can signify the thing that one studies, analyzes, or theorizes (in contradistinction to the subject of the analysis), it can also indicate the aim or goal of the theoretical endeavor, its stakes. Furthermore, in psychoanalysis the object is defined primarily by its instability in relation to the drive, by the constant subjection to displacement that makes it the least substantial indicator of psychical life—working against the tropes of solidity, heaviness, and "thingness" that usually cling to the notion of object.

But to reduce it to its lowest common denominator, its most basic and seemingly transparent sense, it would seem obvious that the object of cinema studies, for instance, is the cinema. Nevertheless, for us now there would seem to be at least two monumental difficulties with this formulation, one with the insistence of historical crisis. What happens to a discipline on the verge of the disappearance of its object, or, to put it more conservatively, in the face of the perception of the death of its object? I am referring here to the emergence of electronic and digital technologies of representation, which threaten to ensure the cinema's obsolescence, or at the very least its outdatedness, in the foreseeable future. What happens when the object begins to lose its contours and its identity threatens to dissolve in a sea of convergence? The second difficulty with positing the object in its purest and most transparent sense, while deprived of such historical pressure, may serve as a potential antidote to—or perhaps sublation of—the first. The cinema, in this basic, originary, innocent, and empirical formulation, *never was* the object of cinema studies. I am not referring to the fact that the cinema has always been subject to accelerating technological mutation so that the cinema of Hugo Munsterberg is not the same as the cinema of Christian Metz (although this is true). Rather, I am gesturing toward the epistemological requirement that theory encapsulate within itself the task of defining its object. The 1970s conceptualization of a cinematic apparatus was by no means unproblematic, but, to the credit of its theorists, it was an effort to actively *think* the limits and identity of an object of knowledge rather than to take for granted the prior existence of self-evident and indisputable objects. The cinematic apparatus was precisely the conjuncture of spectator, theater, screen, projection, and image subtended by a theory of desire. This is not an argument for what has been labeled constructivism. The empirical is very much in play—it is simply not sufficient nor determinant in the specification of the theoretical object.

The second term in my title, *theory,* is arguably no less vexed—historically and epistemologically—than the first. For just as we seem to be on the brink of a postcinematic era, we are also, as David Bordwell and Noël Carroll tell us, already in the age of Post-Theory. The anthology that goes by that name is constituted as an amalgam of cognitive studies approaches, strong critiques of various aspects of what the editors label Grand Theory, and local economic or institutional histories. Its rhetoric is that of antiabstraction and antisystematicity, and its differentiation between Grand Theory and Post-Theory is accomplished through the construction of a series of binary oppositions: empty versus solid, universalizing versus localizing, theory versus stance, homogeneous versus heterogeneous, static versus processual, and dogmatic versus democratic. Post-Theory deals with local problems; it is "piecemeal, problem-driven reflection,"[2] and the terms *middle range* and *middle level* recur frequently. I have elsewhere attempted to trace some surprising affinities between Post-Theory and one of its self-proclaimed adversaries—cultural studies.[3] In its commitment to the local and the context driven, if not in its constant appeal to political imme-

diacy, cultural studies shares with Post-Theory an aversion to the abstraction and perceived totalization or systematization of theoretical constructs.
The strategy of localization also entails a certain proliferation of objects
that are presumed to be "out there," just waiting to be studied (many of
which, for cultural studies, are located in the domain of popular culture).
Both tendencies embrace a certain Taylorization of knowledge production
in their appeal to the soluble problem, the answerable question, the usable
thesis. All of this is at the expense of speculation; of abstract thought, which
risks inconclusiveness: or, in economic terms, the possibility of no return.

The resistance to systematicity emerges as a symptom in much current
work defining itself through its opposition to the hyperabstraction of 1970s
theory. Yet I think there is a more interesting and provocative appropriation of the resistance to systematicity that, while attempting to grapple
with its distillation in the concept of contingency, does not abandon the
theoretical imperative. This work seems to respond to Niklas Luhmann's
question, "Is there a *theory* that can make use of the *concept* of contingency?"[4]
For Paul Willemen and Miriam Hansen, this project takes the form of a return to and rethinking of the historical role of indexicality in the cinema.
Indexicality would appear to ensure the availability of the particular, the
singular, the unpredictable — in short, the antisystematic — within the cinematic domain. In the work of both theorists, the indexical trace as filmic
inscription of contingency is indissociable from affect. In the case of Willemen, that affect takes the precise form of cinephilia. Cinephilia is usually
considered a somewhat marginalized, furtive, even illicit relation to the
cinema rather than a theoretical attitude. It is the property of the film buff
rather than the film theorist. For Willemen, it begins as a fully historical
concept, flourishing from the early 1950s to the later 1960s in relation to
the emergence of a different kind of "mediatic society."[5] It has affinities
with earlier attitudes toward cinema such as that embodied in the concept
of *photogénie* and in the surrealists' celebration of chance. Willemen claims
that cinephilia is a kind of zero degree of spectatorship — it "doesn't do anything other than designate something which resists, which escapes existing
networks of critical discourse and theoretical frameworks."[6] The word indicates the domain of the inarticulable in the film-viewing experience.

What is cinephilia? And as the antithesis of theory how does it come to
embody the hope in a different epistemological grounding of cinematic
pleasure? Cinephilia, at its most basic, is love of the cinema, but it is a love
that is attached to the detail, the moment, the trace, the gesture. Wille-

men, in attempting to specify it, refers to the surrealists' discussion of photography as the "capturing of fleeting, evanescent moments," to Catholic discourses of revelation, to the intensity of a spark, and to the concept of excess.[7] It seems to be most readily localizable in relation to acting or its perceived lack—to a gesture, a body position, a facial expression, or an uncontrolled utterance that somehow escapes scripting. For instance, Jean Epstein isolated as an instance of photogénie the moment when Sessue Hayakawa comes into the room in *The Cheat,* in Willemen's discussion, "his body at a certain angle, in a particular position, opening the door, entering with a particular body language."[8] Epstein was exuberant in the face of the power of the cinema to convey the telltale signs of the body itself: "I can see love. It half lowers its eyelids, raises the arc of the eyebrows laterally, inscribes itself on the taut forehead, swells the massiters, hardens the tuft of the chin, flickers on the mouth and at the edge of the nostrils."[9] Rarely does cinephilia fasten onto a cinematic technique such as a pan or a dissolve— it is to be distinguished from the technophilia Metz glosses as fetishism.[10] And because cinephilia has to do with an excess in relation to systematicity, it is most appropriate for a cinema that is perceived as highly coded and commercialized.

> One way of accounting for the cinephiliac description would be to say that it has to be an aspect of cinema that is not strictly programmable in terms of aesthetic strategies. What is being looked for is a moment or, given that a moment is too unitary, a dimension of a moment which triggers for the viewer either the realisation or the illusion of a realisation that what is being seen is in excess of what is being shown. . . . What matters is that something should be perceived as in excess of the film's register of performance, as potentially undesigned, unprogrammed.[11]

What Willemen gestures toward here is the uncontrollable aspect of cinematic representation, its material predilection for the accidental, the contingent. These moments "show you where the cinematic institution itself vacillates, where it might tip over or allow you a glimpse of the edge of its representation."[12] Or, in other words, you are allowed to glimpse "something you are not meant to see."[13] It is not surprising that Willemen invokes the surrealist discourse on photography, for what is visible but not shown must be a function of the indexicality of the medium, of its photographic base. What cinephilia names is the moment when the contingent takes on meaning—a necessarily private, idiosyncratic meaning neverthe-less characterized by the compulsion to share what is unshareable, inarticu-lable (Willemen refers to the desire to write about the experience as crucial to cinephilia). Whether the moment chosen by the cinephiliac was really unprogrammed, unscripted, or outside codification is fundamentally un-decidable. It is also inconsequential since cinephilia hinges not on indexi-cality but on the knowledge of indexicality's potential, a knowledge that paradoxically erases itself. The cinephile maintains a certain belief, an in-vestment in the graspability of the asystematic, the contingent, for which the cinema is the privileged vehicle.

The apparent indexical guarantee of access to contingency also grounds much of Miriam Hansen's reading of Kracauer's *Theory of Film.* Although she does not invoke the term *cinephilia,* the significance of the cinema in modernity is linked to "the love it inspired along with new forms of knowledge and experience."[14] For Hansen (as for Willemen), cinema is "the aesthetic matrix of a particular historical experience"—the historical ex-perience of modernity, of accelerating technological expansion, of the phe-nomenological and representational dominance of urban space, and of the potential for mass destruction. History here is not a discourse foreign to theory, not evocative of the gradual but certain accumulation of knowl-edge. But the access to contingency, to the imprint of temporality, is made possible by a cinema heavily imbued with historicity. An emphasis upon chance reveals Kracauer's affinity with the surrealists and with slapstick, and it is chance alone "which offers a tiny window, at once hope and obli-gation, of survival, of continuing life after the grand metaphysical stakes have been lost."[15] According to Hansen, it is not the camera's iconicity that ensures its realism for Kracauer but its indexicality, which undergirds the "medium's purchase on material contingency."[16]

What is at stake here, as in Willemen's description of cinephilia, is a *re-lation* between spectator and image, but it is the photographic base that acts as the condition of possibility for such a relation. As in cinephilia, the cinema has the "ability to subject the viewer to encounters with contin-gency, lack of control and otherness."[17] These encounters are always indi-vidual, idiosyncratic, with the flavor of Roland Barthes's *punctum* in photog-raphy.[18] The content of cinephilia is never generalizable—it must be unique to the viewer—but the form of the relation can be specified. The terms of Hansen's discussion of the relation between viewer and film are amazingly similar to those of Willemen's description of cinephilia: "What is at stake is the possibility of a split-second meaninglessness, as the placeholder of an otherness that resists unequivocal understanding and total subsumption. What is also at stake is the ability of the particular, the detail, the incident, to take on a life of its own, to precipitate processes in the viewer that may not be entirely controlled by the film."[19]

For both Hansen and Willemen, the cinematic inscription of contingency constitutes a process whereby history leaves its mark on the film. The content gleaned is not that of history (the historical "fact" is only a subset of all contingencies), but this relation to the film is deeply historical, emblematic of a modernity dominated by a highly technologically mediated rationalization. In this context, the lure of contingency is that it seems to offer a way out, an anchoring point for the condensation of utopian desires. It proffers itself as a way out of systematicity—both that of a tightly regulated classical system and that of its vaguely oppressive abstract analysis.

It is no accident that cinephilia and the consequent return to ontology should emerge as the bearer of such high theoretical stakes now. A certain nostalgia for cinema precedes its death. One doesn't—and can't—love the televisual or the digital in quite the same way. It is as though the object of theory were to delineate more precisely the contours of an object at the moment of its historical demise. Willemen claims that cinephilia is specific only to the historical form of cinema: "The cinephile shares the notion of an ontology of cinema and the less the image has a Bazinian ontological relation to the real (the death-mask notion of the real), the more the image gets electronified, with each pixil becoming programmable in its own terms, the less appropriate cinephilia becomes."[20] It is arguable that cinephilia could not be revived at this conjuncture were the cinema *not* threatened by the accelerating development of new electronic and digital forms of media. Hansen already refers to cinema in the past tense (along with a bewildering variety of other tenses) in claiming that Kracauer's book "elucidates the tremendous significance of cinema, the love it inspired. . . . As we embrace, endure or resist the effects of the digital, the cinematic still remains the sensorial dominant of this century, of a modernity defined by mass production, mass consumption, and mass destruction. At the very least, *Theory of Film* may help us understand the experience that cinema once was and could have been, whatever may become of it."[21] It is the intense and privileged relation to contingency, assured by photographic indexicality in the abstract, that can be loved again, this time as lost.

Is this theorizing of contingency limited to the status of a death knell for the cinema? Does the theory adequate to its object only emerge at the moment of its loss? There is a confusion here of the two senses of object—perhaps a deliberate confusion. If the object is characterized by mortality—it *can* die—it is then the object external to theory, more properly perhaps, the historical object. On the other hand, it is not the cinema as such that is the object of analysis but cinephilia (named in Willemen and suggested in Hansen by the description of a free-floating attention to detail and contingency)—a historical and historicized stance, the historical moment of a relation to cinema. That relation is one which may be definable only negatively—as that which resists systematicity, rationalization, programming, and standardization. It is the leakage of the system, potentially mobilizable as its ruin. Cinema spectatorship, from this perspective, involves cognition, but it is not the cognition of cognitive studies, claiming the illumination of universal processes of reasoning and deduction in film viewing. Rather, it is a knowing through cinema that hinges on the effectivity of contingency.

But is the cinema's relation to contingency really that of the utopian moment other to or in excess of all structure or systematization? Because the theorized object is located by Willemen and Hansen as profoundly historical, I think it would be wise to look again at the historical status of contingency—and indexicality as well—in modernity. In the late nineteenth and early twentieth centuries, the moment of the emergence of cinema, the smooth narrative of a successful and progressive rationalization allied with modernization was also destabilized by an insistent fascination with contingency, indexicality, and chance, which manifested itself at many different levels—in aesthetics, debates about photography, physics, biology, and the growth of social statistics and statistical epistemologies in general. In evolutionary theory, chance becomes determinant, the basis of law. For evolutionary change hinges on an aberration, a contingent difference that is then retained and consolidated as a characteristic of the species. The evolutionary process is motored by chance rather than design. Statistics not only acknowledged the intractability of the contingent, the unknowability of the individual, but it was based on and depended on these affirmations. It allowed the analyst to deal with a plethora of apparently isolated and anomalous events, subordinating their contingency to a lawlike regularity. Statistics hence involves the conjunction of rigorous regulation and the simultaneous acknowledgment of inevitable excess and diversity, of that which is beyond the grasp of epistemology. A technique that might be said to "work indeterminacy," it is, in a sense, the social praxis, in capitalism, of epistemologies of indeterminism. It is one form, in modernity, of the project of making the contingent legible.

Cinema, in its dominant modes in the twentieth century, could be said to be another. The implicit thesis of the Lumière catalogs and the plethora of actualities produced in the earliest years is the indexical guarantee that anything and everything is filmable. The idea of the filmability of the contingent without limit persists and subtends mainstream classical narrative. It explains the overwhelming multiplicity and diversity of detail that contribute to the sense that a film must be experienced rather than described, that it is fundamentally alien to interpretation or translation. It promotes the sense that cinema is the site of newness and difference itself, the focal point of modernity. In the face of the abstraction of time, its transformation into the discrete, the measurable, the locus of value (e.g., in the worldwide standardization of time to facilitate railroad schedules and communication by telegraph as well as in Taylorism), chance and the contingent are assigned an important ideological role—they become the highly cathected sites of both pleasure and anxiety. What is critical is the production of contingency and ephemerality as graspable, representable but nevertheless antisystematic. The isolation of contingency as embodying the pure form of an aspiration, a utopian desire, ignores the extent to which the structuring of contingency, as precisely asystematic, became the paradoxical basis of social stability in modernity.

A cinephilia that hinges on the envisaged death of cinema stipulates the death as that of the photographic base. This is because we tend to see photography as the exemplary instance of indexicality and hence the privileged bearer of contingency. But for Charles Sanders Peirce, who defined the indexical sign, photography was by no means the central example. In Peirce's description, the index is evacuated of content, it is a hollowed out sign. It designates something without describing it; its function is limited to the assurance of an existence. The demonstrative pronouns *this* and *that* are "nearly pure indices."[22] Hence, indexicality together with its seemingly privileged relation to the referent—to singularity and contingency—is available to a range of media. The insistency and compulsion Peirce associates with the indexical sign are certainly attributes of television and digital media as well—witness the televisual obsession with the "live" coverage of catastrophe, the ultimate representation of contingency, chance, and the instantaneous, as well as the logistics of an Internet that promises to put diversity, singularity, and instantaneity more fully within our grasp. From this perspective, the desire fueling cinephilia will not die with the cinema as we know it. Cinephilia is only a slightly illicit subset of a larger and ongoing structuring of the access to contingency.

It might seem that I am simply constructing a metasystem with no outside, characterized by the sheer impossibility of envisaging an exit. But this is not my intention. For the metasystem itself is fully historical and hence could have been different. Willemen and Hansen are attracted to the notion of a love for the cinema that fastens on the contingent because they see it as an homage to the cinema's historical dimension. The indexically inscribed contingency is not the embodiment of history as mark of the real or referent but history as the mark of what could have been otherwise. Hence, the lack of importance accorded to the precise (cinematic) moment chosen by the cinephile. In the manner of all utopian discourses, it is an homage to possibility. In a chapter entitled "Contingency as Modern Society's Defining Attribute," Niklas Luhmann provides an Aristotelian definition of *contingency*: "Anything is contingent that is neither necessary nor impossible. The concept is therefore defined by the negation of necessity and impossibility."[23] There is an apparent contradiction internal to the definition itself, which allows it a productive ambiguity. For it is difficult to think the compatibility of necessity and impossibility except perhaps through their simultaneous negation. What is necessary is difficult to think of as impossible, and what is impossible is hard to imagine as necessary. However, as the negation of necessity cinematic contingency participates in the resistance to systematicity discussed earlier and hence becomes susceptible, ironically, to a form of systematicity. In resisting, it *partakes* of systematicity, locked within the terms of its antagonist. But as the negation of impossiblity, contingency has the potential to become a reflexive concept, to force a meditation on the history of its own impossible fate within modernity. As the negation of impossibility, contingency is a witness against technology as inexorability, a witness that it could have been otherwise. Through the tensions internal to its own definition, contingency might take up a double function—allowing us to derive what is positive, even utopian, from the cinema while not losing sight of what links it to future technologies and the continuing structuring/systematization of chance.

Notes

1 This essay was originally presented at a plenary session on theory at the Society for Cinema Studies Conference, West Palm Beach, April 15–18, 1999.

2 David Bordwell and Noël Carroll, "Introduction," in *Post-theory: Reconstructing Film Studies,* edited by David Bordwell and Noël Carroll (Madison: University of Wisconsin Press, 1996), xiii.

3 Mary Ann Doane, "Radical Nostalgia: Disciplines and the Politics of Method," paper presented at the symposium Cinema Studies in the Age of Global Media, University of Chicago, April 13, 1996.

4 Niklas Luhmann, *Observations on Modernity,* translated by William Whobrey (Stanford: Stanford University Press, 1998), 46.

5 Paul Willemen, *Looks and Frictions: Essays in Cultural Studies and Film Theory* (Bloomington: Indiana University Press, 1994), 228.

6 Ibid., 231.

7 Ibid., 232. For an intriguing discussion of the surrealists' relation to photography, see Rosalind Krauss, "The Photographic Conditions of Surrealism," in *The Originality of the Avant-Garde and Other Modernist Myths* (Cambridge: MIT Press, 1985), 87–118.

8 Willemen, *Looks and Frictions,* 233.

9 Jean Epstein, "Magnification and Other Writings," translated by Stuart Liebman, *October* 3 (1977): 13. See also Jean Epstein, "*Bonjour Cinéma* and Other Writings by Jean Epstein," translated by Tom Milne, *Afterimage* 10 (1981): 8–38.

10 Although Epstein fastens on the technique of the close-up, he is more interested in it as a conveyor of the signs of the body, especially the face, than in its inherent characteristics as a technique. He is not interested in close-ups of objects or of aspects of landscape. The close-up simply magnifies the legibility of the body.

11 Willemen, *Looks and Frictions,* 237, 238–39.

12 Ibid., 240.

13 Ibid., 241.

14 Miriam Hansen, Introduction to Siegfried Kracauer, *Theory of Film* (Princeton: Princeton University Press, 1997), xxxv.

15 Ibid., xxii.

16 Ibid., xxxii.

17 Ibid., xxi.

18 Roland Barthes, *Camera Lucida: Reflections on Photography,* translated by Richard Howard (New York: Hill and Wang, 1981).

19 Hansen, Introduction, xxxi.

20 Willemen, *Looks and Frictions,* 243–44.

21 Hansen, Introduction, xxxv.

22 Charles Sanders Peirce, *The Essential Peirce,* vol. 1, edited by Nathan Houser and Christian Kloesel (Bloomington: Indiana University Press, 1992) 226. Since *this* and *that* are also symbolic signs, Peirce would no doubt have been more accurate in isolating the pointing finger as the "purest" form of the index.

23 Luhmann, *Observations on Modernity,* 45.

CULTURAL INDICES

No Longer Absolute: Portraiture in American
Avant-Garde and Documentary Films of the Sixties

Paul Arthur

When this device is made available to the public, everyone will be able to photograph those dear to them, not just in their immobile form but in their movement, in their action, and with speech on their lips; then death will no longer be absolute.—*La Poste* (Paris), December 30, 1895

Of approximately a dozen tiny films presented by the Lumière brothers for their inaugural program on December 28, 1895, *Le Dejeuner de Bébé* stands out as at once visually distinct and remarkably prescient. Lasting less than a minute, it shows a mother and father from the waist up plying their seated toddler with bits of food. Compared with other vignettes, the scene has a centered, unhurried development. The greater proximity of its subjects, along with their relatively subdued gestures, allows us fleeting access to who they are in the social order as indexed by clothing and setting. It is perhaps the only scene from the early roster of Lumière films whose aura of familiarity deflects the clinical chill of historical distance. Where other scenes are populated by indistinct if highly animated figures, the family of *Le Dejeuner* creates an impression of particularized identity grounded in corporeal fullness and immediacy. At one point, the beaming child thrusts a piece of biscuit directly toward the camera, a gesture that indicates not only the unseen locus of observation but the inchoate fact of complicity between social actors and recording process. We know that the person behind the camera was her uncle Louis, his role in the profilmic already fixed by familial bonds. Thus, in anecdote as well as in the performative exchange between observer and observed, this little glimpse of domestic life can be regarded as the first home movie.[1] For our purposes it is also the primal origin of the Portrait Film, a practice that developed much later in cinema but is latent from the beginning as recording impulse, social desideratum, and pictorial inheritance from painting.

The technohistorical development of home movies converges with that of the portrait film in several important respects. For both practices, conditions of aesthetic possibility were shaped by innovations in camera and recording devices, especially the advent of 16mm semiprofessional equipment in the 1930s and the refinement of lightweight sync-sound camera rigs in the late 1950s. Further, the nearly simultaneous emergence in the early 1960s of documentary and avant-garde approaches to portraiture closely mirrors the explosion in America of amateur film production.[2] Like home movies, portraits tend to be sub-feature-length, present-tense studies of individuals or socially affiliated coteries made by autonomous filmmakers or small collaborative units. However, while home movies are made strictly for domestic consumption, the self-conscious creation of avant-garde and documentary portraits relies on at least rudimentary networks of distribution, exhibition, publicity, and often external funding. It is perhaps not incidental that the creation of new bases of institutional support for avant-garde and independent documentary initiatives—albeit substantially separate and distinct for each movement—coincides with the accelerating growth of portraiture as a mode of filmic organization and as a cultural signifier.

Forty years after its inception, the existence of portraiture as a film-critical category and, in its myriad televisual extensions, popular entertainment is hardly in doubt. Nonetheless, given its longevity and unquestioned body of achievement, there have been surprisingly few attempts to describe, theorize, or historicize the genre as such (admittedly, individual films have received ample critical attention). This essay is intended to redress a long-standing oversight by providing a general account of portraiture's aesthetic, thematic, and social dynamics during the period of its initial flowering as well as offering detailed analyses of exemplary films and filmmakers. Although the discussion is limited mainly to the 1960s, dominant paradigms of organization and the epistemological questions they underwrite have continued to activate portrait films of later decades. Similarly, although I do not assess relations between portraiture and adjacent practices in either American documentary or experimental cinemas, the broader implications of portraiture for the methods and aspirations of these movements should be evident.

Some basic formal elements and motifs, pertaining equally to documentary and avant-garde idioms, can be ventured at the outset. As if taking cues from *Le Dejeuner de Bébé,* the majority of film portraits favor frontal midrange compositions in which a subject's face and hands are privileged foci of information and/or expression. Subjects are usually posed within vernacular settings—as opposed to neutral or patently symbolic contexts—and at times a specific object in that setting will play a role in defining the subject's identity. Portraiture is among the most "literal" or nonrhetorical of filmic genres, yet, as we shall see, there are numerous instances of pointed metonymy forged from the friction between subject and surrounding space. Not unexpectedly, longer takes and relatively straightforward handling of the camera are preferred over the use of montage—an essentially metaphoric device—or expressive or denaturing recording options. Indeed, editing patterns tend toward simple linear or additive structures in which temporal arrangements of shots or scenes abjure dramatic development or rhythmic articulation.

The emphasis in film portraiture on immediacy and present-tense observation will receive a more nuanced, ontologically inflected examination later, but for now it is useful to note the typically 1960s conflation of temporal address with the youthful bearing of many subjects, a correspondence in which *formal* markers of vitality are mirrored in, and implicitly held as appropriate to, a subject's age and social "presence." The idea of living in the present, and its concomitant celebration of creative spontaneity and the rejection of official history, became a potent shibboleth in 1960s art and countercultural activities: happenings, be-ins, protests, improvised music, and spoken poetry were all manifestations of a defiant urge for "newness," and portraiture found a receptive home within this broader cultural ethos.[3] To be sure, the arc of time covered by film portraits is in no way standardized; it may encompass a single "real time" exposure, a sequence of temporally disjunctive shots, or a series of scenes recorded over several months. But, despite public confusion between the portrait form and biography, generated in part by practices of titling and descriptive labeling, portraits do not as a rule dip into a subject's past via still photos, archival footage, or ancillary verbal testimony. In films such as Shirley Clarke's *Portrait of Jason* (1967), there is considerable first-person narration of past events yet the stress is always on the *performance* of piquant stories rather than on a diachronic, inclusive unfolding of biographical information (given this qualification, *Nanook of the North* [1922], despite its ordering by seasons, deserves consideration as a protoportrait while *Antonia: A Portrait of the Woman* [1974] is more properly classed as biography).

There is a further crucial consequence of portraiture's imbrication in the 1960s cult of presentness that harbors a self-reflexive thrust. The dominant subjects in documentary portraits, especially the cinema vérité or direct cinema films discussed here, are public performers, celebrities of one sort or another—including athletes, lawyers, politicians, and salesmen. Aside from occasional family and friends, the focus in avant-garde portraits tends to be on artists: poets, painters, and of course other filmmakers. In both groups, then, there is an implicit, frequently foregrounded, reciprocity between the act of filming (and editing) and a subject's enactment of self before the camera.[4] That is, 1960s portraiture simultaneously champions a particular type of person whose sociocultural status reflects back on, and enters into productive exchange with, the vocation of filmmaking. Moreover, it is not cinema per se that is granted privileged standing in the representation of personal identity but, respectively, two nonmainstream practices bent on posing timely challenges to conventional and/or previous cinematic styles. In the course of valorizing a certain class of subject through specific sets of visual strategies, documentary and avant-garde portraits incorporate the terms of their own parochial agendas and visions of cinematic renewal.

In 1945, André Bazin declared that photography had freed modern painting from the burdens of naturalistic representation, an idea that had already circulated through the European art world of Picasso and his cohort.[5] Although Bazin fails to address the implications of this historical transformation either for cinema or for specific types of painting—portraiture was unquestionably the pictorial genre most deeply and irrevocably transformed by mechanical reproduction[6]—his contemporaneous writings on Italian neorealism prize exactly the sort of linear, present-tense staging of quotidian events that a decade later would galvanize the emergence of portrait films.[7] Cesare Zavattini, a key neorealist practitioner and theorist, posited a sequence that would record for ninety minutes the unexceptional routine of an ordinary person: "I want to meet the real protagonist of everyday life, I want to see how he is made, if he has a moustache or not, if he is tall or short, I want to see his eyes, and I want to speak to him."[8] In this un-realized—in certain respects unrealizable—project, Zavattini anticipates in both method and subject matter the modus operandi of American portraiture of the 1960s.

Tempting as it is to link neorealism with portraiture as historically successive movements, they diverge significantly in their aesthetic and philosophical assumptions. Fueled by the disavowal of classical Hollywood ideals of glamorized, heroic action and unambiguous closure, the Italian films endorsed by Bazin were a politically motivated blend of original techniques and extant fiction and nonfiction practices. Indeed, the roots of neorealism uncover a range of cinematic precedents for the depiction of nondramatic subjects in quotidian settings, which, at least indirectly, are pertinent to portraiture. Newsreels and *actualities* since Lumière trafficked in scenes of famous personages engaged in mundane acts—Tolstoy wandering in his garden, Woodrow Wilson taking tea on the White House lawn. In the 1930s, Hollywood studios churned out supposedly unstaged promotional trailers featuring movie stars in their "normal" off-screen routines.[9] Robert Flaherty's commercially successful documentaries explored the dailiness of exotic individuals whose personal qualities are realized by struggles against a hostile environment. What these nonfiction character studies share is a fascination with *extraordinary* subjects, whereas neorealism prided itself on the portrayal of "everyday protagonists."

Leaving aside disparities in the presentational aims of early examples of crypto-portraiture, the beginnings of a self-conscious practice were sparked by the development of key institutional supports and technological options: primarily, a system for distributing and showing short nontheatrical films and the availability of relatively inexpensive 16mm camera rigs. Hence a full-blown, bifurcated movement of portraiture in the United States derives as much from a confluence of material and cultural factors as it does from any cinematic inheritance. In other words, the independent film scene of the early 1960s was primed for distinctly American treatments of the microdrama of personal identity. As is well known, cinema vérité took advantage of the capacity for sync-sound recording and found a welcome partner in network television's demand for extended celebrity profiles.[10] Later in the decade, a theatrical niche market for full-length documentaries helped reinforce the economic viability of nonfiction production—although portraits were less popular at the box office than were rock concerts. At the same time, the increasing availability of amateur movie equipment, along with the founding in 1961–62 of artist-run film distribution collectives in New York and San Francisco and the opening of new exhibition venues, girded the expansion of avant-garde filmmaking.[11]

As in earlier eruptions of marginal film activity, experimental and documentary cadres of the 1960s derived a sense of purpose through the contestation of Hollywood's aesthetic and ideological formations. Innovations in the institutional patterns of nonfiction production not only helped consolidate otherwise vagrant impulses, they led to mutually beneficial concatenations of visual idioms and social praxis (such an alliance is evident in the manifestos of the New American Cinema Group (NAC) in the programming of alternative exhibition venues and in the early rental catalogs of distribution collectives).[12] If new forms of nonmainstream production and consumption provided a material foothold for the emergence of portraiture, burgeoning public discourses and cultural ideologies mobilized against the authoritarian, top-down exercise of power rehearsed the liberatory potential of "chosen," performative notions of social identity. In both cultural and political arenas, the desire to create new historical subjects entailed a critical dissolution of boundaries between reality and artifice, public image and private behavior, the personal and the political. Convening a theater of everyday life wherein direct participation in social change, as opposed to tacit "representation" (in both senses), various groups proclaimed the necessity of ordinary individuals to "speak for themselves." In this sense, film portraiture may be understood as an inevitable by-product, as well as an ethical tool, of 1960s opposition.

Inverting traditional portraiture's role in the propagation of stable, socially affirmative values—a tradition beginning with the Roman bust and extending through nineteenth-century painting—film portraits of the period served as a democratic forum for the display of alternative lifestyles and social diversity, a utopian gesture toward a future in which everyone really could be famous for fifteen minutes. Ultimately, the faces lifted from the ranks of "everyday protagonists," regardless of their actual locations in structures of power, achieved momentary celebrity as contemporary versions of, as well as antidotes to, the ruling elite's exhausted regime of idealized heroes—a regime intimately connected to the portrayals of classical Hollywood cinema.

Although documentary and avant-garde portraits became similarly entwined with the rebellious energies of the 1960s, the social and aesthetic discourses to which they were originally bound evince, in each case, more conservative "humanistic" underpinnings. Practitioners of cinema vérité openly rejected not only the densely edited, voice of authority structures of 1930s social documentaries but also their partisan political stances. The focus in two early TV series, *Close-Up!* and *Living Camera,* on psychological "crises"—the term employed by producer Robert Drew to designate a dramatic arc deemed necessary for mass appeal by corporate sponsors—marked an abandonment of documentary's traditional burden of exposing collective social ills. This retreat was aided in no small measure by the corporate liberal wing of American social science. Rejecting Left-tinged "partisan" analyses of social inequality or ruling class oppression, the popular discourse of sociologists and social psychologists turned its attention to problems of what Daniel Bell called "intrapsychic identity," namely, the anxieties of a thriving middle class in search of "self and status."[13] David Reisman's "socially oriented psychoanalytic characterology" drew on empirical research methods in the creation of ostensibly nonjudgmental "snapshots" of quotidian life.[14] Not coincidentally, a number of vérité directors had social science backgrounds, and their abundant interviews are sprinkled with the rhetoric of "disinterested science." Frederick Wiseman, for example, speaks of his filming approach as "research" for studies in "natural history."[15] In both theme and method of production, the first-phase documentary portraiture reflected broader demands for a "nonideological" rendering of the American character.

On the surface, at least, the cultural baggage attached to avant-garde portraits is less ideologically fraught. In contradistinction to the history of American documentary, there is scarcely any discernible impulse toward portraiture prior to the 1960s. It is possible to argue that the trance films made by Maya Deren, Kenneth Anger, and Curtis Harrington in the 1940s, in which filmmakers themselves appeared as principal actors, constitute de facto self-portraits of the artistic psyche. Nonetheless, the avant-garde's aesthetic inheritance from poetry and music, in its stress on symbolism and the expression of inner states of consciousness, virtually precluded the kind of close observation of immediate reality necessary for full-blown portraiture.[16] Indeed, the dissonance is evident in Stan Brakhage's description of his third film, *In Between* (1955): "portrait of Jesse Collins: a daydream nightmare in the surrealist tradition." Thus, it is only when experimental film begins to direct its vision outward, divesting itself of the trappings of narrativized drama, that Brakhage's celebrated "adventures of perception" find common cause with the descriptive aims of portraiture.[17] Unlike documentaries, experimental films do not go off in search of newsworthy personalities but draw their subjects from the social environments in which they live and work.

What might be the very first avant-garde portrait, Bruce Baillie's *Mr. Hayashi* (1961), offers a perfect example of the meshing but also the divergence of experimental and documentary approaches. According to Baillie, the film was made as a short, silent, in-camera "newsreel" to advertise the gardening services of an unemployed friend. Its haikuesque editing of shots of Hayashi walking against shots of scruffy foliage signify an overt subjectivity that would be inimical to codes of documentary neutrality. On the other hand, all film portraits are in part *advertisements,* declarations of the quiddity, if not the commodification, of their subjects. The following discussion attempts to recognize and also confound entrenched critical binaries that separate documentary from avant-garde work: objective/subjective, public/private, transparent/reflexive. If exploration of the portrait form has a broader implication for an interdependent study of these two nonfiction categories, it is as an arena in which opposing aesthetic ideologies collapse only to be redrawn along fresh lines.

Perhaps the best way to gauge the sweeping changes in documentary style facilitated by the introduction of mobile sync-sound rigs is to compare two early portraits produced by the National Film Board of Canada. Roman Kroiter's *Paul Tomkowicz, Street-Railway Switchman* (1954) follows the daily routine of a sixty-four-year-old Polish immigrant as he clears trolley tracks in the dead on winter. Over a series of nighttime scenes that are elegantly shot and crisply edited, Tomkowicz's intermittent voice-over narration, framed as an interior monologue, recalls a painful past and offers banal details about his work and home life ("Maybe I'll take a bath, maybe go to a show, maybe stay home"). A jazz score and ambient street noise stitch his low-key meditations into a seamless impressionistic flow. Low- and high-angle long shots isolate his figure against the harsh glare of street lamps and the foreboding shapes of buildings. In a half-dozen sequences, the film creates pseudo-point-of-view editing in which Tomkowicz's off-screen glance is followed by a shot ostensibly from his perspective. Kroiter's method here is clear: to create a heightened aura of intimacy that evokes the quiet dignity of "unseen" lives, balancing individual traits with indices of social type—Tomkowicz as a personification of all hard-working immigrant laborers.

In 1961, Kroiter codirected, with Wolf Koenig, a groundbreaking sketch of pop singer Paul Anka. In scenic design and formal articulation, *Lonely Boy* can serve as template for numerous celebrity portraits that followed in its wake. Bracketed by several terse voice-over passages identifying locations or characters, the film intersperses snatches of live performance and audience reaction with backstage conversations between the rising star and his handlers. A nonfiction treatment of the familiar show biz theme of public adulation versus private isolation, compounded here by the relentless grooming and packaging of a *salable* "image," *Lonely Boy* embraces what would become a dominant trope of celebrity portraits. Unlike later films, there are passages of direct on-camera interviews, yet the overall approach is observational: hand-held, medium-distance, long takes, with occasional zooms for emphasis, map a network of performative relationships in which the camera registers as a separate but homologous observer in a compass of approving spectators. Hyped by his manager as "potentially the greatest entertainer of all time," Anka comes across as a sweet if briskly ambitious semitalent trapped in a publicity machine. Significantly, the choreography of camera and subject fosters sympathy for the singer, and distaste for his staff, while never quite making clear its own function as supplemental promoter. This ambivalent dynamic of neutral recorder/complicit exploiter resurfaces in later portraits such as Richard Leacock's *Happy Mother's Day* (1963), Albert and David Maysles's *Meet Marlon Brando* (1965), and D. A. Pennebaker's *Don't Look Back* (1966).

A series of made for television character studies, produced in 1960–62 under the auspices of Drew Associates, jumpstarted the careers of several key directors as they established important precedents for the direction of documentary portraiture. *Primary,* the series' best-known and most influential work, is a double portrait of John F. Kennedy and Hubert Humphrey on the campaign trail in Wisconsin.[18] Our awareness that actual sync-sound recording is present only in a few scenes, or that scenes are heavily crosscut, belie *Primary's* signal impact. Indeed, what the film inaugurates is less a program of spontaneous "eyewitness" filming than the metatheme of totalized performance, elicited through a counterpoint of campaign appearances and behind the scenes maneuvering (*The War Room,* D. A. Pennebaker and Chris Hegedus's 1993 portrait of two Bill Clinton campaign gurus, is one of several de facto sequels). Both politicians allowed the filmmakers access to hotel rooms, TV studio dressing rooms, and other private areas on the premise that viewers would receive an unprecedented insider's glimpse of the daily rigors of the electoral process. Nonetheless, the reigning impression is that of two figures nearly equally adept at filtering and controlling the image they wish to purvey almost regardless of external circumstances. That is, even in ostensibly private scenes in which exhausted candidates greet yet another well-wisher, there is a powerful awareness of the degree to which the camera's presence—indeed the presence of *any* outside auditor—shapes their resources of self-presentation. Casual postures of vulnerability or introspection aside, these are people for whom the camera is always on or who reserve expression of their least attractive qualities for truly unattended moments.[19]

In its relentless pursuit of figures inured to media scrutiny, social actors and performers from various professional realms, vérité portraits rationalize the recording process as noninvasive if not completely transparent. At the same time, they purport to offer intimate views of personal identity that exceed in truth value those of competing agencies of reportage such as still photos and newspaper or magazine profiles. It is only on those rare occasions when documentaries confront subjects insufficiently skilled in public performance, as with the depressed mom in *Happy Mother's Day,* that the guise of observational neutrality is laid bare. Drew Associates' *On the Pole* (1960) and *Nehru* (1962), like the Maysles's *Showman* (1962) and *What's Happening! The Beatles in the U.S.A.* (1964), reveal momentary breaks in the compact of nonrecognition whereby the recording process is signaled to viewers by word or gesture. However, such instances are often recuperated as markers of spontaneity and noncontrol. In the post-vérité climate of the 1980s and 1990s, especially in the remarkable films of Nick Broomfield, the hidden protocols between observer and social actor are finally thrust center stage, with the portraitist assuming a heretofore unacknowledged position as codependent film subject.[20]

Jane (1962), produced for the Time-Life series *Living Camera,* is among a subset of early portraits in which performance anxiety, the shifting border between public spectacle and confidential self-revelation, is explicitly thematized. In *Meet Marlon Brando* and *Showman,* the burden of eliciting potentially embarrassing information is displaced onto diegetic interrogators, mainly print journalists. *Jane* spins the relationship between camera and subject by interjecting a surrogate observer/confidante, an irritably manipulative stage director. He is rehearsing Jane Fonda for the Broadway opening of a new play and is, coincidently, the actress's current boyfriend. Onstage refinement and revision of a fictional character is juxtaposed with increasingly tense offstage scenes of preparation and ego massage. Fittingly, the play being rehearsed is a romantic comedy about sexual ambivalence and the travails of marriage. The stage couple's scripted relationship is reprised and ultimately mocked by the actual couple's tenuous courtship and by the play's immanent failure. Fonda, whose Hollywood career would soon eclipse her modest theatrical ambitions, labors diligently to ignore the camera as she deftly enacts her primary *cinematic* role as troubled yet deeply committed actress. A clumsy subplot, intercut with the trajectory of opening night, finds newspaper critic Walter Kerr preparing to write a damning review. Through this device, *Jane* summons a second ancillary profilmic observer to foreground and evaluate the dubious ideals of playacting. More cogently, the film installs a double arena for performance in which offstage "unrehearsed" behavior is privileged as the "real," authentic version of Fonda's personality. It is hardly accidental that Jane's preferred self-image, burnished by scenes in which she sits alone reading or applying makeup, is the unmistakable by-product of the camera's fly-on-the-wall fascination with its subject.

For the period, Thomas Reichman's *Mingus* (1967) is unusual in its open display of collaboration between filmmaker and social actor. A chronicle of one long, traumatic night in the life of jazz great Charles Mingus, the film's jagged pace and spiraling structure invite parallels with the composer's signature style. Passages of direct observation abruptly segue into brief episodes of live musical performance, as if Mingus's music were a direct projection of his domestic turmoil. Normally, insertions of outside material or crosscutting serve to conceal temporal ellipses in the shooting process; here gaps in continuity are emphasized by jumpcuts of Mingus speaking or wandering around his impossibly disorganized loft. The musician is about to be evicted, and the film provides him a sounding board with which to rail against injustices in the American system. Like his music, his moods leap mercurially from anger to nostalgia to patient explanation (especially evident in scenes with his young daughter). One minute he is talking about establishing a jazz school for young people, the next he is firing a shotgun into a cluttered closet and threatening armed resistence. Throughout the tension-filled session, Mingus refers to the director as "Tom" or "Tommy," asks him occasional questions, and gestures at or verbally instructs the camera crew. Because the recording process is acknowledged so directly and casually, and the subject is so volatile, moments in which he ignores the camera and turns introspective—looking for some missing object or document while mumbling to himself—make us acutely conscious of a voyeuristic undertow that other portrait films are at pains to disguise.

An interesting contrast to the internal dynamics of *Mingus* is *Don't Look Back,* the popular feature-length study of a Bob Dylan concert tour of England. Here a prominent motif is the contrasting parallels between types of media scrutiny: newspaper, magazine, and radio coverage against the putatively more "natural," sympathetic style of verité. There are numerous scenes of Dylan fielding silly or vaguely hostile questions from straight-laced reporters, reading, or listening to sarcastic descriptions of his personality or music. What these sources can never penetrate, and the film exults in showing, are "private" backstage moments in which Dylan fools around with members of his entourage or, tellingly, plays or sings for the sheer joy of making music. Although the recording apparatus is never visualized as such (in one shot a top-hatted Pennebaker is caught in a mirror clutching his camera), its status as privileged insider, a status conferred in part by the expressive power of images over *mere words,* seals the text and by extension the viewer in self-congratulatory identification with the singer's anti-authoritarian stance. Dylan, in the manner of other verité performers, delivers an ad hoc credo that 1960s documentary would readily claim as its own: "The truth? The truth a plain picture . . . of a tramp vomiting into the sewer."

By the end of the 1960s, two groups of documentaries representing rather different countercultural objectives began to erode the symbiotic

1. Bob Dylan backstage in *Don't Look Back,* D. A. Pennebaker, 1967 (frame enlargement of video)

relationship between public celebrity and portraiture. One group could be dubbed "anticelebrity" or "outcast" portraits since their subjects are neither well ensconced in the popular imagination nor the fleeting protagonists of sensational news stories (e.g., the birth of quintuplets or a headline murder trial). In their social marginality or outright rejection of conventional middle-class values, the anticelebrity operates beyond the scope of normal media attention but receives admiring treatment as the eccentric bearer of an oppositional mystique. In Ralph Arlyck's *Sean* (1969), the precocious four-year old son of Haight Ashbury hippies is fed leading questions about his favorite activities and probed for his blunt assessments of adult romance, drugs, and racial conflict. Making a child the subject of a quasi-serious interview has an obvious polemical function while inadvertently revealing the power of the interviewer to elicit self-serving responses; asked what he thinks about injuring a policeman, the kid responds, "Too bad!" Children as harbingers of progressive transformations in parental authority, and by extension the dynamics of intergenerational authority, are shown in a more ambivalent light in Robert Frank's *Conversations in Vermont* (1971), in which the fierce independence of his two convention-flaunting kids is cause for both respect and anxiety. Frank, an artist whose work has continually straddled boundaries between documentary and avant-garde, made an earlier film about a schizophrenic, *Me and My Brother* (1968), which treated mental illness as the logical, if terribly painful, response to the repressions of bourgeois society. Homelessness is given a similarly resistant role in Ed Pincus and David Neuman's *Panola* (1971) and Bruce Davidson's *Living off the Land* (1972). A paradigm of the theme of inverted celebrity, Clarke's *Portrait of Jason* patiently audits male prostitute Jason Holiday's startling repertoire of impersonations and contradictory selves.

A second group embraced the portrait for more overtly political purposes, positioning itself as cinematic armature of antiwar protest, black liberation, and feminist struggles. Portraiture in this context rechannels public fascination with charismatic leaders as a vehicle for verbal briefs against systemic inequality, allowing the portrait form to double as recruiting tool for rebellious causes. In Newsreel's *Bobby Seale in Prison* (1969), Nicholas Doob's *Set-Up* (1970), and Yolande du Luart's *Angela Davis: Portrait of a Revolutionary* (1971), the element of performance is located primarily in direct-address impromptu speeches in which the recording process rarely interferes with the speaker. Although found footage appropriation is antithetical to the 1960s passion for immediacy, it is worth noting that the period's most hilarious political portrait is Emile de Antonio and Dan Talbot's reclamation of *Nixon's Checker's Speech* (1968).

An exception to the fostering of cinematic transparency in studies of political activists is Michael Gray and Howard Alk's *The Murder of Fred Hampton* (1971). At the risk of trivializing a truly egregious abuse of police power, this film makes palpable the pressure exerted by human mortality on portraiture as a whole. Begun as a study of the Chicago Black Panther Party chairman, it takes a sudden detour when Hampton is killed, in effect assassinated, during a police raid.[21] The second half is shaped as an investigative report and indictment of city officials that opposes the official image of Hampton propagated by police spokesmen and local media with physical evidence and verbal testimony of a brutal conspiracy. To cap the filmmakers' argument, flashback footage reconfirms Hampton's status as smart, dedicated community activist. At their best, Gray and Alk stage a pitched battle between competing versions of the truth about the life of an extraordinary individual. Hampton emerges as a heroic martyr keenly aware that every moment in the spotlight only increases the chances of his extermination.

It would be an exaggeration to say that documentary portraiture played more than a peripheral role in the legitimizing of 1960s political movements, yet the period's central belief in direct self-representation at once spurred the development of the genre as it opened the form to less easily assimilated cultural tasks. Movies emerged as the privileged medium of countercultural expression because they were deemed to be more democratic, more available for appropriation, and were embraced by filmmakers and audiences alike as harbingers of new forms of human connection and communal enterprise.

In a 1963 interview, Richard Leacock proposed a working definition for the kind of documentaries he wanted to make: "A film about a person who is interesting, who is involved in a situation he cares deeply about, which comes to a conclusion within a limited period of time, where we have access to what goes on . . . yeah, that's about it."[22] At nearly the exact moment when vérité portraits were reaching their public apogee, another portraitist was engaged in a radically different approach underwritten by a nearly identical rationale: "I only wanted to find great people and let them be themselves and talk about what they usually talked about and I'd film them for a certain length of time and that would be the movie."[23] The speaker is of course Andy Warhol, and the body of work he produced in the mid-1960s stands as the signal achievement in avant-garde portraiture.

On the surface, Warhol's films merely recast visual concerns traversed by his serial silkscreened images of movie stars and other celebrities: variation within repetition, the face as landscape, material flatness and the illusion of depth. However, in breadth as well as formal diversity, his black-and-white portrait films rival if not exceed the intellectual complexity of the paintings. Leaving aside his embedding of portrait sequences in longer narrative structures—for example, the reel of singer Nico primping her hair in *The Chelsea Girls* (1966)—the Warholian portrait came packaged in an assortment of shapes and sizes: minimalist fixed-frame compositions; wildly improvised, seemingly interminable interviews; art world japes; anonymous "action" portraits (*Blow Job* [1964]); and densely layered image/sound compositions (*Outer and Inner Space* [1965]). There are serial portraits of couples (*Kiss* [1963]) and an open-ended series of individual "Screen Tests" (1964–66). Although the majority are silent, some feature sync-sound monologue, dialogue, or overlapping speech. In terms of temporal scale, they range from three-minute single rolls to feature-length closet epics.

Filmmaker Jonas Mekas was the first to proclaim that "Andy Warhol is taking cinema back to its origins, to the days of Lumière, for a rejuvenation and a cleansing."[24] Considered in relation to his portraits, the remark does not go far enough. In truth Warhol took cinema back to the dawn of still photography. Beginning in 1964, he asked visitors, as a rite of passage into the bubbling Factory scene, to sit for a three-minute silent "screen test." The subject was told to stare into the camera, to not "act" or even blink, until the film ran out.[25] More than *five hundred* of these rolls have been or will be restored by the Warhol Foundation. They were shown to denizens of the Factory on a regular basis, singly or in arbitrary clusters, but unlike other serial projects Warhol never assembled them into longer skeins. When they are currently shown in public, they are grouped in very rough chronological order. If they function as an ironic twist on Hollywood's "casual" auditions for fame and glamour, they are also among the most comprehensive, and witty, documentary records of a vital New York subculture.

Equally significant, the "screen tests" constitute a modernist revision of an archaic photographic practice, the mid-nineteenth-century *carte-de-visite*. In 1853, Nadar opened a portrait studio frequented first by his friends in the Parisian intellectual elite and later by government officials as well.[26]

As several commentators have noted, Warhol's Factory resembled a traditional artist's studio but one that was geared to the (parodic) codes of standardized, mass media production. Following Nadar, Andre Disderi began in 1854 to market small mounted photos for use as calling cards. Not unlike the automated photomat strips cherished by Warhol as pictorial model and image source for his silkscreen paintings, the multipose cartes-de-visite were hastily made, with little attention to lighting or other aesthetic effects, and became a cherished accoutrement of bohemian performers. While camera technology had reduced exposure time from a grueling twenty minutes to several minutes, the sitter was still required to remain frozen in place during the recording process.

Early photographic portraits effectively democratized a genre previously reserved for the rich and powerful as affirmation of their social status. Warhol's "screen tests," along with adjacent portrait practices, served as self-appointed arbiters of subcultural validation as well as a kind of in-house publicity organ for underground "stars." Reabsorbing a photographic tradition in which symbolic representations of power gave way to simple "likeness," Warhol's three-minute exposures limn a "withdrawal of authenticity" that trashes humanist claims—including those of the cinema vérité camp—for the portrait's ability to illuminate an irreducible core of being.[27] In David James's astute assessment, they "do not document their subjects' ability to manifest an autonomous, unified self so much as narrate their

anxious response to the process of being photographed. The camera is a presence in whose regard and against whose silence the sitter must construct himself. As it makes performance inevitable, it constitutes being as performance."[28]

Held in the viselike grip of frontal, evenly lit, eye-level close-ups framed against mostly blank backgrounds, the subjects adopt one of several minimalist performance strategies. Some, like poet Gerard Malanga or dancer Lucinda Childs, attempt to turn their faces into still masks in which even a blink or the perceived tightening of facial muscles has the weight of a dramatic trans-

2. An example of Warhol's screen tests, featuring Gerard Malanga. (Still courtesy of Anthology Film Archives.)

formation. Others appear to have orchestrated little comic fugues consisting of nods, lip movements, eye exercises. A few abandon any pretense of stillness and find ambient means of foregrounding the camera's stare; in one film, Nico smiles seductively and bites her fingers, then rolls a magazine into a telescope to mimic the lens in front of her. Ironically, tests with the least amount of overt movement register the strongest impression of temporal flow, every passing moment reminding us that time is the ineluctable instrument of human change. By strenuously contracting the field of performance, Warhol directs our understanding of latent contradictions between still frame and illusion of motion.

In a number of tests, Warhol's instructions—and it was not always clear who was behind the camera—were blithely subverted: painter James Rosenquist skitters in circles around the frame on a wheeled stool, trying to maintain constant eye contact with the camera; actress Beverly Grant impersonates an anguished silent movie diva, pulling and mangling her thick coils of hair; Harry Smith toys with a cat's cradle of string. In still other portraits, the camera itself gets into the act, creating pixillated motion or performing short zooms. *Eat* (1963), a forty-minute silent study of painter Robert Indiana eating a mushroom, is remarkable in its ambiguous play of looped or repetitive footage and singular moments of "action." Indiana bobs around in a swiveling rocking chair in slight slow motion (his enacted slowness amplified by Warhol's insistence on a slower projection speed). His face is at times shadowed by the brim of a fedora as he shifts the angle at which his chair faces the fixed camera. The effect is that of a "real time" cubist compilation of facial views, the absolute mutability  of deadpan identity heightened by the scattered trajectory of Indiana's off-screen glances. The time it takes to consume what is apparently a single mushroom is distended by Warhol through insertion of freeze frames and repeated images. Thus, the apprehension of a progressive movement toward closure is made doubly complex, with the subject acquiring an almost hallucinatory time-warped veneer.

3. Gary Indiana in Warhol's *Eat,* 1963. (Still courtesy of Anthology Film Archives.)

Especially in Warhol's longer silent portraits, the format of unbroken camera takes prompts the sitter to improvise successive poses around a banal, frequently oral, activity. *Henry Geldzahler* (1964), a feature-length visual treatise on the art of cigar smoking, frames its subject reclining on the infamous Factory couch in a succession of high-angle long takes bathed in starkly dramatic lighting. As in *Eat,* the terminus of the film's unfolding action, here the extinguishing of an ostentatiously huge cigar, is evident from the beginning. The art curator's obvious self-appointed task was to discover fresh ways of composing his face and body in relation to the central phallic prop, not simply allowing time to pass but fondling its shape as a horizon of change. The film's exorbitant duration allows ample time to shift attention to different areas of the frame, to specific parts of subject's body, and to the material surface of the image itself. As if staring into a mirror, we gradually become aware of how the sitter's posture and corporeal fidgeting parallels our own. As in other silent studies, consciousness of the weight and physiotemporal restriction of bodies produces an eerie jab of self-recognition. Yet in sound portraits such as *Beauty #2* (1965) and *Outer and Inner Space,* both featuring the vivacious Edie Sedgwick, the interplay of direct and off-screen speech, coupled with a more densely populated mise-en-scène, redistributes reflexive energies toward the dramatic struggle between subject and various dispersed scenic "directors."[29]

Once again, Jonas Mekas was ahead of the pack when he designated Warhol and Brakhage as "two extremes" of cinema, "the slow and the quick."[30] Not surprisingly, their antithetical approaches to film language are nowhere better illustrated than in their styles of portraiture. As Brakhage cut loose the trappings of oneiric narrative—focusing instead on detailed observations of himself, his family and friends, and isolated Colorado surroundings—portraiture emerged as a primary axis of poetic practice, conjoining the celebration of intimate textures of everyday life with a constructivist, intersubjective view of identity. In this sense, he carries forward the aesthetic heritage of Picasso and other modernists, for whom portrait depictions could no longer serve as record of an external, immutable presence but issued instead from "the artist's personal response to the subject."[31] More cogently, Brakhage adopted practices of filmic inscription commensurate with his literary idol Gertrude Stein's meditation on her own linguistic portraits: "I had to find out inside every one what was in them that that was intrinsically exciting and I had to find out not by what they said not by what they did not by how much or how little they resembled any other one but I had to find it out by the intensity of movement that there was inside in any of them."[32] His overarching method entails the arrangement of short repetitive bursts of imagery, the rapid alternation of adjacent views, superimposition, and the metaphoric linkage of a subject's physical features or movements with objects in an enveloping environment.

Although aesthetic gestures toward portraiture are evident in his work prior to the mid-1960s, they were clarified and intensified when, following the theft of his 16mm equipment, he switched to the smaller, more intimate 8mm format and initiated what would become an ambitious cycle of thirty *Songs* (1964–70). Intended as comparatively unvarnished lyrics, several are explicitly described as "portraits" while others incorporate portrait elements.[33] Brakhage's most concentrated exploration of the form is *Song 15: Fifteen Song Traits* (1965), a silent thirty-eight-minute "gallery" of friends and family in which separate sections develop motifs or visual gestures that recur in other parts and resurface in subsequent *Songs.* In the opening section, poet Robert Kelly is shown in Brakhage's home in a synecdochic flurry of hands cutting cheese, an activity intercut with shots of Kelly's face and an abstract nuclear diagram filmed off a television screen. The rhythmic cascade of hand movements suggests not only a visual affinity between subject and the filmmaker's unseen hand-held camera movements but a visual correlative for the poet's unheard patterns of speech. That is, what defines Kelly for Brakhage is his vocation as creator of verbal images, hence the source of their artistic fellowship. The connective sinew of domestic routine and poetic expression, their mutually invigorating energies, constitutes the dominant trope of *Song 15,* in which homey passages devoted to Jane Brakhage, or Jane and the kids, are paired against brief appearances by poet Ed Dorn and his family, Robert Creeley and Michael McClure, and finally Jonas Mekas. Filmmaking, like the strain of poetry associated with his friends, is confected as a domestic enterprise.

In the fourth section of *Song 15,* daughter Crystal's dark brooding face anchors a series of animal associations, including the mordant image of caged birds. The fifth section, titled "Two: Creeley/McClure," builds consecutive miniportraits out of quite different expressive tropes. As Creeley appears to rise from a chair, Brakhage repeatedly piles positive against negative images of nearly identical movements, inscribing the poet as a fiercely divided personality whose self-control flickers in an imaginary internal argument. McClure's portrait bristles with an apposite tone of manic energy via harsh swish pans, pixillation, and solarized film stock. As McClure tries on an elaborate animal mask, he seems to exude a preternatural shape-shifting function that Brakhage metaphorically connects with both spoken and filmic modes of performance.

Addressed in the context of Brakhage's monumental, amazingly diversified career, the portraits occupy a relatively subdued, even "prosaic," niche.[34] Although underscoring his commitment to direct subjective confrontation with the particulars of daily existence, in scope and execution the portraits remain slightly peripheral to larger imperatives of autobiography, dream, and memory. Nonetheless, their significance can be felt in several ways. They are among Brakhage's most extroverted works, countering intensely solipsistic versions of romantic isolation with a bracingly empathetic recognition of autonomous subjectivities. In an interview discussing *Scenes from under Childhood* (1967–70), created during the same period as the *Songs,* he imputes an almost therapeutic function to the close observation of others: "The first, simple, daily impulse to make it was to *see* my children — to see them as something much more than mine. . . . Photographing them was one way (I'm most intensive and excited when I'm doing that) to begin a relationship of better seeing, or entering their world."[35] For Brakhage, the portrait impulse offered a means of social connexity, a performative act establishing the grounds for renewed kinship in the profilmic. By the same token, a secondary aspect of portraiture, especially evident in *Song 15,* links his project not only to the work of other avant-garde filmmakers but to the philosophical underpinnings of vérité documentary.[36] In this shared commitment, cinema itself is projected as both visual mediation of and instrument for the assuaging of personal alienation and social marginality.[37]

The community sketched in *Song 15* must be seen nonetheless as a utopian gesture whose solidarity is threatened a priori by the transient nature of film portraiture. As it declares subjective affiliation with a group of individuals, this idiom must also acknowledge a horizon of disharmony and dispersion, the imminent release of time from its elaborate scaffolding of presentness. To enter "their world," indeed, the world of any portrait subject, and to see in that image an idealized reflection of oneself is also in some sense to concede the gaping existential chasm separating all human subjects. The tension exerted between identification and detachment, between presence and absence, is all the more vivid in ensemble portraits.

Although there were noteworthy individual sketches made in the mid-1960s — Ed Emshwiller's *George Dumpson's Place* (1965), Baillie's *Tung* (1966), Gregory Markopoulos's *Through a Lens Brightly: Mark Turbyfill* (1967) — the gallery format stands as the avant-garde's consummate and symptomatic achievement. The desire for community and subcultural validation, paramount tenets of 1960s ideology, are embedded in a remarkable range of styles and geographic sodalities. Warren Sonbert, following Warhol, assays ten bohemian couples in *The Bad and the Beautiful* (1967), a series of in-camera "collaborative" glimpses of the underside of stardom. Hollis Frampton enlists a throng of art world acquaintances to sit for *Manual of Arms* (1966), a "14 part drill for the camera" with each section demonstrating different visual treatments of lighting, camera movement, editing, and composition. Markopoulos shot two portrait collections, *Galaxie* (1966) and *Political Portraits* (1969). In the former, thirty luminaries, including Susan Sontag, Eric Hawkins, Allen Ginsberg, and Giancarlo Menotti, are celebrated in camera improvisations linking facial close-ups with particular props or enactments related to their spheres of creative endeavor. Mekas's *Diaries, Notes, and Sketches (Walden)* (1968), although not strictly a work of portraiture, contains numerous brief studies of New York artists. Takahiko Iimura's *Film-makers* (1966–69) blends portrait shots of Brakhage, Mekas, Warhol, and others with shards of spoken dialogue. In one way or another, these works embellish a common subtextual agenda: the fabrication of spectral creative communities in which the filmmaker functions implicitly as a central mediating figure and to claim a place for experimental film within the wider arena of social and cultural transformation.

In lieu of a synoptic conclusion, a problem that undergirds various aspects of the preceding discussion deserves a final sliver of speculative commentary: the intrinsic friction in film portraiture between realist and modernist aesthetic prerogatives. A recurrent thread in the critical discourse on documentary contends that a naturalized formal unity grounded in a rhetoric of transparency, the subordination of dramatic or enunciative functions, serves to preempt modernist pressures to explore material contradictions. However, portraiture, as practiced within the movement of 1960s cinema vérité, carries a distinctly reflexive subtext issuing from the direct negotiation of apparatus and human subject. In many instances, this negotiation is couched in a present-tense conflation of filmic duration and biological time. Hence, material or epistemological questions are addressed not through didactic strategies of visual distortion or analogy—as is the case in documentaries by Dziga Vertov, Alain Renais, or Harun Faroucki—but as they resist the passage from profilmic reality to iconic representation.

The situation is somewhat different for avant-garde portraiture, which aligns itself more readily with the dominant concerns of filmic modernism: the paradox of stillness and motion, the subjective basis of camera recording, fragmentation versus flow. Nonetheless, for both camps the context for such inquiries remains rooted in realist principles of social observation, immediacy, visual pleasure, and accessibility. The status of portraiture as a form dominated by extrafilmic demands, by the myth of nonintervention and deference to the subject, belies an investment in issues of cinematic ontology. Art historian John Welchman contends that facial images, a motif that has "shaped the very conditions of visuality," emerged as "Modernism's repressed token for the whole inheritance of pre-Modernist humanism."[38] In contrast to the contested, denatured terrain of facial representation in modern painting, film portraits reconfigure the face as a hub of shifting, performative expressions of transient identity.

By the same token, deployment of long takes or sequence shots in otherwise disparate portrait styles, intended as guarantees of presentness, paradoxically foreground the problem of indeterminacy. As Warhol's portraits implicitly ask, what limitations can, or must, be placed on a subject's self-representation? All portraits struggle to establish some inner logic for beginning and ending that is without recourse to devices of narrative anticipation or resolution, a struggle in which closure itself is instated as both formal conundrum and biological destiny. By extending the length of individual images, the subject's inexorable decay in time is vivified—not coincidentally, the allegorization of death is a trope linked to portraiture at least since the Renaissance. Since the portrait's temporal scope is inevitably fragmentary, a slice of contingent history rather than a sign of immutable identity, formal alternatives to duration—for instance, the staging of ellipsis through editing—can only partially subdue the uncanny collision of screen time with the temporal sphere of the spectator. For the viewer, a subject is always simultaneously present and estranged and in a manner distinct from that of painting or still photography. Caught in the hesitation between single still frame and the mechanically imposed illusion of continuity, the project of portraiture is sustained by a false promise of nonrepetition as it is endlessly compromised by the fact of material discontinuity. In this sense, the heedless flow of time through the film image, separate from yet mirrored by the consciousness of the viewer, becomes intertwined with the dynamics of subjectivity as a metatextual condition of the portrait genre.

Notes

The epigraph that follows the chapter title is cited in Georges Sadoul, *Louis Lumière* (Paris: Editions Seghers, 1964), 119, my translation.

1 Gerald Mast and Bruce F. Kawin make a similar point about the scene as home movie in *A Short History of the Movies* (Boston: Allyn and Bacon, 1996), 26. In Sarah Moon's omnibus tribute film, *Lumière* (1995), Spike Lee "remakes" *Le Dejeuner* using a Lumière camera to capture his young son having an outdoor meal.

2 See Patricia Zimmerman, "Hollywood, Home Movies, and Common Sense: Amateur Film as Aesthetic Dissemination and Social Control," *Film Journal* 27:4 (summer 1988): 23–44.

3 I address at greater length correspondences between avant-garde film and the counter-culture's emblematic treatment of time in "Routines of Emancipation: Alternative Cinema in the Ideology and Politics of the Sixties," in *To Free the Cinema: Jonas Mekas and the New York Underground,* edited by David E. James (Princeton: Princeton University Press, 1992), 17–48.

4 Although this may seem obvious, making a *film* portrait requires the explicit knowledge, presence, and participation of the subject, whereas paintings, drawings, and literary portraits can be created in their subjects' absence. A counterexample, which had a significant impact on post-1960s styles of avant-garde portraiture, is Joseph Cornell's great found footage tribute, *Rose Hobart* (1939). The "performance anxiety" implicit in vérité portraits is humorously thematized in the voice-over narration of Richard Leacock and Gregory Shuker's *Nehru* (1962).

5 André Bazin, "The Ontology of the Photographic Image," in *What Is Cinema?* vol. 1, translated by Hugh Gray (Berkeley: University of California Press, 1967), 16. Picasso's 1939 version of this dictum is cited by William Rubin in "Reflections on Picasso and Portraiture," in *Picasso and Portraiture: Representation and Transformation,* edited by William Rubin (New York: Museum of Modern Art, 1996), 18: "photography has arrived at a point where it is capable of liberating painting from all literature, from the anecdote, and even from the subject."

6 Rubin, "Reflections," 9.

7 Bazin's reliance on affinities between Italian neorealism and documentary in the representation of everyday life is apparent in "An Aesthetic of Reality: Neorealism" and "De Sica: Metteur en Scene," in *What Is Cinema?* vol. 2, translated by Hugh Gray (Berkeley: University of California Press, 1971), 16–40 and 61–78, respectively. For an excellent discussion of postwar cinema's philosophical investment in the "everyday," see Ivone Margulies, *Nothing Happens* (Durham: Duke University Press, 1996), esp. 21–41.

8 Cesare Zavattini, "Some Ideas on the Cinema," *Sight and Sound* 23:2 (October–December 1953): 225.

9 Stanley Cavell proposes that classical Hollywood itself embodied an aspect of portraiture insofar as "the screen performer is essentially not an actor at all: he *is* the subject of study, and a study not his own" (*The World Viewed,* enlarged ed. [Cambridge: Harvard University Press, 1979], 28). Roland Barthes makes a similar observation in maintaining that Garbo's face "represents [a] fragile moment when the cinema is about to draw an

existential from an essential beauty, where the archetype leans toward the fascination of mortal faces" ("The Face of Garbo," in *A Barthes Reader* [New York: Hill and Wang, 1982], 83).

10   For more on the implications of mobile sync-sound cameras, see my "Jargons of Authenticity (Three American Moments)," in *Theorizing Documentary,* edited by Michael Renov (New York: Routledge, 1993), esp. 188–226. Also in the same volume, see Brian Winston, "The Documentary Film as Scientific Inscription," 37–57. Stephen Mamber provides an informative account of both the development of vérité techniques and the relationship between network TV and independent documentarists in *Cinema Vérité in America: Studies in Uncontrolled Documentary* (Cambridge: MIT Press, 1974), 23–114. Two series on CBS set the stage for the 1960s influx of vérité portraits: *See It Now* and *Person to Person.*

11   By far the best account of the avant-garde in relation to the decade's social and cultural upheavals is found in David James, *Allegories of Cinema: American Film in the Sixties* (Princeton: Princeton University Press, 1989).

12   See the NAC Group's "First Statement," published in 1961 and reprinted in *Film Culture Reader,* edited by P. Adams Sitney (New York: Praeger, 1970), 80–82.

13   Daniel Bell, *The End of Ideology* (New York: Free Press, 1960), 13.

14   David Reisman, with Nathan Glazer and Reuel Denney, *The Lonely Crowd: A Study of the Changing American Character* (New Haven: Yale University Press, 1961), xxvi.

15   Cited in Thomas R. Atkins, *Frederick Wiseman* (New York: Monarch Books, 1976), 56 and 43, respectively. I discuss the relationship of direct cinema and postwar social science in "Jargons of Authenticity."

16   P. Adams Sitney gives the best account of this cultural influence in *Visionary Film: The American Avant-Garde, 1943–1978* (New York: Oxford University Press, 1979).

17   Stan Brakhage, *Metaphors on Vision* (New York: Film Culture, 1963).

18   Stephen Mamber provides a useful account of film credits and authorship within the Drew organization, listing Leacock, Pennebaker, Albert Maysles, and Terrence Filgate as collaborators on *Primary.* For an excellent critique of the film's reputation for verisimilitude and nonmanipulative recording, see Jeanne Hall, "Realism as Style in Cinema Verite: A Critical Analysis of *Primary,*" *Cinema Journal* 30:4 (1991): 24–50.

19   It is telling that Daniel Boorstin's seminal treatise on American celebrity and the "human pseudo-event," *The Image* (New York: Harper Colophon Books, 1961), was published in the same year *Primary* was first broadcast.

20   For a discussion of Broomfield's subversive mobilization of the obsessive, self-debasing nature of celebrity portraiture, see my "Media Spectacle and Tabloid Documentary," *Film Comment* 34:1 (January–February 1998): 74–80.

21   A later film in which death swamps the vaunted immediacy of the portrait project is Wim Wenders *Lightning over Water* (1980), a corrosively morbid dance between Wenders and terminally ill director Nicholas Ray.

22   "Richard Leacock, interviewed by Mark Shivas," reprinted in *Imagining Reality: The Faber Book of Documentary,* edited by Kevin Macdonald and Mark Cousins (London: Faber and Faber, 1996), 257.

23   Cited in James, *Allegories of Cinema,* 67.

24 Jonas Mekas, "Sixth Independent Film Award" (1964), reprinted in *Film Culture Reader,* edited by P. Adams Sitney (New York: Praeger, 1970), 427.

25 Patrick S. Smith, *Andy Warhol's Art and Films* (Ann Arbor: UMI Research Press, 1986), 154–56. In addition, Smith quotes Warhol's instructions to playwright and scenarist Ronald Tavel for one of several films titled *Screen Test:* "Sit and ask him questions which will make him perform in some way before the camera. . . . The questions should be in such a way that they elicit, you know, things from his face, because that's what I'm more interested in rather than in what he says in response" (159).

26 Gisele Freund, *Photography and Society* (Boston: David Godine, 1980), 40–41. See also Beaumont Newhall, *The History of Photography* (New York: Museum of Modern Art, 1964), 50–53.

27 A summary statement of portraiture's enduring humanistic appeal is offered by E. H. Gombrich, describing the effect of a Rembrandt painting: "We feel face to face with real people, we sense their warmth, their need for sympathy and also their loneliness and suffering" (*The Story of Art* [New York: E. P. Dutton, 1972], 332).

28 James, *Allegories of Cinema,* 69. James takes issue with the yoking of Warhol and documentary, claiming that "Far from affirming the possibility of cinema vérité, Warhol mordantly exposes the fallaciousness of both the social psychology on which its assumptions are based and the cinematic codes produced to implement them" (68). Although I address the dynamics of vérité portraits in a less idealized, more performative, and more reflexive manner, his point is well taken.

29 The critical literature on Warhol's films is quite extensive, yet, significantly, very little of it is devoted to issues of portraiture. I trace some additional implications in "Flesh of Absence: Resighting the Warhol Catechism," in *Andy Warhol Film Factory,* edited by Michael O'Pray (London: British Film Institute, 1989), 149–52.

30 Jonas Mekas, *Movie Journal: The Rise of a New American Cinema, 1959–1971* (New York: Collier, 1972), 158.

31 Rubin, "Reflections," 13.

32 Cited in Wendy Steiner, *Exact Resemblance to Exact Resemblance: The Literary Portraiture of Gertrude Stein* (New Haven: Yale University Press, 1978), 183. Stein was quite aware of correspondences between her method and the ontological properties of cinema: "I was doing what the cinema was doing, I was making a continuous succession of the statement of what a person was until I had not many things but one thing" (176).

33 Sitney accurately observes that "the form of the portrait radiates through the *Songs*" (*Visionary Film,* 245). His exemplary discussion and formal analysis of the cycle has been crucial to my understanding of Brakhage's stake in portraiture (238–58).

34 Until the late 1980s, Brakhage continued to make sporadic portraits and self-portraits, including *Clancy* (1974), *Jane* (1985), and a commissioned full-length study of a Colorado politician, *Governor* (1977).

35 Cited in P. Adams Sitney, "Autobiography in Avant-Garde Film," reprinted in *The Avant-Garde Film: A Reader of Theory and Criticism* (New York: New York University Press, 1978), 208.

36 Sixties guru Theodore Roszak summarizes the countercultural agenda as "the effort to discover new types of community, new family patterns, new sexual mores . . . [and] new

personal identities on the far side of power politics" (*The Making of a Counter Culture* [New York: Harper and Row, 1968], 31).

37 When portraiture, and especially self-portraiture, reemerges during the 1980s as a significant avant-garde genre, younger artists such as Peggy Ahwesh, Vincent Grenier, Joe Gibbons, and Marjorie Keller, along with a host of African American, Chicano, and queer film and videomakers, embrace the form as a way of articulating the social constructedness of identity.

38 John Welchman, "Face(t)s: Notes on Faciality," *Artforum* XXVII:3 (November 1988): 131.

In Search of the Real City: Cinematic Representations of Beijing and the Politics of Vision

Xiaobing Tang

Potentially, the city is in itself the powerful symbol of a complex society. If visually well set forth, it can also have strong expressive meaning. —Kevin Lynch, *The Image of the City*

That the city of Beijing presents a perfect spatial embodiment of a traditional culture caught in the maelstrom of rapid and condensed modernization is readily observable, even to a passing tourist. "Beijing is a microcosm of China," so an up-to-date pocket travel book informs its readers and potential travelers. "It combines village and metropolis, Western-style modernization and Chinese tradition, new-fashioned pomp with old-fashioned modesty. It is a showcase of China's policy for reform and opening up to the West."[1] Another contemporary guidebook (from the Travel Survival Kit series) gives more in-depth information: "All cities in China are equal, but some are more equal than others. Beijing has the best of everything in China bar the weather: the best food, the best hotels, the best transport, the best temples. But its vast squares and boulevards, its cavernous monoliths and its huge numbers of tourists are likely to leave you cold. It is a weird city—traces of its former character may be found down the back alleys where things are a bit more to human scale."[2]

Indeed, probably no visitor to Beijing in the 1990s would fail to notice the weird, sometimes mind-boggling character of this sprawling urban center that is becoming increasingly similar to Los Angeles. It is one of the oldest cities in the world, and yet compressed sites or islands of its imperial past are now barely visible under the veil of brownish smog and against the ragged backdrop of masses of prefabricated, international-style apartment buildings or more recent all-glass high-rises. Its broad and often dishearteningly straight, but increasingly jammed and billboarded boulevards, while still stridently reminding you of the scale and aspiration of a recent collective project and central planning, are continually humanized and made lively by an unstoppable flow of millions of bicyclists. If you decide to move across the city, either on foot or by any means of transportation, you will soon find yourself experiencing starkly different sections and neighborhoods (in terms of the appearance of their residents, architectural style, spatial arrangement, and noise level), which, as in almost any other large city in the world, exist side-by-side and form a silent commentary on one another. This "synchronicity of the nonsynchronous," as Ernst Bloch's useful phrase describes it, finds its expression in another space-related human experience, namely, the multiple means of transportation on Beijing's streets, from pedicabs, to overcrowded buses, to the latest Lexus.

Of this uneven but changing cityscape, we find timely and fascinating representations in Chinese cinema since the late 1980s, for which the dynamics and social, if also libidinal, energy of the modern city have become a much-explored theme and created a new film genre. The one particular sequence of images and soundtrack I have in mind is the opening collage in *Wanzhu* (Troubleshooters, dir. Mi Jiashan, 1988). The film's location is emphatically contemporary Beijing. Two enormous characters for the title of the film are projected onto three re-created primitive masks; they are accompanied by a soundtrack that captures a vocal fragment from some traditional opera or storytelling, shifts to a shrill siren that drowns out the narrating voice, and then records some boisterous marketplace where voices shouting out the names of popular magazines can be distinguished. But this brief temporalized sequence of sound effects is only the preface to an explosive juxtaposition of often fragmented but nonetheless spectacular images of the city. Through a zoom lens, the spectacle of traffic congestion is brought much closer, and minimal depth of field underscores a compressed urban spatiotemporal regime; unsteady and fast-moving shots of glass buildings (unmistakable signs of contemporaneity), with twisted reflections of other high-rises and construction cranes, suggest the spatial fragmentation with which an awestruck observer is forced to become reconciled. Then, quickly, the camera is directed back at the hustling and bustling streets where it presents a series of incomplete, unrelated snapshots of crawling vehicles, expressionless old women, hordes of bicyclists, country girls gathering at a labor market, a frowning youth with a punk haircut— all horizontal images of an expanding metropolis from the perspective of an apparently disoriented subject. Over this collage of urban spectacles, contemporary Chinese rock and roll (clearly reminiscent of early Bruce Springsteen) is introduced to make a direct commentary:

> I once dreamed about life in a modern city,
> But I don't know how to express my present feeling;
> Buildings here are getting taller and taller every day,
> But my days here are not that great.[3]

In fact, 1988 saw the production of a series of films on the subject of contemporary city life, at least four of them based on novels or novellas by the popular Beijing writer Wang Shuo. Hence, 1988 has been dubbed "the year of Wang Shuo" in Chinese cinema.[4] These films about the city, mostly directed by members of the Fifth Generation,[5] form a distinct genre and indicate a different intellectual concern and cultural criticism than in earlier Fifth Generation experiments or, indeed, in the tradition of New China cinema. By New China cinema I mean the state-supported film industry that came into being with the founding of the People's Republic in 1949. Its brief and frequently interrupted course of development notwithstanding, New China cinema is mass oriented and generally identified with a formulaic socialist realist aesthetic, "a didactic fusion," as one critic puts it, "of classic Hollywood filmmaking and Soviet Stalinist style."[6] The preferred subject matter for this determinedly revolutionary popular cinema is collective heroism and socialist construction, while its audience is often imagined to be a politically engaged nation instead of sentimental urban dwellers. Consequently, the experiential city fades as a pertinent cinematic theme or field, and the well-lit imagery of contemporary life found in New China cinema invariably comes from either an industrial construction site or the countryside undergoing profound transformations. Even the revolutionary past, when it is projected in New China cinema, is systematically romanticized and made to adhere to the current representational hierarchies. Against this staid tradition of "revolutionary realism combined with revolutionary romanticism," the Fifth Generation of film-makers introduced a fresh cinematic language and vision in the mid-1980s by bringing into focus a remote and obscure location, temporal as well as spatial, that bespeaks a different and yet concrete reality of depth. What enabled their breakthrough was clearly a modernist aesthetics and avant-gardist challenge against didactic mass cinema.[7] Hence, the initial defamil-iarizing impact of *Huang tudi* (The Yellow Earth, dir. Chen Kaige, 1984), *Daoma zei* (The Horse Thief, dir. Tian Zhuangzhuang, 1986), and *Hong gao-liang* (Red Sorghum, dir. Zhang Yimou, 1988), all now considered classics of Fifth Generation filmmaking.

In the new genre of city films that attracted members of the self-consciously innovative Fifth Generation, a central symbiosis is suggested between the experience of discontented youth and a vast, disorienting urban space that invariably provides a symbolic replication of the com-plexity of contemporary sociopolitical life caught in the maelstrom of modernization. Against the spatial complexity of the city, youth, while celebrated as a concentrated expression of the cultural dynamics of moder-nity, is nonetheless frequently depicted on the screen as a disillusioning ex-perience of foreclosed mobility, repressed libidinal energy, and entrenched filial obligation and duties. For instance, in *Troubleshooters,* we see how three young men struggle without much success to run their own service com-pany, whose daily operation and customers bring to the surface the frus-trations and crises deeply embedded in contemporary society. A significant development in the film is that once the story line begins and we are wit-nessing the nitty-gritty of the company's business, the city no longer ap-pears as a spectacle to marvel at. Instead, the urban landscape recedes, as it were, into the distance and turns simultaneously into an untranscendable historical condition and an experiential immediacy that together smother any coherent perception. Put differently, the city becomes both an all-encompassing cultural construct and an inescapable natural environment, one reinforcing the other. By the end of the film, it is clear that the film-maker has persistently refused to present the city as promising a possible perceptual totalization; contrary to the opening collage, the final, slow-rolling shot of people lining up to seek help at the revamped service com-pany conveys a reconciliation, on the part of a besieged and reflective sub-ject, with ordinariness as well as situatedness. The city by now irretrievably recedes into the distance and becomes a grandiose myth no longer rele-vant to the daily lives of its inhabitants. It is now a labyrinthine complex without a coherent pattern, or what Kevin Lynch once promoted as the "legibility" and "imageability" of the cityscape.

However, this film genre, with its critical message about "the estranging city and a paralyzed subject,"[8] did not reach its thematic and cinematic perfection until 1989, when Xie Fei completed *Benming nian* (Black Snow), a sober portrayal of ordinary life in Beijing executed with a film noir sensibility. It may appear coincidental that an outstanding member of the Fourth Generation (here the term refers to the group of Chinese filmmakers who were systematically trained from the late 1950s to early 1960s and reached their professional maturity only in the late 1970s because of the disruption of the Cultural Revolution) had to come in to realize the potential of the new genre, for the directors in this transitional generation of directors are often viewed by critics as forever negotiating for their own artistic identity. Compared to the more cosmopolitan Fifth Generation, they appear as "reluctant, awkward pursuers of the novel and embarrassing believers in cheap humanism and historicism."[9] As the proud, however abused, offspring of New China cinema, they now find themselves, by default, inheriting a battered establishment, and yet they cannot afford to dissociate themselves either emotionally or intellectually from what shapes and defines them. This character profile of the Fourth Generation is closely borne out by another intriguing city film, *Beijing nizao* (Good Morning, Beijing, 1990), directed by Zhang Nuanxin (*Sha Ou* [Sha Ou], 1981; *Qingchun ji* [Sacrificed Youth], 1986). Given their professional training and familiarity with socialist realism, Fourth Generation directors have a strong sense of social responsibility and usually feel more at home dealing with the rural landscape or the contrast between the city and the countryside. Indeed, members of this generation are the ones who made some of the most successful and realistic films about rural China in the 1980s, such as *Rensheng* (Life, 1984) and *Laojing* (Old Well, 1987) by Wu Tianming and *Yeshan* (In the Wild Mountains, 1985) by Yan Xueshu.

Fully accepting his identity as a Fourth Generation director, Xie Fei nevertheless from the beginning exhibited a spiritual affinity with the younger generation. From his earlier, emotionally charged *Women de tianye* (Our Wide Fields, 1983) to *Xiangnü Xiaoxiao* (The Girl from Hunan, 1986), which echoed the ethos of critical cultural root-seeking, Xie Fei established himself as the most sensitive filmmaker of his generation. In *Black Snow,* he not only redirects his own philosophical thinking, but also introduces a new intellectual tension into the city-film genre. As the film critic

Peng Wen observes, while city films by the Fifth Generation express a hidden desire to identify with and belong to the new urban culture, "in *Black Snow*, 'the city' is obviously presented as an estranging and hostile space, to cope with which the filmmaker recommends resistance and disengagement."[10] Still, there is enough continuity to read Xie Fei's intervention as an extension of the general interest in the city. It is mostly a thematic continuity, an increasingly critical examination of an emergent urban culture. "From *Troubleshooters* to *Black Snow*," as another film critic remarks, "Chinese cinema has reached a universal subject matter in world cinema, namely, the experience of anomie and disorientation in a commodity society, also known as the age of market economy."[11] In this light, *Black Snow* deserves a closer look, especially from the perspective of how the city now figures in the everyday experience of unfulfilled youth.[12]

Depth and Social Criticism

While reviewing films about Rome by Vittorio De Sica in postwar Italy, Pierre Sorlin sees the filmmaker as someone who experimented with two different groups of images of the city. In the neorealist cinema of the 1950s, filmmakers "were aware of the blossoming of urban areas and tried to express, cinematically, the complex relationships between old town centers and new outskirts. After 1965 or so, other cinematographers were no longer able to tell, or see, what towns were, and [they] created a blurred image of cities."[13] This blurred vision, according to Sorlin, was first articulated in De Sica's *The Roof* (1956), in which "the strong system which associated the center and outskirts, presented as complementary entities, vanished, and the picture of towns began to lose focus."[14] Subsequently, images of open and formless shantytowns came in to diffuse the neorealist effort that, through cinematic projection, had sought to make sense of an expanding urban landscape and the intricate human lives embedded in it. One classic moment of such neorealist clarity can be found in De Sica's *The Bicycle Thief* (1948), where "extreme depth of field shots accentuate Ricci's isolation: when he searches the thief's home for traces of his stolen bicycle, for example, we see in the background most clearly a neighbor closing her window, as if to cut off all possibility of communication between Ricci and the thief's neighbors."[15]

The loss of such all-encompassing visual clarity in the wake of neorealist cinema, suggests Sorlin, registered a new perception of the European city, a historical moment in which "filmmakers ceased to view cities as potential works of art."[16] Thus, the gradual disappearance of neorealism may point to a general disavowal of allegorical totalization on the one hand and of active social engagement on the other. It may even signal the arrival of a postmodern urban life, for which the source of excitement is no longer the visionary modern city or a neorealist "aspiration to change the world."[17] If this fundamentally moral commitment underlies all forms of the realist ideology, one crucial difference between neorealism and socialist realism may be none other than the former's fascination with, and critical exploration of, the anonymous and multidimensional modernizing city. Socialist realist cinema, at least its Chinese variant, is identifiable insofar as the city on a human scale is disallowed. "The Chinese version of what the Italians called 'neorealism' had been a feature of the 'golden age' of Chinese cinema in the late 1940s," remarks Paul Clark, but it was superseded by socialist realism in the 1950s. As a result, "the urban tragicomedies and social melodramas of the late 1940s were replaced with socialist melodramas set in either urban workplaces or the countryside."[18] In the 1980s, with socialist realism falling into disrepute, the city and its cinematic possibilities returned to the Chinese screen with considerable vengeance.

What I wish to accomplish through a close reading of *Black Snow* and *Good Morning, Beijing,* is to show that the return of the city in late-twentieth-century Chinese cinema once again highlights questions of realism and social engagement. These two starkly different cinematic representations of the city of Beijing articulate separate visions of reality and politics. While in *Black Snow* our view is constantly immobilized by close-ups and focal lighting, *Good Morning, Beijing* moves us with a gratifying story and fluid cinematography. The city in *Good Morning, Beijing,* which may be provisionally described as "neorealist" in style, is amply narratable and eventually comes together as an allegorical social space. In *Black Snow,* however, through the prevalent use of limited field-depth cinematography, Xie Fei focuses our gaze on an embattled individual by keeping his surroundings in a shadowy blur that effectively blocks the city from ever emerging as a graspable totality.

The dramatic tracking shot at the beginning of *Black Snow* immediately sets the chromatic tone and visual structure of the film and establishes itself as an exemplary moment in a conceivable Beijing noir. Hearing first a passing train and then solitary but heavy footsteps, we realize that we are in a dimly lit subway station and following someone, presumably toward the exit. Then the credits begin to roll, and the hand-held camera films to the rhythm of someone walking. Soon we see stairways leading to the ground and a street scene. The person in front of us and at the center of the screen, in the light of the exit, shoulders a stuffed knapsack and wears a bulky coat. Yet the looming, open space is hardly inspiring because the narrow strip of a wintry sky is an impenetrable gray, and a few ghostly bystanders all appear to be uniformly blue or of a nondescript monochrome. As the man (we can assume that by now, judging from his build and the gender-specific hat he is wearing) is about to fully emerge from the subway, the camera quickly shifts, and we see him again, from a slightly downward angle, in some narrow and tortuous lane, which is hopelessly cut short by another train hissing by at the top of the screen. It is a virtual shantytown, void of any human presence at the moment. Then the man walks through a gate, and the camera is noticeably lowered so that the lane becomes even more oppressive and suffocating. There are still no human beings in sight, and the overcrowded space is dominated by an official radio voice announcing first some prohibitive policy and then a train disaster. The impersonal voice fades away as we turn a corner, and an old man's sickly cough, together with a baby's impatient cry, becomes more irrepressible, punctuated only by the sound of flowing tap water. After yet another unexpected turn, we hear a fragment of softened pop rock that seems to float listlessly, and when we are sufficiently lost in this directionless space the man is suddenly stopped by a fence and at the same time the camera comes to a standstill.

But the man quickly pushes open the fence and walks up to a shanty that shows no signs of life. While he struggles with his key in the lock and eventually has to break through the door, a compassionate female voice, probably from a radio next door, gradually replaces the news broadcast and, in the elegant style of the traditional art of storytelling (*pingshu*), either narrates a distant event or proffers a reflective commentary. In fact, this formulaic but mysteriously soothing voice will remain as the predominant background sound, as if supplying a slightly sorrowful historical commentary on present conditions, during the sequence in which the man enters the room, bumps into a few ill-placed objects, examines the disorderly surroundings, and finally takes off his hat and gloves. Only at this moment do we get our first frontal view of him, a sturdy young man in his mid-twenties. Apparently he knows this place, for very soon he finds himself a cigarette buried in a drawer and, while searching for matches, catches sight of a framed picture. He picks up the frame, gazes into it, and blows hard at the dust gathered on it. At this moment, the alarmed voice of an old woman comes from off the screen: "Who is it? Is it Quanzi?"

Li Huiquan is the name of the young man, the hero of the film. He has just returned home after spending about a year in prison, during which time his mother has died. Now he finds himself back in a desolate room, all alone, jobless, and facing the task of starting his life anew. Based on a psychological novel by Liu Heng, the plot of the film is about how hard, and eventually impossible, it is for Li Huiquan the ex-convict to assimilate himself back into society and lead a normal life. Unable to get a job at the factory where his mother used to work, which is now officially declared bankrupt, Li Huiquan decides to rely on himself and sets up a stall at a street market to sell shoes and clothes. After a slow start, his business grows steadily; meanwhile, he gets to know Zhao Yaqiu, an aspiring singer performing part time in a bar. At the bar, he also meets Cui Yongli, a shrewd, self-made broker who profits from clandestine and apparently illegal business deals. While Cui Yongli supplies quantities of popular fashion goods (mostly lingerie), Li Huiquan occasionally escorts Zhao Yaqiu home after her work. With her charming innocence, she seems to restore in him a sense of being respected and even needed. Subsequently, she becomes the object of his libidinal desire. Yet he cannot bring himself to express his tender feelings toward the trusting young girl; instead, he resorts to masturbation at night. At the same time, partly thanks to Cui Yongli's brokering, Zhao Yaqiu becomes relatively successful and grows increasingly indifferent to the young man whom she once obviously admired. Then Li Huiquan's former accomplice and prison mate, Chazi, descends one night from the skylight window, hungry as a wolf after being on the run from the law for about two weeks. Chazi's sudden return devastatingly reminds Li Huiquan of his own solitary existence, which makes his advice that Chazi turn himself in ring hollow. Finally, the fact that Chazi, ruthlessly disowned by his own family, has to run away from him and for his life, together with the knowledge that Zhao Yaqiu has become her agent's mistress, crushes Li Huiquan's fragile world. He badly beats up Cui Yongli, and, in a desperate last effort, he presents the now glamorous Zhao Yaqiu with a gold necklace. His offer is politely turned down, and after aimlessly roaming into a park at night Li Huiquan is robbed and then fatally stabbed by two teenagers. In the film's last shot, we are given a prolonged look downward at his bent body lying among waste paper and garbage on the floor of a deserted open-air theater, which, according to director Xie Fei, constitutes his authorial comment on the vacuity of a purposeless existence.[19]

The senseless death at the end certainly appears to attach an anticlimactic conclusion to the narrative. Yet it symbolically brings to completion the film's critical reflection on the limits and anxieties of city life. A full circle of hermeneutical meaning is thus achieved in terms of both narrative and cinematography. As Peng Wen remarks, the unfolding of the story adopts the pattern of a classical linear narrative, and from Li Huiquan's return (new life) to his death there is a "complete closure."[20] This narrative closure is reinforced by a visual as well as auditory imagery that at the very end recalls the film's beginning. Here is again a prolonged and uninterrupted tracking shot of the young man, his back turned to us and his footsteps echoing hollowly. The movement of the camera suggests unsteady steps, while the muffled and unreal background noise and laughter of a dispersing theater crowd do not divert our attention from the dying hero. The image of the public and the public space itself both fall out of focus and become a grotesque blur. Li Huiquan finally collapses in the empty theater. Through such structural symmetry, this last moment of arriving at his death and his return in the film's beginning powerfully complement each other, the result being a disturbing transgression of given categories and myths about city life. If, at the beginning, Li Huiquan's coming home can be viewed as returning to an interior hopelessly under surveillance (suggested by the harsh radio voice), the ending represents a final disconnection between the public and the private, the environment and its perception by the individual. Only at the moment of his random death, in a deserted public space, does Li Huiquan voicelessly and yet in vain express his individuality and with desperation expose the underlying current of loneliness.

Both critics and the filmmaker himself have remarked on the strong tendency of intellectualizing, obviously in the humanist tradition, throughout *Black Snow*.[21] The whole style of the film, from its predominant melancholy, grayish-blue tone to the virtual absence of external music, reflects the meditative commentary of a sympathetic intellectual. I wish to argue, however, that it is this philosophical interest in the existential condition of an individual in the modern city that leads to the blurring of the city itself, which has the cinematographic effect of keeping the viewer and, by extension, the subject on the screen from gaining a commanding perspective on the urban environment and its relationships. The concerned gaze that the film directs upon the subject and his immediate surroundings is so intense that the rest of the city has to be kept at a distance and as an incomprehensible background. In other words, for the anxiety of the individual subject to be experienced as such, the connection between him and the city must be revealed as nonexistent, and his anguish shown as that of one incapable of identifying himself with the environment from which he nonetheless cannot escape. "But let the mishap of disorientation once occur," Kevin Lynch writes when emphasizing the importance of keeping the city an imageable environment, "and the sense of anxiety and even terror that accompanies it reveals to us how closely it is linked to our sense of balance and well-being."[22]

At this point, we may identify a modernist aesthetics of depth in the film *Black Snow*. Such an aesthetics is usually articulated with a self-conscious, if not ideological, exploration of favorite high-modernist themes of interiority, anxiety, experiential authenticity, and frustrated desire. This "inward turn" that we will discuss in relation to Li Huiquan's experience, however, does not carry the same "politicality" or utopian desire that Fredric Jameson sees underlying the alleged subjectivism in the classics of Western modernism. "Modernism's introspective probing of the deeper impulses of consciousness, and even of the unconscious itself," proposes Jameson, "was always accompanied by a Utopian sense of the impending transformation or transfiguration of the 'self' in question."[23] The anxiety that Xie Fei portrays in his film, while clearly echoing a modernist introspective probing, is generated less by a blocked utopian excitement about transforming the self or society than by a profound uncertainty over the very content of such a transformation. It is a postutopian anxiety in that the interiority explored here resides not so much in some meaningful transitional linkage between tradition and modernity as in a nonspace rejected by, and excluded from, both the past and the future. In the interior space encircling Li Huiquan, while memory or nostalgia offers hardly any comfort, the future is disclaimed with equal dismay. It is the grim reality of a cagelike present that renders anxiety as the experience of inescapability and claustrophobia.

Let us return again to the opening shot to further examine the aesthetics of depth in the film as a whole. One reading of that seemingly endless walk along a tortuous lane in a shantytown is that it suggests the difficult path through which one arrives at the present. It is a metaphor of living through twisted history itself. "If the gray experience of walking belongs to history," the literary critic Chen Xiaoming comments, "then the shabby house as the 'present tense' of the narrative is joined with the 'now' of the character. This small house therefore becomes the starting point for Li Huiquan's self-renewal; it also indicates the end of past history. As a closed space of existence for an individual and a 'present' that must separate itself from its own history, this house has to resist the outside world as much as society."[24] Indeed, what Li Huiquan does here is walk away from the city, from any form of collectivity, and into his own interior space. As he moves into the depths of the shantytown, the camera begins to descend from an encompassing view of the site down to a close tracking shot of the hero. Very soon, we are brought so close to the person walking in front of us that we can no longer have the initial, although momentary, coherent perception of the environs. Our understanding of the situation becomes firmly meshed with Li Huiquan's vision, which quickly turns out to be partial and unmediated.[25] While the sorry images of an overcrowded shantytown evoke poverty as the poignant critique of a failed social project, the failure of the current situation is ultimately presented—by means of camera angles and an evocative soundtrack—as a dead-end entrapment. The only escape seems to be Li Huiquan's home or his private room, but this much-needed interior holds for the young man a memory both too painful and too broken to be of any redemptive value for the present.

This spatial tension, in which depth is embraced out of despair, gives rise to an existential anxiety and at the same time endows that anxiety with social criticism. It also generates two related kinds of visual imagery. The city, when it appears at all, is reduced to fleeting images of empty streets, noisy traffic, dimly lit back alleys, and pale, cold streetlights. All of these images irrepressibly suggest Li Huiquan's unease with the public dimension of the city and even his fear of it. In contrast, the interior into which the individual subject now retreats is continually interrupted and revealed to be vulnerable. Within this second group of images, we can further distinguish two distinct clusters. One consists of those midrange shots of Li Huiquan in his home. Here, the camera always remains at the hero's eye level, and, through a zoom lens, as the director Xie Fei later reminds us, the character is shown in much sharper focus than his surroundings so as to intensify his psychological isolation.[26] Also, invariably, a top light intrudes, which, like the neighbor's loud radio and TV, reinforces a sense of both antisociality and voyeuristic surveillance.[27]

The other cluster of representations of the interior occurs in the bar (another favorite symbol of modern city life that I comment on below) where close-ups of a pensive Li Huiquan, usually in the dark but sometimes under a direct top light, are frequently crosscut with luminous and intensely colorful images of the singer Zhao Yaqiu. The interiority experienced in this situation is of a more emotional nature and is contrasted to the fluidity and vacuity of popular music as a pliable form. The visual proximity of a desiring subject to the object of desire actually underlines the unbridgeable gap between them and forms a disturbing imagery of an emotional and communicational blockage. The profound irony is that commodified art now supplies the expression and appropriates the content of the subject's inmost memory and desire.

If Li Huiquan's ultimate despair is partly attributable to his inability or unwillingness to accept the cruel fact that Zhao Yaqiu is, after all, a popular performer who has to prostitute style for marketability, truthfulness for a universally appropriable external form, his own political identity — or, rather, a blatant lack thereof — constitutes his tragic character. An ex-convict for the crime of aggravated assault, and now the owner of a fashion stall, Li Huiquan finds himself an automatic misfit in a society where a highly moralistic political culture still dominates, while economic activity outside the public sector inevitably smacks of (or rather thrives on) amorality and even illegality (as embodied by the broker Cui Yongli). One defining feature of the dominant political culture is its refusal to recognize the complexity of everyday life, in particular its quotidian ordinariness and mundane needs and passions. Because the crime he committed and the punishment he consequently received appear to be so utterly "petty" in the sense that neither can be explained away by some political misfortune or injustice and thereby rehabilitated and turned into a source of honor, Li Huiquan is at once identified as a dismissable outsider and an invisible member of society. His explosive anger at Chazi's parents, who disown their criminal son so as to be accepted by society at large, directly articulates his frustrated protest against a tightly knit and dehumanizing social fabric. A stunning representation of Li Huiquan's social invisibility comes at the end, when, in that fateful evening in the park, he drags his wounded body through a complacently indifferent crowd. By now a thematic connection is established between Li Huiquan's ambiguous political identity, or the difficulty of narrating his life story, and the blurring or perceived illegibility of the city on which I commented. The unapproachable city, from which Li Huiquan wishes desperately to disengage himself, becomes the gigantic symbol of a social failure.

Urban Relationships Reconnected

The historical significance of *Black Snow* in contemporary Chinese cinema lies in the fact that, better and more focally than other films of the same genre, it presents the city as a social issue and makes visible the deep anxiety it simultaneously generates and suppresses. Private interior space is masterfully shown to be both a necessary shelter and an inescapable entrapment, while realistic images of stark poverty and disrepair quietly depict a demoralized collective imagination. The psychological depth, together with the libidinal frustration, of the individual is sympathetically explored and turned into a metaphor for the anxious, embattled subject of a peculiar historical moment—before a repressive political order ceases to demand homogeneity from members of society, a vibrant market economy sets in to instill anonymity and indifference. If the political reality is embodied in the gloomy urban landscape (predominantly the oppressive shantytown), new and rampant commercialism finds its perfect figuration in the attractive but heartless singer Zhao Yaqiu. The final death of the hero, therefore, while suggesting a strong social criticism, also drives home the impossibility of dissipating individual anxiety through any overarching myth or rationalization, which in recent Chinese history has shifted from an egalitarian vision of socialist paradise to the ideology of economic development and prosperity.

To further understand the politics of such a postutopian anxiety, we should turn to *Good Morning, Beijing,* a noticeably different filmic representation of contemporary life in that city. Here, in contrast to a blurred image of the city, we see a continual mapping of the sprawling cityscape; instead of an aesthetics of depth as social criticism, we find a persistent temporalization of space, linking different parts of the city through narratable, individual experiences. In her preproduction exposition of the film's theme, director Zhang Nuanxin made it clear that *Good Morning, Beijing* would pursue an "expressive, documentary" style to truthfully reflect the flow of daily life, with a sense of humor and light comedy. The soundtrack would be mostly live recording, and the color a shade of pleasantly harmonious gray. Set in a contemporary Beijing awash in the "great wave of the market economy," this film would follow everyday events in the life of a group of young people but in reality would mirror the contemporary social theme of "reform and opening up." It should also convey a refreshing broadmindedness—"everyone's pursuit has its rationality and every attitude to life should be given its due understanding." The director decided to use the title *Good Morning, Beijing* "because this film will present a snapshot of millions of Beijing citizens, depicting the life of those ordinary people quietly working in the most basic strata of our society."[28] Consciously or not, Zhang Nuanxin envisioned her movie largely in terms of a neorealist style of filmmaking, central to which are semidocumentary techniques and social concerns.[29]

This preproduction statement, however, should not limit our reading of the film too much because it was a document intended to secure the film its official approval and funding (in post-1989 China). Still it does strike the keynote for this public-oriented representation of life in Beijing. The plot of *Good Morning, Beijing* may appear complex at first glance. It centers on a young woman, Ai Hong, who works as a bus conductor, and it follows her successive relationships with three young men: first, her coworker Wang Lang, then the bus driver Zou Yongqiang, and finally the currently unemployed but new-fashioned and imaginative Keke. She eventually marries Keke and with him starts a private business. Be-  cause Wang Lang has no definable character of his own, Ai Hong's departure from him is relatively easy to explain, but her break with Zou Yong-qiang, a caring, honest young man who some-how lacks the courage to imagine a different life for them, causes her much soul-searching. Her liaisons with and movement among these three very different young people have an obviously allegorical importance. They repeat, as one critic suggests, a classic narrative format in which the female character, by her departure, either symbolizes negation of an outmoded or objectionable way of life or, through her acquiescence or eventual return, represents affirmation of a certain value system or accepted ideology.[30] In such a narrative tradition, women are made to express rather than create value. The value system to which Ai Hong subscribes in the end is therefore an emergent one associated with the market, which specifically calls for desirable character qualities such as energy, independence, and adventurousness. In the film, Keke, who at first pretends to be an overseas Chinese and wears a Harvard T-shirt, personifies such a new spirit, and his enthusiasm and modern lifestyle will help him win Ai Hong away from a reticent and much-inhibited Zou Yongqiang.

Indeed, the economy of passion in *Good Morning, Beijing* makes it a narrative that explicitly participates in an ongoing and large-scale cultural revolution through which habits, mentalities, and social structures will all be

1. *Beijing nizao* (*Good Morning, Beijing*), 1990. (Still courtesy of Zhongguo dianying ziliao guan, Beijing.)

systematically transformed so as to legitimate the market as an important organizing principle of society. It is also a narrative about social discontent and its mitigation through the introduction of desire.[31] Desire becomes a positive social value in the film, not only in that it expresses a putatively collective vision of a different Lebenswelt, but also, perhaps more crucially, because it sets free the energies and imaginations of individuals. The engendering of this emancipatory desire is narrated and at the same time explained in Ai Hong's departure from Zou Yongqiang and her subsequent fascination with Keke, who appears to move in a more mobile space with unmistakable signs of modernity (taxis, nightclubs, Western-style grocery stores, and general sociability). (The social content of such a desire can be gauged from the fact that, although this can be read as a conventional triangular love story, "love" is never pronounced as of major significance in the plot's unfolding. On the contrary, Ai Hong's affair and eventual marriage with Keke, an odd twist, are auxiliary means for her to discover and assert her own new identity.) As a direct opposite to Keke, Zou Yongqiang belongs to a conformist world in which filial duty and respect for his superior combine to demand from him gratitude and, at the same time, provide him with a sense of security. He lives with his parents in an overcrowded Beijing courtyard where his mother has to continually cut short his only expression of individuality (playing the traditional Chinese violin and later the guitar) out of consideration for the neighbors. Unlike Keke, he shops in a featureless department store, and he expresses his affection for Ai Hong by buying her a practical skirt, whereas Keke enchants her with a Walkman and a tape of American rock and roll.

Thus, these two rivals for Ai Hong's affection are highly symbolic figures, each representing a separate social reality and cultural logic. Yet the residual and the emergent conditions of existence, if we wish to so understand the symbolism here, are engaged in a rhetoric of compromise and tolerance. The ideological emphasis placed on compromise renders untenable a facile dichotomy of tradition versus modernity that seems to suggest itself here as an interpretive framework. On the contrary, this rhetoric of compromise enables the film to sympathetically portray Zou Yongqiang's frustration, the grave social-historical (dis)content of which is now effectively displaced as momentary personal misfortune. As director Zhang Nuanxin puts it, even though he cannot, primarily emotionally, identify with the dominant zeitgeist of the market, Zou Yongqiang maintains his decency and worthiness and continues to work and contribute to society.[32] At the same time, Keke is transformed in the process from a conspicuous consumer of urban culture back into a productive member of society. The film's concluding sequence brings together all the major characters in a dramatic moment when Ai Hong, now an apparently successful self-employed businesswoman, and her husband get onto the bus that Zou Yongqiang still drives and on which Wang Lang still works as a conductor. After a brief and polite exchange of greetings, Zou Yongqiang turns around and starts the bus. Slowly, the camera pulls back to show all four very different young people aboard the same bus peacefully moving along a sunny street in Beijing.

This comforting moment of rapprochement, we are told by a subtitle on the screen, arrives one year after the main action of the film. In this rich final image, the element of time is as important as the central message about the ineluctable coexistence of different modes of production. Time here signifies change, progress, and a healing process as well. Time also becomes identified with the future, or rather with some utopian projections from the present. Actually, even at the beginning of the film, where we are shown Ai Hong still in bed one early morning, time as a major factor is introduced emphatically when the ticking alarm clock goes off. It is time for the young bus conductor to go to work, and the whole interior space is thus redefined and forced open by a universal clock time. Unlike *Black Snow,* where time is subjectivized and locked into a depressing present, *Good Morning, Beijing* is a film about the multiple and contradictory temporal flows in the space of the enormous city. Spatial structures, locations, and relations now acquire a temporal, historical significance to the extent that we can speak of a socially produced "spatiality," which, according to Edward Soja, "like society itself, exists in both substantial forms (concrete spatialities) and as a set of relations between individuals and groups, an 'embodiment' and medium of social life itself."[33] Through the narrative of the film, the uneven and multidimensional spatial relations are mapped and reconnected, and the city of Beijing is brought together as an imaginable totality, as a fascinating collection of images of various social realities that simultaneously exist and interact.

So a central plot in *Good Morning, Beijing* is the movement from the initial spatiotemporal structure of a confining domestic interior (underlined by the close-up shot of a cage with an impatient bird chirping in it) to an open cityscape that is emphatically contemporary and modernizing. Of particular interest in the opening sequence is a stark "crudeness" of the interior space—crude surfaces as well as crude conditions of existence. In this cramped room, we realize that life has to be reduced to its bare necessities; it is an enclosed space kept flat and public by the absence of any refinement or the possibility of privacy. It becomes a most efficient extension of the workplace because "home" now stands less for separation from work than for a direct reproduction of labor. When at home, Ai Hong, as we see later, also has the task of taking care of her invalid grandpa. She readies coal for heating, fixes the exhaust pipe with the help of Zou Yongqiang, and, in the same room where her grandpa lies in bed year round, she prepares porridge for him and washes her hands in a basin next to the window. The same embarrassing experience of scarcity is even more pointedly represented at Zou Yongqiang's home, where, in his parents' makeshift bedroom, the whole family eats supper and watches TV while the father soaks his feet in a basin of warm water. At the end of dinner the son's duty is to take the basin, walk through a dark hallway, and drain the water into a public sink located in the courtyard.

In isolation, such images of impoverishment and severely constrained conditions of existence would not necessarily mean social criticism or cultural commentary. On the contrary, scarce and overcrowded domestic space would only appear "natural" or "realistic" enough, since some public places to which the camera brings us (such as the bus company headquarters, the police station, and the hospital) have surfaces and structures no less shabby and perfunctory. A Third World condition—here the term is used strictly to refer to generalized inadequate living conditions and a pre-industrial, underdeveloped socioeconomic infrastructure—can hardly be grasped as such unless defamiliarized by images of, or references to, a different, more advanced stage of modernization. In *Good Morning, Beijing*, as we will see momentarily, the Third Worldness of the city is candidly acknowledged, together with its explicitly anticipated changeover. It is extremely significant, however, that the Third World condition presented by the film carries with it not so much mere self-loathing (would that be politically incorrect?) or self-glorification (would that be politically correct?) as an almost restless utopian desire for self-transformation. In this sense, the film as a Third World production is also conscientiously for a Third World audience, insofar as an undesirable present condition of existence is both represented as an immediate collective reality and historicized as some fast-vanishing remnant of a better future.[34]

Consequently, the series of images that reveals an impoverished everyday life acquires its historical content when it is juxtaposed with a different sequence, a different set of spatiotemporal structures. We may even argue that history, or a historical understanding of contemporary Beijing, becomes accessible precisely when this juxtaposition of different spatial realities and relationships is employed as a strategy of characterizing an incomplete, in-progress present condition. One way to describe this spatial coexistence or simultaneity could be the architectural notion of "a collage city," where "disparate objects [are] held together by various means" to form a composite presence.[35] In the film, the city of Beijing does become fragmented into a collage of various sites, rhythms, and intensities, but the movements through the city of the characters, in particular Ai Hong, reconnect all these obviously discontinuous moments. Thus, there is still the possibility of narrating one's story in the city, of presenting a spatial experience in temporal terms. As an apt symbol of collective practice, the moving bus, where much of the movie's action takes place, provides an ideal vehicle for linking up different parts and functions of Beijing. From here we see images of Beijing as a political center (Tiananmen Square), a rapidly modernizing metropolis (all-glass high-rises), and an overpopulated Third World city (business districts and shopping streets). In a sense, the moving bus serves as a clever self-reflection on the rolling camera and our viewing experience.

It is, however, Ai Hong's experiences as an individual subject who strives to change her own historical situation that endow the city with a humanizing narratability and a spatiotemporal coherence. We first see her get up early in the morning, run through the empty lane of the neighborhood, and hop onto Wang Lang's bicycle to go to work. Working on the bus is a demanding job, but she gets to meet and observe people. (Here the bus is also a substitute for modern city streets, bound to be occupied by what Walter Benjamin once called an "amorphous crowd of passersby.")[36] One day her friend Ziyun comes onto the bus and proudly tells her that she now works as a typist for a joint-venture company. At her invitation, Ai Hong decides to pay her friend a visit and subsequently finds herself inside a business office on the sixteenth floor of a guarded building. This is one of those standardized, new, international-style offices (polyester carpet, air-conditioning, and low ceilings), equipped with word processors, contemporary furniture, and a coffeemaker. The most astonishing feature of this claustrophobic office, when we recall Ai Hong's home as well as her workplace, are the smooth white walls and shiny objects. The glass coffee table quietly reflects, the sofa extends a comfortably curvaceous line, and the steel sink gives forth a hygienic silver glare. This interior space is totally alien to Ai Hong, and at first she appears intimidated. The polished surface not only outlines a new form of labor no longer associated with bodily discomfort or endurance, but it also suggests a simplification of social relationships to those of an impersonal "cash nexus." Rather fittingly, in this seemingly depthless space, Ziyun, with her own experience, calmly illustrates to her awestruck friend some fundamental aspects of modern urban life: contingency and mobility.[37]

This modern office space can also be taken as an instance of the postmodern "relief" that a world of smooth objects may promote.[38] If it has a shattering effect on Ai Hong because it exposes as "premodern" or "yet to be modernized" the shabbiness of her own world, it also initiates a readjustment of her relation to the city. Her eyes are suddenly opened, as it were, and she is able to experience and perceive the city as an enormous spatiotemporal structure that energetically produces a wide range of social realities and personal identities. In the following sequences, we see Ai Hong enjoy Korean food at a fancy restaurant with Zou Yongqiang and a friend of his; we see her wander into an upper-grade grocery store and find herself followed by an admirer who introduces himself as Keke. Soon she and Keke go to a nightclub, where he performs with passionate emotion and dedicates a song to her. At the end of that evening, he takes her home in a taxi. Finally, as a high point of their romantic affair, and also to divert Ai Hong from her work, Keke suggests that they leave the city and go on a vacation. This series of concrete and very often discontinuous spatialities demands that Ai Hong constantly map and remap the city in order to achieve a coherent perception of both herself and her environment. Indeed, instead of being incapacitated by this new spatial multiplication, Ai Hong insists on keeping the city a legible human space by heroically redesigning herself and rewriting her own story. Her narrative therefore presupposes the possibility of becoming, and it is this conviction that supports a profound optimism about social change and self-transformation, personal as well as collective. In this light, the brief trip that Ai Hong and Keke make to some historical site (now a popular tourist attraction) away from Beijing becomes a significant move. It reintroduces historical time as the untranscendable horizon of experience, and it localizes—albeit in its absence—the city as a reality with reachable limits.

Our reading therefore suggests that the spatiotemporal structure underlying the narrative of *Good Morning, Beijing* remains resolutely accessible to representation, in spite of all apparent conflicts and disjunctures. Ai Hong's story can be read as a narrative of the birth of urban individualism and self-consciousness, and her spatial movement in the city at once reveals and reconnects the complexity of social structures and relations, whether public or private, emergent or residual. Not surprisingly, the cinematic images we witness here are eventually controlled and organized by the subject rather than the other way around. Unlike in postmodern cinema, where representation, according to David Harvey's persuasive analysis, runs into crisis because of a pervasive "time-space compression" engendered by a late capitalism of flexible accumulation,[39] *Good Morning, Beijing*, as a visual representation, is still fascinated by the seemingly infinite possibilities and frontiers promised by a modernizing metropolis. If one dominant theme of postmodern cinema, as Harvey shows through his readings of *Blade Runner* and *Wings of Desire* (respectively about Los Angeles and Berlin), is an impossible conflict "between people living on different time scales, and seeing and experiencing the world very differently as a result,"[40] what we find in this particular Chinese film is rather a "neorealist" arranging of urban relations and a utopian resolution of conflicts arising from city life. By continually moving its characters across the uneven urban landscape, *Good Morning, Beijing* evokes the city itself as an intimate participant that quietly justifies their endeavors and aspirations. It is a film that refuses to let close-up images of the city blur its organizational logic and multiple functions or to allow the city to disappear as a mappable totality. Its general visual clarity, enhanced by continual shots with great depth of field, mirrors the filmmaker's effort to influence and shape our understanding of the changing city.

By way of conclusion, I wish to bring together and compare the different political visions in *Black Snow* and *Good Morning, Beijing*. Both films feature a pivotal scene in a lively nightclub. In *Black Snow*, Li Huiquan as a member of the audience is painstakingly separated from the solo singer, both visually and emotionally. But when Ai Hong and Keke in *Good Morning, Beijing* go to a bar with live music, Keke joins the band and asks to participate. He sings and dedicates to Ai Hong a popular song by rock star Cui Jian, which Ai Hong will also learn to sing, even though she appears to be at a loss when hearing the song for the first time. The interpretation that I would propose, if only too schematically, is that these two different moments express two approaches to the city that are at odds with each other. If we characterize the politics of *Black Snow* as a refusal and contemplation by means of a modernist aesthetics of depth, the rhetoric of compromise in *Good Morning, Beijing* necessarily valorizes cultural and political participation, which in turn articulates the legitimating ideology of a growing market economy. Whereas the market economy arrives to present an open city to Ai Hong and her contemporaries, some deep (well-nigh instinctive) suspicion of the market triggers Li Huiquan's anxious, and to a large extent forced, retreat to interiority. In one case, neorealist techniques are used to rationalize the modernization project, while in the other a hypertrophy of modernist subjectivity emits uncompromising social criticism. Herein lies the cognitive value of *Black Snow,* which may be realized only with critical reflection on the part of the viewer.

These two significantly contradistinct political visions and cinematic languages hardly escaped the notice of the Chinese audience when *Black Snow* and *Good Morning, Beijing* were released in 1989 and 1990, respectively. They were quickly recognized as representative works of the rising city cinema. While *Black Snow* enjoyed the rare distinction of winning both domestic and international honors (Best Picture at the Thirteenth National Hundred Flowers Awards and the Silver Bear Prize at the Berlin Film Festival), *Good Morning, Beijing* was a remarkable box-office success. Quoting Cesare Zavattini, the theorist of Italian neorealist cinema, an enthusiastic commentator commended the second film for truthfully capturing contemporary everyday life in the ancient capital city and in the process revealing a deeper historical meaning.[41] At the same time, the critical recognition of *Black Snow* caused considerable uneasiness among mainstream critics and media. A brief essay in *Popular Cinema,* appearing next to Lei Da's endorsement of *Good Morning, Beijing,* sought to explain why the Hundred Flowers Award won by *Black Snow* did not mean that the film is flawless. In fact, the essayist denounced the film as deeply flawed because, in spite of its artistic achievements, "it does not find (or does not want to find) a new worldview and a new character that new social forces, who represent a new mode of social production, ought to possess."[42] It would be an involved task to unpack the loaded discourse and ideological stances here. Suffice it to say that at stake are some profoundly unresolved questions about artistic and social forms, about representation and engagement, all of which these two films succeed in bringing to the fore by evoking separate intellectual and aesthetic traditions. If our analysis of their indebtedness to either modernism or neorealism shows both films to be an ideological intervention, it should also be clear that we cannot dismiss one on the account of the other.

Rather, these two films should be viewed together, and perhaps between them we will begin to approach the impossible urban reality signified by Beijing.

Notes

1 Don J. Cohn, *A Guide to Beijing* (Lincolnwood, Ill.: Passport Books, 1992), 12.

2 Joe Cummings et al., *A Travel Survival Kit: China,* 3d ed. (Berkeley: Lonely Planet, 1991), 485.

3 The lyrics go on like this: With a friend I always kill some time in a bar, / While the tape player repeats all the hit songs. / You think one way and you talk one way, / Because everyone wears a toylike mask. / What should I say?

4 These four films are *Wanzhu, Lunhui* (dir. Huang Jianxin), *Da chuanqi* (dir. Ye Daying), and *Yiban shi haishui, yiban shi huoyan* (dir. Xia Gang).

5 Two other city films that came out in 1988 are *Yaogun qingnian* and *Fengkuang de daijia,* directed, respectively, by Tian Zhuangzhuang (*Daoma zei,* 1986) and Zhou Xiaowen (*Zuihou de fengkuang,* 1987), two well-established Fifth Generation filmmakers. In 1987, at least two films by directors of the Fifth Generation were also about the contemporary cityscape: *Gei kafei jiadian tang* (dir. Sun Zhou) and *Taiyang yu* (dir. Zhang Zeming).

6 For analyses of some representative film texts from the New China cinema tradition, see Chris Berry, "Sexual Difference and the Viewing Subject in *Li Shuangshuang* and *The In-Laws,*" in *Perspectives on Chinese Cinema,* edited by Chris Berry (London: British Film Institute, 1991), 30–39; Ma Junxiang, "*Shanghai guniang:* Geming nüxing ji 'guankan' wenti" (*The girl from Shanghai:* revolutionary women and the question of "viewing"), in *Zai jiedu: dazhong wenyi yu yishi xingtai* (Rereading: the people's literature and art movement and ideology), edited by Tang Xiaobing (Hong Kong: Oxford University Press, 1993), 127–46.

7 For a genealogical account of the origin of the Fifth Generation and its modernist politics, see Xudong Zhang, *Chinese Modernism in the Era of Reforms: Cultural Fever, Avant-Garde Fiction, and the New Chinese Cinema* (Durham: Duke University Press, 1997), 215–31. See also, for instance, the statement by one of the leading members of the Fifth Generation in the interview "A Director Who Is Trying to Change the Audience: A Chat with Young Director Tian Zhuangzhuang," conducted by Yang Ping, in Berry, *Perspectives on Chinese Cinema,* 127–30.

8 Peng Wen, "*Benming nian:* mosheng de chengshi yu tanhuan de zhuti" (*Black Snow:* The estranging city and a paralyzed subject), *Dianying yishu* (Film art), no. 212 (1990): 41.

9 Xudong Zhang, *Chinese Modernism,* 223.

10 Peng Wen, "*Black Snow,*" 42.

11 Wei Xiaolin, "*Benming nian* de renzhi jiazhi" (The cognitive value of *Black Snow*), *Film Art,* no. 212 (1990): 51.

12 In a 1984 essay, Xie Fei emphasized the importance of representing daily life. Commenting on Raizman's *A Personal Life* (1983), Xie Fei wrote: "No significant events, heated dramatic conflicts, and unusual techniques are used. On the contrary, it vividly de-

picts a variety of characters, touches profound social problems and philosophies, and is obviously a contemporary product." See Xie Fei, "My View of the Concept of Film," translated by Hou Jianping, in *Chinese Film Theory: A Guide to the New Era,* edited by George S. Semsel et al., translated by Hou Jianping et al. (New York: Praeger, 1990), 79.

13 Pierre Sorlin, *European Cinemas, European Societies, 1939–1990* (London: Routledge, 1991), 135.

14 Ibid., 126–27.

15 Bondanella, *Italian Cinema from Neorealism to the Present* (New York: Unger, 1983), 60.

16 Sorlin, *European Cinemas,* 136.

17 After making clear the relationship between the classical realist ideology of the nineteenth century and neorealism, Millicent Marcus, in his *Italian Film in the Light of Neorealism* (Princeton: Princeton University Press, 1986), observes that neorealism in Italian cinema expressed an "immediate postwar optimism about the attempt to shape political reality according to a moral idea" (28).

18 Paul Clark, "Two Hundred Flowers on China's Screens," in Berry, *Perspectives on Chinese Cinema,* 40–61.

19 Xie Fei, " 'Di sidai' de zhengming" (The proof of the "Fourth Generation"), *Film Art,* no. 212 (1990): 23–24.

20 Peng Wen, "*Black Snow,*" 43.

21 See, for instance, Chen Xiaoming, "Daode zijiu: Lishi zhouxin de duanlie" (Moral self-salvation: The breaking of a historical axis), *Film Art,* no. 215 (1990): 105. While describing the difference between *Black Snow* and his earlier films, Xie Fei emphasizes his philosophical beliefs. "Surely there was some change in my conception, but in my artistic creation, I as always held dear my ideals, and stayed with my value judgment as far as the true, the good, and the beautiful versus the false, the evil, and the ugly in our life experiences are concerned." See Xie, "The Proof of the 'Fourth Generation,' " 20.

22 Kevin Lynch, *The Image of the City* (Cambridge: MIT Press, 1960), 4.

23 Fredric Jameson, *Postmodernism, or the Cultural Logic of Late Capitalism* (Durham: Duke University Press, 1991), 312.

24 Chen Xiaoming, "Moral Self-Salvation," 103.

25 The "inward turn" or psychologization of experience that I relate here with the aesthetics of depth can also be observed in the original novel, which opens with Li Huiquan's return to his home and a wintry present. Here is Howard Goldblatt's translation of the first sentences: "A fat white guy was squatting in the yard. Li Huiquan, his knapsack slung over his shoulder, noticed the frosty grin as soon as he walked through the gate, so he walked over and wiped it off. Chunks of coal for eyes, a chili-pepper nose, a wastebasket hat—the same stuff he used as a kid." Liu Heng, *Black Snow,* translated by Howard Goldblatt (New York: Atlantic Monthly Press, 1993), 3.

26 Xie Fie, "The Proof of the 'Fourth Generation,' " 26.

27 See Liu Shuyong, "Zaoxing zuowei yuyan: Qianlun *Benming nian* de yongguang chuli" (Imaging as language: On the lighting technique in *Black snow*), *Dangdai dianying* (Contemporary cinema) 35 (April 1990): 87–91.

28 Zhang Nuanxin, "*Beijing nizao* de daoyan chanshu" (The director's thematic exposition of *Good Morning, Beijing*), *Contemporary Cinema* 39 (December 1990): 53–54.

29 Acknowledging the formidable difficulty in generalizing about neorealism, Millicent

Marcus nonetheless offers a useful description of what constitutes its basic style and techniques: "The rules governing neorealist practice would include location shooting, lengthy takes, unobtrusive editing, natural lighting, a predominance of medium and long shots, respect for the continuity of time and space, use of contemporary, true-to-life subjects, an uncontrived, open-ended plot, working-class protagonists, a non-professional cast, dialogue in the vernacular, active viewer involvement, and implied social criticism" (*Italian Cinema,* 22).

30 Zhang Wei, "Nüxing de guishu yu lishi qianyi: *Beijing nizao* de yuyanxing chanshi" (The position of the woman and historical transformation: An allegorical interpretation of *Good Morning, Beijing*), *Contemporary Cinema* 39 (December 1990): 55–56. One needs to note here that this reading is heavily influenced by Laura Mulvey's critical analysis of classic Hollywood narrative cinema.

31 It is interesting to note that in its subtitled English-language version the film is given a much more suggestive title, *Budding Desires.*

32 Zhang Nuanxin, "The Director's Thematic Exposition," 54.

33 Edward W. Soja, *Postmodern Geographies: The Reassertion of Space in Critical Social Theory* (London: Verso, 1989), 120.

34 There is another group of films in contemporary Chinese cinema whose cultural "Third Worldness" is marketed primarily to First World film audiences. Films by Zhang Yimou (*Ju Dou,* 1990, *Raise the Red Lantern,* 1992) seem to be favorite samples of this group.

35 Colin Rowe and Fred Koetter, *Collage City* (Cambridge: MIT Press, 1978), 139–40. I would like to point out that Rowe and Koetter's vision of a "collage city" expresses a typical postmodernist sensibility and ideology. "Collage city" is offered as a solution to the anxiety generated by both utopia and tradition: "because collage is a method deriving its virtue from its irony, because it seems to be a technique for using things and simultaneously disbelieving in them, it is also a strategy which can allow utopia to be dealt with as image, to be dealt with in *fragments* without our having to accept it *in toto,* which is further to suggest that collage could even be a strategy which, by supporting the utopian illusion of changelessness and finality, might even fuel a reality of change, motion, action and history" (149).

36 Walter Benjamin, *Illuminations,* translated by Harry Zohn (New York: Schocken Books, 1969), 165.

37 While putting on makeup in the office lavatory, Ziyun tells Ai Hong that even though her salary is handsome she has no job security; then, when asked about her boyfriend, she replies that they split up because "it was too demanding for both of us."

38 See Jameson, *Postmodernism,* 313–15.

39 Harvey, *The Condition of Postmodernity: An Enquiry into the Origins of Cultural Change* (Cambridge, Mass.: Blackwell, 1989), 322.

40 Ibid., 313.

41 See Lei Da, "Dangda dushi fengjing xian: Tan yingpian *Beijing nizao*" (Contemporary urban landscape: About the film *Good Morning, Beijing*), *Dazhong dianying* (Popular cinema) 450 (December 1990): 4–5.

42 See Zheng Shu, "Xie zai *Benming nian* huojiang zhihou" (Afterthoughts on *Black Snow* winning the award), *Popular Cinema* 450 (December 1990): 5.

Private Reality: Hara Kazuo's Films

Abé Mark Nornes

While documentary has a decidedly peripheral position in most national cinemas across the globe, the form has enjoyed relative prestige in the Japanese film world. Initially, this was a peculiar side benefit of global warfare in the 1930s and 1940s. However, even in the postwar era, documentary's profile was never lost on the film community. Directors like Imamura Shohei, Teshigawara Hiroshi, Hani Susumu, Yoshida Yoshishige, and Oshima Nagisa moved easily between fiction and nonfiction. Written histories, in both Japanese and English, never fail to include consideration of the most important documentarists: Kamei Fumio, Tsuchimoto Noriaki, Ogawa Shinsuke, and Hara Kazuo. With the deaths of Ogawa and Kamei, as well as the relative inactivity of Hani and Tsuchimoto, the younger Hara Kazuo has taken the lead in pushing the Japanese documentary into new, unmapped territories.

Hara's filmography reveals a considerable variety of subject matter—a portrait of a victim of cerebral palsy, a deeply personal account of his relationships with women, a radical investigation into wartime atrocities, and the biographies of a novelist and a filmmaker. However, it is easy to tease out certain consistencies, particular and peculiar passions. While Hara is always undergoing transformation, the concerns of his films and the style in which these issues are worked out are inevitably affiliated with the film-maker's sense of his own subjectivity as both social actor and artist. Hara's approach to postwar Japanese history eschews any easy realism, as it is a representation of the world linked to the measure of his own sight. The measuring stick of the filmmaker's own look searches out private spaces, piercing them with his presence with a singular obsession. This tendency reveals as much about Hara as a Japanese documentary filmmaker as it does about documentary realism itself. While there have been a number of ex-cellent interviews with Hara and surveys of his life and work, Hara's rela-tionship to his own tradition of documentary has gone unexplored.[1] This essay will discuss the films of Hara Kazuo against the backdrop of Japanese nonfiction film in order to consider larger questions about the realism of the documentary moving image.

Born months before the end of World War II in 1945, Hara came of film-making age during a turbulent time for Japanese documentary. He gradu-ated from high school in Yamaguchi Prefecture and worked for *Asahi* news-paper as a photographer. Through this contact, he was able to move to the capital in 1966 to study at a photography school (Tokyo Sogo Shashin Sen-mon Gakko) while working for *Asahi* at night. However, he quit school after only half a year. According to Hara, the only exercise that taught him anything was a portrait assignment: approach a stranger and take his or her portrait from no more than a meter away, not from behind but full frontal and not carefully but in a "sudden assault."[2] It was absolutely terrifying and positively educational. In a sense, it became the work ethic of Hara's subsequent work in filmmaking.

Hara continued to pursue a career in still photography while working at a school for children with disabilities. He finally staged an individual ex-hibition on disabled children at the Ginza's Canon Salon in 1969. At the same time, he became increasingly interested in making movies, choosing television as his entry point. Television documentaries of the time were experiencing a radical shift in style. At the very moment when the radi-cal films about Japan's massive social protests became iconic for drawing a contrast between the styles of television news reportage and independent documentaries—between styles that *take sides* with either the powerful or the powerless—there were certain spaces in television available for experi-mentation that blurred some of the very same boundaries.[3] Takeda Miyuki, the woman he married in 1968, was also interested in filmmaking and appeared in Tawara Soichiro's documentary *I Sing the Present: Fuji Keiko, June Scene* (*Watashi wa genzai o utau: Fuji Keiko, roku gatsu no fūkei*, 1970) for Tokyo Channel 12. The next year they appeared as a couple with their newborn in Tawara's *Bride of Japan* ("Nihon no Hanayume"), another documentary for Tokyo Channel 12. This was also the year they started filming *Sayonara CP* with Kobayashi Sachiko.

Sayonara CP drew on Hara's experiences working with people suffering from disabilities. The film featured Yokota Hiroshi, a man whose body was devastated by cerebral palsy, leaving much of his body limp. Hara's approach was far from conventional, as his collaboration with Yokota cut straight to issues of the representation of handicapped bodies. With the exception of Tsuchimoto's newly released *Minamata: The Victims and Their World* (*Minamata: Kanja-san to sono sekai*, 1971), documentaries approaching the topic of mental or physical handicaps were toothless exercises that simply allowed spectators to empathize with the subject's plight, policing the borders between the healthy and the ill. The consequences for such a delimitation was ghettoization of the ill from social acceptance and the creation of a culture of shame that excluded the handicapped from full participation as subjects in the social world.

Hara sensed the enormous role cinematic representations had in this process, and so his portrait of Yokota attacked the sensibilities established by conventional images of disability. In the film's most striking and controversial scene, Yokota strikes out into the public realm without a wheelchair . . . and without clothing. He literally drags his naked body down the street. The film has a remarkable level of self-reflexivity, which exposes Hara to, indeed, invites criticism of, the filmmakers' unorthodox strategy of empowerment through representation. For example, in an extraordinary scene, Yokota's wife, who suffers from the same disease, threatens divorce if the filmmaking does not stop. She argues forcefully that such aggressive tactics are only playing to the camera as a monstrosity. This will surely result in nothing other than a perpetuation, if not intensification, of the discrimination they suffer.

Sayonara CP came out in 1972. While it did not achieve the notoriety of Hara's later films, it did make a mark on the history of representations of illness in Japan. This was a tradition that began in the postwar era with Kamei Fumio's use of the atomic bombings as a counterpoint to the aesthetic of healthiness during the war, a tradition continued in the work of Tsuchimoto Noriaki (the mercury poisoning of Minamata disease), Yanagisawa Hisao (disabled children), Haneda Sumiko (Alzheimer's victims), Sato Makoto (Niigata Minamata disease), and other important documentarists. To this very day, Hara and Kobayashi regularly show the film in hospitals, clinics, and medical schools. In addition to raising ethical issues underpinning public representations of the disabled, the film puts into play certain dynamics that characterize all of Hara's work: an exploration of and penetration into the line drawn between the public and the private. This is a vector codified into the very title of his next film, *Extreme Private Eros: Love Song, 1974* (*Kyokushiteki erosu: Renka 1974*, 1974).

Here Hara brought his own life before the camera, using his material existence to represent the larger social world and its politics. Considering how the period of this production coincided with massive changes in his personal situation, it was a brazen move. Hara's disintegrating marriage ended in divorce from Takeda Miyuki in 1973; the same year, he and producer Kobayashi Sachiko gave birth to a baby girl and shortly thereafter entered marriage. Using the camera to retain some vestige of his relationship with Takeda, Hara follows her on an extraordinary journey (with Kobayashi along recording the sound). Takeda leaves a relationship with a woman to travel to Okinawa, where she gives birth to a mixed race child by herself, camera running, on the kitchen floor. Surrounded by a prostitution system set up on the peripheries of the U.S. military bases, she starts a day care center for the working women and gets involved in political action around the brothels. She joins a commune for feminists and ends up working as a stripper at a nightclub for American soldiers.[4] At one level, Hara's film consolidates a long running strand in Japanese documentary: films on the U.S. military bases, which were pioneered by Kamei Fumio with *Children of the Bases* (*Kichi no kodomotachi*, 1953) and *Sunagawa: A Record of Flowing Blood* (*Ryûchi no kiroku: Sunagawa*, 1956) and Higashi Yoichi's *Okinawa* (1968). However, Hara's film was radically different in the way this larger social landscape was intimately tied to his private life. As he explains, "In the sixties and seventies, there was a feeling that if the individual did not cause change, nothing would change. At the time, I wanted to make a movie, and I was wondering how I could make a statement for change. There was much talk of family-imperialism (*kazoku teikokushugi*). One of the strong sentiments of the time was that family-imperialism should be destroyed. I thought that if I could put my own family under the camera, all our emotions, our privacy, I wondered if I might break taboos about the family."[5]

The approach of the film hinges on an exposure of the private and its conversion into public space and event. In its most intimate moments, with Hara making love with camera in hand, it inspires awkward embarrassment. Takeda's single-minded determination to be independent and socially engaged often turns on Hara with a vengeance. For example, at a beach, Takeda and Kobayashi (holding the microphone and wearing earphones) discuss Hara as he films their conversation. Takeda lashes out at Hara, warning the new bride that he is just using her and she is doomed to be thrown away. At one point, Takeda's political activism around the prostitutes gets Hara beaten up. For over a decade, film theory by people like Oshima Nagisa and Matsumoto Toshio had been calling for a documentary foregrounding the artist's subjectivity, but nowhere had this been so thoroughly realized than in Hara's physical and emotional immersion in *Extreme Private Eros: Love Song, 1974*. It may not render an objective accounting of the situation in Okinawa or of Japan in 1974, but it does offer a palpable, embodied knowledge about the life around military bases, the often whimsical sides of political activism, and the deep impact of feminism on adult relationships. This world, Japan in 1974, is measured through the network of human intersubjectivities surrounding Hara Kazuo.

While the film is often seen in terms of documentary voyeurism, it may actually reveal something more fundamental about nonfiction moving imagery itself. William Rothman has recently argued that a dialectic between the public and the private is key to understanding the power of direct cinema style.[6] Drawing on a previous argument from *The "I" of Cinema*, he links the classical Hollywood style to the direct cinema of Drew Associates, unlikely partners indeed.[7] Both, Rothman asserts, share the same philosophical concerns in that they rely on a play of public impression and private response to represent human reality. In the earlier work, he suggests that a stylistic feature such as shot/reverse shot is based on granting access to an internal, subjective, private view of the world—access through the facial "mask" presented in reverse shots. Direct cinema depends on a similar foundation: "The cinéma vérité cameras revealed its human subjects continually putting on masks, taking them off, putting them on again, and so on, as they reacted to the spectacle of the world, prepared their next ventures into the public realm, performed on the world's stage, and withdrew again into privacy to which the camera grants us access."[8]

Thus, the documentary offers up a public world as a "succession of private moments," especially through cinematic devices like the close-up. Viewed by mass audiences in the privacy of their own homes, these private moments again are transformed into public events. *Extreme Private Eros* and *Sayonara CP* share this dynamic to a large degree. However, they also point to a politics of the private in ways that develop the circumstances and implications far beyond Rothman's parallel.

The grounds for such a discourse, which complicate any easy division between the private and the social, were set in Japanese documentary theory itself. Thus, a contextualization of Hara's work—particularly its use of collective for individual modes—is crucial to understanding Hara's singular innovation as a contribution to the transformation of documentary realism in Japan.

In the 1950s, television was fast establishing itself as the dominant form of distribution for nonfiction work, creating an explosion in production that hadn't been seen since the war, when the government forced theaters to show documentary shorts. With a new distribution outlet hungry for material, production companies sprouted up to feed the demand. Because politics is never far from issues of style in documentary, it should not be surprising that this relatively luxurious climate would breed some experimentation and questioning of given forms of realism. As in many other parts of the world, the Left had long made its mark on documentary film. With growing generational rifts between new and old in Japan, tensions grew over the most appropriate ways of representing the referential world. The stakes of cinematic realism felt exceedingly high with the impending U.S. security treaty renewal in 1960, which locked Japan into a bilateral relationship under America's nuclear umbrella.

The epicenter for what would be a shake-up of the Japanese documentary world was the Iwanami Publishing Company. One of Japan's oldest book publishers, it decided to cash in on the new markets for nonfiction film by creating a filmmaking unit. The most prominent of the staff members was the young Hani Susumu. Hani's commitment to innovations in film style is evident in his first two documentaries for Iwanami, which sent shock waves through the Japanese film world. They were called *Children of the Classroom* (*Kyoshitsu no kodomotachi*, 1954) and *Children Who Draw Pictures* (*E o kaku kodomotachi*, 1956), and were observational documentaries shot in elementary school classrooms. With their radical spontaneity, these films mark an important stylistic and theoretical break in the history of Japanese documentary, and we can draw a direct line between them and the practices of Hara Kazuo some twenty years later. Indeed, English-language criticism of Hara's work is quick to compare him to his Euro-American colleagues, from Rouch to Morris. However, these are ultimately arbitrary linkages. Hara has far more in common with someone like Hani than any foreign filmmaker. This is not to essentialize some ephemeral Japanese style of realism but to point to an approach to documentary that has a history that is analogous to developments in other parts of the world while being supported by a rhetoric that was very nearly hermetically sealed from theories from abroad.

Hani is a case in point. His was primarily an observational style. He brought cameras into the classrooms of young students and closely watched their interactions. While they were initially concerned that the equipment and adult camera operators would distract the children—well, children are easily distracted—they quickly forgot about the filmmakers and went about the business of playing, drawing, and learning. Other filmmakers at Iwanami attempted similar approaches to representing the social world, most notably Haneda Sumiko in *Village Politics* (*Mura no seiji,* 1958). In this film, Haneda detailed the activities of a group of women in village Japan as they attempted to balance work and participation in local politics. Following Hani's lead, she took care not to interfere with the women, choosing instead to capture the events transpiring before the camera in an observational mode. The women interact in daily life and discuss local politics in meetings, apparently oblivious to the presence of the filmmakers. The result of this approach was a highly observational cinema, one, I might add, that significantly predates the innovations of Drew Associates and its direct cinema by half a decade.

The spontaneity captured by Hani's films bowled people over in the mid-1950s. Japanese audiences were accustomed to a documentary realism that involved the treatment of human subjects as actors (the cinematic kind). This had roots in both Soviet theories of typage and in long-standing filmmaking practices with a lineage reaching back to the China War. In the 1930s, an enormous amount of energy went into theorizing documentary film. It began with the writings of the Proletarian Film League of Japan in the late 1920s and early 1930s, and when this movement was suppressed by the government, critics from a wide variety of political positions developed the theories until the end of World War II.[9] Some of Japan's greatest philosophers and film theorists wrote on documentary, including Tosaka Jun, Nakai Masakazu, Hasegawa Nyozekan, and Imamura Taihei. The writings of authors like Vertov, Eisenstein, Moholy-Nagi, and Rotha were translated and debated. During the China War, the government introduced forced screenings, providing an unquenchable market for nonfiction, and this energy pushed documentary from fairly straightforward newsreels and compilation films to something far more creative. At this early stage in the history of documentary, this meant a brand of realism closely aligned with fiction filmmaking. Filmmakers would take people in their natural settings and direct them through scenes using rudimentary scenarios; these scenes were embedded in larger, nonnarrative structures of compiled documentary footage. Ironically, while the war feature film drew closer to documentary, the nonfiction form gradually integrated more and more narrative techniques. This tendency was further energized by a translation of Paul Rotha's *Documentary Film* in 1938, which brought news of a documentary movement whose engine was the "creative treatment of actuality." For many, this was none other than the inclusion of scripted narrative with nonactors.

The inertia behind this style of documentary realism propelled it across the apparent breach of 1945, when Japan seemed to undergo an overnight political and social conversion. While the politics of documentary shifted from Japan's wartime brand of nationalism to a postwar democratization — if not radicalization — the largely fictive form of documentary realism remained standard and stable. A postwar film on the democratic activities of a village *looked* little different than a documentary on a similar village preparing for the American wartime invasion. Hani's films began to upset this equilibrium, and people began questioning the claims the standard approach made for an adequate representation of the phenomenal world. The relative freedom of Iwanami's approach to management at all stages of production allowed its employees to experiment within the bounds of the public relations (PR) film. The brightest of the bunch formed Blue Group (Aou no kai), including Kuroki Kazuo, Higashi Yoichi, Suzuki Tatsuo, Tamura Masaki, Tsuchimoto Noriaki, and Ogawa Shinsuke. They discussed filmmaking and theory. They would show rough cuts for feedback and perform experiments. At the same time, they began pushing the limits of the PR film, converting typical shorts on, say, steel factories into massive cinemascope spectaculars. Not surprisingly, working for large corporations soon proved constricting. Their creative and political energies could not be contained, and they fled from Iwanami en masse in 1960 and went independent. They were subsequently joined by Hani himself, who made feature films with a strong documentary touch, such as *Bad Boys* (*Furyo sho-*

nen, 1959), *He and She* (*Kanojo to kare,* 1963), and *Nanami: Inferno of First Love* (*Hatsu koi: Jigokuhen,* 1968).

Hara Kazuo was becoming fascinated with the cinema at precisely this point, as the former Iwanami PR filmmakers began producing completely personal works in the mid-1960s. After leaving Iwanami, they had quickly aligned themselves with the New Left, a political break conjoined to a stylistic rupture. They completely eschewed the reenactments with nonactors, a continuous practice since the 1930s, and explicitly took sides with political movements of one sort or another. Higashi went to Okinawa while Tsuchimoto and Ogawa made films at the universities, behind the lines with the student movement. Then Tsuchimoto moved to Kyushu to record the devastating impact of Minamata disease, while Ogawa and his film collective (Ogawa Pro) joined the farmers in Sanrizuka, who were being evicted from their land for the construction of the new international airport at Narita.[10] With the appearance of these films, the work of older filmmakers appeared marked and inauthentic, and documentary realism experienced a sea change.

This was one of those moments when theory and practice evolved together, when the filmmakers were theorizing their own work. Artists like Matsumoto Toshio and Oshima Nagisa attacked the older styles as nothing more than a continuation of wartime conventions. They held that filmmakers adhering to the standard form of realism exhibited a Stalinist authoritarianism that restricted artistic and political expression for the sake of a faux objectivism. This style of documentary realism, they reasoned, was predicated upon a total suppression of the artist's subjectivity. Ironically, Hani's observational mode also involved a similar kind of suppression, even if it made the artifice of the mainstream style obvious. So, rather than continuing in Hani's direction—and there is no indication that they were aware of American direct cinema or the Rouch-style vérité—they moved documentary toward the avant-garde through an impressive combination of critical discourse and filmmaking practice. Matsumoto, for example, made experimental documentaries like *Security Treaty* (*AMPO Joyaku,* 1960), which shocked the documentary world with a surrealist approach to compilation and an agitprop narration. Other filmmakers followed his lead, both in filmmaking and in criticism and theory. These new experimental documentaries were the films that Hara was watching in the 1960s.

Hara was a fan of every genre of feature film, but it wasn't until he moved to Tokyo that he paid serious attention to documentary. It was probably impossible to miss this form of filmmaking at the time, considering the excitement over the radical student movement films of Tsuchimoto Noriaki, Ogawa Shinsuke, and many others. Like most young people interested in politics, Hara found himself drawn to the films from Ogawa Productions' Sanrizuka series. They were shown in public halls instead of regular theaters. The lines were long, and the energy at screenings was incredibly impressive. The theaters were often decorated for the film; spectators would wear helmets, sing songs, chant, give speeches, and hold after-film discussions. Years later, Hara recalls,

> I was deeply attracted to Ogawa Pro, the collective itself. . . . Actually, I never joined, but did think about it. Still, jumping into the middle of that kind of thing, I just couldn't imagine myself in that kind of collective. . . . Those people were, after all, from the sixties, one generation earlier. Since we were from the seventies . . . there's the question of who exactly is that self that's participating in the struggle. Oneself . . . who are you? We'd face that individual, our self, and ask that question. . . . Who are you, this individual that wants to express something? That's how we thought. For example, even if I entered Ogawa Pro, in the end it is my self that's wrapped up inside there. While I kept thinking that creating things within a collective was incredibly attractive, in the end those Ogawa Pro people were already doing it, so as for me, I might as well try and do it from this place called the individual.[11]

This comment edges us toward the issue that defines Hara's work, the problem that both sets him apart from his contemporaries and places him within the larger stream of Japanese documentary. Theorists, journalists, and filmmakers posed the nonfiction film as the trace of a meeting between human beings, between filmmaker and a collaborating subject. Not surprisingly, the terminology in Japanese is significantly different. Writers and filmmakers always speak of a *shutai* (subject/filmmaker) and a *taisho* (object/filmed). By way of contrast, Euro-American theory speaks of the sign and its bracketed referent. It is the difference between discussing human beings or a material reality. Thus, while the Japanese discourse arguably suffers from a philosophical poverty, it simultaneously focuses on the qualities of representations of human beings in a language available to artists without specialized training in psychoanalysis or other critical systems. In other words, Japanese documentarists take issues of representation extremely seriously and come to their work armed with a body of thought grounded in a politicized sociality.[12]

Therefore, for Hara the very notion of private must be undergirded by a regulation coming from without, which is to say the dynamic between private and public is enforced through mores and social controls that penetrate and construct private space. This renders the binary opposition between the two terms relatively meaningless. Hara feels compelled to uncover this secret relationship of the private and public by using the camera to provoke policing, making the political implications visible and palpable. In this sense, that policing is an activity from the lived world and at the same time a process deeply inscribed in the film: "Within this private area, I think there's something like a contradiction that we hold. . . . To speak of this privacy, we talk about individual people's values and sensitivities. When you look at the sensitivities and feelings of those kinds of individuals, I end up thinking that within their own self-contradictions the establishment or something systemic (*seidoteki*) is thoroughly incorporated. Therefore, regarding that systemic thing, when we strike out with the camera, the target we face is, after all, that world of individual feelings. To this end, what is necessary is stepping into the private sphere."[13]

Extreme Private Eros pointed to a transformation in Japanese documentary from the collective modes of filmmaking best represented by Ogawa Pro and Tsuchimoto to the highly individualized and artisanal practice being pioneered by Hara. This change, turning around a vague point in the mid-1970s, is deeply connected to cultural shifts Japan shared with other localities in the world, a move from forms of committed, collective, social activism and public passions to more private concerns. While a similar vector in the West led to theories and art practices that recognized the political dimensions of the private, forms of so-called private film in Japan ended up largely apolitical. Hara's work stands out for its intellectual vigor and constant provocation of privacy politics. After the unqualified success of *Extreme Private Eros,* he went thirteen years before releasing his next major film. In the meantime, Hara and Kobayashi made *History Starts Here: "Women, Now . . ."* (*Rekishi wa koko ni hajimaru 'Onnatachi wa ima . . .'*), a television documentary for the TBS network in 1975. He survived largely by working as an assistant director for major filmmakers like Imamura Shohei (on *Vengeance Is Mine* [*Fukushu suru wa ware ni are,* 1979] and *Ei ja nai ka* [1980]), Urayama Kiriro (on *The Children of the Sun* [*Taiyo no ko (tedanofwa),* 1980]), and Kumai Kei (on *Sea and Poison* [*Umi to dokuyaku,* 1986]). All the while, he worked on his next film, *The Emperor's Naked Army Marches On* (*Yuki yukite shingun*), which was released to an explosive reception in 1987. In addition to a long run at the prestigious Eurospace Theater in Tokyo,

Hara received the New Director Award from the Japan Film Directors' Association, as well as prizes at the Berlin and Cinéma du Reel festivals. It was one of the first Japanese documentaries to find a distributor in the United States since Hani's *Children Who Draw*.[14]

The film is about veteran Okuzaki Kenzo's search for the truth behind the deaths of two comrades in arms in 1945. Okuzaki is well known in Japan for his loud protests about wartime atrocities and the need for politicians and the emperor to take responsibility for the war. This activism included outrageous stunts like shooting a steel *pachinko* ball at Emperor Hirohito and passing out pornographic leaflets depicting the imperial family. Imamura Shohei introduced Okuzaki to Hara in 1981 after deciding not to make a film about the activist himself. Hara took on the project, following Okuzaki in his single-minded quest.

Okuzaki is, by anyone's measure, relatively insane. In the pursuit of history, he is a "dogged empiricist," to borrow a phrase from Jeffrey and Kenneth Ruoff. Hauling Hara all over Japan, Okuzaki is committed to nailing down the facts about the suspicious deaths once and for all. However, in his pursuit of "truth" Okuzaki resorts to constant "lies." The basic structure of the film revolves around Okuzaki's visits—with Hara in tow—to his old army buddies. One by one, Okuzaki interrogates them about the events of 1945. Gradually, a picture takes shape: Okuzaki was not present because he had been captured in the final months of the war in New Guinea, the two comrades were shot by a firing squad composed of his own unit, and the charges were desertion. The problem is that the desertion charges and subsequent executions occurred after the war was over.

Okuzaki resorts to unconventional interview tactics for the film. He abruptly shows up at the homes of the remaining members of his unit (twelve elderly men from the thirty survivors of a contingent of troops numbering one thousand).[15] His unannounced arrival catches them off guard, and they hesitate in brushing him off. The presence of the brother and sister of each dead soldier probably contributed to their politeness, although Hara's film crew might have had something to do with it as well. In each meeting, Okuzaki and the relatives plead and cajole the men into telling their stories. Each offers a small piece of the puzzle before telling them to let the dead lie in peace. Finally, in the face of such insistent stonewalling, Okuzaki suddenly jumps from his seat and begins beating one of the old men. Hara continued to film.

Needless to say, this raises a spectrum of issues regarding the ethics of documentary representation. From this point on, every encounter is marked by the inclination to use violence on Okuzaki's part and Hara's willingness to provoke and record this violence. Okuzaki now greets the obfuscations with threats that haunt each encounter: "I've shot pachinko balls at the emperor, so don't think I won't beat you up." Okuzaki even attacks one man recuperating from an operation. As a spectator of this violence, we are pushed off balance by the gravity of the final revelations. The two soldiers were indeed executed by their own men after the war. This was a standard practice: the weakest, lowest-ranked, and most problematic members of the unit were singled out for execution and cannibalization. The two men had been eaten.

These revelations are profound, and the force of their disclosure *feels* unfathomable, immeasurably heavy. This epistemological weightiness comes largely from Hara's penetration of the private spaces where this knowledge resided, in that most private realm of human memory. However, this personal form of media also has a deeply social level. The memories protected by such privacy were networked by a national suppression of discourses engaging wartime violence and responsibility. As one of Okuzaki's interlocutors recalls, cannibalism in New Guinea in 1945 was a way of life for the emperor's army. The postwar, mnemonic defenses circled around this knowledge. Its shunting into quiet, private spaces was a complex process connected to other struggles over wartime memory and responsibility, issues such as violence against civilians, the abysmal treatment of prisoners of war, and the military's organized efforts at forced prostitution.

The exposure of this private space relies distinctly on a multivalent performance. Okuzaki's outrageous, flamboyant style is clearly a spectacle de-

signed for his interlocutors and for Hara. He answers threats to call the police by putting in the call himself. When the relatives of the slain soldiers tire of Okuzaki's manner and strategies, he simply has his wife act as the sister and an anarchist friend play the brother. Even the violence itself is performative; they kick and wail and thrash about on the ground. But Okuzaki is more interested in provoking that revelation of memory than in injuring his rhetorical opponent. This use of performance points us to the rhetoric of documentary as well.

1. Okusaki demands the truth in *The Emperor's Naked Army Marches On*, Kazuo Hara, 1987. (Still courtesy of the University of Michigan, Department of Asian Languages and Cultures.)

Susan Scheibler has argued that most documentary is a form of constative event. The constative is a use of language that guarantees authority and authenticity. There is a sticky, snug fit between sign and referent. For Scheibler, the constative is the foundation of traditional documentary realism, which draws on the indexical qualities of the photo-mechanical image to assert a confidence in the adequacy and completeness of its representation of the world. If the traditional documentary is predicated on a constative enunciation, the newer, essayistic forms of documentary are performative. The films of documentarists like Trinh T. Minh-ha, Errol Morris, Jill Godmilow, and Marlon Riggs are characterized by breaks, ruptures, and reflexivity. While the reality effect of most documentary relies on the human desire for the constative, Scheibler argues that the documentaries of these artists capitalize on performative enunciative acts. They circulate around the constative and performative in the form of a "struggle [that] plays itself out in the discursive arena by performatively confronting the constative with its own assumptions of authority, authenticity, veracity, verifiability."[16]

Austin himself called the performative "perfectly straightforward utterances with ordinary verbs in the first person singular present indicative active . . . if a person makes an utterance of this sort we should say that he is doing something rather than merely saying something."[17] Thus, the performative treats facticity as less important; it is an enunciation outside of verification, one that sidesteps binaries like true and false and eschews a straightforward, conventional documentary realism. Bill Nichols appended his modes of documentary with the "performative" to account for them.[18] Michael Renov has more convincingly called them "essayistic" works.[19] However, both Renov and Nichols use their terms to isolate a variety of very recent documentaries and describe their formal and epistemological innovations, Renov to valorize them and Nichols to top off a historical time line. Hara's practice points to the ways in which performance and privacy appear to be fundamental to documentary itself, suggesting that the recent phenomenon of the essayistic documentary is predicated on something more basic.

Hara's action documentary points us toward the performative in the everyday, a performative enunciation that makes documentary itself possible. His films rarely exhibit the experimental qualities of the filmmakers listed above. Rather, in the tradition of his colleagues in the Japanese documentary, his cinema is always the record of a meeting between the filmmaker and the filmed, between subject and object. His films begin with the presence of the filmmaker penetrating private space, exposing it to the glaringly public view of the cinema. The dramas that unfold depend upon a slippery sense that the events unfolding are performative acts rather than observed reality mindlessly captured by the camera. The difference between the violence of, for example, the Rodney King videotape and Hara's films is that the latter are always self-conscious performances for the camera, for the world. The violence is real enough, and it hurts, whether it be Takeda Miyuki berating Hara or Okuzaki Kenzo kicking an army buddy, but it is a violence that requires the documentary cinema.

What Hara's films suggest is that most documentary is constituted by performative enunciations masquerading as constative ones and that the most private-appearing spaces are thoroughly raked by public systems and gazes. The extremes he is willing to go to foreground this triad of film/filmmaker/filmed teases us with the possibility that the documentary as a form relies heavily on the conversion of all human action and language as performative enunciations for the camera. It is only that Hara's cinema teases this performance to the surface by playing with the lines between the private and public space. Without this, documentary would be nothing but surveillance. The lives Hara's subjects offer up are not simply false or fictive, but they are not exactly innocently "true" either—even with Okuzaki's obsessive quest to uncover lies. There is a winking conspiracy between these charismatic social actors, director Hara, and their audiences. His next film, a portrait of the famous novelist Inoue Mitsuharu, sheds light on this problematic.

In the midst of shooting *A Full Life,* I came across Hara in the United States, where he was enjoying an extended visit under the auspices of the Asian Cultural Council and the Cultural Ministry. Based in New York, he was enthusiastically researching the history of documentary at places like the Museum of Modern Art and New York University. Undoubtedly, he was driven in part by a problem that had arisen in his Inoue project: the novelist was dying. A film that was to portray the life and life energy of a charismatic author was suddenly diverted to representing his death. And upon that death how does one go about representing the life no longer present? Hara turned to issues of performance, and that brought fundamental questions about documentary form to the fore.

The first image of the film is a grotesque and amusing dance by Inoue in geisha drag. It then alternates between interviews, scenes of Inoue teaching seminars, and fictional sequences. The latter are dreamy reenactments of the novelist's early years; they emerge full blown from his nostalgic reminiscences, which are laced with the sharp, ironic humor of bragging. Inoue was clearly another charismatic, magnetic personality for Hara. Having been invited in, Hara delights in edging closer and closer to this man's life, loves, and impending death. The filmmaker goes as far as documenting, in close-up, Inoue's open heart surgery.

Finally, upon the novelist's death, Hara's continuing investigation begins to turn up one surprise after another. Inoue's date of birth was inconsistent. He didn't drop out of school. The novelist's story about losing his virginity with a young Korean prostitute was fabricated. All of the key circumstances of Inoue's early life, stories repeated constantly over the years, information featured in the histories of modern Japanese literature, were fiction. The novelist had written his own biography. His entire life was a performance!

Hara exploits this discovery to interrogate the shifting boundaries between fiction and documentary from a new perspective. As an artist, he initially deploys fictional re-creation of history as a constative reiteration of the life described in interviews. There is nothing particularly innovative about this. However, upon the discovery of Inoue's fanciful recollections — the *writing* of his life — Hara brings back his fictional sequences, turning them against the interviews to point to a performance at the heart of the interviews' utterances. He peels away the constative stickiness between oral interview and history. To extend Hara's observations and consider the implications of this for documentary as a form, we might turn to the work of Margaret Morse.

In *Virtualities,* Morse makes a convincing case for understanding the powerful cultural position of television in the late twentieth century. She is interested in the way we have come to grant human qualities like subjectivity to machines, from computers to television. Human beings have a deep need for intersubjective engagement, a desire that television engages as a machine featuring a simulation of human subjectivity. This is effectively accomplished in television through full frontal, direct address by charismatic anchors using words like *we* and *you*. Drawing on Derrida, she argues that the gap between enunciation and meaning is what makes television possible: "The argument to be made here is *not* that once there was something sincere and unmediated called face-to-face conversation of which exchanges mediated by television and the computer are inherently inauthentic or debased simulations. If anything, machine subjects are made possible by the fundamental gap that has always existed between language and the world and between *utterances*—be they subjective or impersonal—and the act of enunciation—whether it is produced by a human subject or has been delegated to machines."[20]

Morse points to a human need for and pleasure in being recognized as a partner in discourse—even if a machine stands in between subjects. This explains one of the reasons why documentary has persisted for a century, even if relegated to a marginalized position, and why it came to settle into modes so reliant on the interview and direct address. Most critical attention in documentary theory has gone to the innovative and politically progressive work of performative documentary (such as *Nitrate Kisses* and *Tongues Untied*), for all the reasons charted by Scheibler. Because of this focus, documentary theory and criticism have not dealt adequately with (post-direct-cinema) television, even though the vast majority of documentary is now distributed through this medium. While the relationship between documentary realism and television has yet to be mapped, we can see that the emergence of interview-heavy documentary coincides with the rise of television as a cultural form. The pleasures of documentary may not be reduceable to the virtual engagement with charismatic on-screen subjectivities, but it certainly is a fundamental starting point.

Hara intrigues because there is no question that the interview—with spectacularly charismatic figures—is his starting point, yet he diverts us to another dimension in intersubjective engagement mediated by cameras and screens. Indeed, from a historical perspective the formal break represented by Ogawa and Tsuchimoto was precisely the search for a style that foregrounded the intersubjective nature of nonfiction filmmaking by immersing the documentary process in social communities under siege. Hara extended their innovations by turning the camera to the self with his "action documentary." Interestingly enough, his 1998 documentary on his mentor, Urayama Kiriro, is the culmination of his increasing reliance on the interview.[21] However, it is significant that Hara chooses his objects so carefully. He clearly takes delight in approaching a highly glamorous and even dangerous object. His own humanity and his desire for discursive exchange with these seductive other subjects are mediated by machines at a different level; his machine is the camera. This is what is so distinctive about Hara's cinema. Recall the opening sequence of *Extreme Private Eros,* where he states this dynamic specifically: "I have this relationship; I was losing her, and couldn't let her go. It seemed the only way to keep our relationship going was to make a film." It is also what he has most strongly in common with his fellow documentarists in Japan, who have—at least in the postwar era—defined documentary practice in terms of a relationship between *shutai* = subject = filmmaker and *taisho* = object = filmed. The film is a vestige of this relationship, captured on celluloid and offered up for a virtual engagement with spectators.

Hara has often said that "documentary is the recording of '*ki*.'"[22] This is an extremely loaded term. The Chinese character itself refers to "spirit, mind, soul, heart; intention; bent, interest; mood, feeling; temper, disposition, nature; care, attention; air, atmosphere; flavor; odor; energy, essence, air, indication, symptoms; taste; touch, dash, shade, trace; spark, flash; suspicion." It is commonly combined with verbs (in a kind of linguistic montage) for various inflections: "doing *ki*" means "be nervous about"; "having *ki*" indicates "having the intention"; you notice something when you "attach *ki*"; "*ki* stands" when you get excited; you "become *ki*" when you worry; and so on. What does it mean to "record *ki*"? I think it has to do with describing a trace of that intersubjective moment of filming, committing it to celluloid or tape in order to offer it up again for another intersubjective moment in the performance at the theater.

Hara brings us to this point by discovering the performance at the heart of documentary, a discovery he makes by aggressively penetrating the private spaces in this most public of media. That is why Hara is the most exciting of all Japanese documentarists.[23] The actors in Hara's last films appear keenly aware that to some inestimable degree, the deployment of fictions approaches a knowledge that is embodied and social and escapes the logic of true/false, real/unreal. Needless to say, this is not the conventional wisdom of the documentary, for Hara carries us back in an arc that touches the pre-Iwanami documentary without bringing us full circle.

Notes

1   On Hara's work, see Kenneth J. Ruoff and Jeffrey K. Ruoff, "Japan's Outlaw Filmmaker: An Interview with Hara Kazuo," *Iris: A Journal on Image and Sound* 16 (spring 1993): 103–114 Akira Iriye, "*The Emperor's Naked Army Marches On*," *American Historical Review* 94:4 (October 1989): 1036–7 Makiko Ogihara, "*The Emperor's Naked Army Marches On*," *Japan Times*, August 4, 1987, 11; Jeffrey Ruoff and Kenneth Ruoff, *The Emperor's Naked Army Marches On* (London: Flicks Books, 1998); and Laura Marks, "Naked Truths: Hara Kazuo's Iconoclastic Obsessions," *Independent* 15:10 (1992): 25–27. In Japanese, see

Sayonara CP (Tokyo: Shisso Productions, 1972); *Yuki yukite shingun Seisaku Noto* (Tokyo: Shisso Productions, 1987); *Zenshin shosetsuka* (Tokyo: Kinema Junposha, 1994); *Gunron Yuki yukite shingun,* edited by Matsuda Masao and Takahashi Taketomo (Tokyo: Togosha, 1988); Hara Kazuo, *Fumikoeru Kamera: Waga Hoho, Akushon Dokyumentarii,* (Tokyo: Firumu Aatosha, 1995); and Hara Kazuo, *Eiga ni Tsukarete* (Tokyo: Gendai Shokan, 1998).

2   Hara, *Fumikoeru Kamera,* 47–49.

3   Clearly, these television documentaries require more comment. However, this is difficult because they have largely been ignored by Japanese film historians and there are no archives holding them for research purposes. Hara himself began this research in late 1998 through the organization of a kind of "short course" on the subject in Osaka. For the last few years, Hara's production office has been buzzing with the energy of young people as they organize what they call Cinema Juku, literally "Cinema cram courses." These are short events in which Hara appears with famous Japanese actors, directors, and cinematographers to discuss various issues. In toto, they constitute an impressive body of research into Japanese film and some of its neglected areas, including television documentary. It culminated in a 16mm documentary produced collaboratively with his students entitled *My Mishima* (*Watakushi no Mishima,* 1999). This signals Hara's turn from the individual to a collective mode reminiscent of the filmmakers he broke with in the early 1970s. Indeed, talk of Ogawa Productions frequently enters his public rhetoric (he was one of the filmmakers interviewed in Barbara Hammer's documentary on the collective, entitled *Devotion* [2000]). Hara's current project, however, is a feature film.

4   Takeda's life is clearly a personalization of politics from a feminist point of view. The women's liberation movement in Japan is often ignored by commentators on Japan, while the sexism of Japanese patriarchy has very nearly become an object of obsession. Takeda points to a far more complicated situation. Her excesses seem to have become stereotyped by more conservative women today, who often associate feminism with obnoxiousness even if their lives embody many of the core values of feminism. Hara himself presents a paradoxical example. In many respects, he is one of the most progressive filmmakers with respect to feminist politics. His work with Kobayashi is clearly a deep collaboration, and I have been impressed, for example, seeing him allow a female staff member to work at the office with her newborn. However, the progressivism of a film like *Extreme Private Eros* is called into doubt by his recent work.

5   Ruoff and Ruoff, *The Emperor's Naked Army Marches On,* 6–7.

6   He actually uses the word *cinema vérité,* but his argument to collapse American and French practices is neither convincing or historiographically useful.

7   William Rothman, *The "I" of the Camera: Essays in Film Criticism, History, and Aesthetics* (Cambridge: Cambridge University Press, 1988).

8   William Rothman, *Documentary Film Classics* (Cambridge: Cambridge University Press, 1997), 119.

9   For a history of prewar and wartime Japanese documentary (forthcoming) Japanee Documentary Film: From the Meiji Era Through Hiroshima (forthcoming) Univ. of Minnesota Press, 2003. see Peter High's *Imperial Screen* and my own *Forest of Pressure* (both forthcoming).

10 Sanrizuka is the name of the village now under the cement of Narita International Airport. When the government announced the eviction of farmers from their ancestral

land, the farmers staged massive protests with the help of the student movement and various activist organizations. The protests involved tens of thousands of people, and were violent enough to cause deaths. The Ogawa Pro collective based itself in the village of Sanrizuka and documented the struggle for nearly a decade. The protests continue today, with farmers refusing to sell strategic lands. Any visitor to Japan should look out the windows of Terminal 2, where they'll see a small patch of mulberry bushes in the middle of the tarmac, bushes tended by a reticent farmer.

11 Hara, *Fumikoero Kamera,* 64–67.

12 This is an exceedingly complicated discourse, with roots in larger debates within Marxism during the occupation period (which in turn is based on prewar social theories within the Left). I discuss the genealogy of these debates over *shutaisei* at length in "The Postwar Documentary Trace: groping in the Dark," in Open to the Public: Studies in Japan's Recent Past, ed. Leslie Pincus, a special issue of Positions 10:1 (Spring 2002): 39–78.

13 Hara, *Fumikoero Kamera,* 8.

14 The film is distributed by Kino International of New York. For countries outside of the United States, contact the Japan Foundation.

15 Ruoff and Ruoff, *The Emperor's Naked Army Marches On,* 11.

16 Ibid., 140. Associating constative forms of documentary realism with nonfiction's plenitude, Scheibler turns to the suture theory of Jean-Pierre Oudart and Daniel Dayan. This seems to me to be a retreat to an earlier brand of film theory, replicating the problematic valorization of Brechtian distanciation as progressive politics and in effect reconstructing the binary difference that Derrida critiques.

17 Quoted in Susan Scheibler, "Constantly Performing the Documentary: The Seductive Promise of *Lightning over Water,*" in *Theorizing Documentary,* edited by Michael Renov (New York: Routledge, 1993), 139.

18 Bill Nichols, *Blurred Boundaries: Questions of Meaning in Contemporary Culture* (Bloomington: Indiana University Press, 1994), 92–106. The original modes were presented in Bill Nichols, *Representing Reality* (Bloomington: Indiana University Press, 1991).

19 For example, see Michael Renov, "The Subject in History: The New Autobiography in Film and Video," *Afterimage* (summer 1989): 4–7.

20 Margaret Morse, *Virtualities* (Bloomington: Indiana University Press, 1998), 14.

21 The documentary was produced for television and is nothing but interviews with the dead director's friends, actors, and relatives. In fact, Hara published a 492-page collection of the full conversations, billing it as an "interview documentary" on the cover: Hara Kazuo, *Eiga ni Tsukarete: Urayama Kiriro* (Obsessed by movies: Urayama Kiriro) (Tokyo: Gendai Shokan, 1998).

22 Hara Kazuo, "Extreme Private Eros—Love Song 1974," in *Japanese Documentary: The 70s,* edited by Yasui Yoshio (Tokyo: Yamagata International Documentary Film Festival, 1995), 30.

23 This is why Hara is more interesting than Tsuchimoto and more like Ogawa. The latter turned to performance and fiction in his last film, *Magino Village: A Tale (Magino monogatari: Sennen kizamino hidokei,* 1987), and after his death it was discovered that his biography, like Inoue's, was largely a personal fiction.

Mike Leigh's Modernist Realism

Richard Porton

We should monotonize existence so existence isn't so monotonous. We should turn everyday life into something anodyne so the tiniest thing would be amusing—Fernando Pessoa

As old aesthetic debates grow moldy, it has become increasingly apparent that polemics both promoting and devaluing the spectral category of "realism" are largely unilluminating. To a certain extent, the polarization between advocates of "critical" and "socialist" realism such as Georg Lukács and champions of modernism, most notably Roland Barthes, was engendered by now outmoded cold war tensions. During his long literary career, Lukács gravitated from near slavish obeisance to the Stalinist status quo to a restrained dissidence that led to his imprisonment during the Hungarian Revolution of 1956.[1] He never, however, wavered from his belief that the modernism of Kafka, Joyce, and Beckett (all of whom arguably derived sustenance from the work of nineteenth-century "realists" such as Balzac and Dickens) was irredeemably "decadent." Conversely, the nausea Barthes felt when confronted with mimesis's "conservative reproduction of already existing signs"[2] was an implicitly Left-libertarian response to the aesthetic conservatism of leftists, of whom Lukács remains the most sophisticated representative.

Contemporary theatrical and cinematic realism, which has spawned hybrid styles and genres, presents even thornier quandaries. Among contemporary filmmakers, no one exemplifies the paradoxes of what might be termed "modernist" realism better than the British playwright and screenwriter-director Mike Leigh. Like Charles Dickens, the most blatantly theatrical of nineteenth-century novelists, Leigh uses comic hyperbole to indict the established order. Usually facilely pigeonholed as examples of British realism, Leigh's films are as indebted to British comic traditions and the theater of the absurd. Seminal Leigh films such as *Life Is Sweet* (1990) and *Naked* (1993) are no more straightforwardly realist than Lars von Trier's *Breaking the Waves* (1996) or Atom Egoyan's *The Sweet Hereafter* (1998). While Leigh's films are as character driven as Dickens's novels, it is useful to recall Theodor Adorno's observation that "Dickens and Balzac . . . are not so realistic after all . . . [and] the whole *Comédie Humaine* proves to be an imaginative construction of an alienated reality."[3] Nevertheless, he has been constantly saddled with often unfair accusations of patronizing his (usually) working-class and lower-middle-class protagonists by turning them into grotesque caricatures. Since much of the critical antipathy toward Leigh's work stems from an inability—or an unwillingness—to come to terms with his eclectic theatrical influences, a brief excursus is necessary to clarify the context that engendered Leigh's idiosyncratic meld of Brecht and Beckett.

Brecht's realism—a nonnaturalistic insistence on "laying bare society's casual network/showing up the dominant viewpoint as the viewpoint of the dominators"—enlivened a broad stratum of British radical and working class theater during the 1960s and 1970s.[4] Consequently, radical dramatists who worked within the commercial and subsidized sphere such as John Arden and Trevor Griffiths, as well as militant collectives like the 7.84 Theatre Company, which spurned mainstream venues like the National Theatre, shared Brecht's desire to "refunction" the bourgeois sphere through theatrical interventions that effaced traditional boundaries between aesthetics and politics. All of the British neo-Brechtians, moreover, followed their mentor's injunction to fuse didactic realism with popular theatrical traditions. In Arden's *Non-Stop Connolly Show,* for example, *Lehrstück* coalesced with vaudeville during a fourteen-hour piece of agitprop chronicling the life of the fiery Irish nationalist, James Connolly.[5] A more diluted Brechtianism is discernible in Arnold Wesker's work, but, paradoxically enough, his social-democratic morality plays were tethered to a hyper-naturalistic aesthetic. Wesker, however, was sophisticated enough to know that strict verisimilitude did not entail an illusory transparency. His most celebrated play, *The Kitchen,* required a meticulously authentic re-creation of a huge restaurant kitchen, but John Dexter, the director of the original production, cannily offset this superficially slavish exercise in naturalism with a highly stylized approach that illuminated the hierarchical division of labor within the service industry. If Brecht sneered at middle-class drama as "culinary" theater, Wesker's portrait of one kitchen's class divisions and ethnic conflicts strives to reveal the sweat and rancor that makes culinary pleasure possible.

For Adorno, Beckett's seemingly apolitical drama captured capitalist alienation and deindividuation with more accuracy than Brecht's didactic plays. Harold Pinter, Beckett's leading British disciple, offered the most influential alternative to Wesker and Arden's social realism. Yet, although Pinter eschews the polemical style of Arden and Wesker, unlike Beckett, his work is marked by what one admirer terms "extreme naturalism."[6] Oddly enough, Pinter's clipped, elliptical dialogue often resembles Noel Coward's repartee, even though the ambiance of his early plays could not be farther removed from the upper-class flippancy of *Private Lives. The Homecoming* is a paradigmatic example of Pinter's blend of detailed naturalism, Coward-like badinage and a mordant view of individuals, who, like Beckett's protagonists, are unable to extricate themselves from the constrictions of what Adorno termed their "wretched realities."

Bleak Moments (1971), Leigh's first feature film, despite its almost documentarylike evocation of the London suburbs, is his most Pinteresque evocation of urban desolation. Leigh's biographer, Michael Coveney, observes that this assured blend of humor and pathos is suffused with a "mood of . . . Slavic despair."[7] The film concerns the plight of Sylvia, a painfully shy young woman whose morbid introspection seems inseparable from her grim neighborhood with its many streets of identical row houses. Like the feuding friends of *Career Girls* (1997), Sylvia owns a copy of *Wuthering Heights,* even though her romantic (or Romantic) urges cannot be expressed with anything approaching the carefree abandon possessed by the later film's heroines. Since everyday life is an onerous burden in *Bleak Moments,* the hapless characters cannot even consider the possibility that it might be even temporarily negated. Oddly enough, it is the mark of Leigh's brilliance that he can render unalloyed depression unnervingly funny. Sylvia's agonizingly awkward date with Peter, a tongue-tied teacher who is nearly as introverted as his paramour, consists of exchanges that are as elliptical as anything in Pinter as well as long patches of silence. Norman, a folksinger whose spectacularly banal renditions of American ditties such as "Freight Train" charm Sylvia and her retarded sister, encapsulates *Bleak Moments*'s comic enervation.

Characters like Peter, Sylvia, and Norman are rendered with both empathy and astringency, but audiences are occasionally unsure whether Leigh is satirizing or celebrating his dramatis personae. This befuddlement can probably be attributed to the fact that Leigh downplays, but does not completely eschew, the Balzacian tendency to, in the words of Erich Auerbach, "accompany his narrative with a running commentary—emotional or ironic or ethical or historical or economic."[8] Nothing quite that nakedly didactic ever surfaces in Leigh's films. He implicitly concurs with Flaubert and "modernist realists" that "every event, if one is able to express it purely and completely, interprets itself and the persons involved in it far better and more completely than any opinion or judgment appended to it could do."[9] The languid exchanges between the characters, often punctuated with generous pauses, are hugely reminiscent of early Pinter plays such as *A Night Out* and *A Slight Ache*—austere but brilliantly paced evocations of marital discord and familial tensions that resemble Beckett-suffused blackout sketches rather than melodrama.

In fact, Pinter's disdain for "the writer who puts forward his concern for you to embrace, who leaves you no doubt of his worthiness, his usefulness, his altruism" is shared by Leigh and suggests why some of his harshest critics were repulsed by his aesthetic stance.[10] Most of his critics have little trouble with Leigh's indebtedness to certain offshoots of modernist dramaturgy; what perturbs them most is the social realist, explicitly naturalistic veneer of films that (although they are ostensibly sympathetic to the Left) abjure Brechtian revolutionary uplift. On the other hand, many observers also fail to appreciate the fact that, while Leigh's actors borrow their gestures and dialogue (improvised in rehearsal and then incorporated into a final shooting script) from empirical observation, their impersonations often partake of a style reminiscent of Brecht's *gestus* or "quotable gesture." Leigh, paradoxically enough, emphasizes his preoccupation with the "detailed study of actual physical, rhythmic speech patterns—like real people, like you and me,"[11] but strenuously maintains that his films promote a clarity through distance that he unhesitatingly labels "alienation."[12]

Paraphrasing Marx, Brecht proclaimed that his Lehrstücke were didactic plays, providing a place for "philosophers . . . who not only wish to explain the world but wish to change it."[13] Conversely, Leigh rejects Brecht's assumption that drama can possess an instrumental "use value." One of his most accomplished BBC films, *Home Sweet Home* (1982), a painfully funny saga of three bumbling postmen, although not detached enough to refrain from offering "didactic" judgments concerning small-town ennui and bureaucratic ineptitude, demonstrates Leigh's departure from—as well as his debt to—Brechtian agitprop. Nevertheless, his penchant for extracting performances from actors that are superficially naturalistic but resemble Brecht's "quotable gestures"—gestures designed to defamiliarize the quirks of "natural" behavior—is also evident.

The central character is Stan, a lugubrious postman who attempts to forget about the wife who abandoned him and his daughter Tina—sadly confined to a foster home—by conducting furtive affairs with his colleagues' wives. Nevertheless, as is often true in Leigh, the more peripheral characters are more central to the film's ideological thrust. The two social workers who visit Stan on behalf of Tina drive home the distance between Leigh's often dyspeptic form of satire and conventional filmic realism and the strange affinities between *Home Sweet Home* and Brecht's more engagé perspective. The sequences featuring these two hapless social workers recall Brecht's fusion of pleasure and instruction, despite the fact that the film's Left-liberal critics were distinctly annoyed by the sardonic treatment of welfare state pieties. Melody, the first case worker (who appears to be two parts hippie and one part yuppie), scolds Stan for neglecting Tina, but her patronizing manner proves as off-putting as it is ineffectual. She smiles incessantly and spouts bromides such as "deviancy is caused by insecurity" while Stan stoically endures the session. Melody's successor, Dave, a young case worker who shares Melody's comic incompetence, chides his predecessor for her "quiche Lorraine" utopianism and mumbles Marxist clichés concerning commodity fetishism and "peripheral substructures" under his breath. In all of these sequences, platitudinous monologues by well-meaning individuals concerned with Tina's plight alternate with close-ups of Stan, whose expression seamlessly combines bewilderment and irritation.

Leigh's scathing thumbnail sketch of an incongruously militant altruist may seem gratuitously cruel. However, like Brecht's conception of the gestus, which fuses the "stylized and the natural," Leigh's seeming "caricatures" are attributable to a similar dynamic. Rather misleadingly, Leigh's preoccupation with how "real people" behave recalls Stanislavsky's detailed advocacy of "physical actions," not Brecht's musings on the gestus. This celebration of what might be termed "behavioral realism" notwithstanding, *Home Sweet Home*'s acerbic depictions of social workers short-circuits the tendency of audience members to empathize with such innocuous eccentrics and promotes disidentification. Instead of galvanizing spectators with proletarianized "consciousness raising" à la Brecht, Leigh's mode of distantiation challenges his nominally "liberal" viewers to see a mirror image of their own condescension in these ineffectual members of the "helping professions." The decision to follow Dave's maunderings with a parodic version of "The Internationale" on the sound track is not a conservative flourish but an indictment of his bad faith leftist rhetoric, which does nothing to effectively puncture the status quo. As Fredric Jameson observes, the "gestus simply identified the nature of the act itself, showing private emotion to be socially and economically functional, and in general revealing the basis of individual psychology in social dynamics."[14]

Playwright David Edgar's accusation that *Home Sweet Home,* with its deadpan focus on Stan's limited aspirations, is dripping with contempt for its protagonists echoes other liberal and left-wing critics' misgivings concerning Leigh's entire career. But, as Andy Medhurst, one of Leigh's most articulate champions, observes, the chorus of critics who maintain that Leigh is patronizing "are only really projecting their own guilty anxieties onto the films he makes . . . as if the (working class) were proletarian pandas in need of protection."[15] In fact, Leigh's refusal to create unblemished working-class icons is congruent with his analogous demystification of middle-class leftists and could be viewed as his own cranky version of *plumpes Denken.* These nuanced portrayals helped prevent Leigh's most sardonic anti-Thatcher films—*Life Is Sweet* and *High Hopes,* from degenerating into one-dimensional tracts. Leigh undoubtedly endorsed Nicola's anti-Thatcherite fury in *Life Is Sweet,* although this neurotic anorectic's self-loathing (fortunately) prevents her from becoming an exemplary heroine.

Leigh's fascination with the often "vulgar" particularities of working-class, lower-middle-class, and nouveau riche life, moveover, coincides with the recent theoretical attraction to "spatial politics," which bears the im-

1. *Life Is Sweet,* Mike Leigh, 1990. (Still courtesy of *Cineaste.*)

print of Henri Lefebvre's influence. The invention of "social geography," however, has its origins in the nineteenth century, particularly the utopian promise of the Paris Commune of 1871. This seventy-two-day experiment in proletarian self-activity exemplified anarchist geographer Elisée Reclus's conviction that "geography is not an immutable thing—it is made, it is remade every day; at every instant, it is modified by men's actions."[16]

Nevertheless, most exponents of spatial politics explore more recent —and dystopian—urban conundrums—flexible accumulation, which resulted in the erosion of the traditional industrial sector; gentrification of working-class neighborhoods; and the rise of the "informational city," with its attendant emphasis on surveillance. While Leigh eventually applied his comic scalpel to these quandaries in films such as *High Hopes* and *Naked,* an early film, *Abigail's Party* (the 1977 film is basically a filmed performance of a Leigh play), examines social geography in a more intimate fashion, revealing the implications of kitsch in all its horrific, and— on occasion—strangely appealing, glory. The play's text begins with detailed stage directions that describe the protagonists' house and party food with pithy humor and on-target sociological accuracy. Leigh calls attention to the couple's "leather three-piece suite, onyx coffee-table, sheepskin rug" and helpfully informs us that the hostess serves "two small platesful of home-made cheese-and-pineapple savories, each consisting of one cube of cheese and one chunk of pineapple on a stick." The focus on cringe-inducing ostentation is not intended to cruelly mock the upwardly mobile but desperately unhappy characters' taste; on the contrary, it entertainingly confirms Lefebvre's belief that "leisure time provides a paradoxical example of alienation within the pursuit of emancipation and the attempt to dis-alienate oneself."[17] Given Leigh's synthesis of the Brechtian and absurdist traditions, he often uses spatial metaphors to reveal the overt injuries of class and the anguish of interpersonal breakdown. In *Home Sweet Home,* the frustration that the working-class Stan experiences as he halfheartedly attempts to establish contact with his daughter are conveyed through ingenious, though unobtrusive, camera placements that circumscribe his milieu's grim topography: "a long shot of Stan and Tina in the scrubland of Stan's back garden, with a full view of the grim, pebbledash back wall, supplies the eloquent vacuum for their halting attempts in communication."[18]

Leigh's fascination with claustrophobic interiors—for example, houses, apartments, and offices—stands in sharp contrast to the much-vaunted realism prized by the British New Wave of the 1960s. Andrew Higson identifies "a tension between the demands of narrative and the demands of realism" in prototypical "kitchen sink" films such as Karel Reisz's *Saturday Night and Sunday Morning* (1960) and Tony Richardson's *A Taste of Honey* (1961).[19] Higson convincingly argues that British realists of the 1960s often deployed landscape shots—especially an "iconographic cliché" he identifies as "That Long Shot of Our Town"—that function more as the departure points for narrative spectacle than as harbingers of the political and historical critique traditionally associated with documentary (a genre not without its own unwitting appeals to the spectacular). Although Leigh himself once voiced ambivalence concerning the films of the period—praising them for their aspirations and taking them to task for the artificiality of their realism— his own films paradoxically achieve a greater verisimilitude by shunning the British New Wave's overt naturalism and embracing a theatrical stylization.[20]

A film like *Meantime* captures these opposing tensions with great savvy, since the film's protagonists—unemployed punks and punk wannabes— belong to a subculture that values defiant posturing, which is itself a form of urban theater. Leigh rejects the moralism of Richardson and Reisz, whose oddly picturesque urban settings served as lyrical preludes to the sermonizing endemic to "social problem" films. *Meantime* certainly indicts Thatcher-era unemployment and its ravaged victims, but the focus on the monotony of life on the dole and static and resolutely unmelodramatic lives is achieved through a scrupulous examination of everyday life that avoids the Manicheanism of much political cinema. Instead of pitting its morose unemployed protagonists—the terminally angry Mark Pollock, his endearingly dimwitted brother Colin, and their parents Mavis and Frank—against a monolithic "system," the narrative highlights circuitous, nonsequiturish conversations and muted confrontations that always end with a whimper rather than a catalytic bang.

Quite often, a minor but intractable problem aptly reflects Leigh's characters' profound social alienation. One of *Meantime*'s most representative sequences, for example, involves a jammed washing machine door. For several minutes of illuminating banality, the siblings and their mother bicker and are unable to solve this simple mechanical flaw. Leigh never stoops to underlining the jammed door as an explicit metaphor. Similarly, although the film does not shirk from that vulgar Marxists term *class analysis,* the distinctions between the working-class Pollocks and the suburban mores of

Mavis's sister are conveyed entirely through what Lefebvre terms "spatial life." But, while Lefebvre's utopian politics assumes that urban slums can be "severed . . . from the governing spatialisation and returned to the realm of 'communitas,'[21] *Meantime* convinces us that the Pollocks' council flat is an alienated space that fails to reveal any hidden liberatory crevices. "Auntie Barbara's" middle-class flat, however, is even less inviting: an antiseptic environment filled with pricey knickknacks that correspond precisely to her desperate cheerfulness.

Leigh's fondness for the accoutrements of domesticity—artifacts of social hierarchy—provides an ironic gloss to the early years of British punk.[22] Ignoring the more militant stirrings of British youth—personified by well-publicized riots in 1981—Leigh prefers to dwell on the external trappings of disaffection, particularly punk fashion. Christopher Prendergast claims that the significance of these trappings is not always entirely transparent: fashion, for example, often "blurs" rather than clarifies the nature of social status. It might be tempting to view Colin's ardent admiration of a snarling skinhead named Coxy—and Coxy's expensive Doc Martens boots —as indicative of misguided working-class rebellion. Yet, in contemporary England, despite a much more deeply entrenched class system than is common in most Western European countries, punk and skinhead costumes appealed to alienated youth from all classes. And Colin's admiration for the skinhead style is probably more a symptom of his desire to strip himself of class-specific traits than an emblem of even nascent class consciousness.

Colin's highly conformist style of rebellion could be viewed as a continuation of what many commentators labeled the British New Wave's tendency to deemphasize overt class conflict.[23] But *Meantime* refuses to embrace its predecessors' enshrinement of upwardly mobile male dynamism and debilitating female passivity. Both men and women are enveloped by defeatism in *Meantime,* but Leigh disdains both essentialist assumptions concerning sexual roles and the naive individualism embodied by films such as Jack Clayton's *Room at the Top* (1959). While a shot of a pram juxtaposed with windblown garbage exemplifies *Meantime*'s downbeat tenor, the film's pessimism is clearly the record of one historical moment, not an expression of eternal, immanent gloom.

Foregoing the taut minimalism of *Meantime,* Leigh's iconoclastic deployment of his own comic variant of Brecht's gestus was wedded to an incisive exploration of the spatial politics of gentrification in *High Hopes* (1988). Despite the superficially gritty delineation of posthippie angst and nouveau riche snobbery during the Thatcher era, the calculated hyperbole of the performances disturbed viewers and critics, who appeared to prefer undiluted—and nonironic—naturalism. In characteristic Leigh fashion, the plight of the protagonists—slightly disillusioned but still idealistic leftists named Cyril and Shirley—was counterbalanced, and on occasion superseded, by the passions of more mercurial minor characters. The cognitive dissonance that ensues when Cyril's doddering mother, Mrs. Bender, is stranded after misplacing her keys in an adjacent row house owned by a preening, absurdly self-satisfied yuppie (and Thatcherite) couple named Boothe-Braine is a case in point. The Boothe-Braines' hypermannered intonations and unselfconscious celebration of conspicuous consumption correspond to what Leigh believes is actual upper-middle-class behavior, while the actors' performance style, however suffused with "authenticity," requires them to revert to a ritualized "third-person" stance that resembles a zany cross-fertilization of Brechtian distantiation and British comic overkill in the tradition of Peter Sellers. The contrast, moveover, between Mrs. Bender's cozy but disheveled flat and the Boothe-Braines's chic, antiseptic brownstone renovation illustrates, in explicitly spatial terms, the chasm in class and status that separates them. Or, to invoke the jargon of radical geography, one commentator observes that gentrification enacts "class constitution through spatial reconstruction."[24]

To a large extent, *High Hopes* reiterates the near impossibility of resurrecting Brechtian-style consciousness-raising in an age when Popular Front verities are often—quite rightly—questioned. Unlike the intransigent certitude of the Lehrstück, *High Hopes* is suffused with political ambivalence. One of the film's most straightforward and moving scenes features Cyril and Shirley's visit to Marx's grave at Highgate Cemetery in London. The final thesis on Feuerbach engraved on Marx's tombstone ("Philosophers have only interpreted the world in various ways—the point, however, is to change it") inspired Brecht's didactic theater and its unqualified affirmation of an esthetic compatible with historical materialism. Leigh, on the other hand, found a 1990 Polish audience's disgust with this scene "confusing and disorientating."[25]

Even though *Meantime* and *High Hopes* refuse to offer false hope, their social milieu still recalls the familial nexus prized by working-class playwrights like Wesker, even though the socialist optimism of an early Wesker play such as *Chicken Soup With Barley* is never discernible.[26] While *Mean-*

time provided a jaundiced gloss on the Pollocks' failure to (in Lefebvrean terms) "regain control over the social reproduction of space," *Naked* revolves around Johnny, an abrasive loner who consciously rejects the humdrum annoyances of domestic life. Like Dostoyevsky's Underground Man, this Mancunian adrift in London celebrates his "own free and unfettered volition . . . inflamed sometimes to the point of madness." Johnny's nocturnal jaunts reveal him as a flaneur at the end of his tether, although this flaneur has none of Walter Benjamin's dispassionate erudition. Instead, his peripatetic outings evoke Georg Simmel's more mundane conception of the flaneur as a passive "*spectator* of the never-ending spectacle of crowded urban life." [27]

Johnny is far from passive, but this voluble, and frequently mean-spirited, hero's meanderings serve as gritty testimonies to how new modes of urbanization have transformed relationships between city dwellers. Edward W. Soja, one of Lefebvre's leading disciples, documents how "old urban cores became increasingly tertiarized, replacing lost industries with an expanding number of corporate headquarters . . . government offices, financial institutions and supportive service and surveillance activities." [28] These affinities between the centralization of corporate power and surveillance assume pungently anecdotal form in *Naked*. At a crucial juncture in the film, Johnny finds refuge in a sterile office building where he alternately befriends—and mercilessly harangues—a gentle nightwatchman named Brian. "You've succeeded in convincin' me that you do 'ave the most tedious fuckin' job in England," announces Johnny to Brian. Brian's job in fact consists of endlessly recording his whereabouts with a security device—a task that makes a grim mockery of the notion of "productive labor," which was treated with reverence in the nineteenth century. As Johnny observes, the corporation might as well have trained "a tall chimpanzee" to perform the same task—"or a small chimpanzee with a bigger gizmo." Johnny expresses his belief that "nobody 'as a future" in apocalyptic terms, aligning his own alienation with the prophetic musings of the Book of Revelations. Yet this peculiar meld of misanthropy and metaphysics cannot disguise the fact that the urban detritus that enrages Leigh's antihero is primarily engendered by material factors. The growth of the "global city," in which the mobility of capital and the power of multinational firms become tied to finance capital and the "informational economy," promotes an extreme polarization between rich and poor. [29] Johnny, unlike a traditional leftist such as *High Hopes*'s Cyril, is constitutionally incapable of militant defiance.

Naked's dissection of alienated sexuality frequently intersects with its evocation of reified urbanism. Throughout the film, Johnny spews forth monologues of sometimes breathtaking, if crazed, eloquence and engages in a series of trysts with troubled women who find themselves initially attracted to his torrent of words but are eventually repelled by his contemptuous abuse. The sex in *Naked* is the antithesis of Hollywood's soft-focus coupling—what Vladimir Nabokov once derided as the "copulation of clichés." Johnny is undeniably a misogynist and some literal-minded viewers and critics made the mistake of assuming that Leigh shared his antihero's disdain (which occasionally reasserts itself, however schizophrenically, as tenderness) for women. Both victim and victimizer, Johnny's generalized misanthropy pales in comparison to

that of Jeremy, a loathsome yuppie woman hater whose pivotal role in *Naked* is one of Leigh's rare aesthetic miscalculations. Jeremy's role as a malevolent deus ex machina almost vindicates the antics of the working-class Johnny, who is nevertheless far from a proletarian hero. Linking, however unobtrusively, these sexual predators with the predatory economic policies of post-Thatcher England, Leigh's emphasis on routinized sex echoes Lefebvre's regret that "with 'modern' eroticism we step outside of the everyday, without actually leaving it: it shocks, it seems brutal, and yet this effect is superficial, pure appearance, leading us back towards the secret of the everday—dissatisfaction."[30] *Naked* acknowledges the everyday dissatisfaction of mechanical sexuality with bittersweet humor. Toward the end of the film, Jeremy lunges at a woman named Sophie who has already endured Johnny's venom. "Here we go again" is her weary response.

This near noirish retreat from Leigh's usual interest in family dynamics was a temporary detour. With *Secrets and Lies* (1996), he returned to the family unit with a vengeance, although this crowd-pleasing soap opera was something of an anti-*Meantime;* the earlier film appeared to take pride in its stoic refusal of melodrama. *Secrets and Lies,* however, does not augment its melodramatic contrivances with the operatic pyrotechnics favored by Hollywood's celebrated auteurs. Leigh's patient appreciation of the quotidian succumbs to an ultraschematic narrative structure that reaches its crescendo with an ending that is apparently designed to be heartwarmingly affirmative. Many critics underline historical affinities between real-

2. *Naked,* Mike Leigh, 1993. (Still courtesy of *Cineaste.*)

ism and melodrama, and it would be naive to view *Secrets and Lies* as Leigh's abandonment of realism (however one defines this admittedly amorphous rubric) or the critique of everyday life. It does seem valid, however, to consider how Leigh's most commercially successful film (not in itself a badge of dishonor) co-opts, either wittingly or unwittingly, his previous achievements.

The film's intricately plotted first half plunges us into recognizable Leigh terrain. The early sequences are preoccupied with Hortense, a middle-class, adopted black optometrist in her twenties who decides to trace her origins; her white, working-class mother, Cynthia; and Cynthia's gentle and more prosperous brother, a portrait photographer named Maurice. Unfortunately, the screen time devoted to Maurice's troubled wife, Monica, exposes the creaky narrative machinery that sometimes threatens to sabotage *Secrets and Lies*. Monica's furtive shame, engendered by her inability to bear children, mechanically rhymes with the film's more significant "secret"— Cynthia's reluctance to confront her long lost child. Leigh's best early films, like the even more downbeat films of the late Alan Clarke, were noteworthy for their minimalist rigor and a concomitant refusal to telegraph prefabricated emotional responses to an audience.

To its credit, *Secrets and Lies* abounds with resonances of earlier Leigh films, and typically scenes that at first seem like irrelevant longueurs are frequently of more interest than the central narrative thread. While the protagonists too often resemble points plotted along an imaginary graph, the minor, eccentric characters often demonstrate how individuals devise stratagems to inject meaning into often superficially meaningless everyday lives. For example, a social worker who resembles a much more sympathetic version of Melody in *Home Sweet Home* subtly conveys an enormous range of emotions; more than just a faceless bureaucrat, she is alternately compassionate, condescending, distracted, nervous, and harried. Partaking of a completely different emotional register, Stuart, the man who sold Maurice his studio, sullenly fulminates against his wife, his mother, Australia, England, and Maurice: he suggests an older, wearier version of Johnny. Nevertheless, despite these privileged moments, *Secrets and Lies* largely abandons the fascination of banality for a diluted, strangely un-English variation of the belief, elaborated in several plays by Eugene O'Neill and Arthur Miller, that confessional zeal functions as balm for the soul. At Cynthia's cataclysmic birthday party (the celebration gone awry is a Leigh motif familiar from previous films such as *High Hopes, Grown Ups*

[1980], and *Abigail's Party*), the film degenerates into a series of confessional monologues that flaunt, with a minimum of irony, more than a few quasi–New Age pieties. Like some nightmarish combination of Bill Clinton and John Bradshaw, Maurice exhorts his family to abandon their "secrets and lies" and "share" their pain. Given this denouement, the film promotes the implicitly patronizing assumption that everyday life cannot be assimilated without sentimental window dressing.

This programmatic conclusion is an aberration within Leigh's work. Most of his films treat daily life with more nuanced grit; *Secrets and Lies,* which shares his best work's character-driven impetus, does manage to evoke "the everyday" through meticulously crafted performances. In this respect, the construction of the Leigh persona recalls André Bazin's characterization of the "Fellinian" protagonist, a figure described as "not a 'character' but a mode of being, a way of living" who the "director can define . . . throughly through his behavior: his walk, his dress, his hairstyle, his mustache, his dark glasses."[31] All of Leigh's scripts are the product of an intimate process of collaboration with unusually talented casts, although it is important to emphasize the fact that his work is no more improvised than Fellini's: after a fairly lengthy rehearsal period, Leigh incorporates the actors' contributions into a final script and remains as much in control as any traditional director. Somewhat disingenuously, or perhaps naively, Leigh insists that his actors don't "simulate something artificially" because their preparation acquaints them with "a history built into the[ir] relationships."[32] In any case, it is possible to set aside Leigh's slightly self-aggrandizing pretensions and maintain that his actors "turn everyday life into something anodyne," making the most minute gestures and habits amusing and invigorating. To cite but one example, Katrin Carlidge's artistry lets us look beyond the masochistic stupidity of *Naked*'s Sophie and the slightly sadistic invective of *Career Girls*'s Hannah. Cartlidge's expertly slurred speech and studied lassitude sum up Sophie's erotic frustration with admirable concision. In a much more manic vein, Cartlidge's karate-chop gesticulations and staccato verbal delivery pinpoint Hannah's personal contradictions — her mixture of anguish and joie de vivre enlivens everyday life despite her weakness for withering put downs.

Lefebvre's fertile category of "everyday life" offers a salutary antidote to the false dichotomy of an idealist construct known as realism and an equally idealized — and monolithic — modernism. Unlike either Lukács or Barthes, Lefebvre claims that the realm of the "trivial" is often a departure point for emancipatory possibilities and the supposedly rarefied terrain of the "marvelous" is actually inextricable from everyday banality. For Lefebvre, "the substance of everyday life—'human raw material' in its simplicity and richness—pierces through all alienation and establishes 'disalienation.'"[33] The 'concreteness,' therefore, of what frequently appears to be humdrum dailiness is not reduced to the platitudes of mainstream sociology but can actually provide a frisson in which critical inquiry and lyrical epiphanies coexist and are in fact inextricable. Employing his usual dialectical brio, Lefebvre ultimately concludes that the Romantic category of the marvelous is not bound up with "exoticism" or the "bizarre" but "operates only on the level of everyday life."[34]

Leigh's *Career Girls*—while a minor work compared to *Meantime* or *Naked*—demonstrates how his tragicomic sensibility commingles superficial realism with a highly stylized emphasis on the juxtaposition of the marvelous with the quotidian. *Career Girls* is a highly schematic memory film in which two former college roommates—Annie and Hannah—look back with melancholy and wistful humor to their fractious youthful friendship, which was redeemed by sporadically happy moments. Strategically placed flashbacks punctuate Hannah and Annie's frequently strained reunion, and these glimpses of the past concretely suggest that everyday life can be "rehabilitated"; the young women combat boredom with a verve that confirms Lefebvre's assertion that "since Baudelaire, the world turned inside out has been deemed better than the world the right way up."[35]

Hannah's verbal facility and quirky (and sometimes cruel) sense of humor enables her and the more withdrawn Annie to—at least provisionally—"turn the world inside out." The two women, like depressive versions of Rivette's Celine and Julie, devise private games and rituals that allow them to endure lives spent in a dreary student flat. One of their favorite rituals uses a dogeared copy of Emily Brontë's *Wuthering Heights* as a magical talisman. By opening the novel at random, "Ms. Brontë" (the anachronistic salutation gently mocks some critics' christening of the writer as a proto-feminist heroine) is able to divine the future and mordantly comment on the present. *Wuthering Heights* was, of course, one of the surrealists' favorite novels: Buñuel's famously over-the-top adaptation is one of his most eccentric films, and Georges Bataille devotes a chapter to the Brontë classic in *Literature and Evil*. The roommates in Leigh's film, however, are mired in the here and now, and their use of Brontë as a tongue-in-cheek *I Ching* highlights the inadequacy of lives that cannot be easily transformed. When

Annie deferentially consults "Ms. Brontë" about her love life, a random flip of the pages reveals the anticipatory words "must come." But when Hannah and Annie's stuttering, overweight friend, Ricky, seeks advice for the lovelorn from the well-thumbed paperback, the book opens, with providential despair, to a blank page. Lefebvre believes that "living is the practice of overcoming alienation"; the comic desperation of Leigh's collegiate outcasts reiterates the fact that this process of overcoming can be rocky and on occasion leads to dead ends.[36]

Years later, when the two women reunite and look back wistfully at their Brontë worship (a visit to the author's home at Haworth is remembered as a seminal event), their pranks and rituals reflect their status as insecure young professionals. Hannah and Annie arrange bogus appointments with realtors to view lavish condos that they have no intention of buying. Like their whimsical consultation of *Wuthering Heights,* this upmarket jape serves as a pointed antidote to daily boredom. When the women visit a soused yuppie's lavish pad, Hannah looks out the window at the surrounding postmodernist skyline and observes that "on a clear day you can see the class struggle from here." Her remark disrupts the received assumptions of the everyday but acknowledges that it is often almost insurmountably difficult to change assumptions that even become embedded in architecture; as Guy Debord once remarked, "urbanism is alienation made visible."

Career Girls offers a useful inventory of Leigh's major themes as well as a capsule view of his highly artificial realism. *Career Girls* eventually resolves the damaged lives of its heroines with relative optimism, but, like nearly all of his previous films, an ironized, truncated version of the classic nineteenth-century bildungsroman can be easily discerned. The protagonists of seminal Leigh films such as *Bleak Moments, Meantime, Life Is Sweet,* and *Naked* do not journey from ignorance to edification in the manner of George Eliot's or Balzac's heroes and heroines; they instead usually progress from personal stasis and despondency to even more aggravated states of personal stasis and despondency. Of course, these films are saved from terminal bleakness by the bracing sting of Leigh's barbed humor, which at least partially alleviates the dreariness of the protagonists' everyday lives. However, the gallows humor of Leigh's most artistically successful films has little in common with the exalted altruism of the classical bildungsroman. Franco Moretti, for example, convincingly maintains that Balzac's novels do not critique everyday life but instead accentuate its "alive and interesting"[37] qualities. Leigh's films are not precisely inversions of nineteenth-century novels that pay tribute to a promise of happiness, but the prospect of happiness has been unquestionably put on hold in most of his best work.

A more buoyant ambience is nevertheless evident in Leigh's most recent film, *Topsy-Turvy,* a meticulous evocation of both W. S. Gilbert's and Arthur Sullivan's exuberant theatricality and the late Victorian era that spawned them. At first glance, a celebration of Tory satirists noted for the escapist frivolity of *H.M.S. Pinafore* and *The Mikado* appears to be far removed from the grittier concerns of *Meantime* and *Naked.* But *Topsy-Turvy* makes it glaringly clear that Leigh, despite being lazily labeled a naturalist by some critics, is primarily concerned with theatrical and cinematic artifice.

Leigh's overweening fascination with the creation of theatrical illusion—and the importance of "quotable gestures"—comes to the fore in an affectionate re-creation of one of *The Mikado*'s most famous set pieces, the "Three Little Maids from School" song. Despite the fact that Brecht's ideal of "the Popular," (a Left-populist affirmation of "forms of expression intelligible to the broad masses") couldn't be more diametrically opposed to Gilbert and Sullivan's stolidly middle-class conception of popular art,[38] *Topsy-Turvy*'s comic rendering of the rehearsal of this innocuous song demonstrates how Gilbert (who serves as director as well as lyricist) shares Brecht's conviction that, after rehearsals, "what . . . comes before the spectator is the most frequently repeated of what has not been rejected."[39] The conservative Gilbert, like the Marxist Brecht, believed that "every performance is a contrivance by its nature,"[39] although, paradoxically, the "Three Little Maids" sequence derives its humor from Gilbert's hilariously misguided attempt to infuse this elaborate production number with authentic "Japaneseness."[40] After Gilbert recruits three Japanese women to demonstrate appropriately demure manners to his befuddled dancing master and cast, it becomes obvious that the company's stiff upper lip emulation of this display is destined to be, in Leigh's words, "as Japanese as fish and chips."[41] This interlude does not merely interrogate Gilbert's own capricious aspirations to realism; it also reiterates Leigh's belief that his work interweaves the flotsam and jetsam of everyday life with a style of dramaturgy and performance that ironizes and theatricalizes the most mundane gestures and incidents.

Topsy-Turvy is a "period" film that also illuminates the spatial politics of modernity and the beginnings of an urban gestalt that has only incrementally changed since the late nineteenth century. The film underlines the importance of the conversion from gas to electric lighting in the 1880s by foregrounding the resplendent Savoy Theater's electrification as a key event in theatrical, as well as urban, history. And, as the historian Joachim Schlör reminds us, electrification only reinforces the allure of the nocturnal city: "Many come 'out of the light' to visit the dark places."[42] Leigh illustrates the allure that the subterranean nocturnal city possessed for the Victorian bourgeoisie by highlighting Arthur Sullivan's (the bon viveur composer who could not abide the temperamental Gilbert) visits to Parisian brothels. Sullivan's hedonistic urges can only be fully satisfied in this netherworld, which serves as an antidote to the above-ground propriety that he and his countrymen are forced to maintain.

This dichotomy between private and public realms not only unifies *Topsy-Turvy*'s disparate narrative strands; it is also a key preoccupation in all of Leigh's films. While it is true that the private/public distinction has eroded somewhat in recent decades, Leigh's films prove how his interest in the public realm casts a backward glance to the great nineteenth-century novelists' and playwrights' preoccupation with the external reproduction of reality, while his interest in private life echoes the concerns of what Erich Auerbach termed modernism's fondness for "internal realism." In addition, if we accept a definition of *realism* that encompasses more than mere naturalism—avoiding, according to Raymond Williams, the literal-minded domain of "static *appearance*" and embracing a "conscious commitment to understanding and describing the movement of psychological or social . . . forces"—there is no contradiction between Leigh's oscillation between the tradition, on the one hand, of Dickens, Zola, and Ibsen, and the twentieth-century counter tradition of Brecht, Beckett, and Pinter on the other.[43] Leigh's modernist realism infuses films featuring detailed portraits of eccentrics, obsessives, curmudgeons, and madmen—characters who sometimes win, but more often lose, a constant battle against monotony. Resolutely iconoclastic, his work straddles Brechtian optimism and Beckett's bleak whimsy. And, like Cyril, the dejected socialist protagonist of *High Hopes,* Leigh remains a man "deeply frustrated by the gulf between how things are and how they ought to be, and how ever-increasingly hard it has become to do anything about it."[44]

Notes

1   For a biographical treatment of Lukács's complex political peregrinations, see Arpad Kadarkay, *Georg Lukács: Life, Thought, and Politics* (Cambridge, Mass.: Basil Blackwell, 1991).

2   This is Martin Jay's paraphrase of Barthes's position. See his *Cultural Semantics: Keywords of Our Time* (Amherst: University of Massachusetts Press, 1998), 120.

3   See Theodor Adorno, "Extorted Reconciliation: On Georg Lukács' *Realism in Our Time*," anthologized in Adorno's *Notes to Literature, vol. 1* translated by Shierry Weber Nicholsen (New York: Columbia University Press, 1991), 228. Several studies have recently outlined affinities between the superficially antithetical realms of modernism and realism. See, for example, Ivone Margulies, *Nothing Happens: Chantal Akerman's Hyperreal Everyday* (Durham: Duke University Press, 1996); and Gilberto Perez, *The Material Ghost: Films and Their Medium* (Baltimore: Johns Hopkins University Press, 1998).

4   This is the first part of Brecht's definition of *realism*. See Bertolt Brecht, *Brecht on Theatre,* translated by John Willett (New York: Hill and Wang), 109.

5   For a comprehensive analysis of trends in contemporary British left-wing theater, including the work of the 7.84 Company and Arden's plays, see Catherine Itzin, *Stages in the Revolution: Political Theatre in Britain since 1968* (London: Methuen, 1980).

6   Martin Esslin maintains that Pinter combines "extreme naturalism . . . with a dreamlike, poetic feeling which, as indeed often happens in dreams, is by no means inconsistent with an uncanny clarity of outline." See Esslin's *Pinter, the Playwright* (London: Methuen, 1984), 270.

7   Michael Coveney, *The World according to Mike Leigh* (New York: Harper Collins, 1996), 85.

8   Erich Auerbach, *Mimesis: The Representation of Reality in Western Literature,* translated by Willard R. Trask (Princeton: Princeton University Press, 1954), 486.

9   Ibid., 486.

10 Harold Pinter, "Writing for the Theatre," in Harold Pinter, *Complete Works: One* (New York: Grove Press, 1976), 13.

11 Lee Ellickson and Richard Porton, "I Find the Tragicomic Things in Life: An Interview with Mike Leigh," *Cineaste* xx: 3 (April, 1994), 12.

12 Leigh's ability to capture behavioral quirks on film constitutes his modest version of realism, but his aesthetic has few affinities with what Ian Watt labels "presentational realism," a more all encompassing stance refined by novelists such as Richardson and Defoe. Watt's recognition that "the tendency of some Realists and Naturalists to forget that the accurate transcription of actuality does not necessarily produce a work of any real truth or enduring literary value" has doubtless helped to discredit the more hubristic claims of realism's proponents. See Ian Watt, *The Rise of the Novel: Studies in Defoe, Richardson, and Fielding* (Berkeley: University of California Press, 1957), 32.

13 Brecht, *Brecht on Theatre,* 80. A Brechtian analysis of Ken Loach's films could also be assayed, despite the fact that Loach was attacked by supposedly Brechtian antirealists such as Colin MacCabe during the 1970s. In a brief book review, Michael Sprinker initiated this project by claiming that "Brecht's plays, like Zola's novels, were experiments conducted with the aim of interpreting the world correctly so that it might in the end be changed. Loach's commitment to this project has never wavered, the putatively regressive mode of his presentation notwithstanding." See Michael Sprinker, "Brechtian Realism," *Minnesota Review* 50–51 (October 1999): 225.

14 Fredric Jameson, *Brecht and Method* (London: Verso, 1998), 104.

15 Andy Medhurst, "Mike Leigh: Beyond Embarrassment," *Sight and Sound* 3:11 (November 1993), 8.

16 Reclus is quoted in Kristin Ross, *The Emergence of Social Space: Rimbaud and the Paris Commune* (Minneapolis: University of Minnesota Press, 1988), 91.

17 Rob Shields, *Lefebvre, Love and Struggle* (London: Routledge, 1999).

18 Coveney, *The World according to Mike Leigh,* 163.

19 Andrew Higson, "Space, Place, Spectacle: Landscape and Townscape in the Kitchen Sink Film," in *Dissolving Views: Key Writings on British Cinema,* edited by Andrew Higson (London: Cassell, 1996), 134.

20 Leigh remarked that "Having grown up in an urban world, it was exciting to know that there was a cinema attempting to deal with that, although one sometimes had reservations about whether it was quite real or slightly artificial." See Porton and Ellickson, "I Find the Tragicomic Things," 15.

21 Rob Shields, *Lefebvre, Love and Struggle,* 165.

22 Christopher Prendergast, *The Order of Mimesis* (Cambridge: Cambridge University Press, 1986), 95.

23 John Hill remarks that for members of the 1960s New Left, "many of the economic changes wrought by 'affluence' were taken for granted. . . . Politically, these tended to lead to a representation of the working class as largely inert and conformist: it is only individual members of the class who are able to rise above or rebel against this general condition." See his *Sex, Class, and Realism: British Cinema, 1956–1963* (London: British Film Institute, 1986), 174.

24 See Peter Williams, "Class Constitution through Spatial Reconstruction? A Re-evaluation of Gentrification in Australia, Britain, and the United States," in *Gentrification of the City,* edited by Neil Smith and Peter Williams (Boston: Allen and Unwin, 1986) 56–77. In reference to gentrification in London, Williams remarks that "the move to establish residence in working-class areas . . . appeared to mark a break from the class-segregated past." He concludes, however, that "far from resulting in a classless society," the process heightened "class consciousness." Williams, 71.

25 Coveney, *The World according to Mike Leigh,* 194.

26 John Hill believes that the portrayal of families in *High Hopes,* and particularly the portrayal of women, "harks back to the tradition of British working-class realism of the 1960s which not only criticized the 'corruption' of the working class by consumerism but characteristically associated superficiality and an 'excessive' interest in acquisition with women characters." Hill is specifically referring to the slightly caricatured figure of Valerie, Cyril's sister. Hill's pronouncements, however, ignore the fact that Valerie, like many of Leigh's characters, is treated with an equal amount of empathy and scorn. While Hill acknowledges the inescapable evidence that her money-grubbing husband is the object of far more contempt, he asserts (erroneously, from my point of view) that the audience is encouraged to share her brutal spouse's disdain. See John Hill, *British Cinema in the 1980s* (Oxford: Clarendon Press, 1999), 194.

27 Zygmunt Bauman, *Modernity and Ambivalence* (Ithaca: Cornell University Press, 1991), 186.

28 Edward W. Soja, *Postmodern Geographies: The Reassertion of Space in Critical Social Theory* (London: Verso, 1989), 179.

29 For an in-depth analysis of the new "global city" in three major cities, see Saskia Sassen, *The Global City: New York, London, Tokyo* (Princeton: Princeton University Press, 1991).

30 Henri Lefebvre, *Critique of Everyday Life,* vol. 1, translated by John Moore (London: Verso, 1991), 35.

31 André Bazin, "The Profound Originality of *I Vitelloni,*" anthologized in *Bazin at Work: Major Essays and Reviews from the Forties and Fifties,* edited by Bert Cardullo (New York: Routledge, 1997), 186.

32 Graham Fuller, Interview with Mike Leigh, in Mike Leigh, *Naked and Other Screenplays* (London: Faber and Faber, 1995), xxv.

33 Lefebvre, *Critique of Everyday Life,* 97.

34 Ibid., 115.

35 Ibid., 123.

36 This paraphrase of Lefebvre appears in Rob Shields, *Lefebvre, Love, and Struggle* 43.

37 Franco Moretti, *The Way of the World: The Bildungsroman in European Culture,* translated by Albert Sbragia (London: Verso, 1987), 35.

38 Brecht, *Brecht on Theatre,* 108.

39 Ibid., 204.

40 Gilbert is quoted in J. Hoberman, "Your Shows of Shows," *Village Voice,* December 21, 1999, 143.

41 Amy Taubin, "Mike Leigh Improvises on History," *Village Voice,* December 21, 1999, 148.

42 Joachim Schlör, *Nights in the Big City: Paris, Berlin, London, 1840–1930,* translated by Pierre Gottfried Imhof and Dafydd Rees Roberts (London: Reaktion Books, 1999), 65.

43 Raymond Williams, *Keywords: A Vocabulary of Culture and Society,* rev. ed. (New York: Oxford University Press, 1983), 261.

44 This is from Leigh's preface to the published screenplay of *High Hopes,* included in Leigh, *Naked,* 186.

Why Is This Absurd Picture Here?
Ethnology/Heterology/Buñuel
James F. Lastra

If the heterogeneous nature of the slave is akin to that of the filth in which his material situation condemns him to live, that of the master is formed by an act of excluding all filth: an act pure in direction but sadistic in form. — Georges Bataille

Near the middle of Luis Buñuel's 1933 film *Las Hurdes: Land without Bread* we witness another in the string of atrocities that make up Hurdano daily life.[1] After learning that their diet consists almost entirely of potatoes, which are all eaten by May or June, and then of unripe cherries, which cause deadly dysentery, we spy a pair of wild goats scaling a precipice. As if to underscore the utter absurdity and precariousness of the Hurdanos' existence, the narrator tells us that goat meat is eaten only when an unlucky creature slips on a loose stone and plummets to its death—an unlikely event that nevertheless promptly occurs. Fittingly, this scene has become the film's most notorious, for spectators invariably notice a telltale puff of smoke from the right edge of the frame, indicating that the goat has, in reality, been shot.

A tiny shift in the camera's position would have obscured this fact, but as if to make sure that no one missed that this sacrifice was staged, Buñuel further theatricalizes the scene by giving us a *reverse angle* shot of the goat falling down the hill. Our only possible inference is that Buñuel had the goat carried back up the hill and dropped to stage this "chance," but representative, event. In a very real sense, the "cause" of the goat's death is the "staging" of Hurdano life as documentary. The very process of ethnographic inscription is thereby indicted as an exercise of brute power mediated through an ostensibly "objective" act of recording.

The power and unresolved affect of this scene draw our attention to the film's other depictions of animals and, more disturbingly, to the numerous sequences in which the Hurdanos themselves are equated implicitly or explicitly with beasts. In this context, the scene of the goat's death suddenly seems one of the film's most characteristic, for it both exemplifies the theme of dehumanization and thematizes the act of ethnographic inscription as such. Because of its surprising violence and duplicity, however, the scene also serves to undermine the film's claims to objectivity, the validity of ethnographic stagings more generally, and, most importantly, our own certainty about where the film stands, morally and politically.

The nature of this act—the slaughter of a goat—resonates with overtones of ritual sacrifice and exile and encourages us to reevaluate the film's attitude toward the Hurdanos. Just as a community might place its sins upon the scapegoat and then expel or slaughter it, the goat here seems a purifying sacrifice.[2] In this case, however, the sins of the documentary are ritually expiated by destroying its pretensions to transparency; the deliberateness with which Buñuel criticizes his own project serves as a kind of mea culpa. Yet, just as resonantly, the goat embodies the Hurdanos themselves, sacrificed on the altar of ethnography in the service of creating a compelling human document. The scene may even be said to crystallize the tenor of the film as a whole—just as the scapegoat (animal or human) was often deified before its expulsion, so, too, the Hurdanos are elevated to a heroic plane at some moments only to be vilified the next. *Las Hurdes* is an unforgettable film, arousing both pity and laughter alike, and it owes its unusual power to this equivocal strategy.

As was the case with *Un chien andalou* and *L'Age d'or*, *Las Hurdes* immediately became the center of controversy, especially in Buñuel's native Spain, where it was banned first by the Republican government and later by the Fascists. Like his predecessors again, critics quickly recognized *Las Hurdes* as one of Buñuel's unarguable masterpieces. While *Las Hurdes* has been extravagantly praised as a scathing and straightforward condemnation of church and capital, its real critical power is inextricable from its darker side—the gamble it takes by emulating aspects of racial and ethnic hate literature. The dehumanization and repudiation of its subjects, which gives it its vehemence and its pathos, condition whatever positive critical or ethical power it possesses.

The Spanish Republic's decision to bar the film upon its initial screening may have been regrettably shortsighted, but it nevertheless was spurred by the film's genuinely violent tendencies. In fact, given the highly charged character of previous scholarship on the region, we might say that the officials who argued for the film's suppression understood only too well what was at stake in Buñuel's particular equivocations—perhaps better than many of the film's champions. Thus, if I emphasize the film's violence more than other critics do, it is in order to reawaken this combined sense of outrage and culpability and to point to the Hurdanos' troubled relationship with Spanish culture and history, for which the symbol of the scapegoat is only too apt.

I propose several frames of analysis through which this darker, but more compelling, reading will become intelligible. The touchstones of my reading are the film's debt to surrealism's ethnographic moment,[3] its implicit response to the cultural politics of the Exposition Coloniale of 1931, its sympathy with Georges Bataille's heterology, and its engagement with its avowed sources, Maurice Legendre's 1926 anthropological study and Miguel de Unamuno's 1922 travel essay. Through these lenses, I see a film that falls on the side of neither pure sympathy nor simple disgust but insists on a constantly double movement, embracing and repelling the Hurdanos at the same time and refusing the stable position we may wish it to take.

Neither Right nor Left?

Buñuel's film, initially an affront to both sides of the Civil War, recalls a literary strategy Denis Hollier has described as "equivocation." Building upon Zeev Sternhell's study of fascist patterns of thought in 1930s France, Hollier identifies a characteristic mode of writing that "never takes the form of a confrontation, but rather that of a *mimetic subversion* that appropriates and diverts the enemy's slogans, that claims to outstrip him on his own grounds, to combat him with his own weapons." He continues: "This resistance, which counterattacks by *identifying with the aggressor,* is a resistance that is literally equivocal, a resistance through equivocation, within which words lose their meaning: it reshuffles the cards, preventing any distinction of the potential aggressor from his victim."[4] Few descriptions better illuminate the technique of Buñuel's curious film. Simultaneously a documentary and a dismantling of the genre, *Las Hurdes* treads a thin and troubled line between revolutionary social critique and nearly fascist revulsion. So, while we are told, for example, that "The only luxurious things we found in the region were the churches," we also hear the Hurdanos described as a "choir of idiots," as "almost wild," and find them equated again and again with animals. So insidiously effective is this strategy that many of the film's most ardent and politicized supporters unconsciously describe the Hurdanos as "backward," "barbaric," and "ignorant," despite the fact that these terms are part and parcel of the oppressive ideological systems whose criticism by the film is otherwise applauded.

Critics have consequently found it difficult to get a firm grasp on the film's attitude toward the Hurdanos. In typical fashion, one critic describes the film as "entirely documentary in style, that is, objective, straightforward presentation of fact," only to denigrate the region later as a "cesspool."[5] Nor is it exceptional for another to describe an impoverished Hurdano family as "sleeping in sexual promiscuity" while informing us that in lieu of work they "*prefer* to remain idly in their beds."[6] These two authors, entirely sympathetic to Buñuel it is important to note, add to these unsubstantiated claims detailed written accounts of scenes whose specifics differ noticeably from their filmic counterparts.[7] Likewise, critics often accept at face value certain of the film's more dubious claims while demonstrating at some length how certain others are clearly tendentious.[8] One of the film's most noted commentators asserts that the Hurdanos "obviously live as the film shows them to us," while noting in the next paragraph that the supposedly typical death of a goat in the film pointedly has been staged.[9] These critical exaggerations and inaccuracies are significant less for the substance of their errors than for the way they demonstrate how even sympathetic critics are carried away by the film's tone and, moreover, by what they are induced to *imagine* occurs in the film or *should* occur. Perhaps most troubling, however, is the frequency with which critics who presume to speak on their behalf attribute laziness, promiscuity, savagery, and cruelty to the Hurdanos.

Responding, it seems, to the film's political slipperiness, in 1937 Buñuel added a conclusion, stating unambiguously that the film's political allegiances were decidedly popular frontist and vehemently antifascist. Franco, Hitler, and Mussolini are blamed directly for the misery depicted in the film, which will be ameliorated "with the aid of anti-fascists from round the world," and replaced with "calm, employment, and happiness."[10] It is tempting to suggest that these lines were added to ameliorate its otherwise troubling equivocations at precisely the moment when the threat of fascist domination seemed greatest. Whatever their presumed function, they rather awkwardly impose a neat order upon an otherwise unruly film. Given, however, the gravity of the issues with which the film engages, explicitly recognized here, why did Buñuel fashion a text so morally, politically, and epistemologically ambiguous?

The "Problem of Man"

However important his "surrealist vision" was for the making of Las Hurdes, Buñuel always maintained that he was primarily interested in "the problem of man."[11] It is not surprising, then, that "man" would play a key role in his decision to leave surrealism: "I was beginning not to agree with that kind of intellectual aristocracy with its moral and artistic extremes, which isolated us from the world and limited us to our own company. Surrealists considered the majority of mankind contemptible or stupid, and thus withdrew from all social participation and responsibility and shunned the work of others."[12] Buñuel's dissatisfaction with surrealism's relation toward others marks a significant shift in his work, signaling a turn toward what, broadly speaking, might be called the "anthropological" concerns that were to animate the rest of his career. If the Parisian working class cafés and flea markets could provide grist for the surrealist mill, the cultures they represented were certainly worth taking seriously as more than objects of appropriation. Buñuel had identified an unfortunate surrealist tendency to "use" bourgeois society's others to negate the cultural status quo, while never giving that negativity its due. In a gesture all too familiar to Buñuel, surrealist good intentions went awry and succeeded, principally, in redeeming these others (workers, criminals, Africans, the insane) as projections of their own desires. It was precisely this redemptive logic that Buñuel began to contest via his emulation of the enemy in Las Hurdes.

Buñuel was not alone in turning his attention to the problems of representing otherness. As James Clifford argues, both ethnography and surrealism shared a "crucial modern orientation toward cultural order" that saw cultural realities not as universal but as "local and artificial, hence susceptible to critique." These concerns were brought to a head by the World's Colonial Exposition of 1931, which, as Herman Lebovics argues, "set the aesthetic and political guidelines for the creation of an imperial culture."[13] Surrealists Louis Aragon, Georges Sadoul, and Pierre Unik responded to this affront by mounting the famous "Anti-colonial Expo." Their inventive approach answered the official exhibit's paternalistic attitudes toward colonial subjects by turning the alienating gaze of ethnography toward their own culture.[14] In a strategy that moved decisively beyond the romantic recuperation of otherness, the surrealists exhibited "European fetishes" and played a combination of Asian music and popular rhumbas, defamiliarizing everyday French life and treating it as strange and exotic.[15]

These rather pointed gestures developed the counterethnography implied by their flea market sojourns in a more explicitly critical direction. Indeed, they simultaneously published a pamphlet entitled "Ne visitez-pas l'éxposition coloniale," attacking its "colonialist banditry" and its vision of an imperial "Greater France."[16] But, although they were bravely forthright in their condemnation of colonial exploitation—France's first important anticolonial manifestation was organized not by Paris's political activists but by its vanguard artists—they were not at other times, above annexing an idealized image of these cultures for their own ends. Artaud's "Letter to the Dalai Lama" is only an extreme example of what has been called the surrealists' "singular lack of knowledge" of other cultures, which allowed them to posit the "exotic East" and "primitive Africa" as romantic utopias.[17]

In Asian and African cultures, the surrealists may have found an exciting fund of exotic formal and ideological alternatives,[18] but, good intentions aside, there was much left to accomplish. Any valorization of L'Art Negre or "black" culture that made no distinction between African American jazz, North African religious relics, and the ceremonial masks of Oceania could only succeed in reducing otherness to the order of the same. In effect, they united and homogenized these traditions through the mere fact that all of them repudiated European norms. In this respect, the surrealists differed little from the contemporary Mission Dakar-Djibouti, which crossed North Africa collecting exotic objects in an attempt to "enrich" French national culture with the booty of a dozen African tribes.[19] In these cultures, surrealists sought a model for a more intuitive and liberated cultural life, but they also *used* them to imagine and create an idealized self-image. In so doing, those looking toward this "phantom" Africa projected onto contemporary peoples an imaginary, archaic culture free from cultural repression or the supposed taint of modernity. In short, understanding the other in this cultural economy risked becoming merely a pretext for reimagining the self.

A dominant culture's power to assimilate even acts of radical negativity had a deeply personal significance for Buñuel, who saw, perhaps earlier and more clearly than many of his compatriots, the futility of purely aesthetic confrontations with bourgeois society. Distressed by the success of *Un chien andalou,* Buñuel asked how the very society he had tried to mortify could find his "passionate call to murder" "beautiful" or "poetic."[20] Returning to the topic in 1937, he wrote, "*Nothing* in this film *symbolizes anything,*" countering the repeated attempts to assimilate its moments of violence and irrationality into a poetic whole.[21] While somewhat disingenuous, this claim is utterly consistent with the filmmaker's repeated efforts to avoid appropriation—literary or political—however futile that avoidance may ultimately have been. By resisting both traditional formal unity and symbolic elevation, Buñuel hoped to respect the radical otherness of the image and allow its singular violence or unreason to disturb the whole in order to think of difference *as* difference and not as the simple negation of the same.

More chilling, though, his next film, *L'Age d'or,* was greeted by cries of "Kill the Jews!" and with ruthless violence that reduced and assimilated this anarchic film to stereotyped and politically effective notions of "rootless cosmopolitanism" and "Bolshevik agitation" that the French extreme Right could only imagine as Jewish in origin. Buñuel and Dali, both Catholic and temperamentally intransigent enough to refuse any kind of doctrinaire political position, thus found themselves and their work appropriated for scurrilous political gain—gains that were amplified when Prefect of Police Chiappe censored the previously approved film. Buñuel learned that even when an artwork's material facts seemed vigorously to defy it hegemonic cultures were capable of the most withering acts of radical homogenization.

One who seemed fully to appreciate the radical negativity of Buñuel's efforts was Georges Bataille, who had praised *Un chien Andalou* extravagantly in his journal, *Documents.* Although Buñuel did sign the 1930 manifesto that so virulently excoriated Bataille for his attack on Breton's idealist (read Hegelian) tendencies, he soon drifted toward Bataille's position.[22] Breton's definition of *surrealism* as the "resolution of these two states, dream and reality, which are seemingly so contradictory, into a kind of absolute reality, a *surreality,*" made explicit the potentially homogenizing tendency of surrealist negation and sublation, which both Buñuel and Bataille rejected, albeit for different reasons.[23]

Among the other renegades moving away from Breton and toward Bataille were Aragon, Sadoul, Desnos, Leiris, Maxime Alexandre, and Pierre

Unik, who soon gravitated with Buñuel toward Bataille's journal. Buñuel, in fact, found both inspiration and at least one collaborator in *Documents*.[24] Besides Unik, who cowrote the narration, the personnel on the film included an old friend, Sanchez Ventura, and an experienced photographer and documentarist, Eli Lotar. Lotar had recently finished working on Joris Ivens's *Zuiderzee*,[25] and he had also recently contributed to *Documents* by furnishing the illustrations for Bataille's short piece, "Abattoir," one of the terms defined in that number's "Dictionary."[26] Fortuitous collage (the very method of the journal, according to James Clifford) draws Lotar's photos toward several others in the same issue.[27] The first, by Boiffard, is famous — "La gros orteil" — illustrating Bataille's essay of the same name. The second, anonymous, is a group of women's legs from the knees down, illustrating a brief piece on the "Fox Movietone Follies" but echoing as well the row of severed hooves against the wall of Lotar's slaughterhouse.[28] The connection between the Lotar, Boiffard, and Fox Follies photos is one of strategy as well as iconography, since each serves to isolate, or to "amputate," a part and employ it to undermine established understandings of the whole through radical fragmentation or enlargement. A similar, unlikely pairing draws *Documents* closer to *Las Hurdes*.

One of *Las Hurdes*' most poignant and disturbing sequences involves a young girl who appears to have been found suffering in the streets of a Hurdano village. As a figure enters the frame from behind the camera and examines the girl, we learn that she is ill, that she has been complaining for days, and that nothing has been done to help her. As evidence of her illness, Buñuel presents us with a close-up of the girl's open mouth. Although critics have described her mouth as swollen, infected, and even "putrefying,"[29] the image itself is hardly unambiguous on this count — it differs little from a healthy mouth. Likewise, when the narrator tells us, without substantiation, that she died shortly thereafter, most interpreters take this assertion at face value. Although it is tempting to read this scene as a brutally self-critical condemnation of the documentarist's morally questionable detachment from the events he "objectively" transcribes — a document of choosing to record rather than help — there are only very weak grounds upon which to build such an (admittedly enticing) argument. In fact, its credibility arises purely from our expectations about the sort of people whose lives are made into documentaries and from our belief in the mode's conventional sincerity. In other words, we must be willing to believe that this sort of thing happens in "places like this" and that the villagers are too stupid, uncaring, or weak to do anything for her. However, while believing exposes our own prejudices about "backward" societies, disbelieving is perhaps even more troubling, implying our desire to ignore their plight. Thus, the simple question of our belief places us on the horns of a moral dilemma; it makes us unable simply to pity or to dismiss them and unsettles familiar attitudes toward ethnographic others.

A strikingly similar image appears in *Documents'* "Critical Dictionary," illustrating Bataille's brief essay, "Mouth." Like Buñuel's film, Bataille's "definition" engages in a curious mode of explanation, de-defining its ostensible subject in the process of analysis and destroying its univocity. It seeks to produce a discourse "beyond" science and philosophy by paradoxically adopting one of its privileged rhetorical modes. Contrary to the standard explanatory goals of stability and transparency, Buñuel and Bataille produce mobility and refraction. Although the relationship between the two images is clearly not causal or logical, neither is it purely arbitrary.[30]

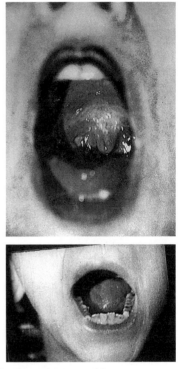

But do these two projects *deploy* their images in the same manner? Instead of addressing questions of normality and pathology, as Buñuel appears to do, Bataille's essay asks, "Where does the human body begin?" Rather than answering this question simply, Bataille leads us through an ever wider series of questions concerning the body, society, and hierarchies of value. Having abandoned our formerly four-legged posture by standing upright, he argues, the human mouth no longer constitutes a proper bodily beginning, nor, henceforth, can *any* unambiguous bodily "starting point" be determined. Therefore, whatever "meaning" or hierarchy is attributed to the human body comes at the expense of what Roland Barthes calls "a violent operation . . . the intrusion of a *value: noble* and *ignoble* (top and bottom, hand and foot)."[31] In other words, lacking any intrin-

1. J. A. Boiffard's mouth, illustrating George Bataille's *Mouth*. (Still courtesy of James F. Lastra)
2. Mouth, in *Land without Bread,* Luis Buñuel, 1932. (Frame enlargement courtesy of James F. Lastra.)

sic hierarchy, the body's order must be imposed arbitrarily. As in a related essay on the big toe, Bataille questions deeply rooted cultural values and hierarchies, especially as these issues are linked to the relationship between animality and humanity. While avoiding any explicit analysis of the body, these are precisely the issues that concern Buñuel.

In the now famous "Big Toe" essay, Bataille "demonstrates" through a series of bravura rhetorical maneuvers that our very definitions of humanity are inextricably entangled with that most base of human features, the foot. Whether defining man as such through its distinction from the analogous organ in primates or by allowing him to stand erect (thereby obscuring his "beginning"), the foot, and more specifically the big toe, enables and even determines the hierarchies of the body and therefore of society, forever favoring the high and noble over the low and ignoble. But, as Rosalind Krauss points out, the toe in Bataille's account *exceeds* the oppositions high/low and noble/ignoble: "[We try] to ennoble the foot, to give it form . . . the foot repays this effort, however, by developing bunions, and corns, and calluses. It becomes splayed, bulbous. It refuses to be ennobled or even to be ignoble. It is, simply, base." [32] Despite our best attempts to integrate it into an expanded definition of an integral whole—the hierarchically ordered body—the toe resists and in so doing disassembles the entire edifice, insubordinately refusing to take its place in a synthetic unity. [33] At the risk of advancing too precipitously, I will suggest that the Hurdanos, in a very real sense, play the same role in Buñuel's national body that the big toe plays in Bataille's physical one.

Spain's Big Toe

The Hurdanos occupied a well-defined, if terribly degraded, place in the Spanish national body. As Spaniards, however, they could also be said to *exemplify* Spanish identity—to express its essence as well as any other group. Nevertheless, elevating them to such a status brought with it immense cultural anxiety, since these "citizens" seemed to embody all the dangers and shortcomings of Spain's social and economic systems. Like Bataille's toe, their exemplary status works to dismantle the existing whole, illustrating how their own arbitrary subjection serves as the basis for the elevation of the national body's "higher" organs. Faced with the prospect that these wretched beasts were, like the wealthy of Madrid and Barcelona, Spaniards all the same, certain factions could only respond by insisting on their demonization—as idiots, as beasts, as foul-smelling laggards. Only by heaping the ills of a nation upon them and relegating them violently to the "outside" of the community could the nation reaffirm its own "purity." Of course, to do so was paradoxical, since the Hurdanos were no alien community but citizens well within the heart of Spain itself.

Buñuel was clearly determined to avoid the idealism embodied in reigning conceptions of the national body's "order" and purity, within which the Hurdanos could be but a debased organ or a parasitical infection. He was therefore extremely wary of presenting the Hurdanos in such a way that they might appear "colorful" or "heroic." In Madrid, at the film's premiere, several officials of the Spanish Republic, chief among them Dr. Gregorio Marañon, argued vehemently that the film was an insult to Spain.[34] Marañon found Buñuel's depiction of the cruel fiesta in which roosters are decapitated particularly objectionable and protested that Buñuel had ignored the fact that La Alberca "has the most beautiful dances in world, and its folk dress in magnificent 17th century costumes."[35] In this apparent admiration for Hurdano culture, Buñuel saw a rather malignant undercurrent of nationalism, noting, "To say the Alberca has the most beautiful dances in the world! That's like claiming your country has the most beautiful women and the bravest men in the world!"[36] In a way, Buñuel's chief task was to avoid the recuperations of national and cultural history but still to give an accurate account of Hurdano life.

While renouncing particular forms of unity, Buñuel's film still pursued some version of conventional documentary truth. Buñuel needed a concrete strategy of heterogeneous analysis, an approach to irrecoverable negativity, and he found a model in an approach that Bataille claimed turned its attention toward that which Hegel (and Breton) excluded: death, filth, sacrifice, loss, meaninglessness, nonknowledge.[37] Against the strategies of science, philosophy, and surrealism, which always recovered the heterogeneous within the homogeneity of reason, Bataille suggested a materialist "science," heterology. Although purportedly scientific in orientation, "when one says that heterology scientifically considers questions of heterogeneity, one does not mean that heterology is, in the usual sense of such a formulation, the science of the heterogeneous . . . above all, heterology is opposed to any homogeneous representation of the world, in other words, to any philosophical system."[38] Bataille may never have succeeded in developing a theory that "excluded all idealism," but his project set the stage for Buñuel, who engages a very similar constellation of concerns in his own investigation of Spain's "big toe," the Hurdanos. Buñuel's problem was to develop a form that respected the otherness of Hurdano life without recuperating it for reason, nationalism, or even humanism, all the while depicting a group supposedly *already* synthesized into Spanish culture. To achieve this, Buñuel concentrates in a disguised and displaced way on those aspects of these peoples' lives that have remained, for hegemonic Spanish (and European) culture, purely material. Despite the Hurdanos' quaint customs, archaic forms of life, and even their heroic struggle to survive, Buñuel's corrosive social critique is of no use to the dominant culture. The Hurdanos do not become symbols of anything, not even of cultural "diversity."

Science and Heterogeneity

Like other, more conventional ethnographies, Buñuel's film assembles a wide array of materials in its quest to portray Hurdano culture. Brief sequences treat education, agriculture, architecture, health, nutrition, geography, morality, religion, folklore, and economics, all of which have their proper place in any ethnographic study. Nevertheless, Buñuel does not arrange these elements in a conventionally linear and/or developmental argument. The images often contradict the voice-over and vice versa, creating a situation in which no single discourse ever fully masters the entirety of the materials. Likewise, succeeding sequences routinely refute one another, as when we are told that the Hurdanos, lacking domestic animals, have nothing to eat but potatoes, only to see pigs running through several shots. Most strikingly, the film contradicts its own title when we see children eating bread, hear that beggars often return from Salamanca with bread, and hear that the sick are given bread soaked in goat's milk. Nor are these contradictions (and there are many) simply the result of ineptitude on Buñuel's part. Had Buñuel wished to present a more conventional documentary, he would simply have omitted, for instance, the patently fabricated death of the goat. Instead, he chose to leave it and all the other contradictions in the film, allowing them to resonate and accumulate a troubling force over the course of its unfolding. By exaggerating the film's heterogeneity, Buñuel refuses to let it settle into any single genre with ease. When it becomes too scientific, it turns toward farce, and when too sympathetic, toward invective. It troubles both generic distinctions and the moral distinctions that are supposed to underwrite them.

Elliot Rubinstein points out that generically *Las Hurdes* is closely related to the travelogue, especially given the fact that for its first screening the commentary was read aloud along with the "silent" picture, as was common for travel lectures. He develops the connection further, arguing that the physical detachment of sound from image is accompanied by an emotional detachment as well. This double detachment reinforces the film's link to the travelogue, which, materially speaking, often consists of a talk with slides and is thus changeable from performance to performance.[39] *Las Hurdes* is, however, best understood as a parody of the form, emphasizing through its detached tone that its images could be narrated differently, could be arranged in a different order, or could even be replaced with other images. In addition, it raises the possibility that structurally there is simply no fixed and cumulative relationship between sound and image—they are only simultaneous, neither one clarifying the other. Instead of the traditional travel narrative, which seeks to integrate and narrativize a heterogeneous set of images, we get parallel threads of exposition, each falsifying the other, casting doubt first on the voice, then on the image. In fact, several of the film's most troubling occurrences (the deaths of four people and eleven animals) are simply asserted on the sound track, without further proof.

The film's credibility, however, does not derive from close attention to its structure or its presentation of evidence, both of which militate against it. Instead, the film seems simply to assert its authority again and again in louder and louder tones, as if, recognizing its own poverty, it seeks not to remedy it but to deny it. It compels belief by adhering to a restricted number of rhetorical ploys that suggest rather than demonstrate membership in various genres like the travelogue, ethnography, or documentary and thereby undermine the autonomy and authority of each.

For example, Buñuel has his way with the so-called arrival scene, which is crucial to both travel writing and ethnography. In each form, it works to create an authoritative impression of personal experience that in turn serves to validate the more "objective" portions of the work.[40] In the film, however, rather than an idyllic encounter between the studiers and the studied wherein a symbolic exchange of presents cements the bonds of humanity across cultures, the investigators stumble into a ceremony described as "strange and barbaric."[41] The newly wed males of La Alberca must wrest the head off a rooster at full gallop and then afterward symbolically share the blood (in the form of wine) with everyone in the village. Rather than reinforcing a sense of shared humanity, the ceremony suggests that a fundamental aggressivity underlies all relations, particularly those between men and women. The apparently unbridgeable gulf between the villagers and the crew (the latter find the former repulsive) is contaminated by this aggression, and, moreover, the ethnographic enterprise is thereafter repeatedly associated with an act of ritualized sacrifice. Furthermore, by symbolically transforming the blood into wine, this sacrificial gesture is inscribed in a Christian economy of resurrection and redemption rather than one of mutilation and loss. This scene, linking violence, cross-cultural encounter, and ethnographic encounter, sets the tone for the rest of the film.

The investigators continue to observe and analyze the villagers but seem to succeed only in widening the rift between them. Describing a baby decorated with Christian pendants, the narrator says, "We can only compare them with those worn by the barbaric tribes of Africa and Oceania," thereby insisting on strangeness where recourse to shared tradition might be expected. Taking their leave of the now drunken villagers, the crew begins the approach to the desolate landscape of Las Hurdes. As if to underscore the antipathy established in Alberca, the second arrival, within Las Hurdes proper, is marked by the phrase, "We are greeted by a choir of idiots."[42] The gulf torn between the investigators and their subjects developed in these encounters justifies and reinforces the film's matter-of-fact tendency to depict its subjects as subhuman brutes. Additionally, the implicit condemnation of the villagers solidifies the authority of the investigators, who offer a comparatively sober analysis while aligning the villagers with drunken dissolution, violence, and irrationality.

In contrast to the familiar style of the ethnographic film or the newscast from a country in the throes of widespread starvation, neither our fascination nor our pity is ever engaged. The spectator is never offered the possibility of either identifying fully with the Hurdanos or of adopting a stance of paternalistic concern. Contrary to generic expectations, the Hurdanos are no "primitive" society within which Western culture can construct an idealized self-image. There is nothing "picturesque" about Las Hurdes; it is a society with the external trappings of our cultures and nothing more, no Western core. Unlike African tribes encountered during the contemporaneous Mission Dakar-Djibouti, the Hurdanos offer no exotic, collectable culture. We quickly find out that while there is, in fact, some bread, there are no songs, that is, no indigenous oral tradition—something even the poorest African community could offer the mission.

While the absence of such "colorful" folklore keeps us from too easily adopting a patronizing curiosity, it also crystallizes the Hurdanos' precarious cultural position. Neither the resources of an oral tradition nor the cultural capacity for self-authorship exist for the Hurdanos, and consequently they suffer continual erasure under the pressure of Spain's dominant cultural models. An alarming episode in a local classroom illustrates the gap between the culture they learn ("They receive the same education that is given in primary schools around the world") and their own specific condition. As the camera shows us barefoot, unkempt, and ragged students, the narrator intones, "To these starving children, the teacher explains that the sum of the angles of a triangle equals two right angles." In the absence of an established, coherent, and powerful indigenous cultural tradition, symbolic resistance to these abstract verities is impossible. The Hurdanos have no wellspring of accumulated wisdom with which to confront and oppose the supposedly universal significance of geometry, no voice with which to talk back to the anonymous and homogenizing voice of reason, no counterknowledge with which to challenge abstract authority.

The Hurdanos, lacking their own means of cultural expression, have no indigenous culture, no "identity," no center from which to speak, no "authentic" voice. The only chance they get to express themselves verbally occurs in the classroom, where the children speak either in the universal language of geometric idealities or in the language of institutionalized, bourgeois morality. One of the students writes on the board, "Respectad los bienes ajenos" (Respect the property of others). It is difficult to imagine a scene that could better illustrate the idea that the subject is never in full possession of, nor does it exist at the center of its discourse. The position from which such utterances could be spoken—supposedly the universal position of the rational, ethical individual—excludes the Hurdanos in advance. The very basis of human identity in language, the subject of rational discourse, robs them of their voice. In Buñuel's film, however, it is precisely the universality of this reason, and, what is more, its objectivity and neutrality, that are put under scrutiny. For Buñuel, "reason" alone may never explain the Hurdanos.

Rather than adopting the unifying voice of reason, Buñuel chooses a strategy that is equivocal to its very core—parody. Parody inevitably results in a polylog, a multiplication of voices that resists the closure of reason. Like Buñuel's oft-repeated slogan, "Thank God I'm an atheist," parody negates but preserves its "host" text, not in a higher dialectical synthesis but in a state of perpetual conflict. Is it a documentary or is it a parody?

Rather than refining a discourse, as scientific falsification does, the logic of the parody multiplies without reconciliation, and like Buñuel's joke it presumes the existence of what it criticizes as an irreducible and necessary fact. Simply negating religion too easily becomes its own religion, just as Bataille's "dead matter" replaces one form of idealism with another. *Las Hurdes* presumes the possibility of a scientific "human geography" in order to criticize its underlying assumptions but not to offer a superior alternative. While always threatening nihilism, the strategy achieves important effects. If nothing else, resisting the closure typical of science is, here, a small victory.

Despite the evidently thorough research and analysis undertaken by Buñuel and his crew, the film profits little in terms of coherence or authority. In short, the difficult work involved in planning, executing, and compiling the film seems almost deliberately wasted—there is no "payoff" in knowledge at the end of the process. At the risk of overliteralizing the term, Bataille's (later) interest in the notion of *expenditure,* or *dépense,* seems illuminating. Against the pragmatic intellectual and cultural investments and profits typical of bourgeois culture (exemplified for him by Hegel), Bataille championed pointless waste and gratuitous expenditure of ceremonies like sacrifice or the potlatch. Yet Bataille's interest is not solely anthropological because *dépense* also implies a kind of "unthinking," a form of thought that provocatively risks all and recklessly avoids the dialectic movement that transforms all negation into profit and embraces waste and destruction. In a manner of speaking, Buñuel's film is likewise profligate with its resources, carelessly risking credibility and sympathy in the quest to think differently, to think beyond the standard oppositions; it revels in its own meaningless, its own rituals, in which science and knowledge are sacrificed and empathy ruthlessly destroyed. In so doing, perhaps, Buñuel avoids transforming the Hurdanos into objects of scientific logic, preferring instead to let them appear as anarchically heterogeneous—as unthinkable.

The doubleness of Buñuel's counterethnography cannot be easily separated from the more general project of equivocation. Both strategies seek to avoid synthesis and to problematize the traditional unities of thought and analysis. Parody is probably the more straightforward of the two, because its tensions can be resolved through laughter, yet, as Bataille demonstrated again and again, laughter is one of the gestures that exceeds reason, that cannot be assimilated by philosophy or science.[43] Here, however, equivocation takes its characteristically troubling form as the mimetic subversion of the enemy's tactics. Dehumanization and racial scapegoating, however, are drastic tools to use at this historical moment, especially since the film's parodic antisynthesis alone would certainly discredit the idealizing and homogenizing tendencies of "normal" science. Why would it seem necessary to go beyond this to depict the Hurdanos as beasts and idiots? Why *not* graft on a socialist critique of their conditions of existence, as many of the film's champions have done? What do we risk by elevating the Hurdanos to exemplifications of Spanish identity? Anthropologist Maurice Legendre's study *Las Jurdes: Étude de géographie humaine* (1926), which served as Buñuel's source, suggests an answer.

Synthesis and Anarchy

The similarities between Legendre's study and Buñuel's film are often striking, particularly in the case of the photographs systematically used by Legendre to illustrate important points. But the function of the photographic evidence, so alike in appearance, could hardly be more different in effect. In his introduction, Legendre apologizes for the lack of a lengthy bibliography but attempts to guarantee the study's truthfulness through recourse to the veracity of photographs. A "bibliography, even when reduced to a small number of volumes can furnish a sufficient number of citations, and the agreement of a range of authors, between themselves and with us, produces a strong enough guarantee of veracity. This presumption is reenforced still more when the photographic illustrations, which can hardly lie, accompany the claims of the travelers."[44] These two modes of inscription, language and illustration, reinforce one another and are guaranteed by the synthesis they produce, since, although "a premature and precipitous synthesis is hateful to sincere and scientific minds . . . it is no less true that the only solid and significant truth is found in synthesis."[45] The importance of synthesis justifies, for him, the presentation of a "*tableau complet*" of the Hurdanos, who are, finally, only examples of well-known Spanish realities. As he states at several points, his "internal critique" is the test of *cohesion*—how well the explanation holds together given what we know about Spain. Within the context elaborated above, however, cohesion and synthesis seem destined to yield only recuperation.

Nothing could be further from Buñuel's representation of the Hurdanos, whom he treats as absolutely alienated from the mainstream of Spanish civilization. *Las Hurdes* not only depicts that alienation but fosters it as well. It offers no gestures aimed at making the Hurdanos more comprehensible that are not immediately discredited. Against the values of cohesion and synthesis, Buñuel concentrates on the collection of concrete particulars. As he points out in an interview, he made a preliminary trip to the area after reading Legendre's study and made a series of "notes," collecting details: "goats," "girl with malaria," "anopheles mosquito," "no songs, no bread."[46] Fernando Cesarman characterizes the results: "Without using a narrative thread, the director has freely chosen significant scenes which meet in a structure apparently owing to chance, and forming a world possessing a [tidy] logic: that of misery."[47] Rather than coordinating these fragments by way of a unifying explanation in the manner of the traditional documentary, Buñuel allows the fragments to clash, contradict, and suggest their own (often opposed) logics. *Las Hurdes* is, in a sense, rigorously materialist in Bataille's sense of the term because by concentrating on a variety of material specifics without providing an organizing explanation it quite literally "is opposed to any homogeneous representation of the world." Yet the cost of heterogeneity is high.

The "logic" of misery described by Cesarman is an antilogic that operates in various forms throughout the film as a kind of nonprogressive negation. The overall rhetorical structure (if it can be called that) is modeled on the following. There is no bread. The teacher gives the children bread. Fearful parents throw it away. They run out of food. There are some cherries. They are unripe and cause deadly dysentery. There is no fertile land. They transport dirt and humus and *produce* land. The river washes it away. Not much food. They raise bees. Even the honey is bitter. A man is bitten by a snake. The bite is not fatal. He fatally infects himself trying to cure it. Again and again, potential solutions to problems amount to nothing. The "thesis/antithesis" structure yields no synthesis here, nor do these individual scenes become organized into a higher level of narrative synthesis. One simply cannot comprehend the Hurdanos; they resist explanation and assimilation to preexisting classifications or modes of understanding.

This irrationality extends across the entire film, distorting its most basic features. Even apparently obvious photographic facts are called into question, as if in Las Hurdes one cannot even trust one's eyes. We are told, for example, that the goitered old woman we see is "not yet thirty-two" but that the tiny young man/boy "is twenty-eight" and that a slain goat has "fallen." This conflict between sound and image is not resolved, nor can we simply choose to trust one against the other. The infamous scene of the goat's death ensures that.

While the scene therefore discredits the voice/image relationship (it is hard to say which is more duplicitous), it stops just short of an absolute nihilism, for, while the film does not "add up" and encourages the dissociation not only of one sequence from another but of sound from image, the illogic established by the film is presented in the very voice of logic, which manages to carry it along. So successful is the pressure of logic and convention that while *everyone* comments on the shooting of the goat, *no one* comments on the even more absurd and cruel shot that follows it—it is simply the shot we expect.

Just as the people's isolation and exclusion from Spanish culture and society suggest their position as national scapegoats, the actual sacrifice of the goat makes the metaphor strikingly literal. And, just as communities were traditionally reinforced by acts of sacralized exclusion, the film, too, achieves some semblance of coherence through this scene. In other words, the overall strategy of the film, including its equivocations and violence, ironically serves to solidify and homogenize the culture that has excluded the Hurdanos, defining them as purely heterogeneous elements in society. The connection between the Hurdanos and the motif of scapegoating is neither coincidental nor gratuitous, I would argue, but goes a long way toward explaining both the irrationality of the people's existence and of the film.

The "Legends" of Las Hurdes

Legendre had studied the region for many years before publishing his book and had accompanied Miguel de Unamuno on the latter's 1921 trip to the region, later immortalized in *Andanzas y Visiones*. The most prominent Spanish intellectual of the left, Unamuno was a friend and sometime mentor to Buñuel, who appears to have introduced him to the Paris surrealists. Buñuel also knew Unamuno's essay, "Las Hurdes," which is a frequent point of reference for Legendre, and it is very likely that he knew other essays and literary works referred to by Legendre as well. Certainly he knew of the "legends" to which both alluded and of the Spanish debate over the region, which provides a crucial but unexplored context whose peculiar character and obsessions shed a penetrating light on the film's politics.

Lope de Vega's *Las Batuecas del duque de Alba* (ca. 1604–14) is often cited as the origin of the legends of Las Hurdes, although it seems to derive from several earlier stories, all of which compare the discovery of Las Hurdes to that of the New World.[48] Despite substantial differences, all versions concur that Las Hurdes and Las Batuecas were unknown, even by their neighbors, and most agree that the region's inhabitants, when discovered, were savages.[49] In Lope's account, two lovers fleeing the wrath of the duke of Alba stumble upon Las Batuecas where, in an Edenic setting, they encounter a valley full of people without culture, without clothing, and without a recognizable language.[50] These stories persisted for centuries.

In our own century, the legends decisively shaped even the more sociological and political discussions of the region. The *Revista de Extremadura,* for example, published a series of articles about Las Hurdes between 1900 and 1902, including a heated exchange on the subject of the legends and their relationship to actual conditions. Luis R. Miguel, intent upon improving the region's social, economic, and hygienic situation, argues strenuously against the belief that the Hurdanos are "a species distinct from those known to the human race" and that they exist in a state of savagery and barbarism.[51] In the interests of his progressive social program, Miguel offers some fragments of another history, suggesting that the Hurdanos simply belong to a *different* cultural lineage. In short, he concludes, what the Hurdanos need is education, money, and social assistance.[52]

In response, José G. Castro enumerates the Hurdanos' debilities in shocking detail in a manner that parallels Buñuel's film in both phrasing and particulars. For example, Castro comments ironically that in these miserable cabins "live in amicable agreement men, women, children, the ass, *if* the family is rich enough to have acquired one, some hens, a pig."[53] The simple listing of the inhabitants in appositive fashion serves to equate the people with beasts of burden linguistically, as Buñuel does visually. The ironic understatement, "if the family is rich" similarly prefigures Buñuel's "The rich families, if we can call them that." The parallels go far deeper than a shared taste for understatement, however. More striking is Castro's use of the "Yes, but . . ." rhetorical strategy identified by Ado Kyrou as characteristic of *Las Hurdes.* To give just one example, familiar from the film, Castro points out that the region is generally bereft of arable land, but by transporting meager quantities of alluvial silt on their backs the Hurdanos build small fields. However, floods inevitably come and wash the fields away. If the floods do not come, he adds, wild boars eat the crops.[54]

While it is striking that, like Buñuel, he repeats this formula several more times, more telling are his discussions of Hurdanos' physiognomy, morality, and daily life. These particular comments give his rhetoric a disturbing chill. According to Castro, Hurdanos have small heads whose foreheads slope as the result of prominent brow ridges. They tend to have big ears with attached lobes and a physiognomy both inexpressive and bearing the "peculiar stamp of the imbecile." "All of these characteristics," he avers, "correspond to the inferior races and even to animals."

Thus begins a familiar, pseudo-Darwinian process of dehumanization, one that Castro embellishes with moral condemnation as well, attributing to the Hurdanos all forms of mental and ethical weakness. In Castro's words, "From the idiot of the lowest sort, whose life is purely vegetative, to the imbecile of lesser gradations . . . many psychopathic states can be found easily in Las Jurdes." He even refuses them intellect, claiming that the Hurdano "consciousness conceives only of ideas generated by immediate perceptions, resulting in judgments of a primitive nature. . . . the powers of reception and assimilation necessary for abstract ideas are non-existent, resulting in the absence of any sense of ethics which might serve as a brake to those egotistical impulses typical of a complete lack of will power." Consequently, he concludes, their appetites for sex and food are greatly exaggerated.[55]

According to Castro, the debilities that best characterize the Hurdanos' degraded existence are sexual, and these include the most brutal of appetites. From the prevalence of incest, which he attributes to the fact that the Hurdanos do not separate the sexes, to their ragged clothing (which permits glimpses of their genitals) and the prevalence of pederasty, these Hurdanos know no shame. The Hurdanos' bestial existence renders them, in Castro's eyes, worthy only of a pity tempered with contempt. In contrast to his progressive interlocutor, he claims that for the problem of Las Hurdes there is but one, final solution: "a complete depopulation of this miserable land."[56]

Twenty years later, Unamuno's essay describes an impoverished but upwardly mobile populace. In the town of Casar, he and his companion Legendre meet with local students, who implicitly request a fairer representation of Hurdano daily life, which Unamuno strives to offer. Traveling deeper into the region, he reports that they encounter "no evidence of the ridiculous legends of savagery" and argues further that, as Legendre says, the area is best thought of not as one of Spain's great *shames* but its *honor*.[57] Like Buñuel and Castro again, he notes that the Hurdanos must work extravagantly to create their small patches of farmland, offering his own account of how the Hurdanos transport the very earth for their crops in sacks across their backs.[58] As if setting a thematic itinerary for Buñuel's film, he reports that before he proceeds further he is cautioned to bring along his own food, since in the High Hurdes there is "nothing, not even bread."[59] And like Buñuel and Legendre again, he comments on the prevalence of goiters and regrets the premature decrepitude of the women.[60] The almost obsessive repetition of the same handful of motifs across a variety of authors suggests that the inflections given in any particular account are crucial.

Perhaps most striking, however, is his discussion of the Hurdanos' strange and powerful attachment to a place that is nothing if not inhospitable. Rather than a nurturing "mother earth," this land, he argues, is a cruel stepmother.[61] They do not flee, he explains, because they love the land, becoming more attached the more difficult the conditions become. Finding in the Hurdanos several characteristic traits of Spanish individualism, he concludes that ultimately they prefer impoverished "independence" to sharecropping. These autonomous, self-defining peasants are a far cry from Castro's beasts but perhaps just as fanciful and self-servingly depicted. As Unamuno admits, amid the poverty the sight of a beautiful young girl recalls in him nothing so much as the writings of Rousseau.[62] We should not pity them, he concludes, since despite their poverty they are "Anything *but* savages. No, no, no, it is truly the paradox described by my friend Legendre . . . they are, yes, one of our country's *honors.*"[63]

Thus, it would seem that there are two basic tropes available to one who would try to offer a picture of the Hurdanos. Either they are beasts unworthy of Spanish or even human identity or they are the very emblems of Spanish dignity and character. The latter option, chosen by Unamuno and Legendre, seems the less obviously pernicious of the two. Buñuel, however, rejects this possibility and veers noticeably in the direction of Castro, ameliorating his film's unsettling qualities only with his harshly explicit condemnation of the social and political conditions that have plagued the Hurdanos. In the context of the available representational strategies, Buñuel's specific form of equivocation comes into sharp focus, for the film's antiscientific or "unknowing" qualities spring from his resistance to the sort of redemptive elevation exemplified by Unamuno and Legendre.

In contrast to Castro's, Unamuno's, and Legendre's accounts, in Buñuel's film, the Hurdanos remain hopelessly obscure, and their situation seems to defy explanation. As even Legendre says, the basic enigma or scandal of Las Hurdes is the very fact that the area is inhabited at all.[64] Legendre's uneasiness with appearing to leave their situation unexplained and unredeemed is assuaged by the curious ending he appends to his introduction. Fearing that his book will lead readers to believe that Las Hurdes is a land without hope, he argues that, as Christians, the people can never be absolutely so. Indeed, he tells us that as he writes (September 14, 1926) the Hurdanos are celebrating their primary holiday, "L'exaltation de la Sainte Croix," which embodies the promise of redemption.[65] Against the values of hope and redemption, however, Buñuel's film embraces irrationality and works carefully to create a sense of hopeless, pointless, irrational, and unrelenting misery supported by a carefully fashioned, nonsynthetic nonsense. But to what end is this irrationality deployed? Perhaps it is directed toward the obviously unasked question, which is simply why don't the Hurdanos leave? Legendre offers us a clue by describing the "singular gravity" of the exaltation of the cross.

Discussing unorthodox forms of worship in the area, Legendre mentions a long-gone Sephardic community in the region, whose former influence explains the abandoned local Jewish cemetery. He tells us that it is "more melancholy" than the other, Christian, cemeteries, noting that among these pillaged tombs there is "no sign at all of hope."[66] While admitting that it is difficult to prove that these are the graves of Jews fleeing the Inquisition, he relates an oft-told story of the interfaith violence of that time, which explains both the lack of hope and the "gravity" of the festival.

Ser Más Malo que los Judíos de Casar

What, exactly, is the connection between *specific* acts of expulsion in the fifteenth century and the more general thematics of scapegoating at play in the film? If the current inhabitants of the region are Christians, as Buñuel tells us, what valence does the specifically Jewish character of the expulsions have for Las Hurdes? Nearly every writer who discusses Las Hurdes[67] tells some version of a single story about the town of Casar—the very town where Unamuno begins his journey in earnest.[68] In a 1931 study of Extremaduran folklore, we find two commonplace sayings that mention Casar. The first alludes to the stupidity of the locals and suggests a tradition within which Buñuel's casual insults ("here's another type of idiot," "the lids on the wall indicate a flair for interior design") resonate historically. The second, "Ser más malo que los judíos de Casar," however, is more complex and illuminating.

What does it mean—"to be more evil than the Jews of Casar"? The *Re-*

vista tells us that according to local superstition to call someone a Jew is equivalent to calling him a wizard or necromancer and even implies that he would be looked upon as a "satanic vampire."[69] In a deeply ambiguous passage, this sinister connection is "explained" by means of a logic that suggests in an all too familiar manner that the victims "asked for it" by rising too high in the government and succeeding too well in their endeavors.[70] In order to justify this hatred, Jews in the region were consistently described as evil and, as most writers on the subject recount, famously so.

In fifteenth-century Spain, Jews were perhaps more fully integrated into society than in any nation in Europe. The distinctive flavor of Spain's "Siglo de oro" has, in fact, often been attributed to the influence of Jews and converted Jews on the Spanish intelligentsia. During the Inquisition, however, even those Jews who had been converts for several generations were prosecuted under "purity" laws and related policies, which sought to eradicate the slightest tinge of racial difference. While the goal of the interrogations, forced baptisms, and expulsions was to "purify" and thereby unify both the Church and the nation—creating "one Spain" out of Castille and Aragon— some "impurity" apparently remained in these people, rendering them unassimilable and no longer "useful" to the new Spanish identity. The expulsion of 1492, in particular, drove many Jews to Portugal and to Las Hurdes, thereby establishing larger and larger settlements in the area.[71]

The uselessness of Jews to the emergent Spanish identity manifested itself at times in various forms of violence. According to both Legendre and Antonio Rodriguez Moñino, in Casar this race hatred was especially intense, though generally kept in check, so that Catholics and Jews lived together in relative calm. On one Good Friday, however, when by law all Jews were required to stay indoors, a small group was discovered playing a noisy game. After refusing to go indoors, the Christian congregation stoned them. Rather than retaliate against the congregation, the rabbi suggested that they attack the village cross. They secretly reduced the cross to splinters, directing their violence against the very symbol of Christian redemptive dialectics.[72] Purely by chance, however, they were discovered by a passing horseman and eventually punished, most by being burned at the stake.

The particularly virulent nature of the local animosity did not subside easily, and Legendre suggests that it became a recurring cause for tension as Christian/Jew, Old Christian/New Christian, and royalist/liberal hatreds renewed with different names the same divisions within the population.

Approximately four years later, during which time more and more Jews fled to Las Hurdes, Casar's Christians took over the local synagogue, re-sacralized it as a church, installed the remains of the cross there, and eventually erected a memorial chapel in its place. They thus completed the violent expulsion of Jews whose only crime had been their difference. These measures find an explicit echo in Buñuel's invocation of the scapegoat, whose expulsion serves symbolically to rid a community of an inner threat, either from the too highly elevated or from its own vilest evil. The larger goal of the ceremony is to (re)establish the boundaries between the community proper and that which is absolutely other, irremediably "outside." Given that scapegoating had taken on a decidedly racial character during the 1930s, especially in fascist Germany, Buñuel's adoption of this motif seems at best a risky maneuver. As Hollier suggests, however, such tactics were by no means uncommon in 1930s France. Citing Maurice Blanchot, he argues that what counts "is not to adopt the old slogans all over again: neither right nor left, but to be truly against the right and the left. In these terms one can see the true form of dissidence is that which abandons a position without abandoning its hostility towards the contrary position or rather to abandon it in order to exacerbate this hostility."[73]

While the historical and political specifics of the phenomena Hollier describes are by no means *directly* applicable to Buñuel's film, the idea of embracing the enemy's tactics in order to move "beyond" particular stifling binarisms of political, social, and aesthetic discourse quite clearly is.[74] Buñuel's "no" to the traditional Left was not a "yes" to the Right but an attempt to "exacerbate the hostility" of each toward the status quo. Given a choice between elevating the Hurdanos in an apotheosis of the "truly human" and a fascist debasement of them as societal waste, Buñuel adopts *and* rejects both in a gesture that avoids both their appropriation and their demonization. In this sense, he situates them, like the scapegoat, on the border between the wholly inside and the wholly outside, as a group hostile to both classifications—radically other – and therefore of no immediate use to either faction. By miming the leftist social critique, he shames us and prevents us from blaming them, but by dehumanizing them he prevents an easy, liberal empathy, too. At a moment when similar violence and hatred were gaining ground throughout Europe, and when Jews were once again to be sacrificial victims in the service of nationalisms of all sorts, Buñuel chose to make *Las Hurdes* and in so doing bore witness to an exemplary moment of cultural scapegoating. He addressed the issue in a manner that would have a precise resonance for Spaniards and a more general one for others, but it does so in a strangely cryptic way, which makes it difficult even to imagine that such issues are at stake. While the film informs us that the present inhabitants of Las Hurdes are Christians, in an interview Buñuel tells us, rather pointedly, that they are the descendants of Jews fleeing persecution.[75] But, scapegoating aside, what evidence does the film give of their Jewishness, especially in light of its crucial role in understanding the film's curious tactics? That is, how might Buñuel have indicated, however obliquely, the stakes of this film? I suggest that one answer can be found in another of the film's unexplained dimensions—one that has remained unjustified. The one mark in the film that gives this knowledge utterance is the altered title on the print he donated to the Museum of Modern Art in New York in 1940. Although he has never referred to this title, nor is it attached to any other version of the film, it carries some authority, coming, as it does, as his personal gift. The new title bears witness to the submerged thematics of racial scapegoating and violent suppression that I have tried to bring to the surface. It is perhaps clearer now why Buñuel so carefully made this a "useless" film—useless to all nationalisms, republican or fascist. To have exalted the Hurdanos, as Unamuno had done, would have falsified the historical reality of their lives and simultaneously enriched the very culture that had so violently excluded them. To blame them, as decades of writers had done, would have been even worse. Thus, the logic of violent equivocation, which risks identifying with the spirit of fascism in order to overcome it, appeared as a possible answer. The new title was, of course, a parody of a famous expression, simultaneously negating and repeating the "original" without reconciliation. It was an expression resonant with exile and unfulfilled redemption: Un*promised Land*.

Notes

The epigraph that opens this essay is from Georges Bataille, "The Psychological Structure of Fascism," in *Visions of Excess: Selected Writings, 1927–39,* edited by Alan Stoekl, translated by Alan Stoekl, Carl R. Lovitt, and Donald M. Leslie Jr. (Minneapolis: University of Minnesota Press, 1985), 146.

1 Although the film was shot in the spring of 1932 and is often dated to that year, it was not screened until spring 1933.

2 On the various traditions of scapegoating, see James George Frazer, *The Golden Bough: A Study in Magic and Religion,* 3d ed., pt. 6, "The Scapegoat" (London and Basingstoke: Macmillan, 1980), esp. chaps. 4–6, 170–274; Jane Ellen Harrison, *Prolegomena to the Study*

of *Greek Religion,* 3d ed. (Cambridge: Cambridge University Press, 1922), esp. 95–114, on the *pharmakos,* Jane Ellen Harrison, *Themis: A Study of the Social Origins of the Greek Religion* (New Hyde Park, N.Y.: University Books, [1927] 1962), esp. 416; and Jacques Derrida, *Dissemination,* translated, with an introduction, by Barbara Johnson (Chicago: University of Chicago Press, 1981), 120–34.

3 See James Clifford, "On Ethnographic Surrealism," in *The Predicament of Culture: Twentieth Century Ethnography, Literature, and Art* (Cambridge: Harvard University Press, 1988), 117–51.

4 Denis Hollier, "On Equivocation (between Literature and Politics)," *October* 51 (spring 1991): 7, my emphasis. See, more generally, pages 5–11. Hollier refers to Zeev Sternhell, *Ni droite, ni gauche,* enlarged ed. (Paris: Éditions Complexe, 1987), particularly the last two chapters.

5 Virginia Higginbotham, *Luis Buñuel* (Boston: Twayne Publishers, 1979), 48, 52.

6 Francisco Aranda, *Luis Buñuel: A Critical Biography,* translated and edited by David Robinson (New York: Da Capo, 1976), 92, 95, my emphasis.

7 Higginbotham, *Luis Buñuel,* 92; and Aranda, *Luis Buñuel,* 95, for example, see on the one hand a picture in the students' textbook of a "typical bourgeois woman, wellfed, welldressed, and content," and on the other a "marquis in a powdered wig, accompanied by his lady." In these and other accounts, the Albercans are described as wearing "gaudy jewelry," the Hurdanos, we are told, "set an infant adrift downstream," "kill the pig as soon as it has a little flesh on it," and so on.

8 Buñuel called the film "tendentious." See José de la Colina and Tomás Pérez Turrent, eds., *Objects of Desire: Conversations with Luis Buñuel,* translated by Paul Lenti (New York: Marsilio, 1992), 35.

9 Ado[nis] Kyrou, *Buñuel: The Man and His Work,* translated by Adrienne Foulke (New York: Simon and Schuster, 1963), 42.

10 See *"Las Hurdes," L'Avant-scène du Cinéma* 36 (1964): 62.

11 "J'ai fait *Las Hurdes* parce que j'avais une vision surréaliste, et parce que je m'intéressais au problème de l'homme. Je voyais la réalité d'une autre façon que je l'aurais vue avant le surréalisme. J'étais sûr de cela, et Pierre Unik aussi" (André Bazin and Jacques Doniol Valcroze, "Entretien avec Luis Buñuel," *Cahiers du Cinéma* 37 [July 1954]: 4).

12 Francisco Aranda, *Luis Buñuel: A Critical Biography,* translated by David Robinson (New York: Da Capo, 1975), 88.

13 Herman Lebovics, *True France: The Wars over National Identity, 1900–1945* (Ithaca: Cornell University Press, 1992), 57.

14 Ibid., 67–83, esp. 79. These new Frenchmen, it was claimed, were people whose names currently sounded strange to Parisian ears, just as Provençal and Gascon names had years earlier, but who would be assimilated just as assuredly. Once again, the political and imperial logic of representation here resulted in a net "profit" for the capital of the empire.

15 Ibid., 105–10. Pages 108–9 offer photographs of the exhibit.

16 On this pamphlet, see Helena Lewis, *The Politics of Surrealism* (New York: Paragon House, 1988), 95; and Lebovics, *True France,* 55–56.

17 Lewis, *The Politics of Surrealism,* 29.

18 Clifford, "On Ethnographic Surrealism," 120.

19 The mission returned with 3,500 objects of unparalleled quality. See *Minotaure: The Animal-Headed Review* (Geneva: Musée d'art et d'histoire, 1987).

20 Luis Buñuel, *La Révolution Surréaliste* 12 (December 1929): 34.

21 Luis Buñuel, "Notes on the Making of *Un chien andalou*," in Joan Mellen, ed. 153. *The World of Luis Buñuel: Essays in Criticism.* (New York: Oxford University Press, 1978), 153.

22 John Baxter, *Buñuel* (New York: Carroll and Graf, 1998), 107. Jacques Prévert introduced Bataille to Buñuel at the former's request.

23 André Breton, "Manifesto of Surrealism," in *Manifestoes of Surrealism,* translated by Richard Seaver and Helen R. Lane (Ann Arbor: University of Michigan Press, 1969), 14.

24 Artaud, Limbour, Masson, Soupault, Vitrac, and Bataille (among others) had abandoned or were banished from Breton's surrealist church at around the same time. See Breton, "Second Manifesto of Surrealism (1930)," in *Manifestoes of Surrealism,* esp. 129–37, 180–86.

25 See *La Révue du Cinéma* 24 (1931): 30; and Aranda, *Luis Buñuel,* 91.

26 Georges Bataille, "Dictionnaire," *Documents* 6 (1929): 330. Lotar had also recently published portraits of Bataille's wife, the actress Sylvia, in *La Revue du Cinéma.*

27 James Clifford, "On Ethnographic Surrealism," 132.

28 Georges Bataille, "La gros orteil," and "Fox Follies," *Documents* 6 (1929): 297–302, 344.

29 Aranda, *Luis Buñuel,* 96.

30 Formal similarity draws together the two enterprises, bridging the gap between one of the signatories of the Second Surrealist Manifesto and one of its chief targets, Breton's "Toe-nail Philosopher," the man Buñuel remembered late in his life as having a face that "looked as if it never smiled." See Luis Buñuel, *My Last Sigh,* translated by Abigail Israel (New York: Vintage Books, 1984), 122.

31 Roland Barthes, "Outcomes of the Text," in *The Rustle of Language,* translated by Richard Howard (New York: Hill and Wang, 1986), 241–42.

32 Rosalind E. Krauss, *The Optical Unconscious* (Cambridge: MIT Press, 1993), 184–85. Krauss's invocation of "form" situates her discussion in relation to Bataille's interest in the *informe,* or that which lacks or resists all form. See also Denis Hollier, *Against Architecture: The Writings of Georges Bataille,* translated by Betsy Wing (Cambridge: MIT Press, 1989), 76–85.

33 As Denis Hollier puts it, Bataille's article provokes "insubordination in the part, which then refuses to respect the hierarchical relations defining it by its integration into the organic system as a whole. [It] makes the organ suddenly emerge as a partial object, irrecuperable for the purposes of constructing a whole body image" (*Against Architecture,* 78).

34 Marañon was an old friend who had served as Buñuel's personal physician during his years at the Residencia.

35 De la Colina and Turrent, *Objects of Desire,* 37: "[Alberca] tiene los bailes más hermosas del mundo y sus charros se visten con trajes magnificos del siglo XVII."

36 Ibid., 37–38. So sensitive, in fact, was the Lerroux government to the film's imagined consequences that it lodged official complaints with all foreign countries that sought to exhibit it. This occurred, of course, during what Buñuel calls a "reactionary parenthesis," which did not characterize the opinion of the Republic at later moments. See ibid., 37–38; and Freddy Buache, *Luis Buñuel* (Paris: Éditions L'Age d'Homme, 1970),

37–39. Despite some confusion, it seems probable that the Spanish embassy in France paid for its sonarization in 1937.

37 It is, of course, important that Breton quotes Hegel again and again against Bataille in the second "Manifesto." In an extended footnote, he also marshalls Marx against Bataille, essentially accusing him of being what the former derided as an "excrement philosopher." Breton: "Marx tells us how, in every age, there thus come into being hair-philosophers, fingernail-philosophers, *toenail philosophers, excrement philosophers,* etc." ("Second Manifesto," 185, emphasis in original). The italicized terms are references to Bataille's essays.

38 Georges Bataille, "The Use Value of D.A.F. de Sade," in Bataille, *Visions of Excess,* 97.

39 Elliot Rubinstein, "Visit to a Familiar Planet: Buñuel among the Hurdanos," *Cinema Journal* 22:4 (summer 1985), 9.

40 Mary Louise Pratt, "Fieldwork in Common Places," in *Writing Culture: The Poetics and Politics of Ethnography,* edited by James Clifford and George Marcus (Berkeley: University of California Press, 1986), 31–38.

41 There are variations among the different versions of the film, but both the French version and one of the U.S. versions say "strange and barbaric." The best-known version, entitled *Unpromised Land,* has a voice-over that is very muted and differs significantly from the earlier French version. Although this print was given to the Museum of Modern Art by Buñuel, he never used the revised title in interviews or memoirs.

42 There are significant differences between the various versions of the film on this point. The version entitled *Unpromised Land* says we are greeted by "hacking coughs." Both English versions differ from the French, which might reasonably be translated as "greeted by a tubercular choir" (un choeur des toux).

43 "Laughter is not the refutation expected by philosophy, that is, the one it has 'in its pocket' in advance. Laughter is a practical refutation, more dangerous when unexpected, that refutes nothing" (Hollier, *Against Architecture,* 101).

44 Legendre, *Las Jurdes: Étude de Geographie Humaine* (Bordeaux: Firet, 1927), xvi.

45 Ibid., xvi–xvii.

46 De la Colina and Turrent, *Objects of Desire,* 38.

47 Cesarman, 104.

48 Legendre, *Las Jurdes* xxiii. Lope's (minor) play is apparently a parody of his *Discovery of the New World by Columbus* (published 1614), which like several other stories compares the discovery of Las Hurdes with that of the New World.

49 Legendre, *Las Jurdes,* xxvi.

50 Ibid., xxiii. See Lope de Vega [Carpio], *Obras Completas,* vol. 11, Crónicas y Leyendas Dramáticas de España (Madrid: Sucesores de Rivadeneyra, 1900), 505–39. The "Observaciones Preliminares" by M. Menéndez y Pelayo are extremely informative on the sources of the Hurdes legends, especially cxxxiv–cli.

51 Luis R. Miguel, "Las Jurdes" *La Revista de Extremadura* 27 (September 1901): 423.

52 Ibid., 426–27.

53 José G. Crotonilo, "Las Jurdes" *La Revista de Extremadura* 29 (November 1901): 509–10.

54 Ibid., 512.

55 Ibid., 510.

56 Ibid., 514.

57 Miguel Unamuno, "Las Hurdes," in *Andanzas y Visiones Españolas* (Madrid: Renacimiento, 1922), 110.

58 Ibid., 112, 114.

59 "allí no hay nada. ¡Ni pan!" (ibid., 112).

60 In fairness to Unamuno, it is important to note that in his discussion of goiter he notes that the purity of the water they drink (its lack of minerals and so on) is extremely debilitating. In order to underscore the problem of excessive purity, he suggests the absurdity of boasting over the "purity" of one's ideas. A race that sought to purify its ideas would be, he argues, ultimately sterile, thereby indicating at least some sensitivity to the politics of purity surrounding the denigration and isolation of the Hurdanos.

61 Unamuno, "Las Hurdes," 113, 114.

62 Ibid., 121.

63 Ibid., 116.

64 Legendre, *Las Jurdes,* xiv–xv: "Ce qu'il est étrange, incroyable et en quelque sort scandaleux, que le pays de Las Jurdes soit peuplé . . . la pays de Las Jurdes, qui ne se prête nullement au peuplement, est peuplé."

65 Ibid., xix.

66 Ibid., xlvi.

67 The list includes Legendre, Unamuno, anonymous writers for the *Revista,* Antonio Rodriguez Moñino (*Dictados Tópicos de Extremadura: Materiales para una Colección Folklórico* [Badajoz: Antonio Arqueros, 1931], Romualdo Martín Santibáñez (*Historia de la Santa Cruz del Casar de Palermo* [Plasencia: Imprenta de Ramos, 1870], an anonymous play entitled *La Santa Cruz del Casar* (Francisco de Torrejoncillo, *Centinela contra judíos, puesta en la Torre de la Iglesia de Dios* [Madrid, 1728], and Vincente Barrantes (*Aparato Bibliográfico para la Historia de Extremadura* (Madrid: P. Muñez Press, 1875–77) vol. 1, 458–59, to name only the few I have been able to discover.

68 Unamuno, "Las Hurdes," 109–11.

69 "Supersticiones Extremeñas: Judíos E Illuminados," *Revista de Extremadura* 25 (1901): 306.

70 Ibid., 306–7, esp. 307, n. 1.

71 The sequence of events in Spain, moving from attempts at conversion to expulsion and, in the most severe case, annihilation, corresponds all too well to the structure typical of Jewish persecution over the centuries, as Raul Hilberg has shown. See, for example, his *The Destruction of the European Jews,* vol. 1 (New York: Holmes and Meier, 1985), 5–28, 53–62.

72 Legendre, *Las Jurdes,* 526–31. This recalls a famous anecdote in Buñuel's life in which he attacked Charlie Chaplin's Christmas tree with a pair of shears, shouting "Down with symbols!" reducing it to nothing but a trunk. Obviously, the consequences were less severe.

73 Maurice Blanchot, "On demande des dissidents," *Combat* 20 (December 1937), reprinted in *Gramma* 5 (1978): 63–65, cited in Hollier, "Equivocation," 11.

74 Most of the essays that Hollier discusses were written well after the original release of Buñuel's film, although several, including Blanchot's "On demande des dissidents," are roughly coincident with the film's sonorization in 1937.

75 Aranda, *Luis Buñuel,* 89.

People understand themselves better than the social fabric; and to see themselves on the screen, performing their daily actions—remembering that to see oneself gives one the sense of being unlike oneself, like hearing one's own voice on the radio—can help them to fill up a void, a lack of knowledge of reality.—Cesare Zavattini

Cesare Zavattini's quest for a cinema animated by a double movement of misrecognition and social adjustment finds its answer in reenactment films, a practice in which a person reenacts earlier events from his or her life for film or television. The goal of the reenactment film is to lead the subject to a different order of consciousness through a dynamic between repetition and alienation. Implicit in this reenactment proposal is the idea that the screen's making public serves not only the performing subject but also others who may learn from his or her errors.[1] The screened life provides a corrective mirror or a model for social action.[2]

Reenactment films conflate repetition with moral revision, and their main outcome is exemplarity. In his own production of *The Lady of the Dugout* (1918), Al Jennings, the famous Oklahoma bandit, and his brother selectively revise their legend: they are seen robbing banks but also, for the bulk of the film, helping out a hungry mother and child in selfish heroic swings. Like most biographies, and especially exemplary ones, reenactment films proceed by careful distillation. The attempt to both respect and re-interpret the original event leads to strained attempts to get the occurrence right but also to correct it. And "getting it right" often involves the repe-tition on camera of some mistaken behavior, which it is the film's work to put on trial.

The activist, communitarian turn is typical of reenactment narratives, providing symmetry between traumatic ordeal and social redemption.[3] In Orson Welles's unfinished *It's All True,* four fishermen reenact their heroic trip on rafts along the Brazilian northeast coast to request social benefits. Their literal retracing of two-thirds of the country's coastal contour con-stitutes a form of religious "promessa," a purposefully long and obstacle-ridden crossing, which is duly rewarded if the believer shows his faith. Dur-ing the filming however, Jacaré, one of the men, dies and Welles continues the shoot with another fisherman playing his role in a touching illustration of film and reenactment's limits in reversing time.

If the film elides its own, most contingent eventuality, it is to have this tale better stand as exemplary. More often reenactment films such as *The Jackie Robinson Story* (1950) or *Ali: The Greatest* (1977) dramatize the pas-sage from life to model biography by including a conversion scene from a prior off-course behavior to a later enlightened self, from individualis-tic concerns to community awareness. This feature likens reenactment to consciousness-raising narratives in militant documentaries: the reference to the past sets a contrast with a present, informed self. Feminist documen-taries of the 1970s or more recent activist work such as Shabnam Vernami's *When Women Unite: The Story of an Uprising* (1996), showing women in rural India struggling against their husbands' alcoholic dependence, repeatedly present vignette reenactments that are strained with a pedagogic and po-litical toll. The performances do double work: they are framed as examples of what happened, and they are intended as models for future action. Often detached from the film's texture through slow motion or freeze frames, such partial reenactment scenes signal the desire to arrest contradictions and provide idealized, exemplary models.

In grafting the notion of exemplarity onto reenactment films, I bear in mind for the term *example* a range of meanings, any of which are signifi-cant for pedagogic or militant films: a person's action or conduct regarded as an object of imitation; appeals to precedents to authorize a course of action; and a signal instance of punishment intended to have a deterrent effect, a cautionary function.[4] Examples are those concrete instances used to support a general statement, a means, according to Aristotle, of producing belief through induction.[5] In ancient rhetoric, the example had a broadly understood mimetic range: "not only does the example picture, it may also induce an imitative reproduction on the part of the audience."[6] As John Lyons notes in *Exemplum,* there is indeed a marked tendency to "fuse" or even "confuse" the cognitive/rhetorical functions of the example with its doctrinal and prescriptive function (the exemplum).[7] In its vernacular usage, *exemplum* means, "a short narrative used to illustrate a moral point." The constant reference in sermons to the ultimate exemplar, the deeds and life of Christ, helps establish the status of the exemplum as a model. Within this self-validating circle, *exemplum* acquires the meaning of a model to be copied and that of the copy or representation of that model—the exemplar.[8]

Following the distinction between *exemplum* and *example* into the nineteenth-century literature, April Alliston points out how the "exemplary realism" of the mid–eighteenth century gives way to the later high mimetic realism. In "exemplary realism" she claims, "the text's status as exemplum takes precedence over its status as representation. . . . the text asks to be read as an example capable of generating real action through imitation, rather than as an imitation of real action" [as mimesis].[9] On the other hand the "characters of mimetic realism are no longer . . . presented as models for imitation, but they are examples in the other evidentiary sense: they are particular instances that prove a maxim or precept—in this case an implicit statement of general truth about reality—by standing for it, representing it."[10]

Because of their expositional logic, partial reenactment scenes in documentary film seem to fit a mimetic realism. Intercalated with talking head interviews or juxtaposed to voice-over commentaries, these scenes introduce the concrete instance that stands for "an implicit statement of general truth." Fully reenacted films are, however, self-sufficient narratives vis-à-vis a framing argument, and they display relatively unbracketed presences whose authenticating effect far exceeds the demands of mimetic representation. Their in-quotations, signified particularity, are rechanneled from a purely evidentiary function toward an exemplary one.

There are significant differences in moving from the general to the particular in film and verbal language, which qualify my use of verbal exemplarity as a model. The shift from descriptive mimetic toward a modelar exemplarity is key to an understanding of reenactment. Reenactment radically refocuses the issue of indexicality. The corroborating value of reenactment does depend on our knowledge that these particular feet walked these particular steps. But it is the intentional and fictional retracing that *enacted* lends to these faces and places an authenticating aura. This aura, the indexical value of reenactment, is present but at a remove. It is activated but only through a doubling, a replaying that foregrounds the events' most "evident" particulars. The most singular singularity promoted in reenactment is that of a person's identity, a body and face with a first and last name.

This modelar function is sustained by repetition's potential to convert. The narratives discussed here invoke a moral dynamic in which the very act of repetition becomes relevant, not because it copies the original situation, providing its best and closest illustration, but because by repeating it produces an improved version of the event. Inflected by a psychodramatic (or liturgical) belief in the enlightening effects of literal repetition, reenactment creates, performatively speaking, another body, place, and time. At stake is an identity that can recall the original event (through a second-degree indexicality) but in so doing can also re-form it.

I image reenactment films as modern morality tales, and the main question I pose to the films is how they grant an exemplary dimension to the screened individual. This essay analyses the rhetoric of exemplarity in four reenactment films: two from the classic realist school of cinema, the episodes by Zavattini and Francesco Maselli and by Michelangelo Antonioni in the omnibus film *Love in the City* (1953), and two from contemporary films, Zhang Yuan's *Sons* (1996) and Abbas Kiarostami's *Close Up* (1990).

This Is Your Life: *Love of a Mother* and *Attempted Suicide*

Neorealism—as I understand it—requires that everyone act as themselves.
—Cesare Zavattini, "Some Ideas on Cinema"

Love in the City (1953), an omnibus film with episodes by Alberto Lattuada, Federico Fellini, Zavattini and Maselli, Michelangelo Antonioni, Carlo Lizzani, and Dino Risi, was the first (and only) film installment of a projected series of cinematic magazines entitled *The Spectator*.[11] A voice-over prologue defines the aim of the magazine: "unknown people will play themselves, reality will be followed up close, without any fictive clothing. . . . Each event, faithfully reconstituted, embodies its own lesson, if only because it happened." Charged with proving neorealism alive, *Love in the City* was a film manifesto, an attempt to rigorously apply Zavattini's theory of "*pedinamento,*" the shadowing of everyday facts at close range.[12]

Zavattini learned about one Caterina Rigoglioso, who, unable to support her child, first abandoned him and then regained him—through the "zoom effect" of journalistic sensationalism. "Today all Italy knows what she did and why; few people have not been moved by it," remarks the announcer of *Love of a Mother,* advertising both the film's source—a news item—and the film's ultimate mission, to make it public. After giving up her child, Rigoglioso read the newspaper headline "Heartless Mother Abandons Her Boy," was filled with regret, and became a nurse at the orphanage where the boy had been taken. She then cared not only for her own child but also for the children of others.

In a turn typical of reenactment projects, Caterina's story concludes in social integration and can thus serve as a model tale. Her care for other children literalizes Zavattini's prescription for reenactment as a mode for collectively sharing in one's difficulties. In his writings, Zavattini focuses on the potential of cinema to better the self through repetition, giving reenactment the status of a "second chance." In reliving one's experience through a "kind of ritual," and through "reconstruction with almost scientific aims," one breaks away from that "embarrassment that is always anti-collective, that is too protective of individualistic fact." One can then "acquire consciousness of the collective destiny of our acts, its 'making public.' "[13] For Zavattini, the reenactment of one's life must produce a form of communion—a repetition that distances but also reanimates.[14] Both nonprofessional actors and those who relive their experiences for the camera do so as a way to primarily interpret their human roles in society. The actor that replicates his or her own experience passes from the state of protagonist to that of "officiante."[15]

Love of a Mother obviously aspires to this liturgical dimension. The literal retracing of Caterina's painful path suggests a Christian trajectory. The film's focus is on concrete hardship and Caterina's tribulations: when she looks for and is rejected for work, when she tries to get someone to care for her child. Images of actual physical endurance—scenes of Caterina walking, climbing steps, and waiting—make up most of the film, figuring a kind of via crucis. These nondramatic moments, in which literal performance and acting are the most indistinguishable and cannot be judged in terms of acting, are also the most successful in achieving a ritualistic order. Because these scenes involve the repetition of mundane moves, they pertain to a nondramatic register and invoke meaning through a deliberately nonaestheticized repetition. When she abandons her child, however, the reverse is true. Convoluted camera movements such as a crane shot closing in on Caterina crying and abrupt shifts between long shots and a close-up of Caterina peeking back at her child after leaving him, are obvious attempts to color this event through melodramatic conventions. These scenes are insufficient to elicit emotion even when they strain to do just that. Rigoglioso's flat performance and the uninteresting cinematic treatment by Maselli give every situation an unintended distance.

Always attuned to the vicissitudes of realism, André Bazin delineates the contradictory requirements at the core of Zavattini's project in "Le Neorealisme se Retourne," his review of *Love in the City:* "if this story constitutes itself an appropriate scenario the minute faithfulness can only undermine the dramatic construction, and also only an incredible luck could predestine the real protagonist to her employment in the film."[16] Indeed, even Zavattini was disappointed with Caterina's less than true to life performance. "Caterina did not seem to 'take' to the cinema. But wasn't she 'Caterina'?"[17] The dramatized mise-en-scène sets in relief the main dilemma in reenactment's reach for exemplarity. As Caterina is asked to be what she is not, an actress, her identity, one of the authorizing principles for exemplarity, wavers. At the same time, her inability to act spoils any chance for verisimilitude and thus compromises the believability of another possible form of example, the "fictitious narrative that nevertheless could have occurred."[18]

If Caterina has failed, against expectations, to "represent" Caterina, how does the film fulfill its "making public" mission? It becomes increasingly obvious that it is not the identity of the original event's protagonist alone that guarantees an exemplary narrative. "We know" states Bazin, that "the assassin doesn't look necessarily like a criminal. Forcibly we have to note that reality goes here beyond all the cautions of art. Not because the witnessing in its brutal reality renders art derisory, but on the contrary because being given this scenario (real or not) no interpretation and no mise-en-scène could better show its value."[19] Bazin's remark underlines the fact that the evidential force of reenactment does not depend on resemblance or acting skills. That this kind of story (even if fictional) can only be served by literal reenactment emphasizes the interdependence between the body's presence and particular kinds of model narrative. It is the tale of error and penance that fits reenactment. Bazin's choice of a criminal metaphor also alerts us, inadvertently, to the link, implicit in all of Zavattini's rhetoric, between reenactment and atonement.

In *Zavattini: Sequences from a Cinematic Life,* the screenwriter recounts one of his film ideas of 1944. He proposed going on a truck with Lattuada, Fabbri, and Monicelli and stopping in a destroyed village where the people are slowly beginning to resume life among the ruins.

> We talk to them in the square; I'll say I'm guilty of this and that, at first they'll consider me a monster, but this is the only way I'll be able to act also as accuser, attribute to each his responsibilities, we'll be constantly dramatizing . . . some of those present try to justify themselves and they don't realize I'm offering them a chance to get it all off their chests. . . . We set a primitive screen in the center of the square and show some bits of film . . . the narrator tries to make the people in the square understand that these other men also weep, die, kill, run off . . . the spectators get tired, they tell the moralist to go to the devil . . . Mussolini's voice appears from the rubble and we hear applause coming from that man smoking his pipe. It lasts five minutes . . . they would all like to shut up the voice from the loudspeaker but they don't know what to do.[20]

In 1949, Zavattini aspires to make a film that is "to be projected against the sky, visible at the same moment in every part of the earth." This "domestic Last Judgement . . . begun by our films just after the war cannot be interrupted."[21] For this is cinema conceived as a settling of accounts, a program for political and historical catharsis. This program is also in line with the consensual view of neorealism as an antifascist front and to a vigilant postwar consciousness to which any "evasion of reality was a betrayal."[22]

These statements, pregnant with the urgency of social and national healing, provide the basic ideological matrix of reenactment. Reenactment is a "moral remake": it is "the cognitive intent of cinema that can give moral force to the anti-spectacular remake of the 'first time around'."[23] When Zavattini postulates cinema as promoting a comparative, humanist frame, when he arrogates himself as both a narrator and father confessor, when he proposes his candid camera (pedinamento) theory with its disturbing connotations of detective work and wrongdoing, he shapes a basic scenario for his intervention and the relevance of his methods: "making public" presupposes a social reality in need of redemption.

The terms of judgment that are so prevalent in Zavattini's discourse suggest that the moral superiority warranted in resistance was continuously mobilized in neorealist rhetoric but particularly so in the early 1950s. During this moment of definition and survival for the Italian film industry, neorealism's social agenda and aesthetic credentials were questioned from both the Left and the Right.[24] Two related ideological and aesthetic debates emerged. The first, staged in the party line and leftist criticism, has to do with the embrace of social realism as a model.[25] The second one, more pertinent to Zavattini's methods, argues for the needed passage from neorealism to realism. Guido Aristarco's *Cinema Nuovo* is the main voice for a cinematic version of Lukács's theories of literary realism: "Chronicle, document, denunciation. All this constitutes solely the preface to true realism, which by its nature can only be critical, historical."[26] Under the Lukácsian doxa, the immediate record of the everyday is deemed a flawed, insufficient version of realism. Again and again Zavattini's projects are chastised for bordering on naturalism, for being unable to say anything more than something about "this or that person, this or that situation."[27] *Love in the City* is cited variously as an extreme and failed experiment. Visconti's *Senso* instead exemplifies a true, epic realism in which characters embody broader historical forces.[28]

In *Il Cinema Italiano*, Carlo Lizzani states that "by 1953 . . . every movement . . . wanted to decide for the life and death of realism."[29] The First Convention of Parma, in December of that year, was devoted to a critical evaluation of neorealism, and there was a manifest "attempt to replace the lack of effective unity [among the various positions] with the greatest display of verbal unanimity and voluntarism."[30] The resistance to the departures from a single neorealist model figured in the works of Fellini, Rossellini, and Visconti was acutely enacted in Zavattini's appeal to uncontroversial positions, for instance, his equation of neorealism with a moral vocation.[31]

Zavattini's dramatization of cinema as an expiatory apparatus is aimed, in the Parma Convention, at those who dare declare neorealism and its raison d'être dead. His discourse returns to the key theme in the immediate postwar debate: the motif of the alienated intellectual and the need "to overcome this condition inherited from idealism [of the fascist era] through a direct contact with the popular, proletarian and urban reality."[32] Reenactment becomes a ritualized plea for the redemptive potential of the film medium. Based on a named, particular body, reenactment becomes a method of social reparation, a way to socially redistribute attention: "One should remember that in the registry we all have names, and therefore are all interesting."[33] In Zavattini's rhetoric, reenactment is the way to reinstate neorealism as a social barometer, to redirect its focus on inequality in a more diffuse and complex social reality, and to return it to its more immediate, socially conscious, postwar vocation.

Reenactment also works, significantly, as an attempt to absolve Zavattini, the scriptwriter, from his own ability to tell stories and create drama. Suggestions for the elimination of a script, and for the closer and closer share in the subject's life ("make a hole in the ceiling, live in the house in front, also pretending to be a worker, etc.") are all attempts to circumvent an intellectual/artistic mediation that for Zavattini coincides with a bourgeois point of view.[34] After *Umberto D*'s critical success, Zavattini can only state that "the same persons who lived a story and *not the script,* must tell their story"[35] His emphasis on literal reenactment points, faintly, to a transformative dimension located in happenings, in one's bodily experience, an attempt perhaps to reinstall art into the social body. This ritualistic, performative dimension is nonetheless continuously compromised by Zavattini's talent for creating stories with a social moral. As Sam Rohdie notes, the story of *Love of a Mother* replicates the same cycle of abandonment for the sake of love as *Umberto D.*[36] More importantly the significance of real time representation in each project is finally not so different. Both films use radical ellipsis to compensate for the long takes representing mundane events.[37] As redemptive tales, both films depend entirely on the representation of material, physical ordeals. And only the painstaking repetition of gestures, dialogue, and moods can provide the Christian connotation on which Zavattini's morality rests.[38]

The patronizing attitude of the commentator in *Love in the City* reveals the link between the Italian Left and Catholicism: the thread implicitly uniting Caterina Rigoglioso's story to the stories comprising Antonioni's *Attempted Suicide,* another episode in the omnibus film, is absolution through public confession. For both filmmakers, film is figured as a screening process for purging mistakes and for the conversion of subjects. And yet there are significant differences in each filmmaker's road beyond (or back to) neorealism.[39]

Attempted Suicide casts reenactment in a psychoanalytic light, providing an indication of Antonioni's interest in staging social alienation through individual impasse and crisis. Given the limits of literal repetition, a suicide attempt is an admittedly interesting case for reenactment. As an exhibitionist spectacle, a performance whose closure is lacking, the sole evidence of good conscience in a suicide attempt is the performer's demise. An attempted suicide (and that is Antonioni's position on the matter) suggests a desire for effect rather than substance, especially if its frame is feminine despair. And, indeed, in each of the episode's four case histories the suicide attempt marks a crisis in the representation.

In one of the stories, a woman starts off walking silently while a voice-over narration relates her history. As the tale moves toward its climax, and toward the present tense, she stops on a riverbank, turns to the camera, points to the river, and says, "That's where I did it." The shift from representation to presentation, to direct address, significantly coincides with the problematic repetition of her actions. The filmmaker represents the sui-

cide attempt through an insert of an abstracted shot of the river's troubled waters. It represents her drowning but is unclear as to its agency.

In another story, that of Donatella, the shift to direct address is dramatized in a simple stroke —a close-up inserted within the reenactment of the woman's actions. After the narrator describes her disappointment in love, Donatella goes through the motions of slitting her wrist in a medium shot. A close-up of her wrist shows the stitch marks of the suicide attempt and, over the stitches, a small dark drop. This shot is inserted in the film's flow through analytic editing. However, in a clear movement of display the woman turns her wrist to the camera, as if doubling the denotative aspect of the film shot. It is as if the close-up were stating, "Here is the representation of a suicide attempt," almost in mockery of reenactment's pretense. This shot encapsulates the limits of reenactment: the blade cannot trace the same path twice without literally producing a wound.

1 and 2. Donatella reenacting the slicing of her wrist in *Attempted Suicides,* Michelangelo Antonioni, 1953 (frame enlargement of video)

3. Donatella displays to the camera the scar on her wrist in *Attempted Suicides,* Michelangelo Antonioni, 1953 (frame enlargement of video)

After this shot, Donatella addresses the camera. She is lying in bed, and a cut in the action shows her wrist, still turning in the display position. She holds the blade, telling us what happened next. Asked why she has agreed to reenact this event, she reveals what is at stake in a successful reenactment: "the feeling of being more open about it . . . a second chance." Finally, Donatella says that the only thing she wants to do is to "be an actress, not through a contest but seriously . . . enter the academy."

This sequence presents a vertiginous slippage of representational registers that make the film's therapeutic project explicit. The reenactment of one's past behavior is interrupted suddenly. Instead of a risky acting out, the film proposes the working through of a talking cure. Both Breuer and Freud attributed a cathartic force to verbal expression, suggesting that "language serves as a substitute for action . . . [through] its [the language's] help an affect can be 'abreacted' almost as effectively . . . speaking is itself an adequate reflex, when for instance, it is a lamentation or giving utterance to a tormenting secret, e.g. a confession." [40] Substituting repetition for verbal enunciation, this scene works as proof of the recovery power of reenactment. The foolishness of repeating such a gesture is noted, and reflective talk substitutes for action. The impossibility of literal repetition can only lead to safe and even creative forms of repetition: to tell a story or to become an actress.

Acting is the constitutive aporia of reenactment. To make public means to perform, but any nod toward theatricality calls into question the authenticity of one's gestures. It is when Caterina acts that she casts suspicion as to who she is. Antonioni himself treads a precarious route in his choice of subject. He states his own distrust about the exhibitionist nature of the suicide attempts by commenting at the film's start that "one may ask why these people have decided to come forth and make their stories public." He stages his protagonists against a white background. Each woman—and only women tell their stories—starts talking in this setting before the film cuts to the reenacted events. Ostensibly a sound studio, the neutral backdrop is also eerily reminiscent of a police lineup. The authenticity of one's gesture—namely, the suicide at-

4. Women line up before reenacting their stories in *Attempted Suicides,* Michelangelo Antonioni, 1953 (frame enlargement of video)

tempt—is an object of social interest, but in his mise-en-scène Antonioni's subjects are on trial.[41] His mise-en-scène indicts these city dwellers, suggesting their incommunicability.

Something else emerges from Antonioni's treatment of suicide. The depiction of a suicide attempt calls direct attention to a needed shift from representation to presentation. In addition, this passage from enactment to verbal description or confession can be seen as Antonioni's own move toward a different register for his cinema and realist cinema in general. The person does not simply illustrate a general condition but is, at points, heard. Women voice their own particular reasons. "Those were cases that had to do with psychology, not morality" states the filmmaker in defense of his emphasis on particular, psychological causes. In a letter to Aristarco about *Attempted Suicide,* he carefully weighs these two terms, acknowledging the theme's challenge: "I cannot bring myself to sharing the opinion that if someone kills himself it is to some extent everyone's fault. Suicide is such an enigmatic gesture. . . . It is true that suicide has a moral significance and that psychology cannot ignore morals, but it is also true that morality cannot ignore the teachings of psychology. . . . the Church itself grants its sacraments to a suicide affected by madness. This demonstrates that it is not possible to leave special causes aside and the special is the proper domain of psychology."[42]

The interest of Antonioni's film lies in the clarity through which it negotiates the terms of a change in neorealist representation. Almost in compensation for its focus on "special causes," the film strains to channel the representation of one's consciousness for the public good. "They've agreed to come to our studio only because they felt that this moment of sincerity, this examination through another's gaze of the sole irreparable act in a man's life, would be useful for him and for others," the commentary remarks.[43] At its close, the segment returns to the film studio. The group of men and women once physically alienated from each other wander out chatting against the white studio background in a visual representation of the "making public" effects of reenactment—a communion of interests, a sharing in each other's problems.

The casting option in *Love of a Mother* and *Attempted Suicide* can be understood as a move to disturb the bland generality of fictional representation, a move toward the singular representativeness of the original exemplar oxymoronically produced through reenactment.

The potential for disturbance generated through reenactment—a surplus of artificially produced authenticity—is nevertheless tamed. The decrease in authorial presence and voice advocated by Zavattini in his repeal of script acting and "fairy tales," and staged through Antonioni's on-camera revelations, is heavily qualified by the films' interrogating and adjudicating voice-over commentary. This voice-over, which introduces the film spectator and each of the cases portrayed, comments and interrogates, creating a moralistic frame that transforms the extended sections of reenactment into illustrative material. The singularity of each identity and case is here at the service of an idea, a message.

In their enlistment and containment of excessively singular bodies and voices, *Love of a Mother* and *Attempted Suicide* introduce, in 1953, key issues facing realist representation, issues that become, interestingly enough, most evident in cinema vérité practice and in later, 1970s consciousness-raising documentaries.

The exclusive attention to the everyday, a hallmark of neorealism, is radicalized in reenactment through the validating presences of authentic bodies. A similar search for the authentic voice (direct address to the camera or unmediated record) leads in cinema vérité to a concentration on private narratives. Freely combining interview, commentary, and reenactment, Antonioni's segment anticipates in its mixed address French cinema vérité's approach to the staging of truth.[44] Jean Rouch and Edgar Morin's *Chronicle of a Summer* (1960), for instance, presents the silent reenactment of a Renault factory worker's daily routine along with other participants' extensive verbal "relivings" of the past.

And yet the neorealist reenactments resemble most, in their social vocation, the consciousness-raising American films of the 1970s. As Bill Nichols has suggested, the unframed voices of cinema vérité generated an intense focus on the private sphere but with a parallel loss of context. The need to create collective ramifications for these statements leads to the use of voice-over commentary.[45] In the neorealist episodes, the voice-over narration works to generalize. The example's subordinate quality and its structural function as an illustration of a more general precept are evident. The filmmakers' difficulty in giving their subjects an unbracketed voice works as a paradoxical "this is your life" gift. Framed by a clearly moralistic commentary, these exemplary narratives return one's life as a fully amended property. The commentary works as a censure, while the women's confessing bodies serve as negative examples. It is finally this other body, produced by reenactment and in support of a moral precept, that allows it to work as exemplum.

In yet another way, these films resemble the consciousness-raising films.

Their lesson is voiced in the gap between an enlightened present and a mistaken past. With astonishing consistency, projects that use reenactment repeat a "before and after" structure in an allegory of change and improvement. Whatever fissures appear in the representation—Caterina Rigoglioso's bad acting or the obvious shifts between actors and actual people—are co-opted as formal analogues for passing modes toward a more stable, aware self.

This stabilizing tale of self-construction is the positive residue of a loss: the unavoidable perception that reenactment can only produce another image and that the closer it recalls the original the more it distances itself from it. And yet this inbuilt impossibility should be viewed as reenactment's pedagogical asset. Reenactment projects only succeed as dystopian versions of *Back to the Future* (1985): it is by showing that it is impossible to go back in time to avert a particular event or change a particular situation that they disseminate their lessons and warnings.[46]

In Antonioni's film, the scar establishes the limits of reenactment. Through this corporeal impasse, reality cross-checks realism: the scar stands as proof that reenactment cannot affect reality, cannot reverse time. The pedagogic potential of reenactment depends, however, precisely on the irreversibility of time. That one cannot change the past but can merely, and barely, reproduce its appearances is the implicit drama of reenactment as well as its explicit, working moral.

One might term this example-setting approach "doomed repetition." Repetition, the enabling feature of reenactment, haunts its liberating promise. In its moralistic version, reenactment films often qualify the reenacted events as a thing of the past, an error left behind. Reenactment is meant to produce at once an image of the past and a redeemed, conscious presence. The genre's built-in, inescapable, and cyclic return is instead problematized in two contemporary films, to which we will now turn.

Reenacting Heredity: Zhang Yuan's *Sons*

I'm like your grampa, and you are like me, genetics.—Li Maoje to his son in *Sons*

In *Sons* (1996), an entire family reenacts events leading to the alcoholic father being committed to a mental asylum.[47] Zhang Yuan, the filmmaker, briefs us as to how the two Li brothers, Tou Zi and Xiao Wei, his young neighbors, ask him to make a film in which they would act themselves.

Asked why they chose *Sons* and not *Father* as the film's title, the brothers reply that all men are sons but not all men are fathers. This remark is especially significant in a film about hereditary behavior, about what gets passed on naturally from father to son (in this case, alcohol addiction and abusive behavior).

The film relentlessly immerses itself in family drama. The father's contorted face is often intercut with the family tensely avoiding him, the sons sitting in their room, the door closed, his voice booming through the rooms. With the father's drunkenness as a continuous, high-pitched backdrop and his face distorted in the frame's foreground, a parallel narrative gradually emerges that focuses on the sons' behavior.

As the title announces, *Sons* is only ostensibly about the father's alcoholism. Initially, the film introduces the household's routine, a series of admonitions and reproaches directed at Li Maoje by mother and sons. But soon we watch the effects of the home's disintegration in the sons' lives. They exhibit a slightly perverse sexuality, are seen in bars, and often come home climbing over the wall or the compound's gate.

In its peculiarly didactic economy, the film promotes a direct causality between the father's affliction and the sons' vio-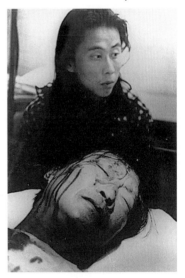lence and addiction. As if in direct response, scenes showing the sons' erratic behavior follow scenes with the father. Oedipal scenarios are staged, the most explicit one being when Tou Zi, the older son, shocked after finding his mother drunk and lying close to his father, breaks into their room and crashes a chair over the father's head. With blood streaming down his face, Li Maoje states: "Thank you my good boy, thank you my good boy." In the hospital, he refuses anesthetic and dramatically declares: "I want to keep it and look at it; this is a permanent mark of a son hating his old man." At home, Xiao Wei cares for his father and tries unsuccessfully to remove the bloodstain from the sheets. The collapse of parental authority is stressed three times: by the father's saying "An unpious son is the father's

5. Father and son after the physical attack in *Sons*, Zhang Yuan, 1998. (Still courtesy of Photofest.)

fault"; by the sons, who commission the reenactment; and by Zhang Yuan, whose frame composition foregrounds the ineffectual cleaning of the stain, branding it with extra signification.

The stain that is so accented by both the characters and the filmmaker exacts, at this later point in the film, a number of meanings. First, this bloody scene presents one of many transgressions of the boundary between acting and being. In reenactment, all the quandaries of realism are amplified, and *Sons* thrives on scenes that especially depend on a careful demarcation between fiction and reality, between pretense and actual bodily change and harm: the father's ingestion of alcohol, the sons taking drugs and having sex, and finally the chair that splits open the father's head. These are scenes whose literal repetition may have real consequences, demanding, therefore, greater artifice. But the bloody scene also caps the film's violent crescendo. It dramatizes the uselessness of repeated admonitions.

The film is structured as a series of unheeded warnings. All of the dialogue delineates the father's inability to stop drinking and the sons parallel junkie paths. In the first, most explicit sermon, Li Maoje, the father, talks to Tou zi: "I failed because of drinking. I have my own reasons . . . work . . . interpersonal relations. I've told you this many times, I'm like your grandpa. Your grandpa glutted, drunk, gambled, and philandered. Almost every night someone in the family had to look for him in the night. Each time he came he disturbed the family. My genes are from your grandpa. . . . Anyway I don't like you both drinking." The next shot shows Tou Zi unequivocally using drugs silhouetted against what looks like a fraternity corridor. This two-scene sequence — the father's warning, the son's transgression — underlies the exemplary structure that the film pursues thematically. "Like father like son" sums up the film's expositional tactics.

Several other counseling scenes follow: between the mother and the younger son, between Tou zi and the neighborhood counsel. The addictive cycle that affects father and sons is presented contiguously to a series of warnings underscoring their ineffectiveness. Scenes in which Tou Zi and Xiao Wei criticize the father's drinking alternate with those in which the father and mother reproach them in turn. Scenes in which the father makes the family's disgrace even more public — by moving his cot into the compound's courtyard — are followed by others in which the sons also fall, vomit, and sleep in the streets. This compact succession is ironically critical.

The violent scene between Tou Zi and his father also suggests the extent to which the filmmaker and the family are willing to go in their display of private matters. Bridging actual fact with storytelling reenactment allows for multiple elisions, and in its choices of what to present *Sons* makes its intention of exposure glaringly manifest.

Sons is part of a wave of personal exposés and confessions by ordinary people on television and in newspapers characterizing the "reemergence of the realm of the private in China" in the late 1980s and 1990s.[48] Rey Chow has discussed how Fifth Generation filmmakers had begun to defy the traditional Chinese taboo agafinst self-display and exhibitionism. She notes that the Chinese phrase that epitomizes this taboo, translated as "don't air your dirty laundry in public," has to be understood in a specific way: "it puts the emphasis not on the dirty laundry but on the very act of showing, brandishing, exhibiting (to the outside)."[49]

The fact that *Sons* has been censored in China and its director blacklisted proves *Sons'* transgressive exhibitionism.[50] But it is its calculated exhibitionism, signaled by its use of reenactment, that interests me here. Reenactment purposefully makes public what might have otherwise remained private. By virtue of its use of reenactment, *Sons* doubles its violation of the party's perfect image promoted under communism.

Milan Kundera has described the lack of privacy under socialist authoritarianism as parallel to "the ideal of the exemplary family: a citizen does not have the right to keep any secret from his father or mother."[51] Zhang Yuan's project is quite other. The flaunting of a dysfunctional family beset by addictive behavior differs substantially from "the orgy of criticism and confessions" through which "the Chinese tended to internalize the party charges of ideological unhealth" during the Cultural Revolution.[52] The filmmaker facilitates the acting out of familial dynamics in what amounts to public exposure, but there is no narrative of conversion in the film. Signs of resistance to any authority or norms are everywhere. Tou Zi's refusal to admit his drug taking to his counselor is only the most obvious. That the son at one point almost kills the father is only one of the barely averted crises. What gets exposed is, in fact, the negative of a model exemplary family.

On the surface, the film embraces the therapeutic thrust of reenactment. The very act of reconstructing the painful days preceding the family's decision to commit the father suggests a conviction that reenactment has beneficial aspects. Zhang Yuan has stated that he "tried his best to help the family recall and portray what happened in their past life, and that during the film it was nice to see them establishing new contacts with one another and coming closer again."[53] Since this rapprochement between the family members is glaringly missing to the film's very end, it is not immediately clear how reenactment operates as healing in it.

For if the film's excess of sermons and admonitions continually renders reenactment's cautionary prospect vacuous, what, then, is marked in this filmic return? The family visits Li Maoje in a mental institution. He claims that the doctor says he's OK. The family insists that he stay longer. At the film's end, Zhang Yuan mentions in a voice-over that he has come to visit in an attempt to amend the family's vicious circle. The film is a perverse version of this filial amendment.

Zhang Yuan is a member of the Sixth Generation of filmmakers and part of a countercultural movement. Their films often tap into marginalized topics, and they are produced without government funding. Zhang's choice of themes—the mentally retarded in *Mama* (1992), gay life in *East West Palace* (1998), the everyday and the routine of control in Tiananmen *The Square* (1994), and his record of rock star Cui Jian in *Beijing Bastards* (1993)—is in line with other critical attempts to register and expand a consciousness rebellious toward tradition.

This characterization of filmmaking in the broad terms of a generational conflict is magnified by *Sons'* excessively narrow, almost too exclusive focus on the family. The film's paradoxical combination of crisis and paralysis, its depiction of resistance to change, and its high-pitched display of irrational responses recalls the melodramatic genre. The genre's erratic rhythms as well as its tendency to define its conflicts as a struggle with patriarchal authority are perfectly matched to *Sons'* content. In its own act of reconstruction, the film phrases and rephrases the fate of those foregoing advice. The structure—If only they'd listened . . . but of course they don't—sums up the pathos of both melodrama and reenactment. This double pathos is especially poignant in the stain cultivated by the film's careful framing, for reenactment can only teach by repeating precisely that which seems irrevocable.

Sons is an example of family melodrama, one of the dominant forms of expression in Chinese cinema. In his essay "Symbolic Representation and Symbolic Violence: Chinese Family Melodrama of the early '80s," Ma Ning has historicized the ways in which the genre's popularity follows from the significance of the family as a social unit in Chinese culture. Given the ways in which melodrama has been quick to register the progressive restructuring of family size—extended versus nuclear—as well as its internal conflicts and dynamics, Ma Ning has suggested how in melodrama the family has often worked as a means for the "public enactment of socially unacknowledged states."[54]

This displacement theory is especially tempting in analyzing a film that explores a single topic—the collapse of parental authority—so relentlessly. *Sons'* melodramatic tone and its single-minded insistence on the ineffectiveness of handed down models tips its realism from a microportrayal of urban disaffection in Beijing toward the possibility of a broader comment on Chinese society. The excess of admonitions as well as their failure in promoting any positive change become signifiers of a contemporary problematic, a confused but insistent refusal to submit to the bankrupt traditions of filial and party devotion.

Reenactment's built-in repetitive structure is doubled in *Sons'* own thematics of inherited addiction. The film's portrayal of an addiction cycle suggests two nonexclusive causes—genetics and social disaffection. Both inherited and socially acquired bad behavior constitutes radical indictments of a liberating mimesis and consequently of a redemptive reenactment.

Undoing the Trial Optic: Kiarostami's *Close Up*

The close-up limits and directs the attention. . . . I have neither the right nor the condition to be distracted. Present imperative of the verb understand.—Jean Epstein, *Écrits*

Like Zhang Yuan, Abbas Kiarostami also uses reenactment to undermine the hierarchy of original models. Mixing reenactment and documentary scenes, *Close Up* retraces the arrest and trial of Ali Sabzian, an unemployed man who was accused of impersonating the well-known Iranian filmmaker Mohsen Makhmalbaf. Sabzian's love for film has led him to replace a director whom he physically resembles and whose work he admires.

At first, the film follows and reenacts the chronology of the original events. In a prologue before the film's opening credits, Sabzian and the mother of the Ahankhah family reenact their initial encounter. Sabzian holds a book written by Makhmalbaf, and once he notes that he's been mistaken for the filmmaker he assumes that identity, signing a dedication and giving the book to the Ahankhah mother. Next we see an excited journalist telling a cab driver about a story he has got, a "windfall for a journalist." He has come with two policemen to arrest the impostor. A very simple scene follows, played out almost in real time: behind the walled house, we wait with the cab driver. The driver tries to peek over the wall, looks up at a plane passing overhead, picks flowers from a garbage dump, casually kicks a can. Kiarostami cuts to this can, which rolls a few feet along the sidewalk, stopping two or three houses down. This long scene, in which barely anything happens, will become more significant later, when the events inside the house, which happen in a faster tempo, are replayed. At this point, Sabzian appears, flanked by the two policemen. The reporter takes pictures, then asks neighbors if he can borrow a tape recorder. As the reporter waits for an answer in front of yet another walled house, he, too, kicks the can, which rolls a little farther down the street. As Gilberto Perez notes, the second time the aerosol can is kicked, it rolls much faster than before and we "don't stay with the can on its rolling course but cut to a printing press . . . putting out the paper with the reporter's story." This sequence establishes "not a connection of cause and effect . . . but a metaphor: the unremarkable detail of everyday life given the kick, the spin of publication." [55]

At Sabzian's trial, the film's central scene, we learn how Sabzian performed his director's role. Lacking the means of production—a film crew, even a camera—he had to limit his impersonation to rehearsals and what he portrays as location scouting: he inspects all the rooms in the Ahankhah's house (this is what leads to their suspicion that he is a thief). He has family members walk back and forth in the house, and he even proposes cutting down a tree that might block a shot of the facade. Asked how far he intended to take this act, Sabzian says he would have gone to final production if the Ahankhahs had raised the money.

The Ahankhahs seem disappointed to be deprived of stardom. But it is the pretender's beliefs and motives that Kiarostami probes the most. Sabzian admits that it was hard to maintain the fiction of being a famous film director when he had to take the bus back to his own shabby home every night. He also describes how, led by a strange compulsion, he became addicted to his new, powerful identity: "They did everything I told them to. Before I had never succeeded to get anyone to do anything. Move the cupboard, they did. I ordered, they obeyed."

During the trial, members of the Ahankhah family describe how they began to suspect Sabzian; conversely, he reveals that he knew he would soon be detected. At this point, Kiarostami breaks the film's linear chronology to insert a reenactment of Sabzian's futile attempt to keep up the pretense while the family waits for the police to arrest him. Elaborate blocking and terse dialogue suggest the family's response to being duped.

They reenact their own little act of fooling Sabzian by pretending they don't know he is an impostor when, as both social actors and characters in Kiarostami's film, they already know everything. Thus, Kiarostami grants them this token compensation for having been taken in. Meanwhile, playing himself playing Makhmalbaf, Sabzian reveals his skill as an actor. These skills are mobilized in the symbolic atonement implied by his participation in the reenactment, an expiatory performance that seems to motivate the acquittal scene that follows.

The scene inside the house is a dramatic tour de force. Nowhere are Sabzian's sufferings more poignant than in his attempt to play Makhmalbaf after all his audiences have been tipped off. Kiarostami has mentioned that the return to the house for the would-be director was very emotional despite ineffective attempts by the filmmaker to lighten the situation as he prepared to film. Sabzian performs his failure to convince successfully; his performance conveys his own dwindling belief in his pretense, and, given the reenactment's necessary belatedness in relation to the event—the arrest and the acquittal—one reads this awareness against his own shattered hopes.

This little theater of punishment and penance is only the first layer in Kiarostami's *detournement* of reenactment. The scene is the main instance in which Sabzian reenacts his impersonation of Makhmalbaf. Its placement after the trial, its bitter expressions of disappointment, and its quality as a repetition of an event grant it a special function: instead of creating a distancing effect, the reenactment of the arrest co-opts the representational *mise-en-abyme* as a dramatic effect. Here reenactment magnifies the drama of deceit. We watch the family's agitation as the father first receives the reporter, then stalls for time to allow him to bring the police. The camera stays with Sabzian, who is left alone in a poignantly empty long shot. He looks out the window, then sits back down in a corner. Because this scene shows us the drama that was unfolding inside the house as we waited with the cab driver in the street at the beginning of the film, it retroactively feeds dramatic momentum into a rather banal, gratuitous moment—the kicking of the can by the cab driver. By showing this scene from two different perspectives—one in which we know nothing, another in which we know too much—Kiarostami turns witnessing into a clear, costly embarrassment: faced with the scene's elaborate deceit and stark pathos, we almost wish for the earlier, blocked, more innocent view.

Close Up follows Kiarostami's pedagogical method. During the late 1960s and 1970s, he made several documentary films, short and feature length, for the Institute for the Development of Children and Young Adults. Some of these short films contain distinct moral and ethical lessons. The director's basic modus operandi (*Regular or Irregular*, 1981; *Two Solutions for a Problem*, 1975) lies in creating a comparative paradigm, a series of repeated situations (ways of crossing the street, responses to children's bickering) that alternate on the screen. These versions, equally framed, are then placed one after the next so they can be compared. Framing here refers not only to the cinematic composition and mise-en-scène but to the sense of scrutiny enforced upon a given behavior or situation, as these are repeated with significant differences, which then become the object of comparison. In *Fellow Citizen* (1983), Kiarostami selects a situation that itself becomes a vivid representation of a frame—one of Teheran's city gates and the cop who guards it. Traffic in Teheran has become so hectic that the downtown area has been blocked from drivers. Kiarostami continually frames the guard who blocks one of the entrances that leads to a hospital. We then watch the guard's attempts to be strict and fair as he listens to each person's excuse, some more convincing than others, to get through. The degree of personal inventiveness in presenting one's case is central to the comparison effect sought after by Kiarostami. While some of the films suggest a very simple morality—wrong and right, regular and irregular—this, and other films, *Homework* (1990), for instance, add to the predicament of judging by providing so many vicissitudes in arguing that the rigidity of the form breaks down. In this sense, the paradigmatic frame operates as a humanist gauge in which selfish drives and desires are all excused under a benign, understanding gaze.

Close Up is a complex example of the filmmaker's pedagogic humanism. His social critique is pointed. Its trial scene grants a voice to multiple testimonies, but the film remains unperturbed by them. Most redemptive reenactment turns people into culprits. Kiarostami's didactic project reveals a critical sensibility attuned to Sabzian's pathos—to his love of films and his inability to make them.

The last scene shows the real Makhmalbaf waiting for Sabzian as he is released from prison. Sabzian cries, embarrassed; the two men embrace. They climb onto Makhmalbaf's motorcycle and pay a visit to the Ahankhahs. The classical score charges this encounter with a poetic humanist dimension. Filmed with the candid texture of direct cinema—in long shot and with a faltering microphone—the scene stands as an elaborate (and faux) cinema vérité device. Kiarostami created the effect of a badly connected microphone in order to rebalance the power between the two people being filmed. Since Makhmalbaf knew he was being filmed and spoke articulately into the microphone while Sabzian remained unaware that he was being filmed, if Kiarostami had left the scene without manipulating the sound Makhmalbaf would have turned into the protagonist and would be confirmed as the source of Sabzian's drama.[56]

When he shows the two Makhmalbafs, Kiarostami invalidates the notion of source. He hints at the unfairness of social hierarchies suspending the definition of who, of these two, is the original. Kiarostami thus renews his complicity with Sabzian's genuine desire to be another. This complicity, possibly triggered by their common cinephilia, leads him to warn Sabzian, at the start of the trial, that one of the two cameras, mounted with close-up lenses, is there for Sabzian to tell the audience facts and feelings that are legally unacceptable but nevertheless true.[57] Kiarostami's intervention transforms the trial from an accusation of fraud into an exploration into the nature of belief. His camera probes for Sabzian's motives with relatively restrained close-ups beyond the actual one-hour trial. After that, Kiarostami "borrowed the accused and continued to interrogate him, in closed quarters for almost nine hours" and "reconstituted a great part of the trial with the judge absent."[58] Compare, then, Kiarostami's optics to Jean Epstein's advocacy of the close-up in a cinema imagined as a normative apparatus."[59] "Enlarged twenty times . . .

revealed to be a neuropath by his psychiatrist, made public, bare, and confused, man finds himself through the cinematic camera cut off in all his lies . . . shameful and perhaps truthful. Mental health, the judicial inqui-

6. Original and impersonator, Makhmalbaf and Sabzian, visit the duped family in *Close Up*, Abbas Kiarostami, 1990 (frame enlargement of video)

7. Sabzian on trial, filmed in a medium close-up shot, *Close Up*, Abbas Kiarostami, 1990 (frame enlargement of video)

8. Sabzian addresses Kiarostami in a more truthful close-up in *Close Up*, Abbas Kiarostami, 1990 (frame enlargement of video)

sition will someday use this confessing film where the subject sees himself as object. When will there be dramatists to do this?"[60]

The efficiency of this confessing apparatus is purposefully lacking in *Sons* and *Close Up*. Differently than the moral exemplarity deduced in the neorealist episodes in these contemporary films the ostensible culprits are not framed as examples. The films are void of redemption but also judgment. Instead, they reenact cases that are pervaded by forms of repetition already existent in reality: in *Close Up*, the disturbing physical similarity between Sabzian and Makhmalbaf; and in *Sons* the heredity (social, genetic) of addiction, presented through the film's relentless "like father like son" expositional tactics.

These natural and social injustices are extracharged in the films' clever reconstructions. *Sons* offers no narrative of redemption and at least two years later, at the time of the hospital visit and the filming, no sign of familial healing. Kiarostami's focus on the double points to the constitutive impotence of representation to surmount real social distinctions. Reenactment works, in the film, as a poor vindicating mirror. It promotes the awareness of the similarity between impersonation (Sabzian posing as Makhmalbaf) and acting (Sabzian as Sabzian as Makhmalbaf), along with the recognition of the absolute chasm enacted in this doubling.

Notes

The epigraph that opens this essay is from Cesare Zavattini, "Some Ideas on the Cinema," in *Film: A Montage of Theories*, edited by Richard Dyer MacCann (New York: E. P. Dutton, 1966), 222. The essay "Alcune Idee sul Cinema" was translated by Pier Luigi Lanza as "Some Ideas on the Cinema" and first published in *Sight and Sound* in October 1953. It originally appeared as the preface to the script of *Umberto D*, published in *Rivista del Cinema Italiano*, December 1952.

1 See "Che Cos'E Il Film Lampo," and "Film-Lampo: Sviluppo del Neorealismo," in *Neorealismo ecc*, edited by Mino Argentieri (Milan: Bompiani, 1979), 86–88, 89–91, and "Some Ideas on the Cinema"). The term *film lampo*, or "lightning film," denotes a desire for a reportagelike immediacy.

2 Bertolt Brecht, who had imagined extracting images from films in order to apply them to different social contexts, an archive classifying every known form of behavior, foresaw this cautionary function. Models not only of socially accepted actions—an after-dinner speech, for example—but of antisocial conduct could be isolated and studied. The quotable, representative images of the "pedagogium," as he called it, stand as a terse image for the corrective delirium of reenactment films. These images clearly represent an almost maniacal expansion of the exemplary potential of

film. See Ben Brewster, "The Fundamental Reproach (Brecht)," *CineTRacts* 1:2 (summer 1977): 52.

3 In the made for TV film *Victims for Victims: The Story of Teresa Saldana* (1984), for instance, Teresa Saldana, an actress who was stalked and stabbed, relives her story for the film, including her later involvement with an organization for the victims of crime.

4 For a comprehensive study of the notion of exemplum, see John D. Lyons, *Exemplum* (Princeton: Princeton University Press, 1989). See also Alexander Gelley, ed., *Unruly Examples: On the Rhetoric of Exemplarity* (Stanford: Stanford University Press, 1995).

5 According to Aristotle, "there are two kinds of examples: namely one, which consists in relating things that have happened before, and another in inventing them oneself" (*Rhetoric* 2.20.1393), a–b.

6 "An example from the past will most probably contain a pattern that will be pertinent to the situation under deliberation." And it is its "potential for further occurrence or replicability that allows [its] rhetorical use" Lyons, *Exemplum*, 8. See also Gelley, *Unruly Examples*, 3.

7 Often associated with medieval literature, the term *exemplum* denotes any narration in an oratorical or preaching situation.

8 Gelley, *Unruly Examples*, 3.

9 April Alliston, "Female Sexuality and the Referent of Enlightenment Realisms," in *Spectacles of Realism: Gender, Body, Genre.* Edited by Margaret Cohen and Christopher Prendergast. (Minneapolis: University of Minnesota Press, 1995) 13–14.

10 Alliston, Ibid., 14.

11 Marco Ferreri and Riccardo Ghione introduced the idea of *The Spectator* in their short-lived journal *Documento Mensile: L'Avant Scène du Cinema* 289–290 (1982): 62.

12 The pedinamento theory can be summed up like this: "One should succeed in seeing on the screen a sort of documentary of private and public facts with the rigor and readiness of a mirror and the analytical dimension of the cinema which reveals all the spatial and temporal dimensions of these facts" (Argentieri, *Neorealismo ecc,* 75). Zavattini states that "there will be a moment we'll watch what a man does in his most quotidian and minute actions, and we'll be as interested in that as we did once in going to see a greek drama." Cited in Armando Borelli, "Le idee de Zavattini," *Rivista del Cinema Italiano:* 3:11–12 (November, December, 1954) 74.

13 Argentieri, *Neorealismo ecc,* 90.

14 Maurizio Grande, "Personaggio," in *Lessico Zavattiniano: Parole e Idee su Cinema e Dintorni,* edited by Guglielmo Moneti (Venice: Marsilio Editori, 1992), 194.

15 Maurizio Grande, "Attore," in Moneti, *Lessico Zavattiniano,* 32.

16 André Bazin, "Le Neorealisme se Retourne," *Cahiers du Cinéma* 69 (March 1957): 46.

17 Zavattini, "Some Ideas on the Cinema," 227.

18 Both Aristotle and Cicero suggest three basic forms of examples: the historical, an "account of actual occurrences remote from the recollection of our own age"; the argument, "a fictitious narrative which nevertheless could have occurred"; and the fable, a "narrative in which the events are not true and have no verisimilitude" (cited in Lyons, *Exemplum*, 8).

19 Bazin, "Le Neorealisme," 46.

20 Cesare Zavattini, *Zavattini: Sequences from a Cinematic Life,* translated with an introduction by William Weaver (Englewood Cliffs, NY: Prentice-Hall, 1970), 10–11.

21 Ibid., 26.

22 Cesare Zavattini, cited in Saverio Vollaro, "Zavattini e il Neorealismo," *Rivista del Cinema Italiano* 7 (July 1954), 25.

23 Grande, "Personaggio," 194.

24 See Gian Piero Brunetta on the general mobilization in February 1949 to press for legislation in favor of national industry in *Storia del Cinema Italiano dal 1945 agli Anni Ottanta* (Rome: Editori Riuniti, 1982), 147–52.

25 See ibid., 152–53.

26 Guido Aristarco, *Neorealismo e Nuova Critica Cinematografica, Cinematografia e Vita Nazionale: Tra Rottura e Tradizioni* (Florence: Nuova Guaraldi, 1980), 82.

27 Armando Bonelli, "L'idee di Zavattini," *Rivista del Cinema Italiano* 11–12 (November–December, 1954), 75.

28 Aristarco, *Neorealismo,* 85–87, 90–98.

29 Carlo Lizzanni, *Il Cinema Italiano: Delle Origine Agli Anni Ottanta* (Rome: Editori Riuniti, 1982), 165.

30 Adelio Ferrero, "La 'Conscienza di Se': Ideologia e Verita Del Neorealismo," in *Il Neorealismo Cinematografico Italiano: Atti del Convegno della X Mostra Internazionale del Nuovo Cinema,* edited by Lino Micciche (Venice: Marsilio Editori, 1975), 219.

31 Ferrero, "La 'Conscienza di Se'," 245–46.

32 Brunetta, *Storia del Cinema Italiano,* 137.

33 Cited in Vollaro, "Zavattini e il Neorealismo," 36.

34 For more on Zavattini's positivism, see Sandro Petraglia, "Cesare Zavattini: Teorico del neorealismo," in Micciche, *Il Neorealismo,* 219. See also Grande, "Attore," 36.

35 Cesare Zavattini, "Il Neorealismo Secondo Me," *Rivista del Cinema Italiano* 3:3 (March, 1954): 20.

36 Sam Rohdie, *Antonioni* (London: British Film Institute, 1990).

37 In *Love of a Mother* Caterina is seen climbing a welfare agency's steps, taking a number to wait in line, number 181. At this point there is an ellipsis as we see her approach the office's agent.

38 On Zavattini's apostolic vision, see Vollaro, "Zavattini e il Neorealismo," 38–39.

39 In "The Road beyond Neorealism," Federico Fellini argues for the inclusion of other forms of reality besides the objective social chronicle of the everyday in neorealism's agenda. (In *Film: A Montage of Theories,* edited by Richard Dyer MacCann (New York: E. P. Dutton, 1966), 377–84.

40 See J. Laplanche and J. B-Pontalis, *The Language of Psychoanalysis,* translated by Donald Nicholson (London: Hogarth Press, 1973), 61.

41 Francesco Bolzoni sees *Attempted Suicide* as the extreme conclusion of Antonioni's discourse in his "Un ritrato di Antonioni," *Rivista del Cinema Italiano* 10 (October 1954): 61.

42 Michelangelo Antonioni, "*Attempted Suicide:* Suicides in the City," in *Architecture of Vision: Writings and Interviews on Cinema,* edited by Carlo di Carlo and Giorgio Tinazzi (New York: Marsilio Publishers, 1996), 72.

43 Defensively, the filmmaker claims to have "aimed directly at the substance of the

theme," trying to provoke "an aversion to suicide in the public through the spiritual squalor of the characters" (ibid., 73).

44 Antonioni does not, however, subscribe to either cinema vérité's or direct cinema's ideology. In "Cinema Direct et Realite," he clearly voices his suspicion of the notion of an objective camera (in *Etudes Cinematographiques,* 36–37 (Paris, 1964): 3–6.

45 Bill Nichols, "The Voice of Documentary," in *Movies and Methods,* vol. 2, edited by Bill Nicholas (Los Angeles: University of California Press, 1985), 258–73.

46 In its overly compressed juxtaposition of barely averted catastrophes and a pretense of service to the community, the reality TV series *Rescue 911* makes the relationship between cautionary tale and the body especially clear. In one episode, a child pours gasoline on himself and accidentally sets himself on fire. When an actor is used to simulate an accident, the spectator subliminally perceives the threatening event as affecting at least two people—the victim and his or her body double. Performed by an actor, the fire incident becomes the example in a detached, pristine form.

47 *Sons* was directed by Zhang Yuan in 1996, after three fictional/documentary hybrids and prior to an emphatically fictional project, *East West Palace: Behind the Forbidden City.* Although the film does not make it clear, it depicts events that took place two years earlier. The crew had to get the father out of the hospital for the making of the film. I'd like to thank Elaine Charnov, director of the Margaret Mead Film Festival, for calling my attention to *Sons.* I'd also like to thank Yiling Mao for facilitating contact with Zhang Yuan.

48 Orville Schell, "The Re-emergence of the Realm of the Private in China," in *The Broken Mirror: China after Tiananmen* (New York: St. James Press, 1990), 419–28.

49 Rey Chow, *Primitive Passions: Visuality, Sexuality, Ethnography, and Contemporary Chinese Cinema* (New York: Columbia University Press, 1995), 152–53. Rachel Dornhelm was the first to note the relevance of this taboo to *Sons'* "making public" private matters ("The State of Censorship: The Government Politics Surrounding the Chinese Film *Sons,*" *Oxford International Review* [winter 1997–98]: 22–29).

50 Dornhelm, "State of Censorship," 22–29.

51 Schell, "Re-emergence," 422.

52 Ibid.

53 Zhang Yuan, press release for "Outsiders and Antiheroes: Recent Films from Taiwan, Hong Kong, and China," a film series guest curated by Yi Ling Mao of the Asia Society.

54 Ma Ning, "Symbolic Representation and Symbolic Violence: Chinese Family Melodrama of the Early '80s," *East West* 4:1 (December 1989): 79–83.

55 Gilberto Perez, *The Material Ghost: Films and Their Medium* (Baltimore: John Hopkins University Press, 1998), 264.

56 Kiarostami, interview with Stephane Goudet, *Positif* 442 (December 1997): 95.

57 Kiarostami states that "in *Close Up* I describe the face to face encounter between law and art. . . . Art has more patience. . . . The film apparatus rests on two cameras: the camera of the law, that shows the tribunal and the process in juridical terms, . . . and the art camera that approaches the human being to see him in close up, to probe . . . his motivations his sufferings" (ibid.).

58 Ibid.

59 Jean Epstein complements Zavattini's faith in cinema as a corrective mirror, seeing the close-up as the bearer of alterity. As his agile reasoning shows, the notion of cinema as an unmediated path to stable identity can quite simply backfire: "The first feeling in seeing oneself as 'he'd been seen through the lenses . . . is always the horror of perceiving and hearing oneself as a stranger to oneself" ("Photogenie de L'inponderable" in *Ecrits* (Paris: Editions Seghers, 1975), 1:249.

60 Ibid., 128.

Pasolini On *Terra Sancta:* Towards a Theology of Film

Noa Steimatsky

What I tell you in darkness, that speak ye in Light. — Matthew 10:27

Location as *Terra Sancta*

Winter 1960–61 marks the beginning of Pier Paolo Pasolini's work as a filmmaker; it is also the time in which he began to travel.[1] Filmmaking and traveling were to become closely linked in the following years, when the search for locations itself became a key creative moment of the film-work, while the cinema in turn served as a pretext for further exploration of foreign cultures and remote landscapes, from the margins of Europe (Anatolia, Palestine) onward to the Arabian peninsula and Africa.[2] Even a superficial glance at the films reveals this mutual implication of the two activities — filmmaking and traveling — as fundamental to Pasolini's work. This ambition appears dormant in such early works as *Accattone* and *Mamma Roma,* but it can be identified even in these films' exploration of the Roman *borgate* — the subproletariat neighborhoods — as sites of marginality: vital, exotic landscapes external to hegemonic Italian culture. Here the borgate inhabitants, often southern immigrants or their descendants, who in Pasolini's mythicizing view still bear the traces of archaic physiognomies and premodern cultural forms, could enact saints' tales of martyrdom.[3] Later, in a complementary motion, classical and medieval texts will be "exported" beyond Europe and adapted to historical and social processes at work in the Third World of the present. The presence of an archaic past within contemporary life complements in Pasolini's oeuvre the representation of the present in an allegorical vision of the past.

Il Vangelo secondo Matteo (*The Gospel According to Saint Matthew*, 1964) can be located at the crossroads of these two complementary modes: between the original scripts located by and large in contemporary Italy and the works of adaptation shot largely abroad.[4] The latter were often preceded by elaborate *sopraluoghi:* "location hunting" voyages of exploration documented in writings and diarylike films. In fact, Pasolini's documentary cinema consists almost entirely of such work done in preparation for his adaptations (some left unrealized). These relate the search for actors and locations, the faces and places that are the materials of Pasolini's work. Three of the travel documentaries constitute in this respect a trilogy, launched by the *Sopraluoghi in Palestina* (*Locations in Palestine*, 1963) and followed by the *Appunti per un film sull'India* (*Notes for a Film on India*, 1968) and the *Appunti per un'orestiade africana* (*Notes for an African Oresteia*, 1969–70). Rather than historical reconstruction toward a "natural" faithfulness to his source texts, Pasolini's travels led him to experiment with geographical, contextual, and stylistic displacements that resulted in a jarring, heterogeneous textuality. In the years following *Il Vangelo,* with the experience of sopraluoghi travels and the production of *Edipo Re* (1967) and *Medea* (1969–70), notions of "analogy" and "contamination," elaborated in his theoretical work, were to further inform this practice of adaptation. In the location-hunting documentaries, one finds Pasolini's most forceful reflections on analogical adaptation as a working principle and an instantiation of the relation between representation and represented in the cinema. The passage, from the *Sopraluoghi in Palestina* to *Il Vangelo secondo Matteo* serves to clarify this relation; in the course of this passage we may glimpse the evolution and crystalization of a film aesthetic and practice.

The story of the production is complex. In October 1962, as a guest in Assisi of the Pro Civitate Christiana, an institution for the promotion of Catholic culture in contemporary (including leftist and liberal) Italy, Pasolini read the gospel he found at his bedside there. In an exchange of letters with his producer, Alfredo Bini, and members of the Pro Civitate,

Pasolini described his response in glowing terms that connote a sense of religious possession, interchangeable in his mind with an aesthetic revelation.[5] In view of such enthusiasm on the part of a notorious cultural figure, the directors of the cinema office of the Pro Civitate, upon consultation with priests, theologians, and biblical scholars, agreed to support Pasolini's project.[6] In preparation for this, they sponsored Pasolini's expedition to Palestine under the guidance of Don Andrea Carraro and Dr. Caruso of the Pro Civitate. A representative of Alfredo Bini's production company and a cameraman accompanied the tour to Israel and Jordan, which took place between June 27 and July 11, 1963. Pasolini returned with six reels of film, which he hastily spliced together toward a meeting with investors. The fifty-five-minute *Sopraluoghi in Palestina* remains edited in rough chronology, patched with musical excerpts and with improvised voice-over adding to the few sync-sound dialogues in the film.

The dominant impression, repeatedly articulated in the *Sopraluoghi,* is of the humility of the places that the gospel designates as the grand stage of the preaching and Passion of Jesus. Nazareth, Mount Tabor, the Jordan River, Capernaum and the Sea of Galilee, Bethlehem, Jerusalem with its sites of Gethsemene, the Via Dolorosa, and the Holy Sepulchre—Pasolini had envisioned these as manifesting the archaic grandeur not only of the gospel but of the accumulated weight of centuries of elaboration and representation. The modern, industrial aspect of Israel was, as Pasolini states in the *Sopraluoghi,* "a practical disappointment." This became the ostensible rationale for filming the gospel elsewhere.[7] But the plain concreteness of the holy places in Palestine, the modesty of their dimension and placement, bearing neither the epic nor dramatic impact that Pasolini had expected, ultimately constituted "an aesthetic revelation," one that left its traces in the ultimate choices of location and shooting style of *Il Vangelo secondo Matteo.*

> The first impression was of a great modesty, a great smallness, a great humility. . . . The area is frightfully desolate, arid. It seems one of those abandoned places in Calabria or Puglia. And down over here is the Sea of Galilee, tranquil under the sun. What impressed me most is the extreme smallness, the poverty, the humility of this place. And for me—who was expecting this place, this Mountain of the Beatitudes, to be one of most fabulous places in my film and in the spectacle that Palestine would have offered me—it has been an incredible impression of smallness, I repeat, of humility. A great lesson in humility.

After all, I am thinking that all that Christ did and said—four small Gospels, preaching in a small land, a small region that consists of four arid hills, a mountain, the Calvary where he was killed—all of this is contained in a fist.[8]

The repeated emphasis, pressing toward an oxymoron, of the "great humility" of the Christian sights recalls Pasolini's most characteristic trope. The grandeur identified in a ruinous landscape of contemporary poverty pertains to his notion of contamination, borrowed from Pasolini's linguistic studies, where it describes the interlacing of voices, high and low, literary Italian and dialect intertwined in free indirect discourse without thereby neutralizing the specificity of each voice.[9] Nor would Pasolini want to compromise the connotations of tainting, contagion, and violation that accompany this term, setting it most emphatically against the sanitized Italian of fascism or the technocratic language of consumer culture. Contamination in Pasolini's film practice finds its primary moment in the use of Bach's *Matthäus-Passion* over the scene of a pimp's fight in the dust in *Accattone*. Here, in the *Sopraluoghi,* Pasolini alludes to this trope as already immanent in the landscape.[10] The intertwining of humility and grandeur perhaps reflects, on the most fundamental level, the contamination of actual archaeological remains—scattered, dusty fragments—by the mythic-visionary connotations whose claim to authenticity and meaning is of an altogether different order. Where a truly secular artist might have located here a debunking of theological dogma and myth or, conversely, a rationale for ignoring altogether the traces of the past, Pasolini embraces both the humble material concreteness of such traces and the grand resonance of the myth. Their mutual contamination forms, rather, the basis of an adaptation in which the landscape of poverty and allusions to the gorgeous riches of Christian art, the contemporary and the archaic, the actual and the phantasmic, intersect rather than negate each other. It may also be seen to reflect, as we shall see, the oscillation of the cinematic image as such between its photographic-realist claim and its amenability to myth.[11]

Pasolini's notion of contamination recalls Erich Auerbach's analysis of the Gospel according to Mark in terms of a mingling of voices. He demonstrates how realistic "low-life" elements, traditionally used for comedic modes, are here endowed with "high" design and purpose. The interweaving of styles serves to portray "the birth of a spiritual movement in the depths of the common people, from within the everyday occurences of contemporary life." This, Auerbach suggests, "was rooted from the beginning in the character of Judeo-Christian literature, it was graphically and harshly dramatized through God's incarnation in a human being of the humblest social station, through his existence on earth amid humble everyday people and conditions, and through his Passion which, judged by earthly standards, was ignominious; and it naturally came to have . . . a most decisive bearing upon man's conception of the tragic and the sublime."[12] This model of biblical contamination is adopted by Pasolini, informing his work of adaptation on all levels. His film production of the gospel will not be historically faithful but will employ instead a heterogeneous stylistics — a deliberate mingling of Christian and other cultural references, of high and low voices, of everyday detail and a visionary outlook — that echoes the thematic contamination at the heart of the text. Adaptation involves, then, not reconstruction but a new cinematic amalgam of materials and connotations synecdochically tied to the Holy Land and analogous to its biblical rendering.

For early on, possibly prior to his trip, Pasolini realized that the "actual" sites of Jesus' life and Passion in the Holy Land would not do. The expedition to the Holy Land informs Pasolini's notion of analogy, which, complementing contamination, enhances our sense of the project as deeply grounded in Christological tradition. Analogy determines Pasolini's adaptations and use of locations throughout his career, shedding some light as well on his idiosyncratic theories of film.[13] The *Sopraluoghi in Palestina* becomes in fact a pilgrimage wherein the impressions, indeed filmic traces, of the original place are collected to be resited in a more radical gesture of contamination than that afforded by the humble grandeur of Palestine itself. In physically retracing Christ's journey, Pasolini already rehearses the prospect of returning whence he came, bearing the sacred loot of his pilgrimage. This loot, inscribed in the *Sopraluoghi,* is in this way comparable to the mobile value of relics and icons that the pilgrim brings home; it will in turn serve to consecrate the Italian sites through which Pasolini will perform a second location hunt and on which, eventually, Jesus' movements will be rehearsed.[14]

In conversation with his guide, Don Andrea, Pasolini confesses that being face to face with the views that Jesus himself might have seen exerts an impact for which his film would have to compensate. What Pasolini perceives as an aesthetic issue, Don Andrea articulates from a religious outlook: "But given that it is here that these scenes took place — on these places, on this land—here the earth had been treaded [by Christ]. . . . There is a sort of geography of Palestine, a geography of the *Terrasanta*. And I think that one has to walk over it, thinking, reflecting, meditating, in order to absorb its spirit. Only then one could re-invent it in some other place, re-imagine it, adapting it even to one's own sensibility, to one's own imagination. Then it will become a new thing; because I really believe that one cannot speak of a "photograph" of these places."[15] What underlies this meditation is of course the notion of *terra sancta:* a sacred topography, a configuration of sites locating a religion in the mapping of its founding myths.[16] The attachment of value to a geography, and more specifically the sacral attributes of Palestine, is clearly not the singular domain of Christianity. Most religions privilege certain sites as meeting places between heaven and earth: most typically, elevated spots (e.g., Mount Sinai or Golgotha) are associated with events paradigmatic to the religion. Christianity has also come to designate catacombs and saints' tombs as bridging this and another world. The spaces of ritual, structured according to hierarchies of sacred and profane, privilege and prohibition, are among the common constitutive characteristics of religious practice, organizing the world by its order and orienting the believer in its apprehensible cosmos.[17]

Pilgrimage to the Holy Land, in particular the passage through the stations of the cross, culminating in the Holy Sepulchre as part of a liturgical order wherein one retraces with one's own body the sacred topography, rehearses a trajectory well established in Christianity. But actual pilgrimage to Jerusalem is only the most literal form in which the Terra Sancta serves the believer. The holy places are incoporated in other modes of veneration: the bringing of relics from original sites to European churches, the construction of models of the Holy Sepulchre to scale, or the placement of small replicas on the altars of local churches. By translating the connotations of a place into the narrative-temporal dimension of the liturgical order, a resiting of the sacred becomes possible. The original pilgrimage gives way to a procession between local European sites in an established ceremonial order that, in the liturgical year, retraces the trajectory from Annunciation through Pentecost.[18] These possibilities of the transposition of the sacred may be identified at the heart of Christian theology, playing a major role in its historical dissemination.

Peter Brown describes the historical shift from pilgrimage, "the movement of people to relics," to "the movement of relics to people"—a movement of "translation" that holds center stage in late antiquity and early medieval piety.[19] While pilgrims perceived the sites of the Holy Land as themselves sacramental, the theological possibility of "translation," the migration of the sacred, allowed for the unparalleled dissemination of the faith through the prevalence of secondary sites that partake in the sacramental value of the original but remote holy places. For this, Christianity is indebted to the growth of monasticism in the fourth century and to popular and pagan influences and practices associated with the veneration of both relics and holy men. Catacombs outside city walls, as well as remote and desolate places where hermits had retreated, were thus consecrated, serving to shift the balance of earlier maps of civilization toward a new holy geography. Sacred places became more common by virtue of the sheer number of saints and the distribution of relics, which was soon authorized. By stressing the popular roots of these cult practices and their vast impact on Christianity, Brown questions simple dichotomies that distinguish official Christian history, dogma, and hierarchy from popular manifestations initially associated with pagan or "vulgar" superstition such as the veneration of relics and icons. We see echoed here, in effect, a model of contamination whereby high and humble, dogmatic and domestic, intermingle, as they do in Auerbach's account of the Gospel's stylistics. The secondary, local site can be consecrated and hence endowed with the value of the original. This may be seen to conform, finally, with the doctrine of the Incarnation at the heart of Christianity, wherein the son of God partakes in a historical (and geographical) mortal fate even as he is fully God and as such eternal and omnipresent. The historical and the eternal, mortal flesh and the spirit, are identified in the Christian sacraments, as they are in the Christian understanding of time, place, and the image.

In the migration of the sacred and the tracing of a new holy topography, one may ground Pasolini's specific notion of analogy as it complements the principle of contamination: Jerusalem "was the old part of Matera, which now, alas, is falling into ruin, the part known as the *Sassi*. Bethlehem was a village in Apulia called Barile, where people were really living in caves, like in the film, only a few years ago. The castles were Norman castles dotted round Apulia and Lucania. The desert part where Christ is walking along with the apostles I shot in Calabria. And Capernaum is made up of two towns: the part down by the sea is a village near Crotone, and the part looking away from the sea is Massafra."[20]

> For the major choices this was not difficult once the mechanism of analogy had been established. For the pastoral, agricultural, feudal world of the Jews I substituted wholesale the analogous world of the

Italian South (with its landscapes of the humble and of the power-ful). . . . But for the small, minor choices, that often come up unex-pectedly on the set on a given day—that was much more difficult. So, for the Roman soldiers at Christ's preaching in Jerusalem, I had to think of the *Celere* [Italian police units for the control of dem-onstrations, strikes, etc.]; for Herod's soldiers before the Massacre of the Innocents I had to think of the Fascist mob; Joseph and the Ma-donna as refugees were suggested to me by refugees in many analo-gous tragedies in the modern world (for example, Algeria) etc. etc.[21]

The analogical location, grasped as sharing in the sacred charge of the origi-nal, endows the cinematic image itself with consecrating power. Pasolini can now approach the most humble of sites in southern Italy, places quite remote from official holy centers, and endow them with an authentic sacral value personally imported, *translated,* so to speak, from the Terra Sancta.

The sites visited in Palestine have been rejected ostensibly because of the obtrusive modernity of 1963 Israel; in the Italian south, Pasolini seeks the underdeveloped aspect of the present seen as a premodern past and therefore in no need for reconstruction. For, he emphasizes, it is not re-constructed history that interests him but rather the persistence of archaic forms within a contemporary world. These he finds on the margins of Italy of the early 1960s in a disinherited world denied active participation in hegemonic culture. The archaic is understood as a condition; it is more of a geographical, not a chronological, designation; and it bears, as well, an ideological charge. In an exchange with Jean-Paul Sartre, Pasolini explained the implications of this analogical mode by drawing a comparison between his choice of the Italian south and what Algeria as a location for a film of the gospel would mean to a French audience.[22] The Italian south is here still perceived as a colonized, Third World entity, bypassed by modernity even as it is exploited by northern industrial and consumer culture. It is here, Pasolini implies, that one may locate an authentic revolutionary potential that is not contradicted by the enduring power of the Christian myth in the rural subproletariat. Rather than posit the archaic against progress, Paso-lini embraces it as a vital and even dialectical force, analogous to what he reads in Matthew's gospel as Christ's challenge to his contemporary estab-lishment. In both historical and art historical terms, Pasolini seeks, then, a setting that has somehow escaped the desacralizing rationality of the En-lightenment and bourgeois capitalist culture. Only in such a place can an act of consecration have any meaning. As an aesthetic project, it can even be grasped as somehow realistic.

The Face of the Earth

The concept of analogy now assumes a breadth that sustains it as an aesthetic and ideological, but also practical, working principle. Leafing through Pasolini's film-theoretical writings, one encounters this term repeatedly. It may be employed to read his theory for what it is: not really a semiology but a theology of the cinematic image. As film partakes of reality through photographic reproduction, so reality, according to Pasolini, is a potential profilmic partaking of an expansive notion of cinema. Reality speaks, it is spoken through, and its word and flesh are identified and may thus be transcribed in a particular film. Analogy defines the relation between the audiovisual cinematic sign and its source in the profilmic—in the camera's field of vision. Film communicates as the "written language of reality," a reality itself perceived as an already formed textual and aesthetic entity, inscribed by death as the ultimate editing device, endowing meaning. Both represented and representation, profilmic and its inscription in film, are understood as analogical sections of a single spectrum; both participate in reality, grasped not as some raw natural entity but always an expressive, human, cultural, and ideological realm. Reality has therefore, in Pasolini's thinking, an immanent human meaning embodied in everything and available to expression. As an inscription of the profilmic, film assumes reality's fullness of meaning, its expressivity, the sacral plenitude of its materials. Moreover, the articulating devices of framing and editing, among other techniques, afford not simply a transparent, "naturalistic" reflection of the profilmic but an analogical transposition to a different level, a potentially higher order. In this theoretical system, the sign does not stand for an absent referent but rather makes it manifest: the cinematic sign is reality's own heightened articulation.[23]

Pasolini recognizes how his account of cinematic signs as meaning incarnate rehearses an archaic, religious, and, one might even say, infantile perception: "My fetishistic love of the *'things' of the world* makes it impossible for me to consider them natural. Either it consecrates them or it desecrates them violently, one by one; it does not bind them in a correct flow, it does not accept this flow. But it isolates them and adores them."[24] And again: "along with this method of reconstruction by analogy, there is the idea of the myth and of epicness which I have talked about so much: so when I told the story of Christ I didn't reconstruct Christ as he really was. If I had reconstructed the history of Christ as he really was I would not have produced a religious film because I am not a believer. . . . But . . . I am not interested in deconsecrating: this is a fashion I hate, it is petit bourgeois. I want to re-consecrate things as much as possible, I want to re-mythicize them."[25] The mythicizing veneration of reality, the "fetishistic love" that emphatically disrupts any sense of natural, "correct flow," positing in its place an isolating and thereby consecrating analogical representation; this is set against a transparent cinematic style of continuity editing but also against the neorealism of the long take. Pasolini's attachment to the "things of the world" and to their incarnate images is manifest in the twofold commitment to the "realist" and the "reverential," deeply intertwined in Pasolini's thinking, the one contaminating the other. Film's indexicality—its claim to a causal bind between representation and represented—may implicate a realism, yet for Pasolini it is the very access through the cinematic image to the direct light of reality that also effects an attitude of veneration. The art historical models underlying this vision and its attendant techniques may now be explored.

The indexicality of cinematic representation can be seen, then, as binding Pasolini's realism with a reverential perception. In the context of an adaptation of the gospel, this confronts us with the doctrine of the Incarnation and, more specifically, with the theology of the Christian image. It is the Byzantine icon that may be seen to appeal for its dogma to an indexical/iconic tie—a causal link as well as a resemblance between representation and represented—which is why it has lent itself to comparisons with the photographic image.[26] In the cosmological order of late antiquity and early Christianity, the image of Jesus is defined as one in a series of stages issuing downward from God, connecting the infinite and abstract with the historical and corporeal. Incarnation, the possibility of God's materialization in Jesus, defines Christianity and its promise of redemption vis-à-vis Judaism, for example. The icon repeats at a secondary level this anthropomorphic incarnation, celebrating the divine descent into form and flesh. The icon, like the relic, is a memento left by Christ as a promise of the vision of God in eternity; it is seen to provide visual evidence for the incarnation of the sacred in the world. The iconic image is not simply "symbolic" or "allegorical" in relation to meaning, as it would be in a Protestant system that severs the manifest and the hidden, the flesh and the spirit. Rather, it is grasped as participating in what it represents: it is an index of Christ's humanity; in partaking of his body, it incarnates God.[27] The doctrine of the icon was formulated in the same period when the transposition of the sacred to new sites in Europe triggered the dissemination of Christianity — this I described earlier as a model for Pasolini's move from Palestine to the Italian south.

And, once again, the "materialism" of pagan and popular cult veneration of icons inflected, historically, official monotheistic dogma.[28] In this tradition, the icon that most forcefully proclaims this theology of the image is the *acheiropoieton,* the icon "made without hands." Following the Eastern Mandylion, the Veronica, or *vera icona,* is the Western rival to the status of archetype of the sacred portrait of Christ from the early thirteenth century. The *acheiropoietic* icon, typically depicting the Holy Face on a cloth, is believed to have received the image by *direct* physical impression, whence its indexical status, causally linking the image and its model, sustaining the sacral presence, the original moment of contact, the identity of represented and representation. Moreover, the Veronica, a mechanical reproduction of sorts, lends its testimonial value to its copies: the contact of image and image, like the "original" contact of body and image, is seen as retrospective proof of the first image's origin, endowing the copy, too, with miraculous power.[29] The icon has, by implication, the properties of what it represents: hence, it is venerated, it participates in processions, and it is expected to heal and to perform miracles. In this way, it inherits the functions of a relic.

The sacral value ascribed to the icon is dependent on certain stylistic conventions: the predominance of an upright, frontal depiction finds its supreme expression in the acheiropoieton. The face of Christ is depicted on the stretched veil whose surface parallels that of the icon as an object of veneration. The ceremonial frontality of the icon, which it shares with ancient portraiture, offers itself to the devout's bowing and prostration. It does not draw the viewer into its space but is directed forward: depth is conceived not as behind but in front of the icon, in the space of the devout.[30] This stylistics of frontality is apparent through Byzantine and medieval images, modified though not altogether obliterated as it reaches into the Italian Renaissance. It may also be identified in certain depictions of gospel scenes that do not rely on the emblematic portraitlike positioning of holy persons but on narrative representation within an increasingly realistic environment. Here the relation of figures to the background, grasped as a flat upright surface, the distinctness of forms and isolation of figures in space, may still be described as the remnants of the ceremonial portrait images of veneration.

Pasolini's pervasive frontal mode may be traced back to the Byzantine icon and followed through Italian descendents such as Duccio, Giotto, Masaccio, and finally Piero della Francesca, whose positioning of figures within an already perspectival system is a major source of allusions for *Il Vangelo secondo Matteo*. Those are fundamental theological-aesthetic principles grasped at the very source of his art historical allusions that Pasolini succeeds in adapting on film and that he identifies, moreover, as underlying a possible insertion of a cinema into the Christological tradition of the image. While they are explicitly thematized in *Il Vangelo*, these principles may be traced almost throughout Pasolini's work and inform as well his theory of film. Pasolini's sense of a reverential capacity inherent in the camera's relation to the profilmic summons this art historical context, which inflects the plastic properties of his work. A flat, frontal organization of mise-en-scène and framing, the ceremonial distinctness of figures in relation to each other and to the background, is pervasive in his compositions and made even more emphatic by the choice of lenses and camera work. The frontal assault of his camera on the profilmic yields an image that seems to press forward onto the screen and endow the subject matter with corporeal presence. The landscape enframed by the movie camera as if it were a backdrop supports a rich texture of faces, bodies, headgear, and costumes; it evokes the gilded vertical surface of the icon receptive to the incarnation of a divine—that is, corporeal, human—figure. In grafting his general privileging of a frontal mise-en-scène on the thematics of the gospel, Pasolini in this film defined and historicized his cinematic aesthetic as a whole.

His 1966 "Technical Confessions" describes the inception of this aesthetic as early as *Accattone,* leading to the conscious choice of techniques in *Il Vangelo.*

> Sacrality: frontality. And hence religion. . . . Also the lenses were, rigorously, the 50 and the 75: lenses that render the materials heavy, exalt the modelling, the *chiaroscuro,* give weight and often an unpleasantness of worm-eaten wood or porous stone to the figures, etc. Especially when one uses them with "stained" lighting, backlighting (with the Ferrania camera!), that hollows out the orbits of the eyes, the shadows under the nose and around the mouth, to the effect of widening and

graining of the images, almost as in a dupe print, etc. Thus was born, in the ensemble of the film [*Accattone*], in its figurative machinery, that "grave aestheticism of death." . . . The principal lens [of *Il Vangelo*] had suddenly become the 300. Which obtained simultaneously two effects: that of flattening and then rendering the figures even more pictorial (*Quattro-* and *Cinquecento*), and at the same time the effect of endowing them with the casualness and immediacy of a news documentary.[31]

The increase of focal length in *Il Vangelo* does not always allow for centralized composition, but the sense of frontality is nonetheless accentuated. Interestingly, frontality thus becomes almost independent of the sheer positioning of the actors and their attitudes. This is accomplished through the flattening of the image, the deliberate effacing of illusionistic depth, and the collapsing together of figure and ground by means of focal length and framing—so much so that even a vast and spacious landscape that would allow a penetrating, perspectival view is transformed into a backdrop pressing up in front of the camera. Against this backdrop, the figures appear to be impressed or, one might simply say, projected. As in the colliding surfaces of visage, cloth, and the pictorial surface of the acheiropoietic icon, figure and setting as well as the screen surface tend to coincide in *Il Vangelo secondo Matteo*. Pasolini's "casual" effect of immediacy borrowed from news or sports reportage results in an iconlike presentness of the image, a distinctness of figures projected on a surface. Beyond the erratic shifts of a hand-held camera, of zoom and telephoto lenses, of quasi-journalistic cinematography, beyond the heterogeneous texture and ultimate reflexivity of this mechanical style, Pasolini achieved an unforeseen contemplative detachment and calm that enveloped the sense of the whole in *Il Vangelo secondo Matteo*. Interestingly, the archaic sacrality and overtly mechanical style are here consistent, complementary. In this ideology of representation, his prebourgeois aesthetic models allow Pasolini to bypass the naturalist fallacy in favor of an immanence of vision that embraces not only the represented profilmic but the materiality of the medium itself.

Pasolini's awareness of the eloquence of the frontal style as exceeding the matter-of-factness of documentary and naturalist stylistics and leading right back to a rich Christological figurative tradition is articulated in the comments that accompany the script of *Mamma Roma,* already envisioning the biblical landscapes of *Il Vangelo.*

I cannot conceive of images, landscapes, compositions of figures out-side of my initial *Trecento* pictorial passion, which has man as the cen-ter of every perspective. Hence, when my images are in motion, it is a bit as if the lens were moving over them as over a painting: I always conceive of the background as the background of a painting, as a backdrop, and therefore I always attack it frontally. . . . The fig-ures in long shot are a background and the figures in close up move in this background, followed with pan shots which, I repeat, are al-most always symmetrical, as if within a painting—where, precisely, the figures cannot but be still—I would shift the view so as to better observe the details. . . . I seek the plasticity, above all the placticity of the image, on the never-forgotten road of Masaccio: his bold *chiaro-scuro,* his white and black—or, if you like, on the road of the ancients, in a strange marriage of thinness and thickness. I cannot be Impres-sionistic. I love the background, not the landscape. It is impossible to conceive of an altarpiece with the figures in motion. I hate the fact that the figures move. Therefore, none of my shots can begin with a "field," that is with a vacant landscape. There will always be the figure, even if tiny. Tiny for an instant, for I cry immediately to the faithful Delli Colli to put on the seventy-five: and then I reach the figure: a face in detail. And behind, the background—the background, not the landscape. The Capernaums, the orchards of Gethsemene, the deserts, the big, cloudy skies.[32]

Like the surface of a painting, the profilmic is "attacked frontally": figure and background converge in a static ceremonial composition designed for veneration. While the ostensible attitude of a figure may be in profile, the relations of masses and the orientation of the mise-en-scène as a whole conform, as it were, to the setting and the picture plane: bodies, costume, architecture, natural landscape, all seem adapted to each other, coinciding into a complete, full frontal scene.[33]

Pasolini acknowledges Masaccio as his prime pictorial referent: here one detects the overlapping planes emerging, endowing figures and groupings with a frontal orientation. The indications of depth and sense of flattening frontality oscillate in Masaccio's characteristic enclosure of a scene in a shal-low foreground even as the molding of figures and foreshortening of archi-tectural elements already belong to a perspectival order. Masaccio's settings participate in this ambiguous tendency: the hills in the *Tribute Money* and the *Baptism of the Neophytes* and the architectural elements in the *Story of Theophilus* constitute the natural or urban landscape as backdrop to a frontal composition brought forth for the viewer. Masaccio's *Adoration of the Magi* renders the processional scene laterally; yet the mountainous background (with only a bit of sky at the top suggesting further depth) lends the painting a ceremonial frontality quite independent from the ostensibly "profile" depiction of the majority of the figures within the shallow, foregrounded space. Pasolini's equivalent gospel scene shifts from a similar organization set up against a nearby hillside (fig. 1) to a consummating high-angle shot taken from behind the Madonna and Child (fig. 2). A boy bearing gifts approaches from the back of the procession to the front, the camera tilting down and zooming toward him as he kneels in front of Mary. From this second, over the shoulder, point of view shot—which no longer connotes a pictorial but a properly cinematic order—the figures now appear to crowd and fill the frame as if the length of the procession, grasped from up front, was pressed forward. Between the lateral view of the processional spectacle wherein the relation to the landscape suggested a ceremonial pictorial space, and this condensed elevated view that transports us to an explicitly cinematic order we witness in a nutshell Pasolini's aesthetic of frontality.

The frontal effect is largely dependent, then, on the relation of figure and ground on an upright, flat, pictorial plane where both meet to face the viewer. Pasolini's camera amplifies this effect by the use of narrow-angle lenses that suppress depth and with it the dynamism of movement. The subduing of movement is also achieved by the camera's following characters—often in close or medium shots—in such a way as to keep them practically steady, in a constant relation to the frame. Another technique involves the deliberately exaggerated use of zoom motions that mechanically enact the colliding of figure and ground. But even his deliberate severing of sound and image, the ceremonial isolation of voices, the frequent use of music to displace all "natural" background sounds, and most radically the moments of complete silence—these far exceed the effects of the Italian postsync tradition, depriving the cinematic space of its resonance in complementing Pasolini's icon stylistics. Early on in *Il Vangelo secondo Matteo,* one identifies paradigmatic instances of these devices. An almost silent soundtrack over the first few shots and counter shots of Joseph and Mary isolates the image from any natural sense of depth or context beyond the highly pictorial frame. The mute frontal portrait of the young pregnant Mary, modeled perhaps on Piero's *Madonna della Misericordia,* is shot against an arch construction in a stone wall that enframes her as would the iconic beam or panel structure (fig. 3). Such enframed areas, as suggested by arches, windows, and doorways—frequently used in the cinema to enhance additional planes in deep-focus composition—are, as in this early

portrait, frequently blocked in Pasolini's film. Rather than lead the eye into depth, such compositions serve here to enframe while pressing the figures forth as if onto the screen surface, oriented toward our space.

As the opening sequence proceeds, Joseph is framed a few shots later in medium shot from the back, his torso a dark shape against the bright background: his silhouette seems stamped upon the view of Barile, the Apulian hill village that serves as the analogue for Bethlehem. The landscape, which seems projected right up behind him, fills the frame almost entirely, with very little definition of sky at the top to barely suggest distance and dimension. Throughout the film, the framing of the landscape rarely allows more than this bit of sky to define the contour of a hillside. Indeed, wherever there is some sky apparent over the landscapes of *Il Vangelo secondo Matteo* it is overcast so as to present an opaque, full, and flattened surface upon the screen, never a vacant recess through which our glance might pierce. Preparing for Joseph's dream, a pan tracing the undulating rhythms of the hill describes the expanse of natural features and architectural elements—ruins, caves, paths— blending into each other in this setting. Joseph's own motion of turning and kneeling to sleep repeats, with his entire body, the movement of the descending pan. The landscape is thus grasped as synonymous with the

1. Lateral view of the Magi from *Il Vangelo secondo Matteo,* Pier Paolo Pasolini, 1964. (Frame enlargement courtesy of Noa Steimatsky.)

2. Frontal view of the Magi. (Frame enlargement courtesy of Noa Steimatsky.)

3. The young Mary. (Frame enlargement courtesy of Noa Steimatsky.)

4. The angel against a hillside view of Barile, Apulia. (Frame enlargement courtesy of Noa Steimatsky.)

human body and in this way also partaking in Joseph's dream. Following this logic of identity between body and landscape, the angel's appearance seems naturalized against the humble setting (fig. 4): the natural and the miraculous contaminate each other.[34] The angel is barely distinguishable from the children shown playing in this setting earlier; it emerges as if it had been all along part of this scene, as if the landscape had been waiting for this instance to offer to view its sacred burden, its underlying *figure*, as I will describe it below. Already at these opening shots, then, Pasolini's camera can be seen to seek relations of repetition, identity, and reciprocity between the landscape and the figures, as if those were drawn by a single hand with no abyss, no shadow, separating one from the other but both overlapping, colliding on the screen.

The importance of this kind of landscape, similarly enframed, which re-appears in variation throughout the film in sites that stand for Capernaum and Jerusalem, cannot be overemphasized. It is the archetypal ground of Pasolini's *Il Vangelo secondo Matteo,* rising vertically against the screen, filling the frame with little or no sense of depth, lending itself to the function of an iconic backdrop. Figures and faces, often static and portraitlike, appear stamped or hovering over the hillside view, as does the Holy Face upon the acheiropoietic cloth. Mountains and jagged rocky precipices, terraces and slopes, crevices, cave mouths, and archways served the Byzantine tradition and its Italian descendants well through the fourteenth century. Such landscape elements have traditionally been coupled with a high horizon line, so that the background would appear to rise vertically as the unifying ground where different dimensions, high and low, far and near, divine and human, are juxtaposed and compressed upon the plane.[35] When they take the place of the iconic veil or gilded background, the symbolic function of such vertical landscape features—their connecting of heaven and earth—is accommodated by their backdrop frontality whereby surfaces converge. The dense hill-town crowding some of Giotto's frescoes in San Francesco at Assisi can be seen to make such "backdrop" use of the terraces and elevated facets of the hillside, with each plane seeming to emerge out of the other as the lot confronts the view of the surface as a whole. These depictions of hill towns appear to be modeled *after* the natural conditions of such environments, yet the vertical frontality also refers back to the gilded or veiled iconic background before the windows of linear perspective were opened.

The zoom lens, an overtly mechanical device imposed upon the ar-

chaic setting and sacral connotations, contributes conspicuously to Pasolini's contamination of the reverential style by "journalistic" devices: it
underlines a frontality already prescribed by the landscape and composition.[36] A pronounced use of the zoom may be seen in the opening of the
Baptism scene: a vast expanse of mountainous landscape is traversed as the
camera seems to plunge from its high-angle position by means of a series of
zoom-in motions into the deeply set Chia Creek near Viterbo: features of
the landscape appear to spread and flatten in their approach, pressing against
the screen surface. All sense of depth, of the distance just "traversed" by the
zoom motion, is optically eliminated as figures and ground are crowded in
a shallow, flattened, enclosed space that remains at the end of the lens's motion. The curious spatiality and the postures of John in these surroundings
recall, once again, Pasolini's prime pictorial referent: Masaccio. The zoom-
in motion, and the final position of the lens in very long focal length, Pasolini notes, "obtains effects even dearer to my boy's-eyes trained on Masaccio, flattens the images even more, renders them more warm and burdened.
It leavens them like loaves, massive and light . . . just as the painter's brush is
light, almost sparkling in creating the most massive *chiaroscuri* of the model-
ling, that has man as its center and as its light, the Universal Light."[37]

Narrow-angle telephoto shots as of the crowd at the marketplace by
the city gate of Matera—Jerusalem's analogue—achieve similar results. The
camera's technique appears to "adjust" itself to the landscape—the hill
slopes, the ascending paths, the *gradoni* (hillside ramps and terraced paths)
leading toward the city gates. The high-angle telephoto lens inhibits depth
and motion, flattens the view, magnifies our sense of an upright, opaque
backdrop, its negative spaces full in the thick of the figures and objects that
crowd the frame. In this tapestrylike impression a multitude of elements is
compressed upon the plane, within the frame. Space is rendered concrete,
full, offering itself forward to the viewer.

The choice of Matera, an ancient hill town in the Basilicata region, as
the setting for Jerusalem constitutes an especially concentrated instance in
Pasolini's grasp of the location as a *terra sancta*. Its resonance in the film
may serve to bring together and conclude many of the themes explored
in this study: contamination and analogy as film-aesthetic principles, the
consecration of the profilmic, and the iconic stylistics that formalize these
concerns. The opening panoramic shots of Matera—placed at the center
of the film and signaling the beginning of the Passion—associate it with
Barile, the location for Bethlehem that offered our paradigmatic image of

the landscape for *Il Vangelo secondo Matteo*. The geographical proximity of Jerusalem and Bethlehem in the Judea Mountains accounts in part for this analogous choice of the paired southern Italian hill towns, as does Pasolini's preference for the severe beauty of the Sassi side of the town, where cave mouths intersperse with arches, windows, and doorways and the hillside *gradoni* lead the eye or the camera along, dictating the rhythm of the view.[38] The local stones that have sectioned and terraced the hillside for centuries to prevent landslides, the fusion of rock surfaces and stone houses with the natural rhythms of the place—those are traced by the camera like a pictorial surface. The Mediterranean hill town is in this way seen as fully inserted in the landscape, which, while arid and hard to cultivate, has nonetheless been inhabited, tamed, for centuries—if only, at times, by the sheer repetition of footsteps along the same paths—into a reserved moderation that is the root of its beauty. Densely built on top and thinning out down the hill, such towns—like Arab villages in the pre–Six Day War Palestine that Pasolini had observed in the *Sopraluoghi*—seem to emerge out of the landscape like an expression of the place itself. The town repeats and embodies the landscape, which is in turn crystalized in the duration of a film shot.[39]

In one of the few shots in the film explicitly designated as Jesus' point of view, a caressing undulating pan over the landscape of Matera is matched in a delayed countershot by a close-up of Christ, the direction of his funereal yet gentle look repeating the pan. As in the earlier matching of Joseph's body movement with that of the pan, in this reciprocity with the landscape there is a sense of full recognition and submission, marked by Christ's ultimate lowering and shifting of the eyes away from the view—a view at once so humble and so charged. As this motion is responsive to the view, so the landscape appears here as if touched by the look—of Jesus as of the camera. The view is predicated upon the consecrating look turned upon it. In this way, the landscape is humanized; it is figured in human features.[40] Pasolini's own cinematic look equates itself here with a divine vision for which the "things of the world," touched by the look, fully incarnate the sacred. In this quintessential instance—the shot/countershot reciprocity of Jesus facing the view of Matera as a whole, "taking it in" while caressing it with his eyes—the spirit of the place may be understood as incarnated in his human features, even as his divine look is figured in the landscape. Like the iconic screen, Matera becomes, then, at once backdrop to the impending Passion and itself not only an object of divine contemplation but its compassionate witness. In this, it reflects our own role opposite it. Béla

Balázs eloquently described just such reciprocity between the landscape and human physiognomy, between the view and the human look in the cinema: "The film, like the painting, thus offers the possibility of giving the background, the surroundings, a physiognomy no less intense than the faces of the characters. . . . It is as though the countryside were suddenly lifing its veil and showing its face, and on the face an expression which we recognize though we could not give it a name."[41] This is the figuration of the sacred in the landscape. The face of the earth—its expression, its presence of soul, its return look—is unraveled by a consecrating, divine perception, now identified with the movie camera.

As the sacred is transported from the authentic Terra Sancta to this place, so does its incarnation in the humanity of Christ bear upon the landscape that grounds his image. The sacred is figured upon the face of the earth, which affords a more profound, more enduring expressivity than that of one human face alone. Pasolini seeks to capture in the filmed world a glimpse of the iconic image of God: seen but not quite nameable, exceeding the particular and the historical in its apotheosis in the landscape. *Il Vangelo secondo Matteo* claims a divine presence concretely figured in the physiognomies of its actors and locations: it transpires on film, it is not abstracted as text, it denies the arbitrariness of signs. The word is incarnated in flesh, and light is animated in the "things of the world." According to such a theology, analogy as working principle is complemented by anagogy,[42] the work's participation in divine meaning, where what has been told in darkness is screened in light.

Notes

Unless otherwise noted, translations from the Italian are mine with the help of Paolo Barlera and David Jacobson, whose generous conversations also enhanced my thinking on Pasolini. Thanks to Ivone Margulies, Charles Musser, Maria Georgopoulou, and Lance Duerfahrd for strong readings of these pages.

1   Barth David Schwartz notes in *Pasolini Requiem* (New York: Pantheon, 1992), 360, that in January 1961, having just started work on his first film, *Accattone,* Pasolini traveled to India with Alberto Moravia and Elsa Morante. Impressions of this trip were collected in Pier Paolo Pasolini, *L'odore dell'India* (Milan: Longanesi, 1962).

2   In using the name Palestine I follow Pasolini's designation for Israel and parts of Jordan. By this, he wishes to designate a larger geographical area than that of Israel before the Six Day War. In reference to more specific locations, he does name Israel and Jordan as such: thus, his usage is not politically inflected, nor is mine in this text.

3   P. Adams Sitney describes the hagiographic models in Pasolini's early work in *Vital*

Crises in Italian Cinema: Iconography, Stylistics, Politics (Austin: University of Texas Press, 1995), 173–84.

4   As has been noted often, the film's original title omits (as does the gospel itself), the word *saint*. It is primarily for this reason that I refer to the film by the Italian title, reserving the English for allusions to the biblical text.

5   Pier Paolo Pasolini, *Il Vangelo secondo Matteo, Edipo Re, Medea* (Milan: Grazanti, 1991), 13–14.

6   One may recall here Pasolini's preceding, "scandalous" treatment of a crucifixion story in the short *La Ricotta* (1962–63). One adviser of the Pro Civitate confirms, however, that the short does not manifest contempt but rather a serious contemporary exploration of the subject. See "Lettera di P. Grasso S.J. a Pier Paolo Pasolini," in Pasolini *Il Vangelo,* 17–18. It is indeed only upon superficial view that *La Ricotta* would appear to "deconsecrate." Its conceit describes the Passion of a starving film extra tormented by the indifferent powers of a film industry that, even in producing a film of the Crucifixion, cannot recognize a Passion when it sees one.

7   Here, as in his subsequent work, Pasolini's yearning for the scrap of the archaic in the contemporary world accompanies an ambivalent attitude toward modernity and progress. In the *Sopraluogho,* this is also apparent in the gentle irony that tinges Pasolini's image of kibbutz family life, implicitly juxtaposed with the resonant biblical image of the mother and child.

8   *Sopraluoghi in Palestina* soundtrack.

9   See, for example, Pier Paolo Pasolini's essays "New Linguistic Questions," "Comments on Free Indirect Discourse," and "Dante's Will to Be a Poet," all in his *Heretical Empiricism,* edited by Louise K. Barnett, translated by Ben Lawton and Louise K. Barnett (Bloomington: Indiana University Press, 1988), 3–22, 79–101, 102–12 respectively.

10 See Pasolini's own account of the contamination of styles in *Il Vangelo* vis-à-vis the more consistent texture of *Accatone* in the interviews with Oswald Stack included in *Pasolini on Pasolini* (London: Thames and Hudson, 1969), 84. A comparison of the two films' music tracks can also serve to differentiate *Il Vangelo*'s contamination. One observes that it is perhaps only in his last film, *Salò or The 120 Days of Sodom* (1975)—which constitutes such a despairing turning of the back on all his cultural and aesthetic connotations of the archaic celebrated in his earlier work—that Pasolini appears to strive for a homogeneous, consistent, symmetrical style.

11 André Gaudreault's essay, "La Passion du Christ: Une forme, un genre, un discours," in *Une Invention du diable? Cinéma des premiers temps et religion,* edited by Roland Cosandey, Andre Gaudreault, Tom Gunning (Sainte-Foy, Quebec: Les Presses de l'Université Laval, 1992), 91–101, describes in such terms the ontology of filmed versions of the life and Passion of Christ.

12 Erich Auerbach, *Mimesis: The Representation of Reality in Western Literature,* translated by Willard R. Trask (Princeton: Princeton University Press, 1953), 43, 41, respectively. Evidence of Pasolini's familiarity with this text may be found in *Les dernières paroles d'un impie: Entretiens avec Jean Duflot* (Paris: Pierre Belfond, 1981), 140–41.

13 North Africa as well as northern Italy for *Edipo Re,* Anatolia for *Medea,* Naples for the *Decameron,* and the town of Salò for *The 120 Days of Sodom* are among the most cele-

brated examples. Some unrealized adaptations are also worth noting. In the *Appunti per un'orestiade africana,* Pasolini explores how he might "export" the Greek-Mediterranean myth to contemporary sub-Saharan Africa. In his treatment of the life of Saint Paul, published in *San Paolo* (Torino: Einaudi, 1977), modern-day New York would stand for ancient Rome, Paris for Jerusalem, modern Rome for ancient Athens, London for Antioch, and the Atlantic Ocean for Paul's "theater of voyages": the Mediterrenean.

14 Upon his return, Pasolini toured Italy in search of new sites and extras, filming the documentary *Comizzi d'amore* (*Love Meetings,* 1964), which itself emerges as a covert *Sopraluogo* and deserves further study in this light. Only after this did he finally turn to the actual production of *Il Vangelo* in the few selected sites in Calabria, Basilicata, Puglia, and the Lezio region.

15 *Sopraluoghi* soundtrack. Don Andrea emphasizes *photograph* to imply, it appears, a superficial resemblence, even if it is based on the use of the original place.

16 Except when quoting directly from the Italian *terrasanta,* I employ *terra sancta* in the Latin, as it is traditionally cited in English writings, capitalized when a definite article is employed to designate Palestine.

17 See Mircea Eliade, "Sacred Space and Making the World Sacred," in *The Sacred and the Profane: The Nature of Religion,* translated by Willard R. Trask (San Diego: Harcourt Brace Jovanovich, 1959), 20–65.

18 See Jonathan Z. Smith's account of this transposition in *To Take Place: Toward Theory in Ritual* (Chicago: University of Chicago Press, 1987), 94.

19 Peter Brown, *The Cult of the Saints: Its Rise and Function in Latin Christianity* (Chicago: University of Chicago Press, 1981), 88. My summary is based on this study.

20 Stack, Pasolini on Pasolini, 82.

21 Pier Paolo Pasolini, "Confessioni tecniche," in *Uccellacci e uccellini* (Milan: Garzanti, 1966), 49.

22 Maria Antonietta Macciocchi provides an account of this meeting with Sartre, one of the few in the French Left who did not reject Pasolini's adaptation of the gospel. See her *Duemila anni di felicità* (Milan: Mondadori, 1983), 332–33.

23 "The Written Language of Reality" is the title of one of Pasolini's seminal film essays collected in Pasolini, *Heretical Empiricism;* also the title "Is Being Natural" may be evoked here. These essays provoked the negative response of contemporary semioticians such as Umberto Eco. But it is a thinker like Roland Barthes whose affinities with Pasolini come to mind, albeit in more self-conscious theoretical form: "Certainly the image is not the reality but at least it is its perfect analogon and it is exactly this analogical perfection which, to common sense, defines the photograph. . . . This purely "denotative" status of the photograph, the perfection and plenitude of its analogy, in short its "objectivity," has every chance of being mythical" ("The Photographic Message," in *Image Music Text,* edited and translated by Stephen Heath [New York: Hill and Wang, 1977], 16–19), or "In Photography, the presence of the thing (at a certain past moment) is never metaphoric. . . . The photograph is literally an emanation of the referent. . . . A sort of umbilical cord links the body of the photographed thing to my gaze: light, though impalpable, is here a carnal medium" (*Camera Lucida: Reflections on Photography,* translated by Richard Howard [New York: Hill and Wang, 1981], 78–81). For Pasolini, as for

Barthes, reflections on the photographic or cinematographic image ultimately rebound their semiotics into phenomenological—and in Pasolini's case specifically theological—grounds. The mutual acknowledgments of these men starting in the early 1960s deserve a separate study.

24 Pier Paolo Pasolini, "Quips on the Cinema," in *Heretical Empiricism,* 227; italics are mine.

25 Stack, *Pasolini on Pasolini,* 82–83.

26 In the Peircean triad, the indexical sign is causally tied to its referent, which might not resemble it at all as in the example of a weather vane as a sign for the wind; the iconic sign is defined by resemblence, while the symbolic sign is akin to our notion of the arbitrary sign, as in verbal language. Iconicity as a Peircean category should be distinguished here, then, from the historical and theological designation of the icon. The suggestiveness of the doctrine of the icon in relation to photography and film has not been lost on scholars. Hans Belting, *Likeness and Presence: A History of the Image before the Era of Art,* translated by Edmund Jephcott (Chicago: University of Chicago Press, 1994), 4, 11, 53, uses the example of the photograph to describe the powers of proof and authenticity attributed to the icon and describes the cult surrounding one Dr. Giuseppe Moscati (d. 1927), whose larger than life photograph is venerated at the altar of the church of Gesù Nuovo in Naples. See also Barthes, *Camera Lucida;* André Bazin, "The Ontology of the Photographic Image," in *What Is Cinema?,* translated by Hugh Gray (Berkeley: University of California Press, 1967), vol. 1, 9–16; Annette Michelson, "The Kinetic Icon in the Work of Mourning: Prolegomena to the Analysis of a Textual System," *October* 52 (1990): 16–39; and Georges Didi-Huberman, "The Index of the Absent Wound (Monograph on a Stain)," translated by Thomas Repensek, in *October: The First Decade, 1976–1986,* edited by Annette Michelson et al. (Cambridge: MIT Press, 1987), 39–57.

27 My summary relies on Belting, *Likeness and Presence,* as well as Leonid Ouspensky and Vladimir Lossky, *The Meaning of Icons,* translated by G. E. H. Palmer and E. Kadloubovsky (Crestwood, N.Y.: St. Vladimir's Seminary Press, 1982); and Richard Temple, *Icons: A Sacred Art* (London: Element Books, 1989); *New Catholic Encyclopedia* (New York: McGraw-Hill, 1967), under "Icon." While the Roman Catholic conception of the image is distinct from that of the Eastern Church, the stylistics of the Byzantine icon persisted in Italy through the thirteenth century and beyond.

28 Belting repeatedly cites this phenomenon, comparable to Peter Brown's account of the cult of saints and relics.

29 This account is based on Belting, *Likeness and Presence,* 53, 208–9.

30 See Gervase Mathew's *Byzantine Aesthetics* (New York: Viking, 1964), 31.

31 Pasolini, "Confessioni techniche," 44–46. While Pasolini states here as in the Stack interviews that in a crisis experienced at the beginning of the shooting he chose to turn his back on the "sacred frontality," in fact he recognized retroactively the resolution and crystalization of this visual style in *Il Vangelo.* Pasolini's style may, I believe, be associated with primitive cinema and deserves study in this light. François de la Bretèque draws attention to the way in which the shift of early film style from frontal to oblique mise-en-scène recalls the trajectory of Western religious art. See "Les films hagiographiques dans le cinéma des premiers temps," *Une Invention du diable,* 129.

32 The passage is from Pasolini's production diaries, published with the screenplay of *Mamma Roma* (Milan: Rizzoli, 1962), 145–49.

33 This account is indebted to Roberto Longhi's 1927 analyses of the archaic frontality of Piero della Francesca as borrowed from Egyptian and classical tomb painting and inherited via Masaccio: a frontality independent of the attitudes of figures and modified though not contradicted by Piero's experiments with perspective. In *Saint Jerome with a Devout Suppliant:* "The kneeling figure, for example, would be described in common phrase as given in profile, and yet it is the 'prospect' or full view of him which spreads itself out at this moment before the spectator's gaze and stamps itself upon the many-coloured landscape. If we were to be faithful to the concept 'profile'—valid, in truth, solely in an art of mere lines—we might attempt to apply it, not only to the man, but to the tree as well: and failing now to distinguish in the case of the tree a 'profile' from a 'front view,' we should come very near to discovering the secret of the stylistic unity in this painting by Piero. This unity is in fact created by nothing else than by this very immanence of the perspective 'front view' composed upon the plane" (*Piero della Francesca,* translated by Leonard Penlock (London: Frederick Warne, 1930), 42–43); analyses of comparable effects are on pages 46 and 105. As Pasolini studied with Longhi in Bologna before the war, there is no question in my mind as to the influence of such powerful descriptions of *Quattrocento* art on his student's visual sensibility.

34 This is paradigmatic of the representation of miracles throughout the film: the miraculous is inserted into the ordinary succession of events via editing, while the humble and mundane is lifted out of its continuum by virtue of such sudden cuts to silence that we witness here. Pasolini observed (in *Les derniers paroles,* 39–40) that in this premodern rural landscape the miraculous is still part of the perception of the everyday, thus consistent with his "realist" refusal to reconstruct the biblical world. Still he was to regret his incorporation of miracles in the film as "almost counter-Reformation Baroque, repellent . . . disgusting pietism" (Stack, Pasolini on Pasolini, 87).

35 Such scenes are perhaps mediated in Pasolini's mind by Duccio's *Temptation of Christ* or his *Entry into Jerusalem.* My summary of Byzantine stylistics here is indebted to Mathew, *Byzantine Aesthetics,* 33–34. Cave mouths, common in medieval nativity scenes, reveal, as in Pasolini's film, no depth, but they constitute a dark ground against which figures may be depicted.

36 Pasolini lists in "The Cinema of Poetry," published the year following *Il Vangelo* and describing it indirectly, the range of mechanical devices contributing to a poetics of contamination (in *Heretical Empiricism,* 184): "The alternation of different lenses, a 25mm and a 200mm on the same face; the proliferation of wasted zoom shots, with their lenses of very high numbers which are on top of things, expanding them like excessively leavened bread; the continuous, deceptively casual shots against the light, which dazzle the camera; the hand-held camera movements; the more sharply focused tracking shots; the wrong editing for expressive reasons; the irritating opening shots; the interminable pauses on the same image, etc."

37 Pasolini, "Confessioni techniche," 45. One may compare to Pasolini's scene Masaccio's *Baptism of the Neophites,* in which the mountainous background appears to press close behind the crowded figures; another allusion may be to *Tribute Money,* in which the

frontal ceremonial composition of figures set up against the mountainous landscape oscillates but is not canceled by perspectival indications. *Universal Light* is a term that Pasolini adopts via Roberto Longhi's "*lume universale*" to designate the even, omniscent, ideal light of Renaissance painting before it was particularized and thereby naturalized in the transition to the Baroque.

38   Pasolini's investment in this kind of landscape is articulated verbally and in his controlled camera demonstrations in the short 1974 television documentary *La Forma Della Città,* directed by Paolo Brunatto, about the hill town of Orte in the Lazio region.

39   This description is partly indebted to Norman F. Carver Jr., *Italian Hilltowns* (Kalamazoo, Mich.: Documan Press, 1979).

40   My dissertation "The Earth Figured: An Exploration of Landscapes in Italian Cinema," New York University, 1995, expands on the notion of a figured landscape in a range of Italian postwar films. It also describes the status of Matera in monastic culture whereby hermits from Palestine, Syria, and Cappadocia who escaped prosecution found precisely in this isolated spot features "analogous" to their native lands. Rock chapels containing frescoed icons were uncovered in excavations here from 1959 through 1966—surrounding the period of the production of *Il Vangelo.* Their embedded presence just under the filmed surface Pasolini might have interpreted as articulated in the landscape's outward features. See Edward Allen's *Stone Shelters* (Cambridge: MIT Press, 1969); and La Scaletta, *Le Chiese Rupestri di Matera* (Rome: De Luca Editore, 1966).

41   My sense of the anthropomorphism of the landscape is clearly indebted to this formulation by Béla Balázs in *Theory of the Film,* translated by Edith Bone (New York: Arno Press, [1952] 1972), 96–97. More famously, Walter Benjamin describes the "ceremonial character" of the aura, associated with a distant, reverential contemplation, as resting on the return look of the inanimate or natural object thus humanized. See his "On Some Motifs in Baudelaire," in *Illuminations,* edited by Hannah Arendt, translated by Harry Zohn (New York: Schocken Books, 1969), 188.

42   Pasolini is certainly familiar with Dante's formulation of the fourth sense of reading in the *Convivio,* excerpted in *Critical Theory since Plato,* edited by Hazard Adams (New York: Harcourt Brace Jovenovich, 1971), 121: "The fourth sense is called anagogic, that is, above the senses; and this occurs when a writing is spiritually expounded which even in the literal sense by the things signified likewise gives intimation of higher matters belonging to eternal glory." Millicent Marcus defines the four levels as the basis for Pasolini's adaptation in *Filmmaking by the Book: Italian Cinema and Literary Adaptation* (Baltimore: Johns Hopkins University Press, 1993), 112–13. Her emphasis on a vertical textuality, informed by biblical hermeneutic tradition, may be juxtaposed with my model: the flat frontality of the iconic image.

Ecstatic Ethnography: Maya Deren and the Filming of Possession Rituals

Catherine Russell

We are watching a mental alchemy which makes a gesture of a state of mind—the dry, naked, linear gesture all our acts could have if they sought the absolute.—Antonin Artaud

Maya Deren's interest in Haitian possession rituals preceded her first film, *Meshes of the Afternoon,* and eventually outlasted her filmmaking activities. Neither the first nor last filmmaker to be fascinated by the scene of possession, Deren was attracted to an ethnographic spectacle that is both theatrical and empirical. Absorption into the pulsating rhythm of the dance may be a threat to ethnographic distance and objectivity, and yet this is precisely what interests filmmakers in search of a subjective entry into the ethnographic scene.[1] It is Deren who, along with Antonin Artaud, has articulated most clearly the modernist fascination with possession. She understood trance as a hallucinatory realism in which reality and subjectivity were indistinguishable. It attracted her as an ideal cinematic spectacle, but possession proved finally to exceed the limits of visual representation.

Deren's first trip to Haiti was in 1947 on a Guggenheim grant, and by 1951 she had made four trips. Various explanations have been offered for her inability to edit the film footage and sound recordings that she collected before her death in 1961. Although she had traveled to Haiti to make a film "as an artist," she ended up writing a book, "recording, as humbly and accurately as I can, the logics of a reality which had forced me to recognize its integrity, and to abandon my manipulations."[2] A film could show only the "surface" of the rituals, not their underlying principles and mythology.[3] Nevertheless, the existence of the footage, and the story of her unsuccessful attempt to make a film, offer some insight into the shared territory of experimental and ethnographic film practices.

Her project is, moreover, suggestive of the challenge that possession poses to cinematic epistemologies. The rituals that Deren found in Haiti were an expression of a complex cosmology of highly individualized deities; and the expression itself, the performing bodies, was charged with an eroticism otherwise absent from Deren's oeuvre. Haitian possession consisted of two very different discourses, the invisible knowledge of the gods and the visible evidence of the possessed body. Her failure to make a film is ultimately a failure to reconcile these two forms of representation.

Within the history of avant-garde filmmaking, Deren is a key figure linking the French surrealists of the 1920s and 1930s to the postwar American avant-garde. P. Adams Sitney describes her films and those that she inspired as "trance films." Unlike her surrealist precursors, Deren's psychodramatic films explore an interiority of consciousness. "She encounters objects and sights as if they were capable of revealing the erotic mystery of the self."[4] *Meshes of the Afternoon* (1943), *At Land* (1944), and *Ritual in Transfigured Time* (1945) all engage with dream states and hallucinatory imagery in keeping with Deren's theory of cinema as the meeting of reality and creative imagination—"the creative use of reality."[5] Thus, her interest in possession is not unrelated to her experimental practice.

Stan Brakhage claims that Deren struggled with her Haitian footage for ten years.[6] Regardless of whether this struggle took place in the editing room or in Deren's creative imagination, her project highlights a vivid tension between personal filmmaking and the observational mode of ethnography as it is played out around the phenomenon of possession. Deren used the term *depersonalization* to refer to the effect of ritual on the individualism of creative activity, and it was through this theme of depersonalization that she attempted to transcend the implicit contradiction between the personal and the ethnographic.

Deren describes surrealism as the final expression of "the search for the romantic personality as the core of the work of art."[7] Her interest in ritual was developed not as a counterpoint to individualism but to the conventions of personality and character in film: "The intent of such a depersonalization [in ritual] is not the destruction of the individual; on the contrary, it enlarges him [sic] beyond the personal dimension, and frees him from the specializations and confines of 'personality'." She follows this statement with the more revealing claim that "a ritual is classicist in nature."[8] Ritual, for Deren is "integrated in its own terms," and while it may be drawn from reality, it is in fact "independent of actuality and unrealistic."[9]

In Deren's proposal for the Haitian film, it is clear that ritual constitutes "form," which she apprehended from a strictly aesthetic perspective. The Haitian material was to have been combined with footage of Balinese trance dancing (borrowed from Margaret Mead and Gregory Bateson) and North American children's games. In her thematic statement for the film, she recognizes that the "cultural integrity" of the different rituals had to be preserved within her comparative project in order to maintain the "authority of the form" of each type of ritual practice.[10] However, she also intended to reveal a "homogeneity in variety"—to foreground the similarities between the different rituals. These comparisons included such grand effects as "displacement of identity" as well as more mundane connections such a chalk lines on the ground—a link between Haitian possession rituals and children's hopscotch.[11]

Within her plan for the film, it is not clear whether she intended to shoot the children's games in a documentary or a performative style. In fact, in the little that we know of Deren's plans for the Haitian film there is no discussion of the different effects and possibilities of documentary footage. In her previous films, Deren had great control over the profilmic performance; in her design for the unfinished film, she is interested above all in isolating formal tendencies in "found" rituals. The aesthetics of the film, including a soundtrack that would experiment with "amplification and recording," would be developed at the editing stage.[12] The forms of the rituals would emerge through analysis and comparison.

An ideal of depersonalization may well have led Deren to Haiti and motivated her interest in possession. However, as a canonical instance of the meeting of avant-garde film and ethnography, Deren's foray into the field of the other threw many of the tenets of personal cinema into question. The "reality" that she confronted in Haiti was one that ultimately evaded the terms of visual expression on which her cinematic art was founded. I would argue that the category of the individual subject is not actually challenged by Deren's experimental practice but is masked by a romantic notion of the community and the crowd as an expression of identity.[13] The representation of fragmented subjects in Deren's experimental films are ultimately subsumed by the creative force of the artist, through whose vision they can be reassembled into conceptual wholes.

Maria Pramaggiore has argued that "Deren's promotional efforts helped create an image of the modernist artist-auteur, whereas her multiplied and fragmented film protagonists refuse to 'guarantee' textual meaning through persona."[14] In Pramaggiore's reading of the experimental work, Deren creates "the sense of bodies subsumed by forces different from and larger than the individual will."[15] This impression of the body, at once liberated from the constraints of space and time and from the limitations of self-consciousness, is precisely the effect of possession rituals. And yet the contradictory ambivalence within Deren's artistic persona may also account for her difficulties in editing (or refusing to edit) the Haitian footage. The Haitian material may have grown out of Deren's prior filmmaking practice, but it also challenged many of the assumptions within her aesthetic theory, most explicitly the romantic individualism underscoring her quest for depersonalization.

Deren's ethnographic method, like her aesthetics, is a romantic one that seeks a transcendent form of experience. What distinguishes it from similar programs and manifestos—such as those of Artaud and Brakhage—is the role of the body in her texts. It was her fascination with the actual movements by means of which Haitian dancers invite the gods to possess them that took her to Haiti. Deren pursues the conjunction of art and anthropology much farther than her contemporaries, and articulates, however crudely, the fundamental attraction of the avant-garde to native cultures that has persisted since the surrealists.

Possession and Modernism

The role of possession in the modernist imagination is highly contradictory. The desire to film possession may be motivated by the idea of subjectivity "on display," given theatrical form, and yet it is also a scene of excess, producing something that inevitably escapes representation. The filming of possession rituals was a fundamental aspect of Jean Rouch's practice of "shared anthropology." The scene of possession became the catalyst in Rouch's development of cinema vérité, as it offered a particular profilmic support for the development of a new form of realism, a different order of truth.

In a series of articles and interviews about his filming of possession rituals, Rouch developed a theory of *ciné-transe,* which linked a cinematic ontology with the phenomenon of trance. He argued that the act of filming lifted the filmmaker onto a plane of magic and out of body experience akin to that of the spirit possessed. Or, more precisely, he felt that the filmmaker would appear so to those he or she filmed: "For the Songhay-Zarma, who are now quite accustomed to film, my 'self' is altered in front of their eyes in the same way as is the 'self' of the possession dancers: it is the 'film trance' (ciné-transe) of the one filming the 'real trance' of the other."[16] The utopian, transcendental aspect of Rouch's writing on possession rituals is inspired by the ecstatic character of the rituals themselves, in which individuals are transported out of everyday reality and become others, doubles of the gods and spirits, who take control of their bodies. Possession is itself a form of representation to which the realist filmmaker might aspire, but it is also a *mise-en-abyme* of representation, with its final signified content always beyond reach. The endpoint of the possession semiosis is the subjectivity of the other, the belief in the spirit world of doubles who are "known" only by the possessed. The epistemological grounds of the ritual, the "reality" of the gods, thus resist cinematic representation along with its ideology of visibility. Deren's struggles with her Haitian film footage illustrate this fundamental contradiction.

The conjunction of documentary realism and trance poses a host of contradictions concerning visual evidence, authenticity, and ethnographic subjectivity. The possession ritual is only completed by being witnessed because the performance constitutes a proof of the existence of gods or spirits. As a spectacle, it challenges conventional forms of spectatorship and passive observation, as spectators are often drawn into the trance. While this is part of the attraction of such rituals to filmmakers, films of possession do not necessarily retain the same structure of spectatorship. The difference between possession rituals and the filming of possession rituals is precisely the inscription of technology. The image of ecstasy stands in for the experience of possession.

The sublime transcendence of the indigenous spirit possessed gives a documentary form to a whole range of Western desires for transcendental experience, from drugs to dance to creative trance.[17] For both Antonin Artaud and Jean Rouch, the possession ritual offered an ethnographic instance of a "found surrealism." Artaud's enthusiasm for Balinese theater was informed by an orientalism that resonates in the films of possession. It represented everything that was missing from the Western theater; it expressed something essentially oriental, and his enthusiasm was entirely motivated by the use he could make of it in his reform of European theater. Possession provided Artaud with a valuable model for a performance mode that transcended spoken language and relied solely on "a new physical language." Apparently he saw dancers even on the Parisian stage go into trance, which he described as "deep metaphysical anguish." The dancers' gestures appeared to be directly linked to their souls, without mediation, so that the actors became doubles of themselves. In their mechanical and rigid movements, he saw a strategy of exorcism "to make our demons FLOW."[18] Despite the spiritual and mystical orientation of the performance, Artaud also saw it as a novel form of realism: "For though we are familiar with the realistic aspect of matter, it is here developed to the 'n'th power and definitely stylized."[19]

Deren's aesthetics of depersonalization are in fact characteristic of a modernist fascination with the collective as a crowd: a loss of the self in the "reality" of the collective.[20] The attraction of the crowd and the fascination of possession is the loss and/or rearticulation of identity, a reconfiguration of the tenets of ego psychology. Describing Marcel Mauss's fascination with possession rituals at the turn of the century, Vincent Crapanzano writes: "There are no longer any individuals but just pieces in a machine, spokes in a wheel, the magical round, danced and sung, being its primitive, ideal image. . . . Here the laws of collective psychology violate, desecrate, transgress, rape, the laws of individual psychology."[21]

Mauss and Durkheim were both interested in *mana,* or magic, as "an unconscious category of understanding whose origin as a category is, needless to say, social."[22] At the same time as Freud was mapping the individual unconscious, these anthropologists were studying the power of social rituals and mana in the collective unconscious. The two lines of inquiry inevitably converged in "a new science of the crowd and collective behaviour" that fed directly into the Italian avant-garde and fascist ideology in both Germany and Italy.[23] Like so much of the modernist imbrication of aesthetics and politics, the fascination with the crowd lends itself both to dangerous and progressive social practices. The crowd as a mobilized body politic is at once a savage and eminently modern figure in which psychological structures and social formations obtain dramatic and theatrical form.

Annette Michelson has compared Deren's interest in Haitian ritual with Eisenstein's aborted Mexican project. Both filmmakers apprehended "community" as "a collective enterprise grounded in the mythic," which Michelson casts in the revolutionary rhetoric of the prewar avant-garde.[24] And yet even Michelson admits that once Deren came to explore the communal forms of Haitian culture and "the complex historical processes inscribed within that culture" her project began to collapse. Deren approached her ethnographic subject matter armed only with a theory of forms, which could not retain their autonomy or authority in the context of living history or the representational practice of documentary film.

Hysteria, Therapy, and the (Psycho)analysis of Possession

Before going to Haiti, Deren viewed Margaret Mead and Gregory Bateson's film *Trance and Dance in Bali,* which was shot in 1937 and 1939 and released in 1951. She was so inspired by this material that she planned to include sections of it in her own film and consulted extensively with Bateson on the implications and possibilities of a "cross-cultural fugue."[25] In diary notes on the Balinese footage, she articulates her interest in the visual effects of possession, but she takes issue with Mead and Bateson's interpretation of their footage. *Trance and Dance in Bali* was sponsored by the Committee for Research in Dementia Praecox, as schizophrenia was once known.[26] The proclivity to trance is interpreted by Mead and Bateson as a function of a characteristic egolessness and weakened sense of self caused by particular child-rearing methods in a culture they understood to be endemically schizophrenic.[27] In the trance state, various activities and emotions are acted out that the individuals could not ordinarily express because of their inability to communicate effectively. For the Balinese watching trance rituals, the spectacle has a cathartic effect, dramatizing climactic intensities that are absent from everyday life. Mead and Bateson saw trance as a form of therapy for a sick culture.

Jean Rouch also appealed to a psychoanalytic frame of reference for his film *Les Maîtres fous* (1954–55), suggesting the vital parallelism between the two discourses of possession and psychoanalysis in the middle decades of the century. Possession and psychoanalysis are linked by an (apparently) shared mechanism of hypnosis, and the cinema is the technology that promises to exploit that vital link. This may explain the attraction of filmmakers to possession, but for Rouch it also served to set the colonialist limits of his project.

Les Maîtres fous follows Ghanese Hauka cult members out of Accra to a rural compound; it climaxes with the frenzied eating of dog meat and ends with the "smiling faces" of the Hauka cult members happily digging ditches in front of a mental hospital. An epilogue serves to reestablish the "normality" of the members of the cult, but it has the effect of reducing the ritual to a therapeutic process. Rouch suggests on the soundtrack that the men, who are employed in fairly menial jobs, have found a way of dealing with the stress of modern life. Their "panacea against mental disorders" saves them from the mental hospital, even if their behavior while possessed suggests that that is where they belong. Echoing Mead and Bateson's analysis of Balinese trance, Rouch applies a Freudian paradigm as a means of rationalizing what has been demonstrated as being completely irrational or at least unknowable. Although he has since rejected this ending as a mistake, its inclusion is testimony to the confluence of psychoanalysis and ethnography in the Western representation of possession in the postwar period.[28] The closing shots of the film show the Africans as fully cooperative "working" members of colonial society, and they are indeed seen "like insects" in a colony, cogs in a machine.[29]

From the available evidence, it seems that Deren was unfamiliar with Rouch's extensive filming of possession rituals. In her comments on *Trance and Dance in Bali,* she effectively rejects Mead and Bateson's implied theory of therapy. Not only does Balinese trance performance not have a pathological explanation but Deren finds that it lacks a cathartic form of spectatorship. She points out that there is a complete indifference between spectators and performers in the film, a lack of identification that challenges the conventional spectator-exhibitionist structure of theatrical performance. The term *exhibitionism,* she says, simply does not apply to the Balinese footage.[30] The lack of star performers, along with the lack of a stage with its strict delineation of the space of performance, suggest to Deren a form of egoless theatricality. In Haiti, she hoped to find a similar spectacle that would place new demands on filmmaker and audience alike.

In 1942, five years before she went to Haiti, Deren published an article on the anthropology of dance, in which she develops a theory of possession as a psychological and creative practice. Recognizing a parallelism between hysteria and possession, Deren makes two important points that make a real break with the analytic framework developed by Mead and Bateson. One is that "in our culture hysteria is an anti-social phenomenon; in Haitian and African culture, possession is not at all antagonistic to its social environment but rather a part of it."[31] Second, the communal context of possession constitutes an active and validating form of spectator-ship, "for when the objective surrounding, or community, confirms the subjective impression of the individual, the concept upon which those two forces are in agreement constitutes, within that particular frame of refer-ence, a reality."[32] Deren insisted that, despite the parallels between posses-sion and psychopathological states, possession was neither "delusional" nor abnormal in Haiti. Both hysteria and possession occur in social contexts, she argues, but possession is culturally determined whereas hysteria is pri-vately determined. She hoped that the social confirmation of a hallucina-tory reality could in some way be achieved in modern American dance.[33] Although she arguably outgrew the orientalism of this article, she remained guided by the theory of hysteria as a key to possession phenomena.

After viewing the Balinese material, Deren went back to her earlier article and found that, despite her critique of Mead and Bateson's use of psychoanalysis, her own theory of possession as "an hysterical release of a subconscious system of ideas" still held.[34] Throughout her writing on ritual performance there is the sense of it as a return of the repressed: "Psycho-somaticism is the re-creation in immediate terms of unrecollected mem-ory."[35] For Deren, "primitive" forms of spirituality differ from modern ones only in their degrees of intensity, and thus the experience of possession in Haiti is not completely alien to the psychology and physiology of ecstasy in other, more "modern" cultures.[36]

Deren's theorization of possession is in many ways emblematic of the Western fascination with the image of possession. In the projection of ori-entalist fantasy, the possessed body tends to become a metaphor for other forms of transcendental experience, including sexual ecstasy, political re-sistance, liberation, and escape from the restrictions of reality.[37] Possession rituals clearly lend themselves to a theorization of the return of the re-pressed, breaking through both colonial and sexual oppression. The image of the possessed, like the hysteric, might thus be read as a melodramatic structure of expression. Possession, like melodrama, is a structure of rep-resentation in which the body itself becomes a form of writing. In Peter Brooks's theorization of melodrama, it is a modernist aesthetic of excess in which signification itself becomes a struggle: "There is a constant effort to overcome the gap, which gives a straining, a distortion, a gesticulation of the vehicles of representation in order to deliver signification. This is the mode of excess: the postulation of a signified in excess of the possibili-ties of the signifier, which in turn produces an excessive signifier, making large but unsubstantial claims on meaning."[38] The "moral occult," which Brooks identifies as "the center of interest and the scene of the drama," is in the possession ritual a properly metaphysical system. Only when it is filmed and transformed into a new level of language, does the moral occult become "the repository of the fragmentary and desacralized remnants of sacred myth"—the moral occult of bourgeois melodrama.

This is not to say that possession rituals are melodramatic but that they share with melodrama a structure of representation that helps to explain the Western fascination with possession. Once the possessed body is filmed, it becomes a signifier in a language that we know as melodrama. The image of the possessed becomes, in the language of modernist cinema, a hysterical, ecstatic, body in which truth functions not as "evidence" but as the return of the repressed. Melodrama also provides the analytical tools to read this discourse of excess as an inscription of the other's resistance in and of representation. This is the radical potential of filmed possession as experimental ethnography: a discursive system in which subjectivity is produced in the field of the other.

Possession is thus a delirious language, a form of "reason in action," that is more truthful (more authentic) than the realism of photography.[39] It offers a new regime of veracity to cinematic representation, an alternative realism that filmmakers have been drawn to for different ethnographic and aesthetic ends. Filmmakers like Deren and Rouch are drawn to the scene of possession because it replicates the utopian drive of the cinema: to produce a total hallucination, a complete illusion of reality. Participants in the rituals enter another reality, another body, but the spectator of the film of possession sees only a document of a hallucination, a mise-en-abyme of realities in which the filmic reality is wanting, lacking the ecstatic potential of the ritual. Thus, the filming of possession tends to be marked by contradiction and compromise.

Given the parallels between her experimental films and her writing on possession, what Deren hoped to find in Haiti was a means of making the mind visible. In uniting the spectacle of the body with a dream state that tended toward the somnambulistic, possession seemed to share basic metaphysical properties with the cinema. From her background in dance and her interest in psychoanalysis,[40] she viewed the bodies of the possessed dancers as manifestations of the mind, as images of the unconscious. To really understand possession, it had to be experienced subjectively—by an artist like herself.[41]

Divine Horsemen: The Footage and the Book

Deren eventually wrote a book that supplanted the film as the more adequate representation of Haitian voodoo. *Divine Horsemen* is written from the perspective of the initiate, and its slogan is "When the anthropologist arrives, the gods depart." In her introduction, Deren establishes her credentials to write about possession on the basis of her status as an artist. Since her métier was to deal on the level of subjective communication, she claims to have had an insight into the rituals unavailable to the anthropologist. She also claims an affinity with the marginal status of native peoples vis-à-vis modern industrial culture. Artists, she says, are an "ethnic group" subject to the full "native" treatment—exhibited, denounced, feasted, forgotten, misrepresented, and exploited by a society on which they are dependent.[42] The difficulties she had in completing the film need to be read back into that precarious alignment of artist and "native," which she herself sets up.

Deren was not really interested in the role of voodoo in Haitian revolutionary movements of the early nineteenth century or in the underground African unity discourse that it preserved within slave culture.[43] These are mentioned in passing, only as an explanation for the power invested in and derived from the *loas*—the gods who mount the possessed dancers.[44] Nor is she interested in the conditions of everyday life of the participants in the rituals—what they do when they are not dancing. *Divine Horsemen* reads more like a religious tract than an anthropological study. The detail is extraordinary, but it is concerned solely with beliefs and ritual practices. Each of the loas, who have distinct and dramatic personalities, and each of their ceremonies are described, along with the hierarchies of the priesthood, the metaphysics of the religion, and the music, costumes, symbols, and accoutrements. Deren's writing is inflected with the passion of bringing the gods to life and culminates in the final chapter, in which she describes her own possession by the loa Erzulie.

> To be precise, I must say what, even to me, is pure recollection, but not otherwise conceivable: I must call it a white darkness, its whiteness a glory and its darkness terror. It is the terror which has the greater force, and with a supreme effort I wrench the leg loose—I must keep moving! must keep moving!—and pick up the dancing rhythm of the drums as something to grasp at, something to keep my feet from resting upon the dangerous earth. No sooner do I settle into the succour of this support than my sense of self doubles again, as in a mirror, sepa-

rates to both sides of an invisible threshold, except that now the vision of the one who watches flickers, the lids flutter, the gaps between moments of sight growing greater, wider. I see the dancing one here, and next in a different place, facing another direction, and whatever lay between these moments is lost, utterly lost.[45]

Deren claims that she wrote *Divine Horsemen* in spite of herself. Editing her footage would have been an unpardonable manipulation, while writing about her experience constituted a form of reportage. And yet, as the description of her own possession suggests, the book is clearly much more than reportage. Her language is stylized, expressive, and subjective, and in this passage metaphors of vision, as well as imagery of light and darkness, inscribe the spectacle of race that lies hidden within her project. Writing, no less than filming, is only a means of representing possession, which is itself a form of representation. Deren was apparently able to go into trance, even back in New York, using her body to evoke the Haitian loas at critical moments.[46] She found film to be an inadequate means of penetrating the layers of signification set up by ritual performance, and so she wrote the book as an interpretation of the performances she witnessed. The characters of the loas are not perceptible on film because those who are seen are not those who are present. The loas remain invisible to the film spectator, and since the purpose of the rituals is to prove the existence of the loas the film fails as a document of reality.

The film that was released in 1985 as *Divine Horsemen,* edited by Cheryl Ito, is an attempt to bring Deren's writing, film footage, and sound recordings together. Unfortunately, it resorts to a format of ethnographic filmmaking that runs counter to Deren's perspective on anthropology. Although the narration is taken directly from Deren's book, the explanatory male voice-over is greatly removed from the act of filming. The voice, and the text itself, are of an entirely different order of language—impersonal, objective, authoritative, and oblique. As a narration, Deren's extremely literary writing is heavy and overwrought. A woman's voice-over is used for one passage, but the softer, less expository tone that may have been an attempt to capture Deren's experiential attitude is simply a clichéd feminization.[47]

The disjunction of sound and image in *Divine Horsemen* is more than a function of the production history of the film. A profound ambiguity lies at the heart of the voodoo ritual itself, creating a real problem for documentary representation. When individuals are "mounted" or possessed by a loa they take on that personality and are no longer "themselves," but visually they are still themselves acting differently. When, for example, a man is seen giving out money and people appear to be bumping into him, the narrator says: "The spirit of Ghede is mounting the body of the priest. He is known as a trickster and delights in playing games to confuse people. . . . Clown though he may be, he is also history—the experience from which the living learn—and in this role is as deeply responsible and trustworthy as he is bizarre in his other aspects. . . . Ghede is also a god of fertility. The women bump against him to ensure healthy children."[48] In the cinematic configuration of sound and image, "he" is the man on screen acting as the loa Ghede, impersonating him. The image of the eroticized body is a much more direct and legible signifier than the descriptive language superimposed on it. The Haitian possession rituals that Deren filmed challenge the cinematic construction of performance by exhibiting an unintelligible theatricality.

The Ito version of the film includes a soundtrack composed of Deren's own recordings, but it is overwhelmed by the voice-over and functions more like background music than as an integral part of the ceremonies. Each segment is introduced with a graphic design or painting associated with one of the loas, thus incorporating yet another level of discourse into the film. The editing is fairly quick, moving from different dancers, settings, activities, and practices, even within segments. As a result, the montage of people dancing, ritual animal sacrifices, parades, and so on is reduced to the status of images that illustrate a preconceived commentary. As an ethnographic film, it has a voyeuristic structure that runs contrary to Deren's insistence on the holistic, psychological, emotional, and experiential quality of her approach to Haiti.

Deren's own silent footage, assembled by Anthology Film Archives, runs three and three-quarter hours. It includes a great deal of in-camera editing, and the assembly of rolls of film is complete with flares indicating reel ends. In a curious repetition, the same trio of three people dancing in a clearing recurs after cutting away to quite different scenes, suggesting that some kind of reordering of scenes may have been done. However, because of the lack of intention behind the montage, the lack of structure, this footage can be described as unedited or "raw." Deren's failure to edit it, manipulate it, or subject it to secondary revision leaves us with a document that is not "a film." But neither is it an observational record shot by a nonintrusive surveillance camera. It is an extremely moving and emotional depiction of possession, even though it may not be "evidence" of the presence and activities of the loas.

Deren's shots are long, with constant movement, including hand-held photography, swish pans, and zooms. Close-ups and medium shots predominate over long and establishing shots. The few images of landscape tend not to be integrated into possession scenes. Every new scene begins from the inside, paying close attention to the movements of feet and bodies, often cutting or panning to the drummers. The rhythm of the ceremonies becomes visible, and each new set of dancers is given film time to develop so the transition from dance to possession is often apparent without anyone pointing it out. Details such as the way dancers lose their balance as they are "mounted," their stunned look as they come out of trance, the spitting of liquor, and the incorporation of Euro-American dance steps such as a jig, a jive or waltz are clear as visual signs. Without a voice-over, the image is legible on its own—as a different order of knowledge. Without a soundtrack, the image is a qualified realism, at a distance from the viewer, and the presence of the musicians inscribe a silence and an attendant awareness of limits.

Many sequences are shot in slow motion, perhaps to follow the complex dance steps and body movements. In contrast to the voice-over version, the dancers perform in their own time with their own knowledge intact. It is not a shared time between spectator and profilmic; it is historical time marked by once-only events, particularly the deaths of animals. At least seven sacrifices take place, including those of chickens, goats, and a bull, each of which is carried out somewhat differently. A convention of ethnographic film, bloodletting practices often contribute to the negative stereotype of the primitive, and they can often challenge the norms of Western spectatorship. This is implied even in Artaud's theater of cruelty, but here the cruelty is only in the eyes of the non-Haitian spectator. As Deren says in her book, in the context of Haitian voodoo sacrifice is not "morbid" but a practice of renewal and rejuvenation by means of which the loa is infused with life and vigor.[49] As a cinematic spectacle, animal sacrifice constitutes an indexical inscription of the otherness of time and history as the spectator becomes a witness to that which has occurred only once: it is thus redemptive. In Deren's footage, the frequency of animal sacrifices and their ceremonial integration at once normalizes the practice and challenges the spectator.

As with most possession dances, the Haitian rituals are set in a circular compound, sometimes with a shed roof over it but without a stage or proscenium structure. Spectators surround the dancers, and Deren's camera moves around, to and from different points in the circle. (The footage also includes a number of setups in which people are clearly performing for the camera, especially in the carnival sequences.) Despite the discontinuity of her editing and the lack of a stable spectator position, the bodies of the dancers tend to anchor the view. Their erotic, sensual, and fluid movements function as an attraction—to the loas who eventually possess the most spectacular dancers but also to the spectator. Deren emphasizes the role of the community and its virtual eroticization by the possession ritual, a scene from which the film spectator, in silence, is excluded. One can watch other spectators become affected by the contagion of possession, but it does not spread beyond the frame.

The Spectacle of the Body

Despite the dynamic character of Deren's footage, which culminates in a carnival parade, the different form of knowledge implicit in possession is ultimately unavailable to the film spectator. Haitian voodoo dances involve many explicit expressions of sexuality—flirting, couple dancing, and eroticized body movements. They also frequently involve gender confusion and ambivalence, but this is not apparent to the film spectator. In one sequence, on the level of the visual alone we see a woman dancing seductively with the drummers. We may know from Deren's book that women are often possessed (or mounted) by male loas, and take on their characters, but we cannot see that she is "not herself." As visible evidence, it remains the image of a woman dancing seductively. Sexuality in Haitian possession is indeed a fluid and communal form of expression, and eroticism is not simply carnal but a transcendent form of being. Ghede, says Deren, "is amused by the eternal persistence of the erotic and by man's eternally persistent pretence that it is something else."[50] Ecstatic ethnography, as a genre of ethnographic film, is entirely bound up with this pretence that eroticism is a function of the material, visible, sensuous body.

The fact that Ghede likes to wear sunglasses further suggests that the discourse of desire in Haitian possession is invested in the eye as well as the body. Ritual experience evades audiovisual representation because it is itself a form of representation with an internal structure of spectatorship. Possession, for Deren, is about witnessing, about the communal recognition of a reality confirmed by the spectacle of the body.[51] And yet she found that film was inadequate; in fact, it renders the loas invisible and absent. Her own observations on Mead and Bateson's footage, that there is no identification between dancers and audience, ultimately come back to haunt her; she can only know the loas through her own performance. If it was only by writing that she could bring the loas to life, it was because she could write herself into the scene of possession more easily in words than in images.

Missing from her footage is the spectacle of Deren herself dancing among the Haitians. How could she have filmed this without looking like Osa Johnson among the Africans, Marlene Dietrich in a gorilla suit, or Leni Riefenstahl among the Nuba?[52] Positioning herself behind the camera, she eliminates her whiteness and its attendant discourse of race. But at the same time she eliminates the level of experience that she claimed to be necessary for an understanding of possession. Her subjectivity is reduced to a strictly phenomenological inscription of viewing, a status that irrevocably separates her from the Haitians. Photography is a different form of witnessing than that called for by possession. Through writing, she could overcome the visible difference of race and the phenomenological separation of mechanical reproduction, but only through dance could the mediation of witnessing be removed.

Deren's unfinished film constitutes an experiment with ethnographic language, a document of the limits of cinematic representation. While her written document constitutes a translation of Haitian voodoo into another language—English literary/academic prose—the film footage is an attempt to represent experience directly, without mediation. The result situates the auratic truth of the image out of reach, along with the subjective reality that the ritual ostensibly documents. The ethnographic spectacle is not "evidence" of the loas, which will always escape the attempt to inscribe them in documentary form. The means by which the Haitians are able to become others through the language of the body might be an instance of what Walter Benjamin describes as the "mimetic faculty" that is in decay in modernity: "We must suppose that the gift of producing similarities—for example, in dances, whose oldest function this was—and therefore also the gift of recognizing them, have changed with historical development. . . . For clearly the observable world of modern man contains only minimal residues of the magical correspondences and analogies that were familiar to ancient peoples. The question is whether we are concerned with the decay of this faculty or with its transformation."[53]

The cinema was for Benjamin an inscription of this transformation, in which a language of similarity and analogy is allegorized in mechanical reproduction. For Deren, the auratic potential of cinema was its ability to make the facts of the mind visible. While it was possible in her experimental films to give her own mind, her own subjectivity, imagistic representation, in Haiti the gap between experience and cinematic representation became unbridgeable and the aura disintegrates.

The fascination with possession is bound up with the different order of knowledge and language that it embodies. Its occult and mystical properties ultimately proved more powerful than Deren's faith in cinematic "magic," and yet in its unfinished form her footage provides a rare document of possession. For Artaud, the utopian possibilities of the cinema were invested in the freedom from language and the promise of a direct visceral experience in and through representation: "Raw cinema, taken as it is, in the abstract, exudes a little of this trance-like atmosphere, eminently favourable for certain revelations."[54] Although Deren's "unedited" record of possession can be considered "raw film," it cannot divine the "secrets of the depths of consciousness" that Artaud hopes for. In turning away from her own subjectivity and exploring the mind of the other, Deren's ethnographic imagery can register only the trace of the occult, which becomes in its absence the aura of the subjectivity of the other.

Mimicry, Resistance, and Postcolonialism

The possession rituals performed by native peoples in the expanding horizons of Western knowledge seemed, within the culture of modernism, to represent a transcendent, utopian experience of community. And yet from a postcolonial perspective it inscribes an encounter between the orientalist desire for primitive spectacle and an ethnographic reality that resists representation. Possession poses a challenge to the ideology of realism, confounding the principles of visual evidence. The spectacle of the writhing body, upturned eyes, and frothing at the mouth is visual "proof" of the existence of the gods or spirits that have entered the body of the performer. Thus, the body becomes the signifier of that which has no referent. In resisting referentiality, it marks the limit of visual language and rational thought. For the uninitiated, however, for those who have not learned to be possessed, the spectacle of the spirit possessed is in many ways illegible. For the spectator from "outside," there may be only the signifier of the dancing body and no way of knowing the authenticity of the trance. It thus poses a real challenge to anthropological epistemology, providing an ethnographic spectacle that is ultimately unintelligible.

The image of possession inscribes a splitting of body and consciousness in a language of performance. The possessed can thus be read as an uncanny figure of the doubling of the self and its other, a splitting or fragmentation of the ego, or a structure of mimicry harboring a fundamental ambivalence concerning identity. While this process of doubling points to the role of possession in the modernist imagination, it also suggests how it produces a resistance in the field of the other. Cinema replicates the possession phenomenon in its strict separation of image and subjective experience, reproducing the radical ambiguity of the colonized subject. Homi Bhabha's theorization of "the mimic man" as a figure of colonial discourse refers to the colonial subject of assimilation, "in which to be Anglicized is *emphatically* not to be English."[55] As a figure of ambivalence in colonial culture, the mimic man performs his identity. If the possession ritual represents the most "savage" and "crazed" figure of the other, it also represents a subjectivity that remains uncolonized.[56]

In Rouch's seminal film *Les Maîtres fous,* the Hauka cult incorporates spirit possession into an explicitly anticolonialist drama, using mimicry as a structure of appropriation. The doubling that takes place in this ritual identifies colonial figures (the "governor," the "conductor") with gods and spirits, the ritual participants being the vehicles that make this identification possible. The effect is to render colonial history as an imaginary parallel world separate from the everyday "mortal" world of the African subjects. If each cult member who goes into trance is identified with a particular colonial figure (transformed into a deity), they are also performing their difference, the utter impossibility of them identifying with those colonial figures. The great gap between the Africans and the white men is as great as that between men and gods. Only in the liminal space of the possession ritual can that gap be overcome.

The very mixed reception that *Les Maîtres fous* has encountered since

1. A possession scene from *Divine Horsemen,* Maya Deren, 1985 (Frame enlargement courtesy of Catherine Russell.)

its first screening in 1954 is further evidence of the ambiguity and unintelligibility of the spectacle of possession.[57] Many spectators could only "see" Africans acting as savage, uncivilized, and crazed. And yet Rouch persisted in filming possession rituals, as have many filmmakers, perhaps because of the intrinsic analogy between cinema and possession, film viewing and trance. The strategies of mimicry in *Les Maîtres fous* constitute another point of contact between possession and cinema, which has something to do with resistance and the challenge of possession to the "reality principle" of sociohistorical oppression.

Deren's failure to represent the other's subjectivity is bound up with the primitivist paradigm that aligns native subjectivity only with occult phenomena. Its failure is not unrelated to Deren's profound neglect of the socioeconomic and political history of voodoo. Her purely metaphysical interest in Haitian possession, which enabled her to identify with "the natives," also wrote history out of the picture. The origins of Haitian voodoo are deeply embedded in the history of slavery and the revolution of 1803–4, in which Haiti became the first black republic in the New World. Its forms of doubling and mimeticism, like those of the Hauka cult in West Africa, invoke the memory of colonial history and embody the specific forms of resistance that slavery provoked. Joan Dayan argues that "The dispossession accomplished by slavery became the model for possession in voodoo; for making a man not into a thing but a spirit."[58]

Dayan's account of Haitian voodoo is especially pertinent to the discourse of gender that subsists in Deren's approach to Haiti. Dayan accuses Deren, like Zora Neal Hurston before her, of idealizing the goddess Erzulie as a fantasy along the lines of the femme fatale and other Western paradigms of powerful women.[59] Instead, Dayan argues, Erzulie should be understood as an incarnation of the sexual practices of eighteenth-century plantation life: "The history of slavery is given substance through time by a spirit that originated in an experience of domination. That domination was most often experienced by women under another name, something called 'love'."[60] Whereas the colonial practices informing the Hauka cult in Rouch's *Les Maîtres fous* are masculine rites of militarism and government, voodoo rehearses the sexuality and emotional terror of colonial history.

The goddess Erzulie encompasses the complex meaning of the black maid who was loved by her master and beaten by her mistress. Like many of the loas, she bears the trappings of luxury denoting the colonial scene, and yet Dayan argues that she "is not so much a 'dream of luxury' as Deren wrote, as a mimicry of excess."[61] And it is this structure of mimicry that constitutes the "menace" of possession. Bhabha claims that "The menace of mimicry is its double vision which in disclosing the ambivalence of colonial discourse also disrupts its authority."[62] Possession constitutes a specific form of knowledge, a mythic memory formed by and in a contested history. Haitian voodoo need not be rendered mysterious and impenetrable to be recognized as a language of resistance, enacting the contradictions that lie within colonial practices of domination and submission.

Deren's interest in Haitian possession was of course also framed by her prior work with Katherine Dunham and her African Dance troupe. In Haiti, she was to some extent seeking a more "primitive" form of the African American dance forms that Dunham had developed for American audiences. And yet ethnographic ritual cannot be filmed on a strictly formal level. The documentation of possession is a complex, multileveled form of representation in which subjectivity and history play key roles. This is evident from Deren's "raw footage," in which its own limits are implicitly inscribed: its meaning lies beyond visual representation. In Deren's silent film footage, the spirit of Carnival and the discourse of race are evoked in the terms of a spectacle that hints at a discourse of mimicry, doubling, and ambivalence, but nowhere in Deren's project is this language linked to historical processes or subjects. Not long after Deren's last trip to Haiti voodoo became linked to the oppressive political machine of François Duvalier and the Tonton Macoute cult of violence.[63] Postcolonial history also teaches us that the other subjectivity cannot be idealized as necessarily anticolonial but always needs to be historicized. Perhaps the gap between experience and film, between aura and language, might be overcome if voodoo were understood as a political and historical language not only of resistance but also of institutions. Within Deren's modernist aesthetics, possession remains a metaphor of language, a utopian ideal of a form of knowledge inaccessible to the fallen consciousness of industrialized subjectivity.

Notes

This essay is a modified version of a section of my book *Experimental Ethnography: The Work of Film in the Age of Video* (Durham: Duke University Press, 1999).

1 Bill Nicholas, *Representing Reality: Issues and Concepts in Documentary* (Bloomington: Indiana University Press, 1991), 221.

2 Maya Deren, *Divine Horsemen: The Living Gods of Haiti* (Kingston, N.Y.: Documentext, [1953] 1991).

3 Lucy Fischer, "Maya Deren's Haiti Footage," *Field of Vision* 7 (summer 1979).

4 P. Adams Sitney, *Visionary Film: The American Avant-Garde, 1943–1978,* 2d ed. (New York: Oxford University Press, 1979), 11.

5 Maya Deren, "Cinematography: The Creative Use of Reality," in *The Avant-Garde Film: A Reader of Theory and Criticism,* edited by P. Adams Sitney (New York: New York University Press, 1978).

6 Stan Brakhage, *Film at Wit's End: Eight Avant-Garde Filmmakers* (New York: McPherson, 1989), 112. Brakhage's claim has not been substantiated.

7 Maya Deren, "Notes on Ritual and Ordeal," *Film Culture* 39 (winter 1965): 10.

8 Ibid., 10.

9 Maya Deren, "Film in Progress, Thematic Statement: Application for the Renewal of a Fellowship for the Creative Work in the Field of Motion-Pictures," *Film Culture* 39 (winter 1965): 13. Although this statement is undated in *Film Culture,* Neiman dates it, as originally written, Feb. 9, 1947. See Catrina Neiman, "An Introduction to the Notebook of Maya Deren, 1947," *October* 14 (fall 1980): 5.

10 Deren, "Thematic Statement," 14.

11 Ibid., 16–17.

12 Ibid., 16.

13 "The crowd" is represented in *Ritual in Transfigured Time* as a claustrophobic, superficial cocktail party in which a couple meet and dance into an open space; the collective and the crowd are symbols and metaphors of psychic states in Deren's poetics.

14 Maria Pramaggiore, "Performance and Persona in the U.S. Avant-Garde: The Case of Maya Deren," *Cinema Journal* 36:2 (winter 1997): 19.

15 Ibid., 27.

16 Jean Rouch, "Vicissitudes of the Self: The Possessed Dancer, the Magician, the Sorcerer, the Filmmaker and the Ethnographer," *Studies in the Anthropology of Visual Communication* 5:1 (1978): 7.

17 Deren's footage is "quoted" extensively in a recent Canadian film about heroin addiction, *Curtis's Charm* (John L'Ecuyer, 1995). It provides an important expressive discourse of transcendent experience to the film.

18 Antonin Artaud, *The Theatre and Its Double,* translated by Mary Caroline Richards (New York: Grove Press, 1996 66.

19 Ibid., 59.

20 The attraction to Western modernists is indicated by Walter Benjamin's description of the crowd as the central urban scene in the work of Baudelaire and Poe. For the latter, it is a "figure that fascinates" and "lures" the observer "outside into the whirl of the crowd." The Baudelairean flaneur invents himself in the midst of the Parisian throng in the Arcades; he is an ambivalent figure who gently resists the pull of the crowd, but who is nevertheless in its midst. To be in the crowd is to be "out of place" (Walter Benjamin, "On Some Motifs in Baudelaire," in *Illuminations,* edited by Hanna Arendt, translated by Harry Zohn (New York: Schocken Books, 1969), 101.

21 Vincent Crapanzano, "The Moment of Prestidigitation: Magic, Illusion, and Mana in the Thought of Emile Durkheim and Marcel Mauss," in *Prehistories of the Future: The Primitivist Project and the Culture of Modernism,* edited by Elazar Barkan and Ronald Bush

(Stanford: Stanford University Press, 1995), 101. The text to which he refers is *Esquisse d'une théorie général de la magie,* originally published in 1902–3.

22   Ibid., 103.

23   Robert Nye, "Savage Crowds, Modernism, and Modern Politics," in Barkan and Bush, *Prehistories of the Future,* 42–55. Freud's "Group Psychology and the Analysis of the Ego," published in 1921, is another example of the convergence of psychology and sociology in the early part of the century. For Freud, the group was basically a mass or a crowd, the behavior of which he believed was a natural continuity of the individual ego and could be analyzed according to similar principles.

24   Annette Michelson, "On Reading Deren's Notebook," *October* 14 (fall 1980): 51.

25   Deren-Bateson correspondence, 1946–47, reprinted in "Art and Anthropology," *October* 14 (1980): 16–20.

26   Andrew Lakoff points out that by 1951 schizophrenia had replaced dementia praecox as a diagnostic label, and so the existence of a committee with that name is a bit strange. See Andrew Lakoff, "Freezing Time: Margaret Mead Diagnostic Photography," *Visual Anthropology Review* 12:1 (spring 1996): 1.

27   The film itself does not include an interpretation of Balinese trance. This is separately argued in Margaret Mead and Gregory Bateson, *Balinese Character: A Photographic Analysis* (New York: New York Academy of Sciences, 1942), xvi.

28   Jeannette De Bouzek, "The 'Ethnographic Surrealism' of Jean Rouch," *Visual Anthropology* 2:34 (1989): 301–15.

29   Teshome Gabriel describes Rouch's treatment of African people as "scientific specimens, laboratory subjects, and insects," in *Third Cinema in the Third World: The Aesthetics of Liberation* (Ann Arbor: UMI Research Press, 1982), 75–77.

30   Maya Deren, "From the Notebook of 1947," *October* 14 (fall 1980): 29–30.

31   Maya Deren, "Religious Possession in Dancing," originally published in 1942 in *Educational Dance,* reprinted in *The Legend of Maya Deren* vol. 1, pt. 1: "Signatures, 1917–42," edited by VèVè A. Clark, Millicent Hodson, and Catrina Neiman (New York: Anthology Film Archives, 1984), 491.

32   Ibid., 488.

33   Ibid., 496.

34   Deren, "Notebook," 24.

35   Ibid., 21.

36   Deren, "Religious Possession in Dancing," 482.

37   The Christian tradition has its own imagery of possession (and indeed its own possession cults), including Bernini's statue of Saint Theresa, of which Lacan notes, "And what is her *jouissance,* her *coming* from? It is clear that the essential testimony of the mystics is that they are experiencing it but know nothing about it." The mystic for Lacan, is not "not political" just because it is sexual, and it is a politics of representation, the articulation of subjectivity as a form of knowledge, that is invested in the image of the possessed. See Jacques Lacan, *Feminine Sexuality,* edited by Juliet Mitchell and Jacqueline Rose, translated by Jacqueline Rose (New York: W. W. Norton, 1985), 147.

38   Peter Brooks, *The Melodramatic Imagination: Balzac, Henry James, Melodrama, and the Mode of Excess,* (New York: Columbia University Press, 1984), 199.

39   Michel Foucault, *Madness and Civilization: A History of Insanity in the Age of Reason,* translated by Richard Howard (New York: Vintage, 1973), 97.

40   Neiman develops the links between Deren's films and her writing on possession and also discusses the influence of Deren's father, who was a psychiatrist, on her exploration of psychic phenomena in Catrina Neiman, *The Legend of Maya Deren,* vol. 1, pt. 2: "Chambers, 1942–47," edited by Millicent Hodson (New York: Anthology Film Archives, 1988), 108–9.

41   Deren, "Religious Possession in Dancing," 487.

42   Deren, *Divine Horsemen,* 8.

43   Deren mentions the political context of voodoo briefly in "Religious Possession in Dancing" (485). For an account of the political history of voodoo, see Michael S. Laguerre, *Voodoo and Politics in Haiti* (New York: St. Martin's Press, 1989).

44   Deren, *Divine Horsemen,* 62.

45   Ibid., 259. The description continues for a page and a half, followed by a long footnote discussing the authenticity of the possession. Deren concludes that its authenticity was approved by those who witnessed it, although she points out that such discussions tend to "discuss the actions of a *loa* in great detail without thinking to make a single reference as to whose head that *loa* had entered." It is not customary to refer to "my possession by such and such a *loa*" in a proprietary manner (322 n).

46   Brakhage, *Film at Wit's End,* 104–5, 108.

47   Ito's version of *Divine Horsemen* is ostensibly structured somewhat like Deren's book, divided into sections that correspond to individual loas. The divisions are marked by black leader and introductory images of chalk drawings or paintings representative of the different gods. The effect is only to further relegate the film footage to the role of illustration of a preconceived commentary.

48   This quotation from the film soundtrack is in Deren, *Divine Horsemen,* 112.

49   Ibid., 216.

50   Ibid., 102.

51   Deren, "Religious Possesion in Dancing," 488.

52   Riefenstahl's Nuba footage has not (yet) been edited or released. A few scenes are reproduced in Ray Müller *The Wonderful Horrible Life of Leni Riefenstahl* (1993), including images of Riefenstahl herself surrounded by dancing Africans.

53   Walter Benjamin, "The Mimetic Faculty," in *Reflections: Essays, Aphorisms, Autobiographical Writings,* translated by Edmund Jephcott, edited by Peter Demetz (New York: Schocken Books, 1986), 334.

54   Antonin Artaud, "Witchcraft and the Cinema," in *Collected Works,* vol. 3, translated by Alastair Hamilton (London: Calder and Boyars [1949] 1972), 66.

55   Homi Bhabha, *The Location of Culture* (New York: Routledge, 1994), 87.

56   It is significant in this respect that possession rituals are often performed by marginalized members of a community, often referred to as "cults," as in the case of the Hauka in Niger, who Rouch filmed. The Balinese dancers in Mead and Bateson's film are members of a special club, and the Fijian dancers in Bill Viola's *I Do Not Know What It Is I Am Like* are members of a disenfranchised ethnic minority (see my essay "Subjectivity Lost and Found: Bill Viola's *I Do Not Know What It Is I Am Like,*" in *Documenting the*

Documentary, edited by Barry Keith Grant and Janine Sloniowski (Detroit: Wayne State University Press, 1998).

57 French anthropologists, including Rouch's mentor Marcel Griaule, were scandalized by the film and demanded that it be destroyed. See Paul Stoller, *The Cinematic Griot: The Ethnography of Jean Rouch* (Chicago: University of Chicago Press, 1992), 153. See also Gabriel, *Third Cinema.*

58 Joan Dayan, *Haiti, History, and the Gods,* (Berkeley: University of California Press, 1995), 36.

59 Zora Neal Hurston, *Tell My Horse: Voodoo and Life in Haiti and Jamaica* (New York: Harper and Row, [1938] 1990).

60 Dayan, *Haiti,* 56.

61 Ibid., 64.

62 Bhabha, *Location of Culture,* 88.

63 "Papa Doc" Duvalier, elected in 1957, exploited the network of "secret societies" organized around the voodoo church. Priests and other high-ranking members of the voodoo church were appointed to key military and civil positions in the Duvalier regime.

Filmic Tableau Vivant: Vermeer, Intermediality, and the Real

Brigitte Peucker

Promoted by the fashionable novels of their day, *tableaux vivants* as a parlor game—the static embodiment of well-known paintings by human actors—came into vogue in the first decade of the nineteenth century. Yet their origins are earlier and twofold, both high and low cultural. One of these is the tableau of Diderot's bourgeois tragedies, a paradigmatic moment of dramatic intensification during which the actors hold their poses and all motion on the stage ceases, a temporally circumscribed and "out of time" moment within the flow of dramatic action. There is little doubt that this form of tableau, in turn, as theorized and practiced by Diderot, is the ancestor of the tableau moment or *apothéose* in the staged melodrama and French variety shows on which Méliès was to rely so heavily in his films.[1] The other origin of tableau vivant is pornographic: the best-known tableaux of this genre may be those staged by an eighteenth-century London sex therapist in which Emma Hart posed scantily clad as a "nymph of health" tableau designed to inspire the performance of clients in a so-called celestial bed.[2] Pornographic tableaux vivants, apparently, have not gone out of fashion, nor has their relevance to cinema gone unremarked, as evidenced in Lyotard's essay "Acinéma."[3] It is in its manifestation as an embodiment of painting that the tableau vivant as visual spectacle is most suggestive for an analysis of intermediality. As we shall see, this does not preclude its erotic lure.

Tableau vivant is a meeting point of several modes of representation, constituting a palimpsest or textual overlay simultaneously evocative of painting, drama, and sculpture. As the staging of well-known paintings by human performers who hold a pose, it involves the "embodiment" of the inanimate image. In other words, tableau vivant translates painting's flatness, its two dimensionality, into the three-dimensional. By this means, it figures the introduction of the real into the image—the living body into painting—and thus attempts to collapse the distance between signifier and signified. Film understood as a medium in which different representational systems at times collide, at times replace, but generally supplement one another suggests that those moments in films that evoke tableaux vivants are moments especially focused on film's heterogeneity. It's interesting to note that in his discussion of the related tableau scenes of early cinema, Noël Burch focuses on what he calls "the unexpected cohabitation in a transition period of two modes of representation,"[4] a "tension between surface and depth."[5] Burch reads this "cohabitation" as evidence of a "collage principle" that suggests "a certain reflexivity" in those films in which "collage" techniques appear.[6] Implicit in Burch's analysis is a concern with the way in which scenes that juxtapose conceptions of space appropriate to several visual modes suggest a deliberate attempt at "collage effects."[7] Broadening the discussion to include more recent film, Pascal Bonitzer reads tableau vivant in cinema as a "composite monster, a sphinx" that poses an "enigma."[8] One aspect of the enigma that is posed, I'd like to suggest, pertains to the hybrid nature of the cinematic medium—itself a kind of sphinx—of which tableau vivant is a deliberate troping.

Elaborating, then, on the idea of tableau vivant as a lens that focuses intermediality, this essay understands tableau vivant in an expanded sense; the discussion is not confined to the stricter definition of tableau vivant as a moment of arrested action that interrupts the flow of images in cinema.[9] Rather, it concentrates on the cinematic reenactment of painting treated as the nodal point of several representational modes, as a means of textual layering that produces a suggestive semantic resonance. In this essay, I draw upon two films, *A Zed and Two Noughts* (1985), by Peter Greenaway, and Wim Wenders's *Until the End of the World* (1991), films that take a postmodern stance toward the cinematic medium. While Greenaway and

Wenders embrace a variety of signifying practices and a multivalent approach to signification—and, perhaps, precisely because they do so—these directors are both intent on locating the place of the real within signification. Although the search for the real and authentic is staged differently by each director, both films "take up" well-known paintings by Vermeer, a painter who worked within an artistic milieu notable for its realism—an added irony being that Vermeer's work is the target of one of this century's most famous cases of forgery.[10] I argue that these films exemplify somewhat different attitudes toward the accumulation of textual systems typical of tableau vivant moments. *A Zed and Two Noughts* examines tableau vivant at the level of the narrative, and its excess of textuality serves as a foil to the simulation of the real. In a perverse troping of tableau vivant, in this film van Meegeren, artist and surgeon, carries his fetishization of the real body within representation to a violent extreme. In Wenders's film, on the other hand, the layering of representational systems within the filmic text itself leads virtually to the point of epistemic collapse, to a near breakdown of representation within which the real is figured as a physiological act of perception. Interestingly—and here a potentially pornographic moment of tableau vivant is signaled—both films use Vermeer's paintings primarily in order to situate women within textuality. In each instance, the real enters the text primarily as or through the female body.

"The Flesh of a Human Presence"

Poised between Greenaway's *The Draughtsman's Contract* (1982) and *The Cook, the Thief, His Wife, and Her Lover* (1989), *A Zed and Two Noughts* has in common with his other films an obsession with the relation of representation to the real.[11] As I have argued elsewhere, Greenaway's drauftsman is a "realist" whose wish to bring the real into the space of his frames is displaced onto and enacted on the body of the woman with whom he has entered into a dubious contract.[12] Both the drauftsman's mimetic drive, acknowledged by the grid imposed upon the image by his viewfinder, and his desire for visual mastery over space that its central perspective implies find their counterparts in *A Zed and Two Noughts*. The interest in the "realist" project of Dutch painting that the still life compositions of *The Cook, the Thief, His Wife, and Her Lover* express is already present in the preoccupation with Vermeer's women that is the idée fixe of van Meegeren, the surgeon in *A Zed and Two Noughts*. Vermeer's work, Greenaway admits in a recent interview, has served as a "treasure chest" for his own production of images and guided him in "project after project" since the 1960s.[13] Following Godard's lead, Greenaway agrees that Vermeer can be seen as the prototype of the filmmaker, since his paintings represent a "world of light," while his rendering of temporality "pins the world down," at once arresting and eternalizing the moment. As Greenaway notes in this interview, his most recent project, "Writing to Vermeer," takes up the relation of writing and image, another of Greenaway's recurrent preoccupations, within the context of Vermeer's letter paintings.

It is obviously not its thematic content alone that makes Vermeer's painting of interest to Greenaway, a filmmaker/painter with a pronounced interest in and knowledge of art theory. We might look to Svetlana Alpers's pivotal study of Dutch art of the seventeenth century, *The Art of Describing,* for an analysis of representational issues that may shed further light on Greenaway's engagement with Vermeer's painting. Written in the wake of Foucault's *Order of Things, The Art of Describing* locates in the painting of this period a system of representation antithetical to that of the Albertian (narrative) model through which painting had hitherto been read. The northern, descriptive mode, as Alpers reads it, lacks a fixed point of view and substitutes the model of the painting as mirrored image for that of the painting as Albertian "window on the world." The Dutch mode of painting, with its mimetic emphasis, thus emphasizes "seeing" the world rather than narrativizing and "reading" it; in Alpers's view, its mode is decidedly not allegorical.[14] Indeed, Alpers claims that the term *descriptive,* as she uses it, can be substituted for *realistic,* and that the realism of this mode can be likened to the "pictorial mode of photographs."[15] This is not to say that Dutch painting of this period shares the impulses of nineteenth-century realism or that it is as accessible to verbalization: Dutch art shows instead that the "realistic" image can serve as a lure for the eye and that "meaning by its very nature is lodged in what the eye can take in—however deceptive that might be."[16] In its most extreme form, approaching trompe l'oeil illusionism, "Dutch art is notoriously subject to confusion with life."[17] Greenaway's van Meegeren—who bears the name of Vermeer's famous forger—is prey to just such confusion.

It is clear that one reason for Vermeer's centrality for the art of filmmaking lies with the enigmatic image of the woman, an image that is voyeuristically explored by artist and filmmaker alike. A surgeon who fancies himself a painter, Greenaway's van Meegeren is obsessed with Vermeer's women: they are said to be his "specialty," both in the medical and in the aesthetic realms. We might well ask whether van Meegeren's goal is to bring Vermeer's women to life or whether, a Pygmalion in reverse, his aim is to kill off the living body into art. As a character, he embodies the voyeuristic attitude toward women that Vermeer's paintings record, both in the earlier work in which, as Lawrence Gowing puts it, "man's attention to women" is depicted in represented acts of spectatorship,[18] or in the later paintings, in which the voyeuristic attention and sexual investment of the artist himself are understood to permeate the scene.[19] In Greenaway's film, van Meegeren's mistress, Catherina Bolnes, bears the name of Vermeer's wife, and she, too, is not the genuine article: unlike Vermeer's wife, who bore him fourteen children, van Meegeren's mistress aborts rather than gives birth, thus paralleling the failed "creative" efforts of van Meegeren. Van Meegeren himself is an inauthentic Vermeer who takes realism to an unprecedented extreme and grotesquely sculpts in human flesh: having amputated one of Alba's legs, van Meegeren is prompted by the lack of symmetry this produces in her body to remove the other.

Vision spells entrapment for van Meegeren, whose desire for the image of Vermeer's women motivates his desire for their transposition into real flesh. To this end, Catherina assists van Meegeren in his efforts to "stitch and suture" the unfortunate Alba into the space of representation —to use her, that is, in various attempts at tableau vivant embodiments of Vermeer paintings. In one tableau vivant sequence, van Meegeren's re-creation of "Couple Standing at a Virginal" is loosely construed, and the narrative of Greenaway's film is by no means arrested. Yet van Meegeren evokes Vermeer's painting cinematically in several crucial respects, including the mirrored image of the woman, a spatial trick that reveals what would ordinarily be hidden from the spectator's eye. Indeed, the act of spectatorship is

1. Vermeer's "Couple Standing at a Virginal," in *A Zed and Two Noughts,* Peter Greenaway, 1985 (frame enlargement of video)
2. Tableau vivant based on Vermeer's "Couple Standing at a Virginal," in *A Zed and Two Noughts,* Peter Greenaway, 1985 (frame enlargement of video)

foregrounded in this scene in a number of ways. Consulting a reproduction of the painting, as though to check on the authenticity of their representation, Catherina and van Meegeren glance repeatedly from a print to the embodied scene. Meanwhile, in the background, the twins Oswald and Oliver view another erotic painting, van Baburen's "Procuress," to which we'll recur in a moment.

But vision is not the only sense that is brought into play here: van Meegeren forces Alba to play the piano/virginal, thus bringing the painting "to life" by means of the introduction of sound. Greenaway claims to see the origin of cinema in Vermeer's oeuvre, and we know that their suggestion of sound is one of the sources of fascination that Vermeer's paintings hold for him.[20] Yet here Greenaway ironically undermines the efforts of van Meegeren to re-create Vermeer's erotic scenario in the "real": the only tune that Alba can play is "The Teddy Bear's Picnic," its infantility no doubt underscoring the regressive sexuality expressed in van Meegeren's compulsive "making real" of these paintings. In Greenaway's film—though not in the painting on which this tableau vivant is most closely based—the scene at the virginal also contains the van Baburen "Procuress" that hangs on the wall in two other Vermeers—in "The Concert" and "A Lady Seated at a Virginal"—thus underscoring in both painting and film the erotic barters understood to be transacted through the seductive medium of music.

This tableau vivant scene is initiated by a montage of close-ups of Vermeer women, details of a series of paintings quickly passed in review that underscore van Meegeren's obsession with a characteristic yellow bodice worn by women in four of Vermeer's paintings.[21] Dressed in the yellow bodice, "stitched and sewn to the music stool," as she puts it, Alba complains that she has become "an excuse for medical experiments and art theory." As a realist "artist" constantly torn between the "truth of the real and the knowledge that representation is only representation," van Meegeren is trapped within the structure that is operative in fetishism, torn between the belief in the fetish and the knowledge of the "real" wound that it is designed to cover.[22] Indeed, van Meegeren stands literally revealed as a fetishist, caught between his needs to operate on the female body and to cover over the wound—a function fulfilled by the yellow bodice as fetish, as an icon that obscures the "view."

It should be noted that the van Baburen "Procuress," represented twice within Vermeer's paintings, is a notable example of northern Caravaggism and that its use within this scene thus also alludes to van Meegeren's obsession with illusionism and the real.[23] If his mistress Catherina accedes to his will regarding the transformation of Alba into a Vermeer woman, van Meegeren tells her, Catherina is guaranteed a place in his "operating theater" and his bed. With this (not unusual) formulation, Greenaway signals another set of multiple allusions of an art historical and theoretical in nature, allusions that layer the real and the representational. Within the context of Dutch painting, surgery as performance calls to mind the foregrounding of spectatorship in Rembrandt's "Anatomy Lesson of Dr. Tulp" (1632). And, within the context of "art theory," as Alba puts it, specifically within the context of shocking realism, we are reminded of Michael Fried's reading of a painting by Thomas Eakins called "The Gross Clinic" (1875). Fried convincingly argues that the portrait of Dr. Gross in the medical amphitheater is a representation of Eakins's personal relation to writing and painting: within the context of this reading, the bloody scalpel in Gross's hand stands in for the paintbrush in that of Eakins. The "nearly overwhelming realism of effect" produced by Eakins's work is parodied in Greenaway's van Meegeren, who operates with an open book of Vermeer reproductions as his guide.[24]

Along with his mistress, Catherina Bolnes, van Meegeren himself enacts a tableau vivant: tellingly, it is "The Artist in His Studio," with van Meegeren, arrayed in a striped black and white doublet, playing the part of Vermeer. Wearing a red hat and nothing else but earrings, Catherina takes the place of the sedate young woman who embodies Clio, the muse of history enacting an allegory of fame in Vermeer's actual painting. The laurel wreath that adorns Clio's head is rejected in favor of the red hat of another erotically charged Vermeer woman, "The Girl with the Red Hat," the hat intensifiying the effect of Catherina's nakedness and giving it a pornographic cast. Thus, van Meegeren—and Greenaway—definitively put aside the allegorical significance of the female figure in this painting (whose allegorical significance is currently in dispute among art historians) in favor of the shock value produced by the woman's naked flesh.[25] The film intensifies the realistic effect that the presence of the human figure already has in Vermeer's painting.[26]

In this scene, van Meegeren, like Vermeer, is positioned with his back to the spectator, and the sequence begins as the film camera pulls back slowly and steadily from an extreme close-up of the black and white stripes of the doublet to reveal the entirety of the scene, clearly marking this tableau vivant sequence as cinematic. Periodically we see the flash of a time-lapse camera imposed on the scene, reminding the spectator of the lights of two other significant deployments of the photographic medium in *A Zed and Two Noughts* that must be brought to bear upon a reading of tableau vivant here. One of these is an experiment with time-lapse photography in which a series of dead animals is photographed in the various stages of decomposition. The other example — in some sense equal but opposite to this one — is a teleological "film within the film" about evolution whose projection within the diegesis is marked by the streaming light of the projector. Motivated by the deaths of their wives, Oswald and Oliver, twin zoologists, are engaged in a study of death and decay. Increasing formlessness, which is now the object of their scientific scrutiny, exists in an inverse relation to their previous object of study, evolution with its ever-increasing complexity of form. But vision has not been left out of the picture. The grids upon which the decay of various animal bodies in their experiment is charted evoke the grid through which Dürer's draftsman famously apprehends his female nude.[27] And, although the flashing of the time-lapse cameras marks the isolated moment of each photograph, these moments occur in sequence. By way of this tableau vivant of "The Artist in His Studio," then, the distinct temporalities of three modes of visual representation are juxtaposed: the celebrated "phenomenon of temporal stasis" implied in Vermeer's paintings is marked by the *punctum* of photography, and subverted by the devolution of narrative in cinema and theater.[28] With death as its temporal limitation, the body remains at the center of Greenaway's concern.

Further, in this re-creation of Vermeer's "The Artist in His Studio," the notion of van Meegeren's operating theater, the *enactment* of this painting in cinema — its sheer theatricality — and the movie theater are fused, suggesting an allegory of Greenaway's filmmaking as postmodern and intermedial. But the semantic resonance produced by these overlapping representational systems stresses simulation rather than making real, since the spectator's awareness of these textualities produces a shock of awareness — the suspension of belief — that realism in art cannot tolerate. Van Meegeren's realist project — with the naked female body at its center — is enclosed within Greenaway's multiple representational brackets, which enhance, but also expose, its simulations.

One more example of the juxtaposition of body with painting in this film — only a tableau vivant in a very expanded sense of the term — needs mentioning. In this scene, which also takes place in van Meegeren's "studio," the naked twins, Oswald and Oliver, sit on chairs positioned under Vermeer's "The Astronomer" and "The Geographer." But these are not exactly the pendant portraits as painted by Vermeer: Greenaway has turned the astronomer around, although, as he is doubtless aware, there's a precedent for this composition in an engraving of 1672 by Louis Garreau.[29] The portraits now face one another, creating a symmetrical arrangement around a central axis. The complexity of Vermeer's rendering of these scientists, surrounded by the tools of their trades, creates an ironic counterpoint to the stripped, exposed bodies of the twins. In this scene, it is suggested that the (here falsified) symmetries of art bear a relation to those of the body. The twins — once Siamese twins, their bodies joined at birth — have decided to reassume their original body symmetry, thus capitulating, it would seem, to a central preoccupation of this film that locates the origin of representational strategies in the body. Van Meegeren, who has amputated Alba's legs, is now asked to stitch the twins together. But the price for this procedure is high: in yet another attempt at "creativity," van Meegeren demands that Oswald and Oliver allow him to stand as father to their own twin sons. In a last effort to grasp the enigma of life and death, form and formlessness, Oswald and Oliver embark upon a joint suicide, having made arrangements to have their own decaying bodies fixed periodically by the lens of the camera. Here we have come full circle to Vermeer's "twin" portraits of "The Geographer" and "The Astronomer." It is clear that the same young man served as a model for both of Vermeer's scientists: interestingly, scholars think that this young man was most probably Anthony van Leeuwenhoek, the Delft microscopist.[30] Greenaway's twin scientists have now themselves become objects of scrutiny under a lens.

At this point, it will be useful to return briefly to the tableau vivant of "The Artist in His Studio" and to the black and white striped doublet worn by van Meegeren/Vermeer. As we may recall, the scene begins as the camera pulls back from an extreme close-up of the painter's striped doublet: this image of the black and white stripes doubles the black and white stripes of the zebra in the previous scene, to which the tableau vivant is connected by way of a sound bridge. What is the link, then, between the zebra and the doublet? Black and white dominate Greenaway's film not only as binarisms to be reconciled, though the spectator takes note, for instance, that Oswald is at first associated with black and image making (photography), while Oliver is associated with white and writing, specifically with the newspaper stories from which he clips phrases and paragraphs. As the twins become increasingly similar and their identities begin to merge, a reconciliation of these representational systems—of narratives and images—is effected, a reconciliation that Greenaway reads in Vermeer's paintings and on which film also necessarily relies. Yet the cut from zebra to artist's doublet has another significance as well: black and white stand for the rigid structures that guide our vision and perception, that allow us to read images and compose them. In Greenaway's view, it is fortuitous that van Meegeren/Vermeer's doublet is black and white.[31] But the artist's task, that of forming and composing, has its counterpart in the twins' preoccupation with the decomposition of bodies—among them that of the zebra and those of the twins themselves—and with the formlessness promoted by decay. At what point, Greenaway appears to be asking, is the structure of the real no longer readable, despite the fact that it is no less real? Perhaps this is one sense in which the van Leeuwenhoek portraits, portraits of a microscopist and lensmaker, have something further to say about the representational practices upon which Greenaway is meditating.

The van Leeuwenhoek portraits also point toward another concern of the film. If we agree with Stephen Heath that the camera itself is bound to the Albertian perspectival system, a system that postulates a spectator prior to and external to the scene viewed, then this system is not easily subverted.[32] In *A Zed and Two Noughts,* Greenaway chooses to expose the Albertian model by working within it, intensifying the effect of central perspective produced by the camera by exaggerating symmetries in the arrangement of the pro-filmic in his frames and thus making his spectator constantly aware of the way in which the scene is laid out before the eye. In scene after scene, for instance, Alba recumbent on her bed is represented at the very center of a symmetrical mise-en-scène, functioning as an ironic cinematic pendant to van Meegeren's attempts to bring her into the space of representation via tableaux vivants. Insofar as Greenaway accentuates Alba's entrapment within central perspective, his mise-en-scène calls the project of Dürer's draftsman to mind, suggesting the camera's difficulty in avoiding a similar appropriation of the female body. There can be little doubt that Greenaway is aware of the restriction that the camera imposes on the representational possibilities of film: his filmmaking is of the "staged" variety precisely because he believes that by juxtaposing a variety of representational modes—hence troping the very idea of representation—this representational excess will expand the boundaries of his medium.

The Keplerian Mode and the Operation of the Eye

As I have argued elsewhere, Wim Wenders's interest in the real and its entry, figured or otherwise, into the space of the text is mediated by an obsession with the photographic image that is well documented in his films and essays.[33] For Wenders, photographs, as "monuments of moments," are privileged objects that link the problem of identity to that of perception and memory.[34] Polaroids hold a particular fascination for Wenders, since their status is ambiguous: as photographs without negatives, they are unprintable and assume something of the status of paintings. But, like other photographs, polaroids, too, arrest the flow of time, "embalming" it, as André Bazin would have it.[35] The representation of time in its cessation: this is one significance that photographs hold for Wenders, whose early short films were shot without cuts, recording the passsage of time by means of what he calls his "phenomenological approach."[36] Wenders's narrative films have their visual origins in the photographs that he takes in preparation for their shooting, but even recent films are shot in continuity, shot "in the present tense."[37] The very title of *Until the End of the World* evokes the collapse of time and space into one another that Wenders's "phenomenological approach" suggests.

The camera's relation to the real, as we are aware, has been read variously and complexly. Like Walter Benjamin, Wenders is fascinated with the physiognomic and topographical aspects of people, places, and things that the camera in the early period of photography — in the photographs of August Sander, for example — is capable of revealing to the eye.[38] A materialist aesthetics similar to that of Benjamin is also promoted by Siegfried Kracauer, with whose work Wenders is obviously familiar, and who asserts film's unique capacity to "picture transient material life."[39] Echoing the work of Bazin as well as his own earlier writings, Kracauer's *Theory of Film* claims that films are proportionately more cinematic the more they cling to the surface of things, their relation to reality seeming mystically to extend beyond the merely mimetic.[40] In conjunction with the work of Bazin, *Theory of Film* provides a source for Roland Barthes's contention, in "The Photographic Message," that the photograph transmits "the scene itself, the literal reality."[41] For Barthes, the very nature of the photograph is at once cultural and natural, both susceptible and unsusceptible to being read. In another essay, Barthes contends that the "filmic" itself is most accessible in the still, by means of which film is closest to the photograph and hence most capable of revealing its "uncoded" or natural dimension.[42] This belief in a residual "uncodedness" also underlies Wenders's fascination with the photographic medium, suggesting the question of whether the real is most readily available for scrutiny when the stillness of the photograph intersects the filmic flow.

But it is Bazin's idea that the photographic image and the object "share a common being, after the nature of a fingerprint," and his comparison of the photograph with the death mask[43] that provide us with a key to a fascinating sequence in Wenders's *Tokyo-Ga* and to the relation that it draws between the image and the real. In this quasi documentary, Wenders lingers over a visit to a factory that produces the realistic waxen replicas of foods by means of which Japanese restaurants advertise their dishes. As Wenders writes: "It all starts with real food. Then gelatine is poured over it and allowed to set. The moulds thus created are filled with wax, and these wax shapes are then trimmed, painted, and refined."[44] It is not the simulacral quality of the "fake food" that is a source of interest here, as has been suggested, but rather the molds' ability to carry the imprint of the real.[45] In this the molds resemble the death masks and footprints to which Bazin has likened the photographic image, metaphors that resonate in Baudrillard's description of the polaroid as "a sort of ecstatic membrane that has come away from the real object."[46] My intention in this essay is to look at the other side of the question asked by some critics concerning Wenders's postmodern concern with simulation, and to examine simulation in terms of the place occupied by the real in his filmmaking.[47]

Turning now to *Until the End of the World* and to the way in which the real intersects here with simulation and the painting of Vermeer, it will be useful to recur briefly to *The Art of Describing* and to the expanded notion of realism that we find there. Realism in Alpers's sense refers not only to the mimetic mirror—whose perverse troping we can locate in the activities of van Meegeren—but to representational practices that record the artist's awareness of the effects of the perceptual apparatus on the image. The Northern system is not Albertian, she asserts, it is Keplerian, concerned with optics and perception. Alpers is not the first interpreter of Dutch art to notice this involvement with optics; Gowing's work on Vermeer also gestures in this direction when it refers to a "mathematical net" in which Vermeer's figures seem caught, and to a style that "relies entirely on the retina for its guide."[48] Gowing locates an "optical impartiality," "optical abstraction," and "photographic tonality" in Vermeer, concurring with

Godard and Greenaway about the role of light in his painting when he claims that Vermeer's world seems to "wear to the last the garment of a retinal impression, to claim no greater depth than the play of light."[49] For Gowing, Vermeer's paintings record the apparent deformation of the retinal image, distorted in the manner of images in a convex mirror. Further, since Vermeer is thought by some scholars to have made use of a camera obscura, his paintings are believed to contain optical traces of this device.[50]

In the interview with Greenaway cited above, he seems to have been echoing not only Godard, but also Wenders's earlier remarks that "Vermeer is the only painter there is. He's really the only one who gives you the idea that his paintings could start moving. He'd be the ultimate cameraman, the ultimate top-notch cameraman."[51] It comes as no surprise, therefore, that Wenders makes use of Vermeer paintings in composing an image that, as the narrative has it, is being viewed through a special kind of sci-fi camera that enables "the blind to see" by literally recording the act of perception — the "brain waves" or neurological activity — of the person who views the image through the lens of the camera. With somewhat different intentions from those of Greenaway, in *Until the End of the World* Wenders sets up a tableau vivant loosely based on two Vermeer paintings in recognition, I would argue, of the optical concerns of Dutch art and today's debates concerning simulation and the real. One of the tensions governing tableau vivant issues has its origin in an uncertainty about the boundaries that divide the representational from the real.

The sci-fi apparatus created by the scientist Farber (a name meaning "he who colors or dyes"—or, in this case, paints) has been called a "machine of vision"[52] and a "sight simulator."[53] It consists of a digital camera that supposedly records the neurological activity of the viewer and cameraperson and a computer that translates the images recorded first into electronic images and then into impulses that trigger neurological activity in the brain. In order to transmit the recorded impulses, the viewer/cameraperson must see them again so that the impulses triggered by a reviewing may serve as a corrective on the first set. As the narrative would have it, Farber's blind wife, the object of the experiment, is thus able to see the images previously recorded and transmitted. Not unpredictably if we consider that Wenders's filmmaking is governed by an oedipal trajectory,[54] the images recorded by the camera are images of absent family members. Of these, the most central to this discussion is a sequence containing the daughter, who is dressed like Vermeer's "Girl with a Pearl Earring" in a setting that recalls "Young Woman with a Water Pitcher."

One thing that Wenders shares with Greenaway's false artist, van Meegeren, is his fascination with the image of the Vermeer woman. This may be because Wenders resembles Vermeer in his interest in the "ungraspable nature of the world seen," as Alpers puts it, and so chooses to pose "the basic problem of a descriptive art in the form of repeated images of women."[55] Although, as Thomas Elsaesser has put it, the mother is "wired up to a machine serviced simultaneously by father and son," the person best able both to record and to transmit the images (the most empathic medium?) is another woman, Claire.[56] Since Wenders has repeatedly been criticized for his reluctance or inability to represent women as central to his narratives, it seems somewhat heavy-handed—though not surprising—that he chooses to portray the images and story of a daughter as being recorded and transmitted for a mother through the medium of a would-be daughter-in-law. It should nevertheless be noted that Wenders situates women on both sides of the camera. By various means, then, Wenders's tableau vivant sequence is divested of its pornographic potential.[57]

But what end does Wenders's allusion to Vermeer serve? The sequence is not anachronistic and does not particularly call attention to itself. Unlike a Vermeer woman, the daughter faces the camera, telling her story while her brother and daughter look on as the sole spectators of the scene. She gives voice, that is, to the contained silence of Vermeer's women. Subsequently she is joined by her young daughter, who also faces and addresses the camera and, by extension, the grandmother for whom these images are recorded. Not only does Wenders animate Vermeer's woman, but he violates her isolation by introducing a child into her domestic space, by confirming her ties to the patriarchal family by way of her narrative, and by causing her to look into and acknowledge the camera. During this sequence, the viewer of Wenders's film sees the image of the woman first through Robby Müller's camera and finally through the eye of the sci-fi digital camera within the diegesis; when seen through the digital camera—constructed by a man though used by a woman—a grid resembling that of Dürer's draftsman is superimposed upon the daughter's image. But this grid refers not only to the draftsman's grid—it is also that of the computer. In the sequence prior to the successful visual experiment, we see images on a large monitor in which the actors' bodies appear to be trapped behind a grid that resembles a fence. In the case of Dürer, Vermeer, *and* Wenders, the question remains the same: how is the body, in particular the body of a woman, appropriated by and for representation? Although the daughter moves about in Wenders's sequence, she appears to be no less "pinned to the drawing board" than the draftsman's image of the nude.

Dressed as the "Girl with a Pearl Earring," the daughter is seated near a window with leaded panes. It is a Vermeer composition par excellence, complete with light streaming through the window, a map hanging on the wall, a Persian rug, and a jug on a table. The subject of the daughter's monologue is her amazement that her mother will soon "see her face." By way of a dream that she relates to the camera and her mother, it is made clear that the mother's recognition would serve to confirm the daughter in her identity: in this dream, as she puts it, there is "something wrong with my face" that prevents this recognition, causing her to protest "but I *am* your daughter." Later, when the blind mother is made to see, she will first see colors, then the image of her daughter. Asking Farber if the young woman could be their daughter, the mother enjoins Farber to "look at her face." What has been "missing" from the Vermeer composition, one might say—the *mirror*—is present after all: it is implied in the two sequences that, taken together, comprise the mirror-stage experience that the daughter has hitherto lacked. The mirror is present in the composition as well when the granddaughter and her mother face the camera that will "mirror" their joint image. Another lack is supplied by the blind woman: by way of super-imposed images of the Vermeer-like daughter and her blind mother, the mother's pearl ring notably appears in place of the daughter's absent pearl earring. Somewhat sentimentally, perhaps, mother and daughter are united through the image of the pearl, or tear.

In the initial shot of this tableau vivant sequence, we see Claire, wearing the sci-fi camera that resembles glasses, from behind. Shot from behind, wearing the camera that records images, Claire is in the position of the painter in Vermeer's "The Artist in His Studio" and appears to be, to use Alba's phrase in *A Zed and Two Noughts*, "an excuse for art theory." We know that the daughter, object of Claire's look as artist and cameraperson, is to be transformed into a digital image and, as a gloss on this image, a passage from Norman Bryson's well-known essay, "The Gaze and the Glance," seems particularly apt. Arguing that Vermeer's paintings are examples of the "painting of the Gaze," Bryson uses a pertinent analogy to distinguish such painting from the Albertian model with its embodied viewer, a passage that may even have inspired Wenders in making this film: "An analogy from computer-based video display may help to clarify this difficult spatial transformation. When sectional drawings are 'rotated' on a television screen, the space through which the image turns is purely virtual—perhaps the purest virtual space so far devised: no one has actually seen this space in the real world; ultimately its only 'real' location is within the distribution data in the computer program."[58]

Using "The Artist in His Studio" as his example, Bryson goes on to claim that in Vermeer's work "the viewer [of the painting] and painter no longer inhabit the same continuum, and so far from entering into the perceptual inner field of the painter's body, the viewer sees that body from the outside, from behind."[59] In this painting, Bryson argues, the "bodily address" of the Albertian model is dissolved into a "computative space" in which "unique, discontinuous, disincarnate bodies, move in spatial apartness."[60] Certainly Wenders's sequence, with its layering of several mediums—painting, film, video, and digital images—creates a palimpsest of textualities under which the body might be said to "vanish . . . in the play of signs."[61] It would appear, then, that those who point to Wenders's postmodern emphasis on the simulacrum rather than the real may be right, since Wenders chooses to suggest that the representational determinants of Vermeer's painting are not very different from those that produce the digital image. The "perceptual incoherence" of Vermeer's paintings, as Bryson reads it, is not simply a product of recording acts of perception but an aspect of Vermeer's deliberate exaggeration of the "conflicting grids of transcriptive fidelity."[62] For Bryson, then, Vermeer's work does not participate in any kind of "realism," even in Alpers's expanded sense of "realistic" painting as an art form whose images bear the stamp of the artist's optical awareness.

But what, we must ask again, happens to the digital image in *Until the End of the World* after it is recorded? In Wenders's fiction, the recorded electronic impulses must first reenter the body of the artist/cameraperson, so that neurological activity extraneous to that produced by the desired image may be excluded; they are then introduced into the body of the blind woman who will be their "spectator." Since the electronic impulses produce "biochemical" images, as Farber puts it, the image is grounded in the body once more, producing both a spectator and an image that are "embodied." Although these images originate in a "machine of vision," Wenders ultimately uses this sci-fi camera in order to undo the "damage" done by representation: the camera is firmly tied to the physiological aspect of vision. Though triggered by electronic images, the nerve impulses that produce the mother's vision are real.

But what of the visual qualities of the images that she sees? In the sequence described above, images seen by the mother are either cut with or superimposed upon her eyes, hence deliberately coded as her vision. They are beautiful, flickering images awash with colors that exceed the contours of bodies, colors that keep changing. In these images, bodies in outline are covered with a gridlike design that here resembles the weave of a canvas support. Initially blurred, they come to look like moving versions of Andy Warhol's silkscreen photo portraits, with each image in a series variously colored; the work of Chuck Close and Gerhard Richter also comes to mind.[63] At one point during this sequence, the spectator of the film sees a chain of serial images, each in different tints. As images, they share with Warhol's silkscreens and Richter's paintings, with their photographic origin, an ambiguous status between the photographic and the painterly. Moreover, Warhol's silkscreens are at once photographic in origin, mass produced, and hand tinted.[64] If Wenders deliberately alludes to Warhol in these transformations of Vermeer-like tableau, then he may do so in order to further reinforce the simulacral quality of these images by connecting them with Pop. Yet, as in a Dutch realism understood to be produced by the recording of optical effects within representation, the visual qualities manifested by these images are decidedly realistic. They are marked as neurological, anchored in the real. For the spectator of the film, however, like Warhol's silkscreens these manipulated images come precariously close to being "art." Wenders chooses, it would seem, to create painterly images that compete with Vermeer on his own territory.

Why Tableau Vivant?

In their filmmaking, both Greenaway and Wenders openly experiment with the variety of representational systems—photographic, electronic, digital—available to film. Sequences that focus on images of writing and print are as common as painterly compositions and allusions in Greenaway's work, and they are evident in Wenders's films as well. Moments that seek figuratively to *split* the image from acts of narration coexist with what I have called tableau vivant here, with moments of representational layering in which painting is brought into the picture. As he has implied, Greenaway reads Vermeer as a realist who addresses senses beyond that of sight, whose paintings depict moments of arrested action and hence closely resemble film stills. In the figure of the surgeon, van Meegeren, Greenaway has created a horribly literal version of the realist, a false Vermeer who does not create in paint but uses the flesh itself as his material. Wenders, too, reads Vermeer as a realist painter, one whose paintings share the properties of the photographic image. It's interesting, then, that both of the films under discussion animate the paintings to which they allude; at no time do they draw upon the possibilities of tableau vivant to halt the action of film. Instead they "make real": they introduce the body (of the actor) into representation.

Embodiment is the theoretical focus of attention and, in the case of both films, the questions that it generates are taken to an extreme: the decomposing bodies of *A Zed and Two Noughts* will finally exist only at the microscopic level; the neurological activity that allows the blind to see in *Until the End of the World* is submicroscopic. What concerns Greenaway is a dialectic between composition (which has an analogue in the harnessing of representational systems that produce a scene) and decomposition, the real taken to its extreme endpoint (with its analogue in the separation of representational systems that produce a scene). By means of the "technologically advanced" sci-fi camera of *Until the End of the World,* Wenders reduces vision to its material determinants and vision becomes wholly internalized. This process can be reversed: a further sci-fi development allows Wenders's characters to record the neurological activity produced in dreaming. Their neurological impulses are converted into electronic images, allowing them to externalize and watch their dreams on a monitor. Thus, dreams are rendered material and portable.

In a talk on high-definition television given in Tokyo in 1990, Wenders discussed the applicability of terms such as *the original* and *reality* to the images produced by contemporary technology.[65] Wenders tells us that the high-vision dream images of *Until the End of the World* are based on photographs taken in Wenders's and Solveig Dommartin's childhoods, highly personal images.[66] The images that we see on the screen, comprised of up to one hundred layers, with image superimposed over image, have the look of animated watercolors. But this layering of different types of images— what I have referred to as representational layering—can be said to produce a "spatialization of the moving image," an "image cluster" that lends the image a kind of material density.[67] Here science fiction's world of the future mirrors the beliefs of the aborigines of the film, who hold that a man's "bad dreams" can be "taken away" by sleeping next to him. When science fiction, primitive magic, and the cutting edge of technology meet, the final irony may be that these "material images" look painterly. In more than one sense, then, the "new images" produced by today's technology are evocative of tableau vivant.

Notes

1 Noël Burch, "Building a Haptic Space," in *Life to Those Shadows,* edited and translated by Ben Brewster (London: British Film Institute, 1990), 167. See also Ben Brewster and Leah Jacobs, *Theater to Cinema: Stage Pictorialism and the Early Feature Film* (Oxford: Oxford University Press, 1997).

2 Susan Sontag, *The Volcano Lover, a Romance* (New York: Farrar, Strauss, Giroux, 1992), 179.

3 Jean-François Lyotard, "Acinéma," in *Narrative, Apparatus, Ideology: A Film Theory Reader,* edited by Philip Rosen (New York: Columbia University Press, 1986), 356.

4 Burch, "Building a Haptic Space," 170.

5 Ibid., 183.

6 Ibid., 176.

7 It is typical of Burch that he would see in such effects a "striking anticipation of Magritte's 'visual puns' " (ibid., 168).

8 Pascal Bonitzer, *Décadrages: Peinture et cinéma* (Paris: Cahiers du Cinéma, 1985), 31.

9 See my discussion of this in *Incorporating Images: Film and the Rival Arts* (Princeton: Princeton University Press, 1995), 143–56.

10 Ian Haywood, "Crusaders against the Art Market: Hans van Meegeren and Tom Keating," in *Art and the Politics of Forgery* (New York: St. Martin's Press, 1987), 105–30.

11 "Flesh of the human presence" is quoted from Svetlana Alpers, *The Art of Describing: Dutch Art in the Seventeenth Century* (Chicago: University of Chicago Press, 1983), 167.

12 Peucker, *Incorporating Images,* 157–59.

13 Peter Greenaway Web site, December, 1998; René Kurpershoek, "Cinema begint bij Vermeer," interview with René Kurpershoek, translated by Bruno Bollaert.

14 Here Alpers departs from the readings of Dutch art that view it as emblematic and didactic.

15 Alpers, *Art of Describing,* xxi.

16 Ibid., xxiv.

17 Ibid., xxvii.

18 Lawrence Gowing, *Vermeer* (London: Faber and Faber, 1970), 54.

19 Edward Snow, *A Study of Vermeer,* rev. ed. (Berkeley: University of California Press, 1994), 101.

20 Kurpershoek, "Cinema begint bij Vermeer."

21 These include "The Concert," "Couple Standing at a Virginal," "Young Woman with a Water Pitcher," "Soldier and Young Girl Smiling"—in all four of which the woman is wearing the yellow bodice—and "Woman in Blue Reading a Letter."

22 Mary Ann Doane, "The Moving Image," in *Femmes Fatales: Feminism, Film Theory, Psychoanalysis* (New York: Routledge, 1991), 194.

23 Leonard Slatkes, "Utrecht and Vermeer," in *Vermeer Studies,* edited by Ivan Gaskell and Michiel Jonker (New Haven: Yale University Press, 1998), 81–88.

24 Michael Fried, *Realism, Writing, Disfiguration: On Thomas Eakins and Stephen Crane* (Chicago: University of Chicago Press, 1987), 64.

25 Eric Jan Sluijter, "Vermeer, Fame, and Female Beauty: The *Art of Painting,*" in Gaskell and Jonker, *Vermeer Studies,* 265–83.

26   Alpers, *Art of Describing,* 167.

27   See Albrecht Dürer, *Unterweisung der Messung,* 1538.

28   Irene Netta, "The Phenomenon of Time in the Art of Vermeer," in Gaskell and Jonker, *Vermeer Studies,* 262.

29   Ben Broos, "Un celebre Peijntre nommé Verme[e]r," in *Johannes Vermeer,* edited by Arthur K. Wheelock Jr. (New Haven: Yale University Press, 1995), 57.

30   Wheelock, *Johannes Vermeer,* 172.

31   The black and white doublet might very well have been worn by an artist during this period. See Marieke de Winkel, "The Interpretation of Dress in Vermeer's Paintings," in Gaskell and Jonker, *Vermeer Studies,* 332.

32   Stephen Heath, "Narrative Space," in *Questions of Cinema* (Bloomington: Indiana University Press, 1981), 27ff.

33   Brigitte Peucker, "Wim Wenders' Berlin: Images and the Real," in *Berlin in Focus: Cultural Transformations in Germany,* edited by Barbara Becker-Cantarino (Westport, Conn.: Praeger, 1996), 125–38.

34   Tony Rayns, "Forms of Address: Interviews with Three German Filmmakers," *Sight and Sound* 44 (winter 1974–75): 6.

35   André Bazin, "The Ontology of the Photographic Image," in *What Is Cinema?* vol. 1, edited and translated by Hugh Gray (Berkeley: University of California Press, 1967), 14.

36   Jan Dawson, "An Interview with Wim Wenders," in *Wim Wenders,* translated by Carla Wartenberg (New York: Zoetrope, 1976), 10–11.

37   Walter Donohue, "Revelations: An Interview with Wim Wenders," *Sight and Sound* 12 (May 1992): 10. See also Charles Hagen, "From the End of the World to Smack Dab in the Middle: An Interview with Wim Wenders," *Aperture* 123 (spring 1991): 90.

38   Walter Benjamin, "A Small History of Photography," in *One-Way Street and Other Writings,* translated by Edmund Jephcott (London: New Left Books, 1979), 251ff. Wenders makes use of Sander photo portraits in *Wings of Desire.*

39   Siegfried Kracauer, *Theory of Film: The Redemption of Physical Reality* (London: Oxford University Press, 1960), ix.

40   Siegfried Kracauer, "Die Photographie," in *Das Ornament der Masse* (Frankfurt am Main: Suhrkamp, 1963), 21–39.

41   Roland Barthes, "The Photographic Message," in *Image, Music, Text,* translated by Stephen Heath (New York: Hill and Wang, 1977), 16–17.

42   Barthes, "The Third Meaning," in Barthes, *Image, Music, Text,* 64–65.

43   Bazin, "Ontology," 15. See also Hugh Gray's introduction to *What Is Cinema?*, in which he writes "Bazin holds that the cinematic image is more than a reproduction, rather it is a thing in nature, a mold or masque" (6).

44   Wim Wenders, "Tokyo-Ga," in *The Logic of Images: Essays and Conversations,* translated by Michael Hofmann (London: Faber and Faber, 1992), 65.

45   Nora M. Alter, "Documentary as Simulacrum: *Tokyo-Ga,*" in *The Cinema of Wim Wenders: Image, Narrative, and the Postmodern Condition,* edited by Roger F. Cook and Gerd Gemünden (Detroit: Wayne State University Press, 1997), 143.

46   Jean Baudrillard, *America,* translated by Chris Turner (London: Verso, 1989), 37.

47   See, in particular, Alter, "Documentary as Simulacrum," and Alice Kuzniar, "Wenders' Windshields," in Cook and Gemünden, *The Cinema of Wim Wenders,* 222–39.

48 Gowing, *Vermeer,* 18, 19.

49 Ibid., 22, 56, 61, 65.

50 In a recent essay, Jean-Luc Delsaute claims, however, that "it seems rash to continue to believe that the camera obscura was one of the tools with which he worked" ("The Camera Obscura and Painting in the Sixteenth and Seventeenth Centuries," in Gaskell and Jonker, *Vermeer Studies,* 120.

51 Dawson, "Interview," 23.

52 Thomas Elsaesser, "Spectators of Life: Time, Place, and Self in the Films of Wim Wenders," in Cook and Gemünden, *The Cinema of Wim Wenders,* 254.

53 Kuzniar, "Wenders' Windshields," 230.

54 Here I part company with Alice Kuzniar, who claims that "Wenders' other films likewise invite an anti-oedipal reading" (ibid., 239), and side with Elsaesser's reading in "Spectators of Life." Much as we might like to claim Wenders completely for the postmodern, his films simply don't bear this out.

55 Alpers, *Art of Describing,* 223.

56 Elsaesser, "Spectators of Life," 255.

57 This contention leaves aside the situation of the lesbian spectator.

58 Norman Bryson, "The Gaze and the Glance," in *Vision and Painting: The Logic of the Gaze* (New Haven: Yale University Press, 1983), 112.

59 Ibid., 114.

60 Ibid., 117.

61 Jean Baudrillard, "Simulacra and Simulations," in *Selected Writings,* edited and introduced by Mark Poster (Stanford, Calif.: Stanford University Press, 1988), 180.

62 Bryson, "The Gaze," 115, 116.

63 I am indebted to Catriona MacLeod for the reminder that Richter's work is pertinent here.

64 Bernstein, "Warhol as Printmaker," 14–15.

65 Wim Wenders, "High Definition," in *The Act of Seeing: Essays and Conversations,* translated by Michael Hofmann (London: Faber and Faber, 1996), 77–78.

66 Shawn Levy, "*Until the End of the World:* Wim Wenders' Dance Around the Planet," *American Film* 17:1 (January–February 1992): 52.

67 Yvonne Spielmann, "Intermedia and the Organization of the Image: Some Reflections on Film, Electronic, and Digital Media," *Iris* 25 (spring, 1998): 65.

Dreyer's Textual Realism

James Schamus

There is a sense in which *The Passion of Joan of Arc* (1928) is not one, but two films; or, as Kierkegaard might have put it, *Joan of Arc* consists of the relation between two films. You could piece together one of the films by pulling out the 174 intertitles, 168 of which are dialogue cards of the judges' questions and Joan's answers, and projecting them in sequence. A perfectly intelligible narrative of a trial and punishment would unfold, since, as the critic Noel Burch has pointed out, the narrative of Joan "has largely been reduced to its own abstraction," to the written texts of the intertitles.[1]

The other film would be the oneiric succession of faces, mostly in close-up, that would remain. And here, too, the story would be more or less intelligible, as we watch what Béla Balázs called "this series of duels between looks and frowns, duels in which eyes clash instead of swords."[2] For *Joan of Arc* also works as a story on a purely visual level. It is, in Siegfried Kracauer's words, "essentially a story told in facial expressions."[3]

These two films—the one made of words, the other of faces—play out a battle for narrative supremacy between text and image that is at the heart not only of Joan's story, as the judges try to trap her with their questions to force her signature on the confession, but also of Dreyer's. Dreyer, who began his career in cinema writing intertitles at Nordisk Films, was pre-occupied with his own relation to the written word: his writings on film return again and again to the question of writing and the film director's role in the translation of word into image. Who, Dreyer wondered, is the real author of the film, the screenwriter or the director? From where does the director, as an artist, derive his own authority?

Dreyer's responses to these questions were always evolving and often contradictory. But he always saw the relation between the written and the filmic orders as an agonistic one, as a constant battle of wills. In 1922, for example, in an article about his favorite Danish director, Benjamin Christensen, Dreyer argued that "the manuscript is the fundamental condition for a good film." But he took issue with Christensen's insistence that the director should write his own screenplays, "for the task of the film is and will remain the same as that of theater: *to interpret other people's thoughts,* and the director's task is to submit to the writer whose cause he is serving."[4] This rhetoric of written mastery and filmic submission would begin to chafe in later years, when Dreyer would picture the power relations as reversed: "And my approach to working with Kaj Munk's *Ordet* has, therefore, always been and still is this: first, to possess oneself of Kaj Munk, and then forget him."[5] But the relationship is still basically the same, so that if in 1920 Dreyer calls for adaptations from great works of literature; and in 1922 demands original scripts from professional authors; and in 1939 thinks that "the screenplay can and should be made by the author and the director in collaboration"; while, in 1950, the "ideal is, of course, that the director writes his own manu-script,"[6] we should remark these inconsistencies not as evidence of a fickle spirit but rather as the symptoms of a lifelong anxiety about authorship and authority. As we shall see, that anxiety informs not only Dreyer's thematic concerns—his repeated focus on heroes and heroines who battle the authorities who attempt to dominate and define them—but also the formal strategies he utilized to present those stories. To understand this dynamic, we should see Dreyer in the larger critical context in which his aesthetic practices can be placed.

Dreyer is most often considered an "avant-garde" filmmaker, a director of difficult "art" films. In most serious studies of his work, such as David Bordwell's, this avant-garde status is thought of as in opposition to the "dominant" codes of Hollywood cinematic realism. On the one hand lie the modernist, truly artistic film works, among which Dreyer's films are figured prominently. On the other hand are the realist films of the mainstream, ideologically suspect because their narratives are constructed so as to appear natural, and the mechanics of their production are kept hidden.

Dreyer's films—at least those after *The Master of the House* (1925)—constantly point to the process of their own making, calling into question the assumptions and ideologies that are usually glossed over in the creation of filmic illusions. We hear the screech of the moving camera in *Ordet,* feel the unnatural weight of the written dialogue in *Gertrud,* account for the constant mismatches in *The Passion of Joan of Arc* as a deliberate deconstruction of filmic space. And such strategies are almost always seen as politically liberating and ideologically progressive. From Brecht to Barthes, mainstream illusion is bad, and formal innovation, the "troubling of the signifier," is good.

Paradoxically, another set of critics, among them the filmmaker Paul Schrader, sees Dreyer's work as anything but revolutionary. His, they argue, is a cinema of the spirit, of transcendence, of, as Father Borgen puts it at the end of *Ordet,* "the good old God, eternal and the same." No matter how formally interesting, this is hardly the work of a dedicated revolutionary, let alone an avant-gardist out to shock the bourgeoisie.

Rather than being avant-garde or realist, though, Dreyer was both, working within a realist tradition—that of Ibsen, Strindberg, and others—that was, in its heyday, itself an avant-garde practice. Dreyer was one of the few filmmakers to seriously extend the reach of that practice into film, and his engagement with that tradition was articulated not merely in his many adaptations of realist texts—from Herman Bang's *Michael* to Hjalmar Söderberg's *Gertrud*—but more fundamentally in the way he theorized the interplay between his characters and their textual roots. For the realist character—unlike, say, an allegorical figure in a mystery play—is precisely that aesthetic construct that demands to be more than a construct, more than a collection of phrases in a script. The realist character demands to be, in a word, "real."

Dreyer's quest for the "real" as a base for his own characters was never ending. With *The Passion of Joan of Arc,* for example, Dreyer rejected the original, poetic script written for him by the French writer Joseph Delteil. Instead, he based his screenplay strictly on the actual records of Joan's trial, working closely with the historian who had recently reedited them. The opening shot of *Joan of Arc,* while probably the film's least memorable, is, in this context, its most emblematic: a hand flips through the pages of

 the transcripts, in which, the intertitle tells us, we can discover Joan "as she really was."

That opening shot establishes a rhetoric of realism based not on the transparency of the filmic illusions to follow—*Joan of Arc* is, in fact, too avant-garde for that—but rather on the assertion of the film's respect for historical evidence, as it seeks to represent the real spirit of its characters. This realism I call "textual realism," an aesthetic practice based on the authority of its documentary sources.

Just as Dreyer researched the "real" Joan, so in *Gertrud* Dreyer claimed that his heroine was not the Gertrud of Hjalmar Söderberg's original 1906 play but the real woman whom Söderberg himself fictionalized, Maria von Platen. Dreyer went so far as to add the famous epilogue, in which his Gertrud recites words von Platen herself wrote in a letter.

And, odd as it may seem, Dreyer claimed that his adaptation of *Medea* (recently brought to the screen by the young Danish director Lars von Trier) was "not directly based on the tragedy of Euripides, but . . . is an attempt to tell the true story that may have inspired the great Greek poet." The true Joan, the true Gertrud, the true Medea—not to mention the true Mary, Queen of Scots, or the true Jesus, to whom Dreyer devoted nearly twenty years of painstaking historical research (even, in his seventies, learning Hebrew)—they are all of them phantasmatic objects of a reality made accessible only through the artistic transmutation of documents into images.

They are phantasmatic, too, in the fact that so few of them ever saw their shadows reach the screen: to visit the Dreyer archives in Copenhagen is like walking through the imaginary libraries of the blind Borges. File upon file of carefully typed or neatly printed notes, literally thousands if not tens of thousands of sheets. And books—whole specialized libraries on Greece, early Christianity, the Scottish Reformation. An entire warehouse, which evokes an uncanny doubleness of purpose—the Dreyer archives, which are themselves Dreyer's archives: the archives of an archivist.

This endless production of documentary evidence took up far more of Dreyer's lifetime than the production of actual films. In fact, his research for the Jesus project most probably *substituted* for the film itself; it's not far-

1. The textual source of the trial of Joan of Arc in the opening shots of *The Passion of Joan of Arc,* Carl Theodor Dreyer, 1928 (frame enlargement of video)

fetched to say that Dreyer could have made the film had he not kept putting it off to take more notes. Here, the "real" collapsed into its written traces; Jesus remained in a wilderness of texts.

We can picture Dreyer's own career—in his last forty years he made only five films—as a heroic battle, and in many ways a tragic one, to image forth his heroes and heroines out of the documents, the scraps of text, in which they lay. His demand for the "real" posed challenges both thematic and formal and in important ways mirrored his characters' own battles. For the archetypal theme of the realist text itself is the hero's attempt to transcend his or her own textual status—to become a consciousness. The realist hero—or, more often than not, heroine—is thus locked in a life-and-death struggle with the author who penned him, with the authority who controls the words. Dreyer, in constantly trying to "end-run" his authors—Söderberg, Delteil, Euripides, and so on—tried to solve the problem of realism's exorbitant desires by aligning his heroes with their actual, documentary sources, against their authors' secondary formulations.

Strindberg had solved the problem in his own way, in his famous preface to *Miss Julie* (1888), by claiming that the human soul itself is nothing but a collection of texts: "My souls—or characters—are conglomerations from various stages of culture, past and present, walking scrapbooks, shreds of human lives, tatters torn from old rags that were once Sunday best—hodgepodge just like the human soul. I have even supplied a little source history into the bargain by letting the weaker steal and repeat the words of the stronger."[7] Strindberg hoped to neutralize the powerful desire his "characters" have for "souls" by neatly conflating the two terms. Meanwhile, his narratives stage the "stealing" of his own words. The tragic irony is that in the modern world the "weaker" beat out the stronger more often than not. Perhaps the strongest figuring of such a "weak" soul is the vampire, so ubiquitous in fin de siècle Scandinavian culture, most famously depicted in Edvard Munch's paintings. In Strindberg the vampire is the "soul-murderer," a weaker soul who literally steals the words that make up the soul of the stronger. In Strindberg's version of "source history," the author is vamped by his own characters.

The vamp is of course a feminine figure, and the gender politics of Strindberg's realism are virulently misogynistic: "I say Miss Julie is a modern character not because the man-hating half-woman has not always existed but because she has now been brought out into the open, has taken the stage, and is making a noise about herself."[8] What Strindberg doesn't mention in his preface to *Miss Julie* is that his tragic heroine is in fact based on a real-life woman writer, Victoria Benedictsson. The threat of the half-woman is the threat of the writing woman, the woman who makes "a noise about herself." So, too, in his play *Creditors:* the emasculating Tekla is a writer, her disarmed husband, Adolf, a painter.

The theme of the emancipated woman in Scandinavian realist theater—it is equally prevalent in Ibsen, for example, in *A Doll's House* and *Hedda Gabler*—is thus not just a theme but a textual matrix through which is figured a whole complex of formal and ideological concerns. Realism creates the desire for real characters—characters like those of the "weaker sex" who struggle to produce language of their own—and so creates an internal tension about the adequacy of its own textual authority.

In Dreyer, this realist desire for real selfhood is magnified to truly heroic proportions—and so, too, is its counterpart, the rhetoric of the authoritative, containing text. And this battle between self and authority is invariably gendered. Indeed, virtually every film Dreyer made—from his first, *The President* (1918), to his last, *Gertrud* (1964)—takes as its theme the confrontation of women with the patriarchal powers that attempt to define and dominate them. Dreyer's insistent centering on the female heroine can thus be seen as a continuation both of realist themes and of realist formal concerns. For the authorities these women battle are not only male but, significantly, "textual" authorities—legal, religious, artistic. They nearly always represent specific institutions that use language as a primary means of gaining authority and wielding power.

If *Joan of Arc* clearly depicts this confrontation between woman and word, it enacts that confrontation, too. Remember Dreyer's insistence on basing the film on the actual court records of Joan's trial. His realist textual practice—which takes as a paradigm of authenticity the court document—repeats the forms of discursive power his heroines so resolutely seek to defy, even while making those power relations manifest. "For me," Dreyer recollected, "it was, before all else, the technique of the official report that governed. There was, to start with, this trial, with its ways, its own technique, and that is what I tried to transpose to the film." And so the narrative, the "story" of *Joan of Arc,* is precisely that of its own production, a recording of the dialogue between male authority and the body of its female object. For Dreyer, writing was torture.

Dreyer's heroines are constantly doing battle with authorial figures—their "transcendence" is almost always a martyrdom at the hands of a textual regime. Gertrud, for example, renounces life because her love is too strong to tolerate her lovers' allegiances to their writerly careers—Gabriel and his poetry, Gustav and his law, Erland and his composing. Gertrud's last words in the film, to her friend Axel, are of a supreme irony: "And thank you for your book."

Sometimes, as in the comic vision of *The Master of the House,* the woman's assumption of writerly fluency wins her important victories. Here the wife's ambiguous letters help tame her tyrannical husband. But the threat of male backlash is still, albeit comically, pictured: after Ida is discovered writing, she is inexplicably chased by the gang of old men she nurses.

More often than not, though, the woman simply resists the enforced textual regime rather than write against it. Siri, the heroine of the fourth segment of *Leaves from Satan's Book* (1919), is a telegraph operator who dies rather than tap out a message for the evil communists who hold her children hostage. Her martyrdom—which takes the form of a refusal of forced writing—prefigures Joan's: Joan is sent to the stake for renouncing her signed confession.

Joan of Arc presents the battle between writing and woman at its most fevered pitch. Joan, illiterate (she learned her "Our Father" orally from her mother, as one of the first questions establishes), is tricked by the forged letter from King Charles. And her lowest moment comes when her own signature is forged, with her participation, on her confession. That signature takes place in perhaps the closest close-up in the film, in a shot that is worth pausing over.

Her first mark—a naught, a zero—can be read as a kind of antisign, a hole. Then a male hand descends upon her own and forces her hand through the motions of a signature. Her hand again left free, she finishes with the mark of a cross, the icon on which she shall soon be burned for renouncing her signature. That denial is actually prefigured in the cross itself—Joan often used the sign of the cross in the margins of her dictated letters as a secret sign

2. "The judges and responses of Joan are here transcribed with the greatest accuracy," title card from *The Passion of Joan of Arc,* Carl Theodor Dreyer, 1928 (frame enlargement of video)
3. *The Passion of Joan of Arc,* Carl Theodor Dreyer, 1928 (frame enlargement of video)

that what was written was actually false, a lure in case the letter fell into enemy hands.[9]

Joan of Arc perfectly marks Dreyer's divided allegiance to his authorities and his heroines. Dreyer, as director, must "submit to the writer whose cause he is serving." But, as always, that writer is not the author of the screenplay but the real person, like Maria von Platen or Joan, whose own written traces Dreyer assiduously tracked down and reproduced. The paradox is, as here in *Joan of Arc,* that this writing is always a writing under duress, a forced submission into the verbal order. To re-create the "real" Joan, he must reenact her reduction into text.[10] Only by brutally sticking to the original process, Dreyer believed, could he put on film what he called "the martyr's reincarnation."[11]

And brutal it was. As Richard Abel puts it, Dreyer "turned the shooting process itself into a grueling reproduction of history" in his search "for means of authenticity." The film was shot strictly in sequence, and the cast and crew were worked mercilessly; in the words of one of Dreyer's assistant directors, "We were not making a film, we were living Jeanne's drama, and we often wanted to intervene to save her."[12]

Falconetti's blood was actually drawn, her famous hair actually cut (Dreyer's right to cut it was written into her contract), her real tears photographed. One wonders what would have happened had Dreyer actually filmed the torture scene he originally wrote in the screenplay (a scene suppressed from the Danish and English printed editions of the screenplay).[13]

Dreyer called the realism achieved through this technique "spiritual" or "psychological," a realism unconcerned with verisimilitudinous details and period costuming. And the spirit or psyche he strove to reproduce has as its privileged field of expression the human face. "Gesture endows the face with soul," Dreyer wrote. "Mime is the original means of expression of inner experience—older than the spoken word."[14] Dreyer kept his actors' faces clean of makeup and kept his camera close to them.

By insistently opposing the word to the facial gesture, Dreyer sets up the regime of the two films—of text and countenance—as a way to stage the fight between the letter and the spirit, between the written and the visual. But these two orders are not as separate as they seem.

If there is one feature of *Joan of Arc* that is most consistently remarked, it is Dreyer's use of close-ups. Dreyer, as well as most practitioners and theorists of his time, heralded the close-up as a technique that enhanced both the realism of the cinema (by forcing "the actors to act honestly and naturally. The days of the grimace [are] over"),[15] and cinema's autonomy as an art form, especially in relation to the theater.[16] In the theater, the human face could be little more than a malleable mask. The cinematic close-up, however, gave us the human face in such detail and with such power that old-fashioned, theatrical forms of facial gesturing could be thrown aside: the face could now remain a window on the soul, a field of natural expression instead of the artificial signification of language.[17]

And *Joan of Arc* is the close-up film par excellence. It is, in André Bazin's words, "a documentary of faces."[18] Or, as David Bordwell puts it, in Joan "every action of mind and heart can be read off the face."[19] It seems that no film could be more committed in its use of the unadorned human face in opposition to the abstract order of linguistic power.

But Dreyer in fact thought otherwise, or, rather, he held two contradictory views of the function of the close-up. For while the close-up brought forward the character's "spiritual realism," its use was in fact actually an extension of the technique of the trial.

> There were the questions, there were the answers—very short, very crisp. There was, therefore, no other solution than to place close-ups behind these replies. Each question, each answer, quite naturally called for a close-up. All of that stemmed from the technique of the official report. In addition, the result of the close-ups was that the spectator was [as] shocked as Joan was, receiving the questions, tortured by them. And, in fact, it was my intention to get this result.[20]

Dreyer's happily sadistic reading of the close-up as an effect of torture—of torture by language, no less—runs counter to the simple ideologies of natural expression that inform most critical appraisals of his work. But the term *sadistic* here is not pejorative. As in much of Sade, what is at play is a deadly serious anxiety about the adequacy of writing and of representation to express the self at its moment of purest consciousness—a consciousness in the realist tradition that is paradoxically a consciousness of the self's own textuality. In Dreyer, as in Strindberg, the self is always a "walking scrapbook," but, unlike Strindberg, the heroic self in Dreyer never ceases to desire its impossible freedom from the texts that hold it, and so it dies.

Notes

1   Noel Burch, "Carl Theodor Dreyer: The Major Phase," in *Cinema: A Critical Dictionary*, vol. 1, edited by Richard Roud (N.p.: Nationwide Book Services, 1980), 299.

2   Béla Balázs, *Theory of the Film,* translated by Edith Bone (New York: Dover Press, 1970), 74.

3   Siegfried Kracauer, *Theory of Film: The Redemption of Physical Reality* (New York: Oxford University Press, 1960), 271.

4   Carl Theodor Dreyer, *Dreyer in Double Reflection,* edited by Donald Skoller (New York: Dutton, 1973), 33. Christensen, like Dreyer, also changed his mind constantly about the status of the script; by 1940, he would be arguing Dreyer's earlier position for original scripts. See Benjamin Christensen, "Film før og nu," *Berlingske Tidende,* November 26, 1940, clipping on file at the Danish Film Museum.

5   Dreyer, *Double Reflection,* 165.

6   Ibid., 28, 33, 91, 146.

7   August Strindberg, *Selected Plays,* translated by Evert Sprinchorn (Minneapolis: University of Minnesota Press, 1986), 208.

8   Ibid.

9   Marina Warner, *Joan of Arc: The Image of Female Heroism* (London: Weidenfeld and Nicolson, 1981), 140. My thanks to Richard Einhorn for pointing out this reference.

10 David Bordwell, *The Films of Carl Theodor Dreyer* (Los Angeles: University of California Press, 1981), 90–91.

11 Dreyer, *Double Reflection,* 48.

12 Richard Abel, *The French Cinema: The First Wave, 1915–1929* (Princeton: Princeton University Press, 1984), 488.

13 Carl Theodor Dreyer, *Oeuvres Cinematographiques, 1926–1934,* edited by Maurice Drouzy and Charles Tesson (Paris: Cinémathèque Française, 1983), 64.

14 Dreyer, *Double Reflection,* 135.

15 Ibid., 27.

16 "The close-up has objectified in our world of perception our mental act of attention and by it has furnished art with a means which far transcends the power of any theater stage" (Hugo Munsterberg, *The Photoplay: A Psychological Study* [New York: D. Appleton, 1916], 87–88).

17 The idea is that, for example, when you are scared, you "look" scared, you don't intentionally "make" a scared face. Expressions thus are thought to mean something, even though they don't signify, that is, intend to mean.

18 André Bazin, *What Is Cinema?* vol. 1, translated by Hugh Gray (Los Angeles: University of California Press, 1967), 109.

19 Bordwell, *Films,* 84.

20 Andrew Sarris, ed., *Interviews with Film Directors* (New York: Avon, 1967), 145.

Selected Bibliography

Allen, Richard. *Projecting Illusion: Films, Spectatorship, and the Impression of Reality.* New York: Cambridge University Press, 1995.

Argentieri, Mino. *Neorealism ECC.* Milan: Bompiani, 1979.

Armes, R. *Film and Reality: A Historical Survey.* Harmondsworth: Penguin, 1974.

——. *Patterns of Realism.* Crambury, N.Y.: A. S. Barnes, 1971.

Arthur, Paul. "Jargons of Authenticity (Three American Moments)." In *Theorizing Documentary,* edited by Michael Renov, 108–34. New York: Routledge, 1993.

——. "Media Spectacle and Tabloid Documentary." *Film Comment* 34:1 (January–February 1998): 74–80.

Auerbach, Erich. *Mimesis: The Representation of Reality in Western Literature.* Princeton: Princeton University Press, 1953.

Ayfre, Amedée. "Neorealism and Phenomenology." In *Cahiers du Cinéma, the 1950's: Neorealism, Hollywood, New Wave,* edited by Jim Hillier, 182–91. Cambridge: Harvard University Press, 1985.

Bann, Stephen. "The Odd Man Out: Historical Narrative and the Cinematic Image." In *The Inventions of History: Essays on the Representation of the Past,* New York: 171–99. Manchester University Press, 1990.

Barnow, Dagmar. *Critical Realism: History, Photography, and the Work of Siegfried Kracauer.* Baltimore: Johns Hopkins University Press, 1994.

Barthes, Roland. *Camera Lucida: Reflections on Photography.* Translated by Richard Howard. New York: Hill and Wang, 1981.

——. "The Face of Garbo." In *A Barthes Reader,* 82–86. New York: Hill and Wang, 1982.

——. "The Reality Effect." In *The Rustle of Language,* translated by Richard Howard, 48–71. Los Angeles: University of California Press, 1989.

——. *S/Z.* Paris: Seuil, 1970.

Bazin, André. *The Cinema of Cruelty: From Buñuel to Hitchcock.* Edited with an introduction by François Truffaut. New York: Seaver Books, 1982.

——. *Jean Renoir.* Edited with an introduction by François Truffaut. Translated by W. W. Halsey II and William H. Simon. Rpt. New York: Simon and Schuster, 1986.

——. "Le Neorealisme se retourne," *Cahiers du Cinéma* 69 (March 1957): 46–7.

——. *Qu'est-ce que le Cinéma?* 4 vols. Paris: Editions du Cerf, 1958–62.

——. *What Is Cinema?* 2 vols. Translated by Hugh Gray. Berkeley: University of California Press, 1967–71.

Becker, George, J., ed. *Documents of Modern Literary Realism.* Princeton: Princeton University Press, 1963.

Benjamin, Walter. "The Mimetic Faculty." In *Reflections: Essays, Aphorisms, Autobiographical Writings,* translated by Edmund Jephcott, edited by Peter Demetz, 333–36, New York: Schocken, 1986.

Berger, John. "The Suit and the Photograph." In *About Looking,* 27–36, New York: Pantheon, 1980.

Bonitzer, Pascal. *Le Champ Aveugle: Essais sur le Cinéma.* Paris: Cahiers du Cinéma Gallimard, 1982.

——. "Neorealismo, Quale Realismo?" In *Il Neorealismo Cinematografico Italiano,* Atti del convegno della X Mostra Internazionale del Nuovo Cinema [Proceedings of the Convention of the New Cinema International Show], edited by Lino Micciche, 222–26, Venice: Marsilio Editori, 1975.

Bordwell, David, and Noël Carroll. *Post-Theory: Reconstructing Film Studies.* Madison: University of Wisconsin Press, 1996.

Boyle, Nicholas, and Martin Swales, eds. *Realism in European Literature.* Cambridge: Cambridge University Press, 1986.

Brecht, Bertold. *Sur le Réalisme,* translated by André Gisselbrecht. Paris: L'Arché, 1970.

——. "A Small Contribution on the Theme of Realism," *Screen* 15:2 (summer 1974): 45–48.

Brewster, Ben, and Lea Jacobs. *Theatre to Cinema: Stage Pictorialism and the Early Feature Film.* New York: Oxford University Press, 1997.

Browne, Nick, ed. *Cahiers du Cinema, 1969-1972: The Politic of Representation.* Cambridge: Harvard University Press, 1990.

Bynum, Carolyne. "Why All the Fuss about the Body? A Medievalist's Perspective." *Critical Inquiry* 22 (autumn, 1995): 1–34.

Canella, M. "Ideology and Aesthetic Hypothesis in the Criticism of Neorealism." *Screen* 14:4 (1972): 5–13.

Cardullo, Bert, ed. *Bazin at Work: Major Essays and Reviews from the Forties and Fifties.* New York: Routledge, 1997.

Carroll, David. "Mimesis Reconsidered." *Diacritics* 5 (summer 1975): 5–12.

Cartwright, Lisa. *Screening the Body: Tracing Medicine's Visual Culture.* Minneapolis: University of Minnesota Press, 1995.

Casebier, Allan. *Film and Phenomenology: Toward a Realist Theory of Cinematic Representation.* Cambridge: Cambridge University Press, 1991.

Cohen, Margaret, and Christopher Prendergast, eds. *Spectacles of Realism: Gender, Body, Genre.* Minneapolis: University of Minnesota Press, 1995.

Collas, Gérald, ed. *Cine Europeo: El Desafío de la Realidad.* 42 Semana Internacional de Cine [International Cinema Week]. Valladolid: 1997.

Comolli, Jean-Louis. "Historical Fiction: A Body Too Much." Translated by Ben Brewster. *Screen* 19:2 (summer 1978): 41–53. Originally published as "Un corps en trop." *Cahiers du Cinéma* 278 (July 1977): 5–16.

——. "Machines of the Visible." In *The Cinematic Apparatus,* edited by Teresa de Lauretis and Stephen Heath, 121–42. New York: St. Martins, 1980.

——. "Le miroir a deux faces." In *Arrêt sur Histoire,* edited by J. L. Comolli and Jacques Rancière, 11–45. Paris: Éditions du Centre Pompidou, 1997.

——. "Du Realisme comme Utopie." Introduction to *Cine Europeo: El Desafío de la Realidad* 111–17.

Corner, John. "Presumption as Theory: 'Realism' in Television Studies." *Screen* 33:1 (spring 1992): 97–102.

Crary, Jonathan. *Techniques of the Observer.* Cambridge: MIT Press, 1992.

De Bouzek, Jeannette. "The 'Ethnographic Surrealism' of Jean Rouch." *Visual Anthropology* 2:34 (1989): 301–32.

Dabashi, Hamid. *Close Up Iranian Cinema: Past, Present, and Future.* New York: Verso, 2001.

Daney, Serge. *Ciné Journal, 1981–1986.* Paris: Cahiers du Cinema Gallimard, 1986.

——. *La Rampe: Cahier Critique, 1970–1982.* Paris: Cahiers du Cinéma Gallimard, 1983.

De Certeau, Michel. *The Practice of Everyday Life.* Berkeley: University of California Press, 1984.

Deren, Maya. *Divine Horsemen: The Living Gods of Haiti.* Kingston, N.Y.: Documentext, [1953] 1991.

Derrida, Jacques. "Signature, Event, Context." In *Margins of Philosophy,* translated by Alan Bass, 309–30. Chicago: University of Chicago Press, 1982.

Diawara, Manthia, ed. *Black American Cinema.* New York: Routledge, 1993.

Doane, Mary Ann. "Information, Crisis, Catastrophe." In *Logics of Television,* edited by Patricia Mellencamp, 222–39. Bloomington: Indiana University Press, 1990.

——. "Screening Time." In *Language Machines: Technologies of Literary and Cultural Production,* edited by Jeffrey Masten, Peter Stallybrass, and Nancy Vickers, 137–59, New York: Routledge, 1997.

——. "Temporality, Storage, Legibility: Freud, Marey, and the Cinema." *Critical Inquiry* 22:2 (winter 1996): 313–43.

Dyer, Richard, and Ginette Vincendeau, eds. *Popular European Cinema.* New York: Routledge, 1992.

Eagleton, Terry. "Realism and Cinema." *Screen* 21:2 (summer 1980): 93–94.

Eaton, Mick, ed. *Anthropology, Reality, Cinema: The Films of Jean Rouch.* London: British Film Institute, 1979.

Elsaesser, Thomas. *Cinema Futures: Cain, Abel, or Cable.* Amsterdam: Amsterdam University Press, 1998.

Elsaesser, Thomas, and Adam Barker, eds. *Early Cinema: Space, Frame, Narrative.* London: British Film Institute, 1992.

Epstein, Jean. "*Bonjour Cinéma* and Other Writings by Jean Epstein." Translated by Tom Milne. *After Image* 10 (1981): 8–38.

——. *Écrits sur le Cinéma.* 2 vols. Paris: Éditions Seghers, 1975.

——. "Magnification and Other Writings." Translated by Stuart Liebman. *October* 3 (1977): 9–25.

Foster, Hal. *The Return of the Real: The Avant-Garde at the End of the Century.* Cambridge: MIT Press, 1996.

Fried, Michael. "Between Realisms: From Derrida to Manet." *Critical Inquiry* 21 (autumn 1994): 1–36.

——. *Courbet's Realism.* Chicago: University of Chicago Press, 1990.

Gaines, Jane, and Michael Renov, eds. *Collecting Visible Evidence.* Minneapolis: University of Minnesota Press, 1999.

Gordon, Rae Beth. *Why the French Love Jerry Lewis: From Cabaret to Early Cinema.* Stanford: Stanford University Press, 2001.

Grant, Barry Keith, and Jeannette Sloniowski, eds. *Documenting the Documentary: Close Readings of Documentary Film and Video.* Detroit: Wayne State University Press, 1998.

Grant, Damian. *Realism.* London: Methuen, 1970.

Gunning, Tom. "An Aesthetics of Astonishment: Early Film and the (In)credulous Spectator." *Art and Text* 34 (spring 1989): 31–45.

——. "Tracing the Individual Body: Photography, Detectives, and Early Cinema." In *Cinema and the Invention of Modern Life,* edited by Leo Charney and Vanessa R. Schwartz, 15–45, Berkeley: University of California Pres, 1995.

Hall, Jeanne. "Realism as Style in Cinema Vérité: A Critical Analysis of Primary." *Cinema Journal* 30:4 (1991): 24–50.

Hallam, Julia, and Margaret Marshment, eds. *Realism and Popular Cinema.* New York: Manchester University Press, 2000.

Hampton, Timothy. *Writing from History: The Rhetoric of Exemplarity in Renaissance Literature.* Ithaca: Cornell University Press, 1985.

Hansen, Miriam. *Babel and Babylon: Spectatorship in American Silent Film.* Cambridge: Harvard University Press, 1991.

——. "'With Skin and Hair': Kracauer's Theory of Film, Marseille 1940." *Critical Inquiry* 19 (spring 1993): 437–69.

Hara, Kazuo. "Extreme Private Eros-Love Song, 1974." In *Japanese Documentary: The 1970s,* Yoshio Yasui, ed. Tokyo: Yamagata International Documentary Film Festival, 1995.

Heath, Stephen. "From Brecht to Film: Theses, Problems." *Screen* 16:4 (winter 1975–76): 34–45.

——. "Lessons from Brecht." *Screen* 15:2 (summer 1974): 103–28.

——. *Questions of Cinema.* Bloomington: Indiana University Press, 1981.

Hebdige, Dick, and Geoff Hurd. "Reading and Realism." *Screen Education* 28 (autumn, 1978): 68–78.

Henderson, Brian. "Bazin Defended against His Devotees." *Film Quarterly* 32:4 (summer 1979): 26–37.

Higson, Andrew. "Space, Place, Spectacle: Landscape and Townscape in the 'Kitchen Sink Film." In *Dissolving Views: Key Writings on British Cinema,* edited by Andrew Higson, 133–56, London: Cassell, 1996.

Hill, John. *British Cinema in the 1980s: Issues and Themes.* Oxford: Clarendon Press, 1999.

——. *Sex, Class, and Realism: British Cinema, 1956–63.* London: British Film Institute, 1986.

Jakobson, Roman. "On Realism in Art." In *Readings in Russian Poetics,* edited by L. Matejka and K. Pomorska, 38–46. Cambridge: MIT Press, 1971.

James, David. *Allegories of Cinema: American Film in the Sixties.* Princeton: Princeton University Press, 1989.

——. "Toward a Geo-Cinematic Hermeneutics: Representations of Los Angeles in Nonindustrial Cinema — *Killer of Sheep* and *Water and Power.*" *Wide Angle* 20:3 (July 1998): 23–53.

Jameson, Fredric. *Signatures of the Visible.* New York: Routledge, 1990.

Jarvie, I. C. "Media and Manners: Film and Society in Some Current British Films." *Film Quarterly* 22:3 (1969): 11.

Johnson, Eithne, and Eric Schaefer. "Soft Core/Hard Core: Snuff as a Crisis of Meaning." *Journal of Film and Video* 45:2–3 (summer–fall, 1993): 40–59.

Klotman, Phyllis R., and Janet K. Cutler, eds. *Struggles for Representation: African American Documentary Film and Video.* Bloomington: Indiana University Press, 1999.

Kracauer, Siegfried. *Theory of Film: The Redemption of Physical Reality.* New York: Oxford University Press, 1960.

Kuhn, Annette, and Jackie Stacie, eds. *Screen Histories: A Reader.* Oxford: Clarendon Press, 1998.

Kulterman, Udo. *New Realism.* Greenwich, Conn.: New York Graphic Society, 1972.

Lastra, James. *Sound Technology and the American Cinema: Perception, Representation, Modernity.* New York: Columbia University Press, 2000.

Lovell, Terry. *Pictures of Reality: Aesthetics, Politics, and Pleasure.* London: British Film Institute, 1980.

Luhmann, Niklas. *Observations on Modernity.* Translated by William Whobrey. Stanford: Stanford University Press, 1998.

Lukács, Georg. "Narrate or Describe?" In *Writer and Critic and Other Essays,* translated by Arthur D. Kahn, 110–48. New York: Grosset and Dunlap, 1970.

——. *Studies in European Realism.* Translated by Edith Bone. New York: Grosset and Dunlap, 1964.

MacCabe, Colin. "*Days of Hope:* A Response to Colin McArthur." *Screen* 17:1 (spring 1976): 100.

——. "Realism and the Cinema: Notes on some Brechtian Theses." *Screen* 15:2 (summer 1974): 7–24.

——. "The Politics of Separation." *Screen* 16:4 (winter 1975–76): 46–61.

——. "Theory and Film: Principles of Realism and Pleasure." *Screen* 17:3 (autumn 1976): 7–27.

Macdonald, Kevin, and Mark Cousins, eds. *Imagining Reality: The Faber Book of Documentary.* London: Faber and Faber, 1996.

MacKenzie, Scott. "Mimetic Nationhood: Ethnography and the National." In *Cinema and Nation,* edited by Mette Hjort and Scott Mackenzie, 241–59. London: Routledge, 2000.

Mamber, Stephen. *Cinema Vérité in America: Studies in Uncontrolled Documentary.* Cambridge: MIT Press, 1974.

Margulies, Ivone. *Nothing Happens: Chantal Akerman's Hyperrealist Everyday.* Durham: Duke University Press, 1996.

Marks, Laura. "Naked Truths: Hara Kazuo's Iconoclastic Obsessions." *Independent* 15:10 (1992): 25–27.

Marwick, A. *Class: Image and Reality in Britain, France, and the USA since 1930.* New York: Oxford University Press, 1980.

Melville, Stephen. "Compelling Acts, Haunting Convictions." *Art History* 14:1 (March 1991): 116–22.

Miller, D. A. *The Novel and the Police.* Berkeley: University of California Press, 1988.

Moneti, Guglielmo, ed. *Lessico Zavattiniano: Parole e Idee su Cinema e Dintorni.* Venice: Marsilio Editori, 1992.

Morse, Margaret. *Virtualities.* Bloomington: Indiana University Press, 1998.

Murphy, Robert, ed. *The British Cinema Book.* London: British Film Institute, 1997.

Murphy, Robert. *Realism and Tinsel: Cinema and Society in Britain, 1939–1948.* London: Routledge, 1989.

Nichols, Bill. *Blurred Boundaries: Questions of Meaning in Contemporary Culture.* Bloomington: Indiana University Press, 1994.

——. *Ideology and the Image.* Bloomington: Indiana University Press, 1981.

——. *Representing Reality: Issues and Concepts in Documentary.* Bloomington: Indiana University Press, 1991.

Nochlin, Linda. *Realism.* Harmondsworth: Penguin, 1971.

O'Brian, Mary. *The Politics of Reproduction.* London: Routledge, 1981.

Peirce, Charles Sanders. *The Essential Peirce.* Vol. 1. Edited by Nathan Houser and Christian Kloesel. Bloomington: Indiana University Press, 1992.

Petrey, Sandy. *Realism and Revolution: Balzac, Stendhal, Zola, and the Performance of History.* Ithaca: Cornell University Press, 1988.

Petro, Patrice, ed. *Fugitive Images: From Photography to Video.* Bloomington: Indiana University Press, 1995.

Peucker, Brigitte. *Incorporating Images: Film and the Rival Arts.* Princeton: Princeton University Press, 1995.

Prendergast, Christopher. *The Order of Mimesis: Balzac, Stendhal, Nerval, Flaubert.* Cambridge: Cambridge University Press, 1986.

Renov, Michael. "The Subject in History: The New Autobiography in Film and Video." *Afterimage* (summer 1989): 4–7.

——. *Theorizing Documentary.* New York: Routledge, 1993.

Rodowick, David. *The Crisis of Political Modernism: Criticism and Ideology in Contemporary Film Theory.* Chicago: University of Illinois Press, [1988] 1994.

Rosen, Charles, and Henry Zerner. *Romanticism and Realism: The Mythology of Nineteenth-Century Art.* New York: W. W. Norton, 1984.

Rosen, Philip. *Change Mummified: Cinema, Historicity, Theory.* Minneapolis: University of Minnesota Press, 2001.

Rosen, Philip, ed. *Narrative, Apparatus, Ideology: A Film Theory Reader.* New York: Columbia University Press. 1986.

Rouch, Jean. "Vicissitudes of the Self: The Possessed Dancer, the Magician, the Sorcerer, the Filmmaker, and the Ethnographer." *Studies in the Anthropology of Visual Communication* 5:1 (1978): 2–8.

Ruoff, Jeffrey, and Kenneth Ruoff. *The Emperor's Naked Army Marches On.* London: Flicks Books, 1998.

Russell, Catherine. *Experimental Ethnography: The Work of Film in the Age of Video.* Durham, Duke University Press, 1999.

———. *Narrative Mortality, Death, Closure, and New Wave Cinemas.* Minneapolis: University of Minnesota Press, 1995.

———. "Subjectivity Lost and Found: Bill Viola's *I Do Not Know What It Is I Am Like.*" In *Documenting the Documentary,* edited by Barry Grant and Janine Sloniowski. Detroit: Wayne State University Press, 1998.

Sadoul, George. *Louis Lumiere.* Paris: Editions Seghers, 1964.

Sandberg, Mark. "Effigy and Narrative: Looking into the Nineteenth-Century Folk Museum." In *Cinema and the Invention of Modern Life,* edited by Vanessa Schwartz and Leo Charney, 320–61, Berkeley: University of California Press, 1995.

Scarry, Elaine. *The Body in Pain: The Making and Unmaking of the World.* New York: Random House, 1985.

Schamus, James. "Dreyer's Textual Realism." In *Carl Th. Dreyer,* edited by Jitte Jensen, 59–65. New York: Museum of Modern Art, 1988. Reprinted in this volume.

Schwartz, Vanessa. *Spectacular Realities: Early Mass Culture in Fin de Siècle Paris.* Los Angeles: University of California Press, 1998.

Seltzer, Mark. *Bodies and Machines.* New York: Routledge, 1992.

Shaviro, Steven. *The Cinematic Body.* Minneapolis: University of Minnesota Press, 1993.

Shohat, Ella, and Robert Stam. *Unthinking Eurocentrism: Multiculturalism and the Media.* New York: Routledge, 1994.

Singer, Ben. *Melodrama and Modernity: Early Sensational Cinema and Its Contexts.* New York: Columbia University Press, 2001.

Sitney, P. Adams. *Visionary Film: The American Avant-Garde, 1943–1978.* 2d ed. New York: Oxford University Press, 1979.

Soja, Edward W. *Postmodern Geographies: The Reassertion of Space in Critical Social Theory.* New York: Verso, 1989.

Sprinker, Michael. "Brechtian Realism." *Minnesota Review* (October 1999): 220–27.

Stevens, Tony. "Reading the Realist Film." *Screen* 26 (spring 1978): 13–34.

Stoller, Paul. *The Cinematic Griot: The Ethnography of Jean Rouch.* Chicago: University of Chicago Press, 1992.

Taussig, Michael. *Mimesis and Alterity: A Particular History of the Senses.* London: Routledge, 1993.

Waugh, Thomas. "'Acting to Play Onself': Notes on Performance in Documentary." In *Making Visible the Invisible: An Anthology of Original Essays on Film Acting,* edited by Carole Zucker, 64–91, Metuchen, N.J.: Scarecrow Press, 1990.

Waugh, Thomas, ed. *"Show us life": Toward a History and Aesthetics of the Committed Documentary.* Metuchen, N.J.: Scarecrow Press, 1984.

Welchman, John. "Face(t)s: Notes on Faciality." *Artforum* (November 1983): 131–38.

Wide Angle 9:4 (winter 1987–88). Special issue on André Bazin.

Willemen, Paul. *Looks and Frictions: Essays in Cultural Studies and Film Theory.* Bloomington: Indiana University Press, 1994.

Williams, Christopher, ed. *Realism and the Cinema: A Reader.* London: Routledge, 1980.

Williams, Linda. "Corporealized Observers: Visual Pornographies and the Carnal Density of Vision." In *Fugitive Images: From Photography to Video,* Bloomington: 3–41, Indiana University Press, 1995.

———. "Film Bodies: Gender, Genre, Excess." *Film Quarterly* 44:4 (summer 1991): 2–12.

———. *Hard Core: Power, Pleasure, and the "Frenzy of the Visible."* Berkeley: University of California Press, 1989.

Williams, Raymond. *Keywords: A Vocabulary of Culture and Society.* Rev. ed. New York: Oxford University Press, 1983.

———. "A Lecture on Realism." *Screen* 18:1 (spring 1977): 61–74.

———. "Realism, Naturalism, and Their Alternatives." *CineTracts* 1:3 (fall 1977–winter 1978): 1–6.

Winston, Brian. *Claiming the Real: The Documentary Film Revisited.* London: British Film Institute, 1995.

Zangwill, Nick. "Metaphor and Realism in Aesthetics." *Journal of Aesthetics and Art Criticism* 49.1 (winter 1991): 57–62.

Zants, Emily, and Bertrand Tavernier. *Fractured Narratives and Bourgeois Values.* London: Scarecrow Press, 1999.

Zavattini, Cesare. "Some Ideas on the Cinema." In *Film: A Montage of Theories,* edited by Richard Dyer MacCann, 216–28. New York: E. P. Dutton, 1966.

———. *Zavattini: Sequences from Cinematic Life.* Translated and with an introduction by William Weaver. Englewood Cliffs, N.J.: Prentice-Hall, 1970.

Contributors

PAUL ARTHUR is Professor of English and Film Studies at Montclair State University. He is a regular contributor to *Film Comment* and *Cineaste* and is coeditor of *Millennium Film Journal*. His writings on documentary, film noir, and avant-garde cinema have appeared in nearly two dozen anthologies and catalogs.

ANDRÉ BAZIN was a film theorist and critic. He was the founding editor of *Cahiers du Cinéma* and the writer of seminal essays and books on the cinema collected in *Qu'est-ce que le cinéma?*; and *Jean Renoir, Cinéma du cruaute: Le cinéma français de la libération à la nouvelle vague (1945–1958)*. Many writings have been translated into English, including *What Is Cinema? Bazin at Work: Major Essays and Reviews from the Forties and Fifties*; and *Essays on Chaplin*.

MARK A. COHEN is Visiting Assistant Professor in French Language and Literature at Bard College. He has translated Eric Weil's *Hegel and the State* (1998) and numerous essays from French. He is the author of articles and encyclopedia entries on seventeenth-century French literature and is currently completing a book entitled *La Bruyère and Humanism: The Hermeneutics of Classicism*.

SERGE DANEY was a film critic for *Cahiers du Cinéma* and *Libération*, editor of *Traffic*, and writer of innumerable books of film and television criticism and theory, including *La Rampe: Cahier critique, 1970–1982; Ciné Journal, 1981–1986; L'exercice a été profitable, monsieur*; and *Devant la recrudescence des vols de sacs à main: Cinéma, télévision, information*.

MARY ANN DOANE is George Hazard Crooker Professor of Modern Culture and Media and of English at Brown University. She is the author of *The Desire to Desire: The Woman's Film of the 1940s* (1987) and *Femmes Fatales: Feminism, Film Theory, Psychoanalysis* (1991). She has published a wide range of articles on feminist film theory, sound in the cinema, psycho-analytic theory, and sexual and racial difference in film, melodrama, and television. She is currently completing a book on technologies of representation and temporality at the turn of the century, tentatively entitled *Technologies of Temporality in Modernity.*

JAMES F. LASTRA is Associate Professor of English and Chair of the Committee on Cinema and Media Studies at the University of Chicago. He is the author of *Sound Technology and the American Cinema: Perception, Representation, Modernity,* and is currently writing a book on surrealism entitled *The Persistence of Surrealism, or "Why Is This Absurd Picture Here?"* devoted, in part, to reassessing the films of Luis Buñuel.

IVONE MARGULIES is Associate Professor in the Film and Media Studies Department at Hunter College (City University of New York). She is the author of *Nothing Happens: Chantal Akerman's Hyperrealist Everyday* (Duke University Press, 1996). She has written on experimental film- and videomakers and on theatricality in film. She is currently at work on a book on exemplarity in film entitled *Spectacles of Reform: Reenactment in Film.*

ABÉ MARK NORNES is Associate Professor of Asian Languages and Culture and of Film and Video at the University of Michigan. He was coordinator of the Yamagata International Documentary Film Festival in the 1990s. He is coeditor of *The Japan-America Film Wars* (1994) and *In Praise of Film Studies* (2001). His book on prewar and wartime documentary in Japan in forthcoming from the University of Minnesota Press.

BRIGITTE PEUCKER is Professor of German and Film Studies and Chair of the German De-partment at Yale University. She has published extensively on issues of representation in literature, visual culture and film, including articles on Fassbinder, Wenders, Herzog, Hitchcock, Greenaway, and Kubrick. Her most recent book is *Incorporating Images: Film and the Rival Arts* (1995). She is currently at work on *The Material Image,* a book on film and the real.

RICHARD PORTON is on the editorial board of *Cineaste* and has written on film for a variety of publications. His *Film and the Anarchist Imagination* was published by Verso in 1999. The Spanish translation (*Cine y anarquismo,* Gedisa, 2001) won the Eninci 2001, awarded by the Burgos Film Festival for the best Spanish-language book on cinema.

PHILIP ROSEN is Professor of Modern Culture and Media and Professor of English at Brown University. He has written extensively on films, film theory, and cultural theory. His most recent book is *Change Mummified: Cinema, Historicity, Theory.*

CATHERINE RUSSELL is Associate Professor of Film Studies at Concordia University in Mon-treal. She is the author of *Narrative Mortality: Death, Closure, and New Wave Cinemas* (1985); and *Experimental Ethnography: The Work of Film in the Age of Video* (Duke University Press, 1999). She has also published numerous articles on Canadian film and video and Japanese cinema.

JAMES SCHAMUS is a Professor of Film Theory, History, and Criticism at Columbia Univer-sity, where he was recently a University Lecturer. He was also the 1997 Nuveen Fellow in the Humanities at the University of Chicago. Good Machine, his award-winning pro-duction company, was honored with a ten-year retrospective at the Museum of Modern Art in New York, 2001.

NOA STEIMATSKY is Assistant Professor of History of Art and Film Studies at Yale University. She is completing a book on landscape and the claim of the modern in Italian cinema and has recently started, with the support of a Getty Fellowship, a project on the human face in film. Her research and teaching focus on rhetorical figures in film and film theory, the genealogy and close analysis of film style, and intersections of realism and modernism in cinema.

XIAOBING TANG teaches modern Chinese literature at the University of Chicago. His book *Chinese Modern: The Heroic and the Quotidian,* was published by Duke University Press in 2000. His current research project is a study of the discourse of art in modern China.

Index

Burnett, Charles: *Killer of Sheep,* 13; *My Brother's Wedding,* 13

Caméra-stylo (camera-pen), 28, 31 n2
Capitalism, 86, 139, 166
Career Girls, 166, 177–79
Carroll, Noel, 81
Chaplin, Charles: *The Circus,* 36
Cheat, The, 83
Chelsea Girls, The, 107
Chiaroscuro, 256, 258
Children of the Bases (Kichi no kodomotachi), 147
Children of the Classroom (Kyoshitsu no kodomotachi), 149
Children Who Draw Pictures (E o kaku kodomotachi), 149
Chinese cinema: aesthetics of depth, 129, 132, 140; censorship, 233; city films, 122, 123, 124, 141 n5; "collage city," 137, 143 n35; Fifth Generation, 13, 121, 122, 123, 124, 233; Fourth Generation, 13, 123; humanism in, 123, 128; and melodrama, 234–35; the postmodern in, 139; Sixth Generation, 13, 234. See also *Black Snow; Good Morning, Beijing*
Christensen, Benjamin, 316
Cinema: "art of time," 30; death and/in, 6, 15, 29–31, 33, 38, 40, 50–53, 56, 62, 253, 257; death of, 80, 85, 87; ontology, 3, 9, 10, 29, 30, 31, 35, 42, 46, 48, 52–54, 56, 62, 65, 72, 73, 80, 114, 274; realist, 5, 6, 7, 13, 18, 220, 228; religion/theology, 29; and transparency, 33, 34, 68, 81, 82, 106, 113, 166, 186, 193, 253, 254
Cinema studies, 80, 81
Cinematic specificity, 8, 11, 17, 30, 38
Cinematography, 17, 257
Cinema vérité, 148, 229, 238, 273. See also Portraiture
Cinephilia, 10, 35, 82, 84–88
Circus, The, 36
Citizen Kane, 28
Clark, Paul, 125, 143
Clarke, Shirley: *Portrait of Jason,* 96, 105

Classical Hollywood cinema, 6, 36, 38, 39, 97, 98, 107, 115 n9, 121, 148. *See also* Realism
Clayton, Jack: *Room at the top,* 172
Clifford, James, 189, 192
Close, Chuck, 310
Close Up, 15, 89 n10, 217, 220, 235–40, 243 n57
Colonialism, 190, 277, 278, 287–89
Comédie Humaine, 165
Comizzi d'Amore (Love Meetings), 266 n14
Commodity fetishism, 168
Commoli, Jean-Louis, 4, 5, 17, 44, 46, 62, 66
Conversations in Vermont, 105
Contingency, 3, 4, 9, 10, 12, 14, 35, 82–88, 114, 138, 218. *See also* Cinephilia; Indexicality
Cook, the Thief, His Wife and Her Lover, The, 296
Coveney, Michael, 166
Coward, Noel, 166
Crary, Jonathan, 7
Cultural Studies, 81–82

Daney, Serge, 9, 17
Daoma zei (The Horse Thief), 122
Dardenne Brothers: *La Promesse,* 13; *Rosetta,* 13
Davidson, Bruce: *Living Off the Land,* 105
Dayan, Joan, 288
de Antonio, Emile: *Nixon's Checker's Speech,* 106
Debord, Guy, 179
Decameron, 265 n13
Depth, 1, 295, 306. *See also* Perspective
Deren, Maya, 5, 9, 16, 99; *Divine Horsemen,* 280–84; *At Land,* 271; *Meshes of the Afternoon,* 270, 271; *Ritual in Transfigured Time,* 271. *See also* Body; Ethnography
Descartes, René, 43, 44
De Sica, Vittorio: *The Bicycle Thief,* 124; *The Roof,* 124
de Unamuno, Miguel, 14, 187, 203
de Vega, Lope, 203

Leacock, Richard, 106; *Happy Mother's Day,* 101, 102

Le Dejeuner de bébé, 93, 95

Lefebvre, Henri: critique of everyday life, 164, 166, 171, 175–80; "informational city," 170; spatial politics, 13, 169, 170, 172, 174, 180

Legendre, Maurice, 14, 187, 201–3, 205–8

Lehrstück, 165, 173

Leigh, Mike, 12; *Abigail's Party,* 13, 170, 177; *Bleak Moments,* 166–67, 179; *Career Girls,* 166, 177–79; *Grown Ups,* 176, 177; *High Hopes,* 169, 170, 172, 173, 174, 176, 181; *Home Sweet Home,* 168–70, 176; *Life is Sweet,* 165, 169, 179; *Meantime,* 171–75, 178–80; *Naked,* 165, 170, 174–75, 177–80; *Secrets and Lies,* 175–77; *Topsy-Turvy,* 180, 181

Lenses, 256, 257, 259

Les maitres fous, 276

Life is Sweet, 165, 169, 179

Life of Jesus, 13

Living Camera (TV series), 99; *Jane,* 102, 103, 111

Living Off the Land, 105

Lizzani, Carlo, 220, 224

Lonely Boy, 101

Long take, the, 101, 110, 114, 225. *See also* Bazin, André

Louisiana Story, 32

Love in the City, 15, 217, 221, 222, 225; *Attempted Suicide,* 220, 225, 228, 229; *Love of a Mother,*" 220, 221, 225, 228, 229

Luhmann, Niklas, 82, 88

Lukács, Georg, 77 n25, 164, 165, 177, 224

Lumière, Auguste and Louis, 87, 94, 97, 107; *Le Dejeuner de bébé,* 93, 95

Lynch, Kevin, 119, 123, 129, 143

Lyotard, Jean-Francois, 294

MacCabe, Colin, 44

Makavejev, Dusan: *WR: Mysteries of the Organism,* 61

Makhalbaf, Mohsen, 235, 237, 238, 239, 240

Malraux, André, 43

Mama, 14, 234

Mamma Roma, 245, 257

Manual of Arms, 113

Markopoulos, Gregory: *Galaxie,* 113; *Political Portraits,* 113; *Through a Lens Brightly: Mark Turbyfill,* 112

Marx, Karl, 68, 167, 173

Maselli, Francesco, 15, 220, 222. *See also Love in the City*

Materialism, 4, 5, 255, 304

Materiality, 3, 7, 8, 17, 18

Maysles Brothers: *Meet Marlon Brando,* 101, 102; *Showman,* 102; *What's Happening! The Beatles in the U.S.A,* 102

Mead, Margaret, 278, 285; *Trance and Dance in Bali,* 276, 277

Me and My Brother, 105

Meantime, 171–75, 178–80

Mechanical Reproduction, 5, 47, 52, 64, 68, 96, 253, 285, 286

Medea, 246, 318

Medhurst, Andy, 169

Meet Marlon Brando, 101, 102

Mekas, Jonas, 107, 110, 111; *Diaries, Notes, and Sketches (Walden),* 113

Méliès, Georges, 294

Melodrama, 167, 175, 176, 294; and Chinese cinema, 234–35; and possession, 278–79; socialist melodrama, 121, 123, 125

Merleau-Ponty, Maurice, 71

Meshes of the Afternoon, 270, 271

Metz, Christian, 71, 73, 81, 83

Michael, 317

Michelson, Annette, 276

Miguel, Luis R., 204

Milky Way, The, 40

Mimesis, 2, 164; mimetic drive, 296, 297, 304, 305; mimicry, 15, 285, 287–89. *See also Equivocation*

Minamata: The Victims and their World (Minamata: Kanja-san to sono sekai), 146

Ming-liang, Tsai: *The River,* 18

Mingus, 103–4

Minh-ha, Trinh T., 157

Modernism, 7, 11, 113, 114, 122, 129, 140, 141, 164, 177, 181, 270, 273, 275, 278, 279, 286, 287, 289, 316. *See also* Realism

Modernity, 12, 84–88, 122, 129, 134, 180, 190, 252, 265 n7, 285

Moholy-Nagy, Laszlo, 150

Molière, 28, 29, 31

Montage, 28, 35, 299

Morris, Errol, 157

Morse, Margaret, 159–60

Moszhukin, 28

Mr. Hayashi, 100

Mummy complex, the. *See* Preservation

Munk, Kaj, 316

Munsterberg, Hugo, 81

Murder of Fred Hampton, The, 106

My Beautiful Laundrette, 11

My Brother's Wedding, 13

Myth, 248, 252, 254

Nadar, 107, 108

Nakai, Masakazu, 150

Naked, 165, 170, 174–75, 177–80

Nanami: Inferno of First Love (Hatsu koi: Jigokuhen), 152

Nanook of the North, 96

Narration, 96, 310; direct address, 8, 105, 226, 229; narrative, 53, 57, 58, 62, 296, 297, 298, 301, 304, 306, 307

Nationalism, 195–96, 209–10

National Film Board of Canada, 100

National Theatre, 165. *See also* Theater: British

Naturalism, 96, 165–68, 171, 173, 181

Neorealism, 11, 96–97, 124, 125, 139, 140, 142 nn17, 29, 220–25, 228, 229, 240, 242 n39, 254

New American Cinema Group, 98

News from Home, 11

Newsreels, 32, 97

Nichols, Bill, 157, 229

Nixon's Checker's Speech, 106

Nordisk Films, 316

Nornes, Abe Mark, 14

Nuanxin, Zhang: *Good Morning, Beijing (Beijing Nizao),* 13, 14, 123, 125, 132, 133–40; *Sha Ou (Sha Ou),* 123

Objectivity, 2, 46, 57, 60, 61, 186, 188, 197, 199, 270

Obsolescence, 81

Ogawa, Shinsuke, 144, 151, 153

Okinawa, 147

Ordet, 316, 317

Oshima, Nagisa, 144, 148, 152

Outer and Inner Space, 107, 110

Painting, 16, 47, 50, 51, 68, 258, 259, 264. *See also* Intermediality; Portraiture

Paisa, 3

Panola, 105

Paris 1900, 28, 39

Pasolini, Pier Paolo, 9, 16; *Accattone,* 245, 248, 256, 257, 264 n1, 265 n10; "analogy," 246, 249, 251, 253, 262, 264; *Appunti per un film sull'India (Notes for a Film on India),* 246; *Appunti per un'orestiade africana (Notes for an African Oresteia),* 246, 256 n13; *Comizzi d'Amore (Love Meetings),* 266 n14; "contamination," 246, 248, 249, 251, 262, 268 n36; *Decameron,* 265 n13; *Edipo Re,* 246, 265 n13; film-theoretical writings of, 249, 253, 256; *La Ricotta,* 265 n6; locations of the films of, 245–27, 252, 262, 264 n2, 265 n13, 266 n14; *Mamma Roma,* 245, 257; *Medea,* 246, 265 n13; *Salò or The 120 Days of Sodom,* 265 nn10, 13; "translation," 250, 251, 252. See also *Il Vangelo secondo Matteo (The gospel according to Saint Mathew); Sopraluoghi in Palestina (Locations in Palestine)*

Passion of Joan of Arc, The, 16, 315, 317–18, 320–23

Paul Tomkowicz, Street-Railway Switchman, 100

Peirce, Charles Sanders, 48, 49, 50, 87

Pennebaker, D. A: *Don't Look Back,* 104; *The War Room,* 101

Peucker, Brigitte, 16

Perception, 296, 303–6, 309

Performative, 2, 17, 156–58, 160, 225

Performance, 2, 4, 6, 8, 15, 294, 295, 300; and portraiture, 96, 101–3, 105, 108–9, 112; in possession, 274, 275, 277, 278, 281, 282, 285, 287; and privacy, 156. *See also* Acting

Perspective, 8, 46–48, 49, 50, 75 nn10, 11; Albertian, 297, 303, 305, 308, 309

Phenomenology, 43–46, 49, 62, 63, 67, 70–71, 304

Philosophy, 193, 195, 200

Photogénie, 82, 83

Photography, 8, 29, 30, 96, 107, 114, 115 n5, 266 n23, 304–5. *See also* Image; Intermediality

Picasso, Pablo, 96, 110

Pincus, Ed: *Panola,* 105

Pinter, Harold, 166–67, 181

Political Portraits, 113

Pornography, 294, 296, 300, 307

Porton, Richard, 13

Portrait of Jason, 96, 105

Portraiture, 5, 11, 14; and the avant-garde, 94, 95, 99–100, 106–13, 115 n4, 117 n33, 118 n37; and cinema vérité/documentary, 96, 97, 99, 100–106, 108, 112, 113; and painting, 94, 96, 98, 114. *See also* Contingency

Possession. *See* Body; Performance

Postmodernism, 11, 295, 301, 305, 309

Preservation, 34, 38, 51–59, 61–67, 71, 72

Primary, 101

Profilmic, 2, 4, 8, 9, 55, 57, 74 n8, 75 n10, 94, 103, 112, 113, 253, 256, 257, 258, 262, 272, 273, 283, 303

Promotional Trailers, 97

Psychoanalysis, 43, 44, 76 n12, 80; and possession, 276–79

Ranke, Leopold von, 68, 79 n39

Realism, 113, 125, 270, 274, 275, 279, 283, 286; behavioral, 169; and classical Hollywood cinema, 316–17; critical, 164, 182 n13; didactic, 165–68, 173; exemplary realism, 219; "kitchen sink," 13, 171, 183 n26; mimetic realism, 219; modernist, 165, 167, 181; oppositional, 11, 12; performative, 18 n3; physical, in *The Bullfight,* 28–29; presentational, 182 n12; and the "real," 317–19, 322; revolutionary, 121; social, 166–67, 224; socialist, 121, 123, 125, 164; spiritual, 322; textual, 15, 16, 315–23. *See also* Naturalism; Neorealism

Reception, 4, 6, 7, 8, 18

Reenactment, 2, 4, 5, 15, 17, 152, 159, 295, 296, 300, 301; and literal repetition, 217–18, 220–22, 225–27, 230, 232, 237, 240; retracing, 2, 15, 16, 249. *See also* Acting; Exemplarity; Performance

Referentiality, 1, 4, 5, 11, 12, 14, 17, 18; and the real, 2, 3, 9, 10, 16

Reflexivity, 5, 16, 17, 295

Regular or Irregular, 238

Reichman, Thomas: *Mingus,* 103–4

Reisz, Karel: *Saturday Night and Sunday Morning,* 171

Rembrandt: "Anatomy Lesson of Dr. Tulp," 300

Renoir, Jean, 36, 45, 64; *The Golden Coach,* 38; *La Marseillaise,* 4; *The River,* 38

Renov, Michael, 157

Rensheng (Life), 123

Repetition, 261, 263. *See also* Reenactment

Representation, 33, 34, 35, 40, 246, 247, 253, 254, 255, 257; and the real, 34, 35, 38, 295–96, 299–300, 303–11. *See also* Referentiality

Representational Layering. *See* Intermediality

Resnais, Alain, 113

Revista de Extremadura, 204

Richardson, Tony, 171

Riggs, Marlon, 157; *Tongues Untied,* 160

Richter, Gerhard, 310

Riefenstahl, Leni, 285

Ritual in Transfigured Time, 271

Rodney King trial, 10, 158

Rodowick, David, 7

Rohdie, Sam, 225

Library of Congress Cataloging-in-Publication Data
Rites of realism: essays on corporeal cinema /
edited by Ivone Margulies.
Includes bibliographical references and index.
ISBN 0-8223-3078-4 (cloth: alk. paper)
ISBN 0-8223-3066-0 (pbk. : alk. paper)
1. Realism in motion pictures.   2. Body, Human, in
motion pictures.   3. Motion pictures—Semiotics.
I. Margulies, Ivone.
PN1995.9.R3 R58   2002   791.43′612—dc21   2002012341